PERMITTED DEVELOPMENT

AUSTRALIA
LBC Information Services
Sydney

CANADA AND U.S.A.
Carswell
Toronto • Ontario

NEW ZEALAND
Brooker's
Auckland

SINGAPORE and MALAYSIA
Thomson Information (S.E. Asia)
Singapore

PERMITTED DEVELOPMENT

Second edition

By

MALCOLM GRANT
Professor and Head of Department of Land Economy
and Fellow of Clare College
University of Cambridge

LONDON • SWEET & MAXWELL 1996

First Edition, 1989, by Malcolm Grant

Published in 1996 by
Sweet & Maxwell Limited of
100 Avenue Road
Swiss Cottage
London, NW3 3PF

Computerset by MFK Information Services Ltd,
Hitchin, Herts
Printed in the United Kingdom by
Butler and Tanner Ltd,
Frome and London

No natural forests were destroyed to make this product:
only farmed timber was produced and replanted

ISBN 0 421 55380 4

**A CIP catalogue record for this book
is available from the British Library**

PREFACE

The three statutory instruments reproduced in this book lie at the heart of the town and country planning system in England and Wales. The main controls are set by the *Town and Country Planning Act* 1990, but the fine tuning lies in these instruments. The 1990 Act insists that planning permission be obtained before land development is undertaken. This statutory concept of "development" has two limbs: so-called *operational* development, where some physical change is made to the land, such as building or mining; and the making of a *material change in the use* of the land. Hence the 1990 Act simply puts in place a crudely defined and wide reaching prohibition: the role of these instruments lies in reducing its scope and sharpening its focus through creating a series of exemptions.

They operate in different ways:

> The *Town and Country Planning (Use Classes) Order* 1987 operates by setting a high baseline in its definition of different types of use of land, so that there will be no material change in use (hence no development requiring permission) if a change is made from one use to another in the same use-class.
>
> The *Town and Country Planning (General Permitted Development) Order* 1995 is effectively a nation-wide grant of planning permission for a diverse range of unconnected activities that do constitute development, and whose only common characteristic is that the Government wishes them to be outside normal planning control. Some of the permissions relate to relatively minor normal planning contol. Some of the permissions relate to relatively minor works, such as "householder" development; some to development which is subject to other forms of control or accountability, such as works authorised by private legislation, or works by public utilities, or licensed mining operations; and some to favoured economic sectors, such as agriculture and forestry.
>
> The *Town and Country Planning (General Development Procedure) Order* 1995 prescribes the detailed procedures for obtaining planning permission, including requirements for publicity consultation.

This book brings together the three orders in their most recent form. The two 1995 orders result from the splitting up of the provisions previously contained in the *Town and Country Planning (General Development) Order* 1988. The 1988 order had been the product of a lengthy process of redrafting and consultation, and was a radical departure in its style and content from its predecessors. There had been several important amendments to it subsequently, and although the 1995 orders allowed the amendments to be consolidated with the main text, they contained only relatively minor changes to the substance.

All three orders are highly technical, and have given rise to practical difficulties in their implementation and to extensive litigation. In this book, therefore, they are reproduced as they presently stand, together with full commentary. As with the first edition, published in 1989, the commentary derives from the *Encyclopedia of Planning Law and Practice*, and the purpose of this book edition is to make the text available to readers who do not have easy access to the *Encyclopedia*, and to provide those who do with a more readily portable version. The book is up to date to November 1, 1995, although it contains certain amendments brought about by the Environment Act 1995, which came into force on April 1, 1996.

Malcolm Grant
Cambridge
March, 1996

TABLE OF CASES

TOWN AND COUNTRY PLANNING (USE CLASSES) ORDER 1987

S.I. No.: S.I. 1987 No. 764.
In force from: June 1, 1987
Enabling power: Town and Country Planning Act 1971, s.22(2)(*f*) (now Town and Country Planning Act 1990, s.55(2)(*f*)).
Amendment: The Order has since been amended by the following:
S.I. 1991 No. 1567, which substituted new para (c) (use as a launderette) in art. 3(6) (*sui generis* uses), and amended Class 1A (shops) to include certain laundry uses;
S.I. 1992 No. 610, which introduced use for any registrable works under the Alkali, etc. Works Regulation Act 1906 into art. 3(6) (*sui generis* uses), and repealed Class B3 (special industrial group A);
S.I. 1992 No. 657, which repealed references to hazardous substances, upon the implementation of the Planning (Hazardous Substances) Act 1990;
S.I. 1994 No. 724, which substituted a new Class C1 (hotels), so as to exclude hostels.

COMMENTARY

Introduction

The Use Classes Order 1987 came into force on June 1, 1987, superseding the previous order, the Use Classes Order of 1972. The 1972 Order had followed closely the layout and style of its two predecessors, the Use Classes Orders of 1948 and 1963. But the 1987 Order is a radical revision, intended to achieve a measure of deregulation and also to clarify its presentation.

Background to the new Order

The Secretary of State for the Environment asked the Property Advisory Group in 1985 to review the working of the 1972 Order. In their Report the Group concluded that the Order was in many respects out of date, because it was based still on the 1948 Order, and there had been major changes in the distribution and nature of economic activity since then. The Group cited the decline of traditional industry in most parts of the country, the growth in service industry; major shifts in population and the development of the motorway network. They recommended a major recasting of the retail use class, suggesting four alternative routes through which this might be achieved; a new business class; an expansion of the special industrial uses; a recasting of the old Classes XI to XVIII; a new residential use class and a class to deal with certain uses of open land.

The Government published a consultation paper in June 1986, outlining its proposals based on the P.A.G. Report, though not adopting all its recommendations. Central to the Government's proposals, and now carried through into the new Order, was the recasting of the retail classes and the new business class, which is an amalgamation of the previous offices and light industrial classes. In relation to retail uses, the Government insisted on maintaining the old distinction between uses involving the sale of hot food and other uses, because they were conscious that the P.A.G. recommendations "would allow any corner shop to become a take-away restaurant and create a smell nuisance in a residential area without the local authority having any planning control." The Government also rejected the P.A.G. proposal to include motor showrooms in the shops class, because of the fear that this would allow redundant supermarkets to be used for car and motorcycle sales, with no planning control over the special environmental problems of noise and traffic generation that might arise.

Other reforms foreshadowed in the consultation paper, and carried through into the 1987 Order, include a rationalisation of the various residential, institutional and leisure classes, a new dwelling-house class and a recasting of the new warehouses/repository class as a class for storage or distribution.

Impact of the Order

The effects of the Order are examined in a research report commissioned by the Department of the Environment, titled *An Examination of the Effects of the Use Classes Order 1987 and the General Development Order 1988* (H.M.S.O., 1991; ISBN 0 11 752413 1).

The Report, which was prepared by Wootton Jeffreys Consultants and Bernard Thorpe, looked at the impact of the two Orders by examining the high street sector, the business and industrial sector and the residential sector, and is based on surveys of the providers and users of space, and local planning authorities. The Report found that in general the reforms had achieved their aim of embracing modern concepts of building use, reducing the intervention of planning in a variety of commercial activity and giving greater freedom to owners of property. However, the practical effects were greatest in parts of the country with high levels of development activity. They have also been greatest in the business sector, where the new freedom was seized on by owners of industrial land and buildings in areas of constrained supply, in order to develop higher value accommodation. In areas of high demand, industrial users have been displaced, and existing workshops in mixed use buildings in the cities have been replaced by studio and office uses. But the changes brought about little interference with amenity, since most of the changes had been towards cleaner uses. The new Order contributed to changes that were already under way in 1987, such as the provision of mixed-use, clean production space and a move out of town.

In the high street sector, the Report finds little effect to date on the number and location of financial and professional services, although takeaway operators have benefited by having greater access to food and drink outlets.

In the residential sector, the Order has assisted with the provision of group homes for the Care in Community programme, but had little effect on the provision of hostels and hotels.

On the basis of the report, the Secretary of State announced in a written Parliamentary answer on June 13, 1991, that:

> "... the freedom from planning control currently provided by the Use Classes Order and Part 3 of Schedule 2 to the General Development Order [planning permission for changes between U.C.O. classes] should remain unchanged. However, the Government proposes to continue to monitor closely the effects of the Use Classes Order and General Development Order and we are minded to commission further research in another three to five years."

Function of the order

The Order was made under s.22(2)(*f*) of the Town and Country Planning

Act 1971. The corresponding provision is now s.55(2)(*b*) of the Town and Country Planning Act 1990, which requires that planning permission be obtained for the development of land, including the making of a material change in the use of any building or other land. Subs. (2) prescribes various operations and uses of land which are not be taken for the purposes of the Act as involving "development," and these include (subs. (2)(*f*)):

> "in the case of buildings or other land which are used for a purpose of any class specified in an order made by the Secretary of State under this section, [the use of the buildings or other land or, subject to the provisions of the order, of any part thereof] for any other purpose of the same class."

The Order thus operates by prescribing a number of classes of use at a comparatively high level of abstraction, such as "shop" or "office." Changes of use within each class are then outside planning control.

Two important preliminary points need to be noted. First, the effect of the order is entirely permissive. It does not follow from it that a use change not authorised by the order must constitute development (see, *e.g. Rann v. Secretary of State for the Environment* (1979) 40 P. & C.R. 113; [1980] J.P.L. 109) Development is not involved, for example, merely because a new use would fall within a different class from the previous use, or because one of them would be a *sui generis* use (see further below). The question in each case is whether there has been a material change in the use of the building or other land. If there has not, the Use Classes Order is irrelevant. This may prove to be an important consideration in construing some of the new use classes in the 1987 Order, such as Class C.3 (use as a dwelling-house). The new class permits the use of a dwelling-house by not more than six residents (although there is no numerical limit if they are a family) living together as a single household, but the upper number is entirely arbitrary. Putting a dwelling-house to such a use might not have involved development in any case; and nor necessarily will there be a breach of planning control if the prescribed number is exceeded.

Secondly, not every use of land falls within one or more of the use classes. Some are expressly excluded by art. 3(6); others are *sui generis* in themselves (see further below).

But notwithstanding the strict approach to understanding the function of the Order it is difficult to resist the impression that the courts have been closely guided by the use classes in their interpretation of what does and what does not constitute a material change of use. For example, in *Cynon Valley Borough Council v. Secretary of State for Wales* [1986] J.P.L. 760 the Court of Appeal concluded, though apparently without any supporting argument, that there had been a material change in the use of retail premises when they changed from a fish and chip shop to an antique shop, and again later back to a fish and chip shop (though without indicating whether any change in the primary commodities offered for sale in a shop would constitute a material change in the use of the premises, or whether, as with the Order, the point of distinction was the sale of hot food); and in *Young v. Secretary of State for the Environment* [1983] 2 A.C. 662 the House of Lords similarly were satisfied that there had been a material change in use when premises previously used for a general industrial use were changed to light industrial use (categories which are wholly the creation of the Use Classes Order).

Primary and ancillary uses

The starting point in asking whether development is involved in any change of use is to examine the primary use to which the premises have been put in the past. It is against this, and not against some ancillary use, that the impact of the Order falls to be assessed: see, *e.g.*, *Vickers Armstrong Ltd v. Central Land Board* (1958) 9 P. & C.R. 33; *G. Percy Trentham Ltd v. Glouc-*

estershire County Council [1966] 1 W.L.R. 506; *Brazil Concrete Ltd v. Amersham Rural District Council* (1967) 18 P. & C.R. 396. Thus a commercial property with use rights within the new Class B1 (business class) may also have a staff canteen, which will be an ancillary use to the primary business use and entirely parasitic upon it. It would not constitute a separate use for the purposes of Class A3 (food and drink). Its use could be changed at any time without permission to use for the primary purpose of the undertaking, or for any other purpose ancillary to it.

Legality of the former use

The key to the conferment of rights by the Order is art. 3, which provides that when a building or other land is used for any purpose of a class specified in the Schedule, its use may be changed to a use for any other purpose of the same class. The change does not constitute "development" because it is excluded by the principal Act, s.55(2)(*f*), and hence no planning permission is required for it.

There is no requirement in the Order that the rights it confers should be limited to cases where the existing use is lawful. An existing use of land may be unlawful, and either susceptible to enforcement action by the local planning authority, or immune from it. The true question therefore is whether enforcement action is still possible in respect of an unlawful existing use of the land. If it is, then it must be equally possible in respect of any use introduced in purported reliance on the Use Classes Order. But any unauthorised material change of use, or breach of a use-restricting condition, is immune from enforcement action if it occurred before the beginning of 1964, or, in the case of change of use of premises to use as a single dwelling-house, more than four years previously. By virtue of the Use Classes Order, a change from an immune use to another use in the same class would not be taken to involve development of the land, and hence the immunity from enforcement action would remain undisturbed. Under s.171B of the principal Act (introduced by the Planning and Compensation Act 1991, s.4) a 10 year rolling period is substituted for the 1964 rule, and immune development is deemed to be lawful (s.191(3)).

"Building or other land"

The effect of the Order is not confined to buildings: some uses may be undertaken entirely in the open, such as storage or vehicle maintenance. The P.A.G. Report urged that there should be three new use classes to cover open land uses, but the Government's consultation paper rejected this proposal, observing that "there does not seem to be any great demand for the introduction of these new use classes." In the 1972 Order, the light and general industrial classes were expressed in terms of buildings, although that term was defined so as to include other land; whilst the special industrial uses were defined in terms of "building and other land." That narrow distinction has been abandoned in the new Order, and the former approach adopted for all cases.

But difficulties may still arise in the case of uses which are carried on partly in buildings and partly on open land. By virtue of art. 3(2), references to a building are to include references to land occupied with the building and used for the same purpose. The 1972 Order contained a similar definition, which referred to "land occupied therewith and used for the same purpose." In *Brooks and Burton Ltd v. Secretary of State for the Environment* [1978] 1 All E.R. 733 the Court of Appeal declined to give this provision the narrow construction sought by the Secretary of State, who argued that it should be confined to land which was dependent upon or otherwise ancillary to the industrial building. The Court of Appeal rejected the notion of dependence, and observed (*per* Lawton L.J. giving the judgment of the Court, at 743):

> "The test is the use to which the land occupied with the building has been put. If it has been used for the same purpose as the building it can be regarded planning-wise as one unit with the building; but if it has not been so used it cannot be. In our judgment that is the plain meaning of art. 2(3). If policy requires a more restricted meaning to be put on the article, the order will have to be amended."

Use change under the General Development Order: the ratchet effect

The use changes which may be authorised by the Use Classes Order are all bilateral: any change in use within one of the use classes will always be reversible without constituting development. But the General Development Order builds onto that structure a number of specified unilateral use changes for which planning permission is deemed to be granted under the GDO. In each case, the change which is permitted is one which would generally constitute an environmental improvement. A new Class III in Sched. 1 to the Town and Country Planning General Development Order 1977 was substituted by S.I. 1987 No. 765, but it was superseded by the Town and Country Planning General Development Order 1988, which was superseded in turn by the Town and Country Planning (General Permitted Development) Order 1995 (S.I. 1995 No. 418), of which Sched. 2, Part 3, now grants planning permission for the following changes in use:

PART 3

CHANGES OF USE

Class A

Permitted development	**A. Development consisting of a change of the use of a building to a use falling within Class A1 (shops) of the Schedule to the Use Classes Order from a use falling within Class A3 (food and drink) of that Schedule or from a use for the sale, or display for sale, of motor vehicles.**

Class B

Permitted development	**B. Development consisting of a change of the use of a building—** **(a) to a use for any purpose within Class B1 (business) of the Schedule for the Use Classes Order from any use falling within Class B2 (general industrial) or B8 (storage and distribution) of that Schedule;** **(b) to a use for any purpose falling within Class B8 (storage and distribution) of that Schedule from any use within Class B1 (business) or B2 (general industrial).**
Development not permitted	B.1 Development is not permitted by Class B where the change is to or from a use falling within Class B8 of that Schedule, if the change of use relates to more than 235 square metres of floorspace in the building.

Class C

Permitted development	**C. Development consisting of a change of use to a use falling within Class A2 (financial and professional services) of the Schedule to the Use Classes Order from a use falling within Class A3 (food and drink) of that Schedule.**

Class D

Permitted development	**D. Development consisting of a change of use of any premises with a display window at ground floor level to a use falling within Class A1 (shops) of the Schedule to the Use Classes Order from a use falling within Class A2 (financial and professional services) to that Schedule.**

Class E

Permitted development	**E. Development consisting of change in the use of any building or other land from a use permitted by a planning permission granted on an application, to another use which that permission would have specifically authorised when it was granted.**
Development not permitted	E.1 Development is not permitted by Class E if— (a) the application for planning permission referred to was made before the date of coming into force of this order; (b) it would be carried out more than ten years after the grant of planning permission; or (c) it would result in the breach of any condition, limitation or specification contained in that planning permission in relation to the use in question.

The development now permitted under the 1995 Order is summarised in the following Table:

From	To	Class in GPDO
A1 (Shops) (any purpose)	a mixed use of A1 (any purpose) and use as a single flat (subject to restrictions)	Class F (introduced in 1995). By virtue of Class G, the change is reversible.
A2 (professional and financial) (any purpose)	a mixed use for A2 (any purpose) and use as a single flat (subject to restrictions)	Class F(b) (introduced in 1995). By virtue of class G, the change is reversible.
A2 (professional and financial) where premises have display window at ground floor level	A1 shop a mixed use of A1 and use as a single flat (subject to restrictions)	Class D (introduced in 1988). Class F(c) (introduced in 1995). By virtue of Class G, the change is reversible.
A3	A1	Class A (appeared in the 1972 UCO as a right to change from use as shop for the sale of hot food to shop for any purpose, and was recast by the 1987 Order).
A3	A1	Class C (introduced by GDO 1988).
B1 (business)	B8 (Storage and distribution)	Class B(b) (introduced by UCO 1987); limited to change in use relating to not more than 235 square metres of floorspace.
B2 (general industrial building).	B1 (business)	Class B(a) (introduced by UCO 1987; original limitation to 235 square metres lifted by GDO 1988).
B2 (general industrial)	B8 (storage and distribution)	Class B(b); limited to change in use relating to not more than 235 square metres of floorspace.
B8 (storage and distribution)	B1 (business)	Class B(a) (introduced by UCO 1987); limited to change in use relating to not more than 235 square metres of floorspace.
Sale of motor vehicles (*sui generis*)	A1 shop)	Class A (former right under UCO 1972 to change to any shop use from use for sale of motor vehicles; recast by 1987 Order).

Apart from those authorised by Class F, these provisions are all one-way, and they may therefore have unintended consequences. A temporary, interim, use of general industrial premises for a more environmentally acceptable business use (Class B1), for example, may be permitted under these provisions, but not a return to the former general industrial use. The former use rights may thus be lost, whether they are established use rights or arise from an express planning permission.

But there is a complex relationship between the ratchet provisions and the scheme of existing use rights preserved by s.57(3) of the principal Act (formerly s.23(8) of the 1971 Act).

Section 57(3) provides that where planning permission to develop land has been granted by a development order, subject to limitations, then planning permission is not required for the use of that land which (apart from its use in accordance with that permission) is the normal use of the land, unless the last-mentioned use was begun in contravention of planning control.

The provision works clearly in the case where a development order grants the right to use land for an interim use, subject to a time limit. An example of this is Part 4 of Sched. 2 to the General Permitted Development Order 1995, which grants permission for the temporary use of land for any purpose (except as a caravan site) for not more than 28 days in total in any calendar year. It is then possible to identify both the "limitation" (*i.e.*, the time limit) and the "normal" use of the land.

But it has never been clear how that provision might operate in the case of other possible limitations on permissions under what is now the General Permitted Development Order, such as the floorspace limitation on the permission in Part 3. In some cases involving the enforcement of planning control (see, *e.g. Garland v. Minister of Housing and Local Government* (1969) 20 P. & C.R. 93; *Rochdale Metropolitan Borough Council v. Simmonds* [1981] J.P.L. 191) the courts have declined to recognise these as "limitations," preferring instead to categorise them simply as part of the definition of the permitted development. But in *Cynon Valley Borough Council v. Secretary of State for Wales* [1986] J.P.L. 760 the Court of Appeal adopted a far broader interpretation. Dealing with the right under Class III of the (then) General Development Order 1977 (as it related to the 1972 Use Classes Order) to change from use as a hot food shop to use as an ordinary shop, the court insisted that the right was subject to a "limitation" because "what was permitted by article 3 of the 1977 Order was a change of use from a fish and chip shop to use as a shop for any purpose except as a shop for the sale of hot food and certain other specific purposes." Thus, in the opinion of the Court, the permission was subject to limitations, the limitations being the excepted shop purposes. Hence, there was a right after all to revert to the previous lawful use.

There are many difficulties with the interpretation, not least the fact that the Court appears not to have addressed the question of what was the "normal" use of the land, which is a pre-requisite to the operation of s.57(3). It appears to have been simply assumed that the antique shop was the "normal" use, notwithstanding that there had been a five year period during which the premises had been used for another purpose. Second, if *exceptions* to a permission granted by the General Permitted Development Order are to constitute *limitations* for the purposes of s.57(3), than all of Part 3 must be regarded as being subject to limitations. The relevant limitation in the *Cynon Valley* case remains as part of the definition of the Class A1 shops use in the new Use Classes Order, together with several other similar limitations; and Class B of Part 3 of the General Permitted Development Order 1995 is also subject to limitations, including the overall limitation based on floorspace. Hence, provided the former use was lawful (*i.e.*, not in breach of planning control) then following *Cynon Valley* there will always be a right to revert to it, following a change of use for which permission is granted by Part 3, provided it can be said to be the "normal" use of the premises. The effect of the Court of Appeal's interpretation would be therefore largely to destroy the intended ratchet effect of Part 3 of the General Permitted Development Order. The better argument, therefore, is probably that the introduction of the word "exceptions" in what is now the General Permitted Development Order 1995, art. 3(2) is deliberate, and intended to offer an alternative to characterising the definitions of the classes as "limitations" at all. Under the 1995 Order, the excepted shop use in *Cynon Valley* would constitute as "exception" rather than a "limitation" to the permitted development, and the argument based on s.57(3) would not arise.

In any event, the *Cynon Valley* analysis clearly does not, given the wording of s.57(3), provide an answer in the case where the preceding use of the premises was unlawful. It is therefore necessary to consider whether such a case might come instead within s.57(4) of the 1990 Act, which provides that where an enforcement notice is served in respect of any development of land, planning permission is not needed for any purpose for which it could lawfully have been used if that development had not been carried out.

In *Young v. Secretary of State for the Environment* [1983] 2 A.C. 662, premises had been used as a laundry from 1912 to 1969, when they changed to use for food processing. The former was a general industrial use; the latter light industrial (now under the business class, B1). Under the (then) General Development Order permission, the change constituted permitted development. But the premises were then used again as a laundry, without planning permission; and a further change was subsequently made to another light industrial use. The House of Lords held that the premises had no subsisting use rights. The protection under s.57(4) was limited to an immediately preceding use. The subsection would, for example, have allowed a reverter to light industrial use upon the serving of an enforcement notice when the premises went back to laundry use; but once the second unauthorised change had been made, the protection of the subsection was lost.

Sui generis uses

Not all uses of land fall within the specified classes. In *Tessier v. Secretary of State for the Environment* [1975] J.P.L. 39 Lord Widgery observed that it was not desirable that the use classes should be stretched to embrace activities which did not clearly fall within them. In this case a building had been used as a sculptor's workshop, the sculptor having operated industrial machinery and tools for cutting out huge stone masonry blocks and other sculpting activities. The Divisional Court held that this was not an industrial use, because the primary activity of the sculptor was the artistic work of sculpture and not the making or manufacturing of an article in the course of a trade or business.

But in *Forkhurst Ltd v. Secretary of State for the Environment* (1982) 46 P. & C.R. 89; [1982] J.P.L. 448, Hodgson J. expressed dissent from Lord Widgery's observations as to interpretation of the Order. In his view there was no warrant in the Act for either stretching or restricting the Use Classes Order, nor could it be said to be either a good thing or, for that matter, a bad thing to treat unusual activities as *sui generis*. The activity either came within the use specified or it did not, and he did not think there was any scope for the measurement of the problem in terms of fact and degree. Once the use had been identified it was not a question of fact and degree whether it came within a given use class. But the dissent is perhaps overstated. Lord Widgery's observations amounted to no more than a caveat against attempting to stretch the classes so as to encompass uses which were in fact *sui generis*; and thus were entirely in line with Hodgson J.'s assertion that there was no warrant for stretching the language of the Order. Further, whilst it may be right that there is no room for the doctrine of fact and degree "once the use had been identified," that does not touch upon what is often the true practical difficulty, to which that doctrine must remain relevant, which is in identifying it—or, more accurately, in assessing whether there has been a material change in use which might, by virtue of the Use Classes Order, be taken not to have involved the carrying out of development.

An innovation in the 1987 Order is to be found in art. 3(6), which effectively declares a number of *sui generis* uses, including theatres and amusement arcades. The list is not, of course, exhaustive; nor, as DOE Circular 13/87 (W.O. 24/87) points out (para. 13), does it imply that such uses should always be regarded as environmentally undesirable and thus liable to be refused permission. Other uses which the courts have held in the past to be *sui generis* include use as an, *e.g.*, packing station (*Kuxhays v. Secretary of State for the Environment* [1987] J.P.L. 675), a non-teaching service unit for a Polytechnic (*Wolff v. Enfield London Borough Council* (1987) 281 E.G. 1320) and a motor vehicle hire service (*Farm Facilities Ltd v. Secretary of State for the Environment* [1981] J.P.L. 42; and see now art. 3(6)(f)). See also Ministerial decisions: [1980] J.P.L. 282 (agricultural contractor's yard, builder's yard); [1985] J.P.L. 884 (garden centre).

Actual implementation of the former use

Before the Order can be relied upon to legitimise a change in use, there must be an existing use within one of the classes. In some contexts in the 1971 Act the word "use" has been taken to include not only actual physical use, but also the legal right to implement a use. The right to use land for a particular purpose continues, for example, even if that use ceases for some time; provided that it has not been supplanted by a change to another use.

But in order for rights to arise under the Use Classes Order, the courts have insisted that the property must at some stage have actually been put to the use upon which the claim to a right to change is based. A mere right to that user, under an unimplemented planning permission, is not enough; and nor, it seems, will a purely token implementation of that right suffice. Thus, in *Kwik-Save Discount Group v. Secretary of State for Wales* [1981] J.P.L. 198, planning permission had been granted for the erection of "a self-service petrol filling station, carwash, car showroom, and tyre fitting bay". The property was then sold to a company who operated retail supermarkets. Upon completion of the building, they offered a motor retailing company a concession for the sale of cars from the premises. It was admittedly a device, undertaken on professional advice so as to bring the Use Classes Order into play. The use lasted for just over four weeks, and the buildings were then put to use as a supermarket. Enforcement action followed, and the inspector in the course of determining the enforcement appeal observed that "the offering of five cars for sale for a period of about one month in a building with a floor space of about 20,000 square feet amounted to no more than a token use of the appeal premises as a shop for the sale of motor vehicles, so minimal as to be of no planning significance." The High Court, and subsequently the Court of Appeal, upheld his finding that there was therefore no effective use of the new premises until they were used as a retail store. It followed that there had been a material change in use from a non-use, requiring planning permission, and not an authorised change from a use within the Use Classes Order.

But provided there has been physical user at some time in the past, it would not need to have continued on the ground right up to the time of the introduction of any new use.

Intensification of use and the Use Classes Order

The courts have recognised that there may be a material change in use when an existing use has been intensified sufficiently for it to be possible to say that the new use is of a different character from, though of the same description as, the former use. There is likely to be a considerable difference, for example, in the planning implications stemming from a caravan site for 3 caravans, and one for 103 caravans.

In the case of a use falling within a class of the Use Classes Order, the doctrine of intensification is qualified by the working of the Order. Despite a process of intensification which would normally constitute development, there will be no development involved if the intensified use is still within the same use class as the former use (see, *e.g. Brooks and Burton Ltd v. Secretary of State for the Environment* [1978] 1 All E.R. 733.). Further, art. 3(4) allows some degree of intensification of a particular use on a site which has a mix of uses falling within classes B1 and B7, so long as the area used for a purpose falling either within class B2, or classes B3 to B7, is not substantially increased as a result.

Hazardous substances

The 1972 Order was amended in 1983 so as to exclude any use for a purpose involving the manufacture, processing, keeping or use of a hazardous substance in a notifiable quantity on land (see now art. 3(5)). Separate site licensing controls for uses involving hazardous substances were introduced by the Housing and Planning Act 1986, Part. IV and are now contained in the Planning (Hazardous Substances) Act 1990.

Planning conditions excluding benefits of the order

It is clear that, as a matter of law, the benefits of the Use Classes Order are capable of being excluded by a planning condition in an appropriate case: see, *e.g. City of London Corporation v. Secretary of State for the Environment* (1971) 23 P. & C.R. 169 (condition requiring that premises should be used for no use other than as an employment agency); and a planning condition excluding the benefit of the 1972 Order has continuing effect in relation to this order (*R. v. Tunbridge Wells Borough Council, ex p. Blue Boys Developments Ltd* [1990] 1 P.L.R. 55). But the Secretary of State has, as a matter of policy, established a presumption against such conditions, and will regard them as unreasonable unless there is clear evidence that the uses excluded would have serious adverse effects on the environment or on amenity, not susceptible to other control (DOE Circular 11/95, Annex, para. 87; DOE Circular 13/85, para. 12). And the courts have insisted that, to have such an effect, a condition must be sufficiently clear and unequivocal: *Dunoon Developments Ltd v. Secretary of State for the Environment* [1992] E.G.C.S. 24.

Effect on existing planning permissions and conditions

The changes made in the 1987 Order cut across pre-existing planning permission and established use rights. Where a building or other land had an existing use for light industrial purposes, for example, it could be used for office purposes—or for a mix of the two—without further consent, upon the coming into force of the Order. But there are three specific cases which call for further analysis:

(1) *use rights arising under a still unimplemented planning permission*: no reliance could be placed upon the 1987 Order unless and until the planning permission had been implemented, and by more than a purely token implementation (see above). Thus an extant but unimplemented permission for offices provided no basis for use for light industrial purposes until it had first been implemented or a further planning permission applied for and granted. Significantly, DOE Circular 13/87 (W.O. 24/87) urges local planning authorities to "take

account of the spirit of the new Order in considering such planning applications" (para. 11).

(2) *new use prohibited by planning condition*: the 1987 Order did not override any existing planning condition which specifically prohibited the new use. It had been common, for example, for some local authorities to impose conditions when granting planning permission for new industrial development, limiting the proportion of ancillary office space to some prescribed percentage of the whole. But the advice in DOE Circular 13/87 (W.O. 24/87) as to the "spirit" of the 1987 Order relates specifically also to applications for the discharge of conditions limiting changes of use within any of the expanded classes, and also refers back (para. 12) to the advice in DOE Circular 11/95 that there is a presumption against imposing conditions designed to restrict future changes of use.

(3) *planning permission limited to specific use or purpose*: in the absence of a specific use-limiting condition, the range of uses allowed by a planning permission is a matter for interpretation. If the permission is for the erection of a building, the permission may specify the purposes for which it may be used, and if no purpose is specified, the permission is to be "construed as including permission to use the building for the purpose for which it was designed." (1990 Act, s.75(2)). Thus if permission is granted for a dwelling-house, it will carry use rights for use as a private dwelling; but a more specific purpose may be specified, such as "an agricultural dwelling," or "old person's accommodation." That specification then becomes the baseline for assessing the materiality of any subsequent change in use. But it may be of limited effect: it would not necessarily follow, for example, that there would be a material change in use if an agricultural worker's dwelling were to be occupied by persons having no connection with agriculture (see, *e.g. Wilson v. West Sussex County Council* [1963] 2 Q.B. 764); and use as a dwellinghouse without any occupational limitation is now within class C.3. In some cases the specified use may correspond to a class defined in the order, either expressly by name or by implication from the description used: see, *e.g. Midlothian District Council v. Stevenson* [1986] J.P.L. 913 ("counter-service restaurant").

Effect on existing contractual arrangements and leases

In *Brewers' Company v. Viewplan* [1989] 45 E.G. 153, the court was asked to construe a provision in a lease which permitted the demised premises to be used for the purposes of the tenants' business and (with the consent of the landlord, such consent not to be unreasonably withheld) for "any other use within Class 3 of the Use Classes Order 1972". The landlords maintained that the reference should now be construed as including a reference to the new business use class (Class B1) introduced by the 1987 Order, and that the reviewed rent should accordingly be higher. The court rejected the submission. Although there was no presumption either way as to whether a reference in a deed to an enactment should include a reference to the law for the time being in force, the specific reference to the 1972 Order contrasted with references elsewhere in the lease to "the Planning Acts", pointing strongly to an intention that the user clause should be narrowly construed. The clause conferred an additional benefit on the tenant, and it was readily understandable that the landlord should have wished to confine that benefit within a range of which he knew at the time of the lease.

Compensation

Whenever any amendment is made to the General Permitted Development Order which has the effect of restricting or taking away any planning permission granted by it, there is an entitlement to compensation if such permission is refused on a subsequent application (1990 Act, s.107; formerly 1971 Act, s.164). But those provisions do not apply to changes to the Use Classes Order, and as a general rule therefore any loss of potential use rights when the 1987 Order came into effect, or any subsequent amendment made, is not compensatable.

However, certain use rights were formerly defined for compensation purposes under the Third Schedule to the 1990 Act. Section 114 provided that the local planning authority were liable to pay compensation where, on an application, planning permission was refused by the Secretary of State for the carrying out of development of any class specified in Part II of Schedule 3, and it could be shown that the value of the interest of any person in the land was less than it would have been if permission had been granted. Part II included:

> "6. In the case of a building or other land which, at a material date, was used for a purpose falling within any general class specified in the Town and Country Planning (Use Classes for Third Schedule Purposes) Order 1948, or which, having been unoccupied on and at all times since the appointed day, was last used (otherwise than before January 7, 1937) for any such purpose, the use of that building or land for any other purpose falling within the same general class."

The 1948 Order specified a range of use classes which were significantly different from those of the 1987 Order, although for the most part it was narrower and more restrictive in its scope. In some cases, however, the classifications were different, such as in the case of theatres which under the 1987 Order are now *sui generis*, but in the 1948 Order were grouped with cinemas and music halls; and "turkish or other vapour or foam baths" (no longer to be found in the 1987 Order), and concert halls and public halls which are now in different classes but in the 1948 Order were both in Class XXII.

The special compensation provisions for Third Schedule development were repealed from July 25, 1991 by the Planning and Compensation Act 1991, s.31(2).

Citation and commencement

1. This Order may be cited as the Town and Country Planning (Use Classes) Order 1987 and shall come into force in June 1987.

Interpretation

2. In this Order, unless the context otherwise requires:—

"care" means personal care for people in need of such care by reason of old age, disablement, past or present dependence on alcohol or drugs or past or present mental disorder, and in class C2 also includes the personal care of children and medical care and treatment;

"day centre" means premises which are visited during the day for social or recreational purposes or for the purposes of rehabilitation or occupational training, at which care is also provided;

[*"hazardous substance" and "notifiable quantity" have the meanings assigned to those terms by the Notification of Installations Handling Hazardous Substances Regulations 1982*;]

"industrial process" means a process for or incidental to any of the following purposes:—

(a) the making of any article or part of any article (including a ship or vessel, or a film, video or sound recording);

(b) the altering, repairing, maintaining, ornamenting, finishing, cleaning, washing, packing, canning, adapting for sale, breaking up or demolition of any article; or

(c) the getting, dressing or treatment of minerals;

in the course of any trade or business other than agriculture, and other than a use carried out in or adjacent to a mine or quarry;

"Schedule" means the Schedule to this Order;

"site" means the whole area of land within a single unit of occupation.

COMMENTARY

AMENDMENT

The words in italics were repealed by S.I. 1992 No. 657 from June 1, 1992.

GENERAL NOTE

By virtue of the Interpretation Act 1978, s.11, words used in the order which are defined by the parent Act (section 336 of the Town and Country Planning Act 1990) bear the same meaning in the order unless a contrary intention appears.

"hazardous substances" and "notifiable quantity": see the Notification of Installations Handling Hazardous Substances Regulations 1982, *ante*.

"industrial process": the definition is largely unchanged from the definition in the old Order of "industrial building", which was defined in terms of the processes carried out therein, except that the making of a film, video or sound recording is now expressly included in the list of industrial processes. The process must in all cases be one which is carried on in the course of a trade or business other than agriculture, but the courts have been prepared to give this expression a broad interpretation, so as to include horticultural activities involving the sorting, grading and despatch of plant bulbs (*Horwitz v. Rowson* [1960] 1 W.L.R. 803) and the cooking of school meals (*Rael-Brook Ltd. v. Minister of Housing and Local Government* [1967] 2 Q.B. 65). A business need not be a commercial business: see *Newbury District Council v. Secretary of State for the Environment* [1981] A.C. 578, at 614 *per* Lord Scarman.

Use Classes

3.—(1) Subject to the provisions of this Order, where a building or other land is used for a purpose of any class specified in the Schedule, the use of that building or that other land for any other purpose of the same class shall not be taken to involve development of the land.

(2) References in paragraph (1) to a building include references to land occupied with the building and used for the same purposes.

(3) A use which is included in and ordinarily incidental to any use in a class specified in the Schedule is not excluded from the use to which it is incidental merely because it is specified in the Schedule as a separate use.

(4) Where land on a single site or on adjacent sites used as parts of a single undertaking is used for purposes consisting of or including purposes falling within any two or more of classes B1 to B7 in the Schedule, those classes may be treated as a single class in considering the use of that land for the purposes of this Order, so long as the area used for a purpose falling either within class B2 or within [classes B4 to B7] is not substantially increased as a result.

[*(5) No class specified in the Schedule includes any use for a purpose which involves the manufacture, processing, keeping or use of a hazardous substance in such circumstances as will result in the presence at one time of a notifiable quantity of that substance in, on, over or under that building or land or any site of which that building or land forms part.*]

(6) No class specified in the Schedule includes use—

(a) as a theatre,

(b) as an amusement arcade or centre, or a funfair,

[(c) as a launderette,]

(d) for the sale of fuel for motor vehicles,

(e) for the sale or display for sale of motor vehicles,

(f) for a taxi business or business for the hire of motor vehicles,

(g) as a scrapyard, or a yard for the storage or distribution of minerals or the breaking of motor vehicles.

[(h) for any work registrable under the Alkali, etc. Works Regulation Act 1906]

[(i) as a hostel.]

COMMENTARY

AMENDMENT

Para. 6(c) was substituted by S.I. 1991 No. 1567 from July 31, 1991. The paragraph formerly provided: "(c) for the washing or cleaning of clothes or fabrics in coin-operated machines or on premises at which the goods to be cleaned are received direct from the visiting public." Use for the washing or cleaning of clothes or fabrics on the premises, and use for the reception of goods to be washed, cleaned or repaired, is now included in Class A1 (Shops).

Para. 6(h) was inserted, and the words in square brackets in para. 4 substituted by S.I. 1992 No. 610 from March 31, 1992. Para. (5) was repealed by S.I. 1992 No. 657 from June 1, 1992.

Para. 6(i) was inserted by S.I. 1994 No. 724 from April 4, 1994.

GENERAL NOTE

Para. (1) is the key to the operation of the Order, and it follows the language of the 1990 Act in providing that use changes within classes "shall not be taken to involve development of the land."

Analysis of the other provisions of this article is included in the General Note to the Order above, and in the General Note to the individual use classes.

Change of use of part of building or land

4. In the case of a building used for a purpose within class C3 (dwelling-houses) in the Schedule, the use as a separate dwelling-house of any part of the building or of any land occupied with and used for the same purposes as the building is not, by virtue of this Order, to be taken as not amounting to development.

COMMENTARY

General Note

The 1987 order is intended to operate in cases where there is a sub-division of the planning unit, except for dwelling-houses. It was held in the Divisional Court in *Winton v. Secretary of State for the Environment* [1984] J.P.L. 188 that the Use Classes Order 1972 conferred exemption from development control only when the former and the new use related to the same planning unit. It did not, therefore, allow the sub-division of an industrial building into smaller units, even though the use of each unit before and after might be within the same use class.

A provision contained in the Housing and Planning Act 1986 amended s.22 of the 1971 Act (now s.55 of the 1990 Act) so as to override that decision and to make it clear that the rights conferred by the order should, subject to the provisions of the order, extend not only to the whole, but also to any part, of the buildings or other land to which it was applicable.

This article qualifies the new general rule, but only in respect of dwelling-houses. It is clumsily expressed but the use of the double negative is necessary to maintain the principle that the order does not define what does constitute development, but merely carves out some areas which do not. In the case of dwelling-houses, there is an express provision in s.55(3)(a) of the 1990 Act which provides that the use as two or more dwelling-houses of any building previously used as a single dwelling-house involves a material change in the use of the building and of each part thereof which is so used. This article ensures that nothing in the Use Classes Order is capable of undermining that provision.

Revocation

5. The Town and Country Planning (Use Classes) Order 1972 and the Town and Country Planning (Use Classes) (Amendment) Order 1983 are hereby revoked.

SCHEDULE

Part A

Class A1. Shops

Use for all or any of the following purposes—
(a) for the retail sale of goods other than hot food,
(b) as a post office,
(c) for the sale of tickets or as a travel agency,
(d) for the sale of sandwiches or other cold food for consumption off the premises,
(e) for hairdressing,
(f) for the direction of funerals,
(g) for the display of goods for sale,
(h) for the hiring out of domestic or personal goods or articles,
[(i) for the washing or cleaning of clothes or fabrics on the premises,]
[(j) for the reception of goods to be washed, cleaned or repaired,]
where the sale, display or services is to visiting members of the public.

COMMENTARY

Amendment

Paras. (i) and (j) were substituted from July 31, 1991, by the Town and Country Planning (Use Classes) (Amendment) Order 1991 (No. 1567).

General Note

Introduction

This shops class represented a long overdue updating of the former Class I. References in the 1972 Order to tripe, pets shops and cats-meat shops have disappeared, and these uses are now brought in to the shops class. The definition is now inclusionary, not exclusionary, though the following are excluded by art. 3(6):
—amusement arcades, amusement centres, and funfairs;
—launderettes, though under new paras. (i) and (j) use for the reception of goods to be washed, cleaned or repaired remains within the class and dry cleaning has also been brought within it.
—motor fuel, motor vehicles and car hire.

The nature of a shop

The 1987 order does not contain the former extended definition of a shop, which included "any other purpose appropriate to a shopping area" (now to be found in Class A.2 below); and there is a new requirement (though probably implicit in each of the categories of the former definition) that the sale, display or services be to visiting members of the public.

In *Cawley v. Secretary of State for the Environment*[1990] 2 P.L.R. 90, the High Court held that the word "shop" used in the heading to this Class showed an intention to restrict its scope to uses which take place in buildings. The Order did not therefore authorise changes in retail uses on open land, such as between (in the *Cawley* case itself) use in connection with a garden centre to use for the storage and sale of caravans.

In *R. v. Thurrock Borough Council, ex p. Tesco Stores* the court (Schiemann J.) held that a "warehouse club" was not a shop for the purpose of this provision. Because there was a restriction on those who could come to the premises and buy, the premises were not *prima facie* for the sale of goods to "visiting members of the public" and hence did not fall within Class A1:

"... the relevant phrase in the Use Classes Order is not intended to catch a situation where the sale is, not to any member of the public who cares to come along, but only to those who, being eligible, have first become members of a restricted group. The Use Classes Order in effect exempts from planning control those who are within one of its specified categories and want to move within that category. I see no reason to construe the words of the Order very widely so as to enable them to embrace categories which they do not naturally embrace."

The retail sale of goods

The concept of retail sale of goods does not extend to the showing of films in coin-operated cubicles, and nor would that constitute a lawful use as ancillary use to a retail use (*Lydcare v. Secretary of State for the Environment* (1985) 49 P. & C.R. 186). Nor does it encompass a bureau de change, which is more appropriately classified under Class A2: *Palisade Investments Ltd v. Secretary of State for the Environment* [1994] E.G.C.S. 188, C.A.

The ratchet provisions of the General Permitted Development Order

Premises used for the sale of food or drink for consumption on the premises, and takeaway hot food shops, are expressly excluded, but are within the ratchet provisions of Sched 2, Part 3 of the General Permitted Development Order 1995, which grants planning permission for a change in the use of such premises to any use within this class (Class A1) of the Use Classes Order. So too premises used for financial and professional purposes, having a ground floor level display window (this provision was introduced by the 1988 General Development Order), and premises used for the sale (or display for sale) of motor vehicles. But once that permission has been implemented the former use rights may be lost, even where they have been granted by an express planning permission, unless there is a right of reverter under s.57(4) of the 1990 Act (s.23(8) of the 1971 Act): see further the discussion of *Cynon Valley Borough Council v. Secretary of State for Wales* [1986] J.P.L. 760 *supra*.

The retail sale of goods does not include showing films in coin-operated cubicles and nor would that constitute an incidental use to a retail use (*Lydcare v. Secretary of State for the Environment* (1985) 49 P. & C.R. 186; (1984) 272 E.G. 175).

Class A2. Financial and professional services

Use for the provision of—
(a) financial services, or
(b) professional services (other than health or medical services), or
(c) any other services (including use as a betting office) which it is appropriate to provide in a shopping area,
where the services are provided principally to visiting members of the public.

COMMENTARY

GENERAL NOTE

This was a new class in the 1987 Order, designed to meet the needs of uses, such as banks and building societies, which do not fall clearly within either a shops or offices classification. The Government rejected the most radical of the P.A.G. proposals for shopping areas, which would have amalgamated high street offices with shops, and ultimately also with other professional services such as solicitors and estate agents. Instead, the Order has the two separate classes of shops and financial and professional services, so as to allow local planning authorities to maintain control over conversion of shops into non-retail uses. The General Permitted Development Order 1995, Sched. 2, Part 3, grants permission to change into this Class from Class A3 (food and drink); and also to change from this Class to Class A1 (shops), but only in respect of premises having a display window at ground floor level.

The range of uses contained in this class is broad. It includes all professional services provided principally to visiting members of the public. An office use not satisfying that last condition would fall within Class B1. Health or medical services are excluded (and are in Class D1), and so are taxi businesses and motor vehicle hire businesses (art. 3(6)). The courts had already taken the view that a radio-controlled hire car business was not an "office" use within the 1972 Order: *J. Toomey Motors Ltd v. Secretary of State for the Environment* [1981] J.P.L. 418.

In *Palisade Investments Ltd v. Secretary of State for the Environment* [1993] 3 P.L.R. 49 the High Court upheld an inspector's finding that a bureau de change fell more naturally within Class A2 of the Order (provision of financial services) than Class A1 (shop use, including the retail sale of goods to the public). Although the sale of currency was no doubt a commercial transaction like the sale of any other commodity, its planning implications were more akin to those of a bank than to an ordinary shop. Like banks, a few can add to the attraction of a retail area by providing an ancillary service, but too many can cause its decline. This approach was endorsed by the Court of Appeal in refusing leave to appeal (see [1994] E.G.C.S. 188).

Class A3. Food and drink

Use for the sale of food or drink for consumption on the premises or of hot food for consumption off the premises.

COMMENTARY

General Note

Shops for the sale of hot food were excluded from Class I of the 1972 Order (an exclusion which before then had been limited to fish and chip shops), and this new class continues that exclusion, but at the same time providing an amalgamation with cafes and restaurants.

Planning permission is granted by the Town and Country Planning (General Permitted Development) Order 1995 (S.I. 1995 No. 418), Sched. 2, Part 3, for change of use from this Class to Class A1 (shops); and to Class A2 (financial and professional). The latter right was first introduced by the 1988 Order.

PART B

Class B1. Business

Use for all or any of the following purposes—

(a) as an office other than a use within class A2 (financial and professional services),

(b) for research and development of products or processes, or

(c) for any industrial process,

being a use which can be carried out in any residential area without detriment to the amenity of that area by reason of noise, vibration, smell, fumes, smoke, soot, ash, dust or grit.

COMMENTARY

GENERAL NOTE

This Class amalgamates the former two classes of offices and light industrial use. The change was prompted partly by the changing relationship between industrial and offices uses, particularly in high technology uses; and partly also because light industrial uses, which were always by definition uses which were capable of being carried on in a residential area, appeared to have no significantly different environmental impact from office uses. A composite use comprising office and industrial elements otherwise than in a primary/ancillary relationship was formerly *sui generis*: *British Paper and Board Industry Research Association v. London Borough of Croydon* (1969) 210 E.G. 461.

Office uses within Class A2 are expressly excluded, although the dividing line will often be difficult to draw, since it may depend entirely upon the extent to which services are, or have been, provided to visiting members of the public: see, *e.g. Kalra v. Secretary of State for the Environment, The Times*, November 13, 1995 (C.A.).

Planning permission is granted under Part 3 of Sched. 2 to the Town and Country Planning (General Permitted Development) Order 1995 (S.I. 1995 No. 418) for a change of use into this class, from any use falling within class B2 (general industrial) or B8 (storage or distribution).

In all cases the use must be one which can be carried out in any residential area without detriment to the amenity of the area by reason of noise, vibration, smell, fumes, smoke, soot, ash, dust or grit. This limitation is based on the 1972 Order's definition of light industrial use, except that in that context it was the processes carried on or the machinery installed which had to be such as could be carried on or installed without detriment to amenity. The new formula encompasses the use itself. It is couched in terms of the potential environmental impact of the proposed use, and may well prove in practice to be subjective and difficult to apply. Two general points of interpretation were established with the previous limitation, and remain relevant.

First, the reference to "any residential area" is general, and not specific to the actual area surrounding the site. It is irrelevant therefore that the actual site may be in a noisy area, or in a primarily industrial area, or that the particular geography of the site may result in the nearest neighbours being protected from emissions (see, *e.g. W. T. Lamb Properties Ltd v. Secretary of State for the Environment* [1983] J.P.L. 303, where the building in question was situated adjacent to Gatwick Airport). The residential area is purely notional. Second, the definition is focused not on the inherent qualities of the proposed industrial process, but on the impact of the use. It follows that the design of the particular building, and especially any measures incorporated into the design to minimise noise emissions, are highly relevant factors. Thus a builder's yard used for joinery and metal fabrication is more likely to be detrimental to amenity and thus outside this class (see, *e.g. Essex County Council v. Secretary of State for the Environment* [1974] J.P.L. 286) than a properly insulated building put to the same use. Account may be taken of the measures (like noise insulation and dust extraction) which can, and now customarily are, put in place to control the escape of offensive emissions and mitigate their polluting effect (*Blight & White Ltd v. Secretary of State for the Environment* [1993] 1 P.L.R. 1). In a Ministerial decision reported at [1978] J.P.L. 781 the Secretary of State held that the use of an industrial building had changed from general industrial to light industrial upon the installation of a new boiler which stopped emissions of smoke and grit.

The Circular (DOE 13/87 (W.O. 24/87), para. 21) observes that, because the new formula encompasses all aspects of the use rather than merely processes and machinery, there will normally be no material change of use requiring planning permission until an intensification or change in the nature of the use is such that the use would no longer satisfy the limitation.

Class B2. General industrial

Use for the carrying on of an industrial process other than one falling within class B1 above [*or within* [*classes B2 to B7 below*].

COMMENTARY

General Note

This Class remained unchanged from the 1972 Use Classes Order. The reference to Classes B3 to B7 was revoked by S.I. 1995 No. 297.

Class B3. Special Industrial Group A

Use for any work registrable under the Alkali, etc. Works Regulation Act 1960 and which is not included in any of classes B4 to B7 below.

Class B4. Special Industrial Group B

Use for any of the following processes, except where the process is ancillary to the getting, dressing or treatment of minerals and is carried on in or adjacent to a quarry or mine:—

(a) smelting, calcining, sintering or reducing ores, minerals, concentrates or mattes;
(b) converting, refining, re-heating, annealing, hardening, melting, carburising, forging or casting metals or alloys other than pressure die-casting;
(c) recovering metal from scrap or drosses or ashes;
(d) galvanising;
(e) pickling or treating metal in acid;
(f) chromium plating.

Class B5. Special Industrial Group C

Use for any of the following processes, except where the process is ancillary to the getting, dressing or treatment of minerals and is carried on in or adjacent to a quarry or mine:—

(a) burning bricks or pipes;
(b) burning lime or dolomite;
(c) producing zinc oxide, cement or alumina;
(d) foaming, crushing, screening or heating minerals or slag;
(e) processing pulverized fuel ash by heat;
(f) producing carbonate of lime or hydrated lime;
(g) producing inorganic pigments by calcining, roasting or grinding.

Class B6. Special Industrial Group D

Use for any of the following processes:—

(a) distilling, refining or blending oils (other than petroleum or petroleum products);

(b) producing or using cellulose or using other pressure sprayed metal finishes (other than in vehicle repair workshops in connection with minor repairs, or the application of plastic powder by the use of fluidised bed and electrostatic spray techniques);

(c) boiling linseed oil or running gum;

(d) processes involving the use of hot pitch or bitumen (except the use of bitumen in the manufacture of roofing felt at temperatures not exceeding 220°C and also the manufacture of coated roadstone);

(e) stoving enamelled ware;

(f) producing aliphatic esters of the lower fatty acids, butyric acid, caramel, hexamine, iodoform, napthols, resin products (excluding plastic moulding or extrusion operations and producing plastic sheets, rods, tubes, filaments, fibres or optical components produced by casting, calendering, moulding, shaping or extrusion), salicylic acid or sulphonated organic compounds;

(g) producing rubber from scrap;

(h) chemical processes in which chlorphenols or chlorcresols are used as intermediates;

(i) manufacturing acetylene from calcium carbide;

(j) manufacturing, recovering or using pyridine or picolines, any methyl or ethyl amine or acrylates.

Class B7. Special Industrial Group E

Use for carrying on any of the following industries, businesses or trades:—

Boiling blood, chitterlings, nettlings or soap.

Boiling, burning, grinding or steaming bones.

Boiling or cleaning tripe.

Breeding maggots from putrescible animal matter.

Cleaning, adapting or treating animal hair.

Curing fish.

Dealing in rags and bones (including receiving, storing, sorting or manipulating rags in, or likely to become in, an offensive condition, or any bones, rabbit skins, fat or putrescible animal products of a similar nature).

Dressing or scraping fish skins.

Drying skins.

Making manure from bones, fish, offal, blood, spent hops, beans or other putrescible animal or vegetable matter.

Making or scraping guts.

Manufacturing animal charcoal, blood albumen, candles, catgut, glue, fish oil, size or feeding stuff for animals or poultry from meat, fish, blood, bone, feathers, fat or animal offal either in an offensive condition or subjected to any process causing noxious or injurious effluvia.

Melting, refining or extracting fat or tallow.

Preparing skins for working.

COMMENTARY

AMENDMENT

Class B3 was repealed, and the words in square brackets in class B2 substituted by S.I. 1992 No. 610 from March 31, 1992. The remaining special industrial Classes, B4, B5, B6 and B7, were revoked from March 9, 1995 by the Town and Country Planning (Use Classes) Amendment Order 1995 (S.I. 1995 No. 297).

GENERAL NOTE

Review of special industrial use classes

The Department of the Environment in 1987 commissioned technical research into the special use classes in the Use Classes Order, and then accepted that there might be little benefit in retaining the classes in their present form. The *Report* (undertaken by Roy Waller and Associates) recommended that the special classes should be abolished, and that uses equivalent to the current special industrial uses be unclassified. For the medium term, the definition of Class B2 General Industrial should be changed to include uses which could be carried on without detriment to the environment of existing or projected neighbouring land uses, and planning permission for the future for industrial development should always refer to Class B1 or B2, except for *sui generis* uses. The Order should remain in its present form in the short term pending refinement of the proposed Class B2 definition and formulation of the necessary supporting guidance, which might take two to three years to implement; but in the interim there was a need for clarification of government advice.

The Government then put forward three alternative reforms for consultation, whilst acknowledging that retention of the status quo would also be a possibility.

Consultees gave a mixed response to the options, and were then asked to consider a further possibility. This entailed replacing Classes B3 to B7 with two new special classes, based on the schedule of processes to be prescribed for the Environment Protection Act 1990. These would tie in respectively with Part A processes (which are subject to integrated pollution control administered by Her Majesty's Inspectorate of Pollution) and Part B (the air pollution control powers administered by local authorities).

The Department saw the advantages of this proposal as being that it should benefit industry by providing greater flexibility, and that it would at the same time continue to provide a degree of certainty about the characteristics of potential future industrial neighbours. Local planning authorities could continue to exercise planning control on grounds of general amenity over change of use from light and general industrial processes to others with recognised pollution potential. It would also allow industry to adapt and change uses on sites whose suitability for potentially polluting industry had already been accepted. Development control would remain over changes of use between classes of industrial process on the basis of pollution potential, including those outside the Environmental Protection Act 1990 but which nevertheless had implications for local amenity and the environment, such as dust and smell.

A further consultation paper in 1993 (see the December 1993 *Monthly Bulletin*) sought views on the repeal altogether of Classes B3 to B7, and that was the course eventually taken in 1995.

Class B8. Storage or distribution

Use for storage or as a distribution centre.

GENERAL NOTE

This is a reworded version of the old class X, which included "Use as a wholesale warehouse or repository for any purpose." The substituted reference to a storage or distribution centre is merely a different description of the same use. The word "repository" had been given a broad interpretation by the House of Lords in *Newbury District Council v. Secretary of State for the Environment* [1981] A.C. 578, rejecting the Court of Appeal's view that it implied a storage use as part of a business. The House ruled that, so long as storage was the principal use of the premises, there need be no business element involved. That point is now reinforced by the use of the word "storage," and Circular 13/87 (W.O. 24/87) (para. 23) also observes that the definition of the class by reference to land use instead of building type "should help to make it clear that warehouses—where the main purpose is the sale of goods direct to visiting members of the public—will generally fall within the shops class however much floorspace is used for storage."

As with "warehouse or repository," "storage and distribution" implies no rights to retail use, except to some limited incidental extent. It would not, for example, include use as a shop (*Decorative and Caravan Paints Ltd v. Minister of Housing and Local Government* (1970) 214 E.G. 1355; *Monomart Warehouses Ltd v. Secretary of State for the Environment* (1977) 34 P. & C.R. 305) or as a "cash and carry warehouse" (*LTSS Print & Supply Services Ltd v. London Borough of Hackney* [1976] Q.B. 663).

A further feature of the new class is that uses within it may be conducted entirely on open land (which a "warehouse" use formerly could not: *Hooper v. Slater* [1978] J.P.L. 252), although the Government rejected the P.A.G. proposals for new open land use classes.

There is planning permission under the Town and Country Planning (General Permitted Development) Order 1995 (S.I. 1995 No. 418), Sched. 2, Part 3, for change to this use from any use within class B1 (business) or B2 (general industrial).

Part C

[Class C1. Hotels

Use as a hotel or as a boarding or guest house where, in each case, no significant element of care is provided.]

COMMENTARY

Amendment

This Class was substituted from April 4, 1994, by S.I. 1994 No. 724.

General Note

Background

This Class derives from Class XI of the 1972 Use Classes Order, which extended to: "Use as a boarding or guest house, or an hotel providing sleeping accommodation." The 1987 Order initially was wider in its scope, in including hostel use. It extended to: "Use as a hotel, boarding or guest house or as a hostel where, in each case, no significant element of care is provided". The 1994 amendment once again excluded hostels from the Use-Class. The exclusion is purely prospective, from April 5, 1994, and does not affect cases where the use of premises had already changed to use to or from a hostel (though preventing any future reversion to the former use without planning permission). The reason for the amendment was given by the Minister of Planning and Local Government as being that there was a real threat to the amenity of tourist areas from the establishment of hostels, which have been attracting large numbers of benefit claimants, in traditional hotel areas.

The distinction between hostels and hotels

Hostel use is now *sui generis*, except where a significant element of care is involved, in which case it falls within Class C2 (use for the provision of residential accommodation and care to people in need of care). Change of use from use of premises as a private dwelling-house, or as a block of flats, to use as a hotel or hostel, is capable of constituting a material change of use and thus requiring express permission: see, *e.g. Birmingham Corporation v. Habib Ullah* [1964] 1 Q.B. 178; *Panayi v. Secretary of State for the Environment* [1985] J.P.L. 783 (which also contains a detailed discussion of the meaning of "hostel"); and *Mayflower Cambridge Ltd. v. Secretary of State for the Environment* (1975) 30 P. & C.R. 28 (change from hotel to bed-sitting rooms a material change in use). So too a change between hotel use and use as a residential club (*English Speaking Union v. Westminster London Borough Council* (1975) 26 P. & C.R. 575), or as a house in multiple occupation (*Breachberry v. Secretary of State for the Environment* [1985] J.P.L. 180). A redistribution of ancillary activity within a hotel does not require planning permission: *Emma Hotels Ltd. v. Secretary of State for the Environment* [1979] J.P.L. 390; [1981] J.P.L. 283.

Class C2. Residential institutions

Use for the provision of residential accommodation and care to people in need of care (other than a use within class C3 (dwelling houses)).
Use as a hospital or nursing home.
Use as a residential school, college or training centre.

COMMENTARY

GENERAL NOTE

This class is an amalgamation of two classes, XII and XIV, of the 1972 Order. Except for schools, the principal distinction between uses in this class, and those in class C1, is the provision of residential accommodation and care to people in need of care. "Care" is defined in art. 2 as meaning:

> "personal care for people in need of such care by reason of old age, disablement, past or present dependence on alcohol or drugs or past or present mental disorder, and in class C2 also includes the personal care of children and medical care and treatment."

The definition thus goes beyond the mere provision of services, such as might be provided in a hostel within class C1. The provision of a "significant element of care" will take a use out of class C1, and (provided the people to whom it is provided are actually in need of it) bring it within this class, or class C3.

Class C3. Dwellinghouses

Use as a dwellinghouse (whether or not as a sole or main residence)—
(a) by a single person or by people living together as a family, or
(b) by not more than six residents living together as a single household (including a household where care is provided for residents).

COMMENTARY

GENERAL NOTE

This is a new class. Much of the area of use change that it authorises would not in itself constitute a material change of use requiring planning permission, but it does clarify the position in cases where unrelated residents live together as a single household. This will include, say, students or other young people sharing a dwellinghouse, as well as small group homes for disabled and mentally disordered people living in the community rather than in institutions (see further D.O.E. Circular 13/87 (W.O. 24/87), para. 27). There had previously been doubt about the appropriate classification of uses involving residential care: see, *e.g. Rann v. Secretary of State for the Environment* (1980) 40 P. & C.R. 113; *Torbay Borough Council* (1986) 1 P.A.D. 269.

The control limit of six persons defines the scope of the right, but does not imply that any excess in numbers *must* constitute a breach of planning control. Where, for example, premises have been put to this use and six people have lived together as a single household, there will subsequently be a material change in use only where the total number of residents increases to the point where it can be said that the use has intensified so as to become of a different character, or the residents no longer live together as a single household (which may then fall to be regarded as a hostel use, or house let in lodgings). Where the household is one where care is provided for residents it remains in this class (provided the limitations are met) rather than class C2 (residential institutions). The Secretary of State does not accept that the distinction depends upon the extent of the care provided: see the appeal decision at [1992] J.P.L. 489; and the High Court has confirmed that the Class does not require that the staff providing care for residents need themselves be resident (*R. v. Bromley London Borough Council, ex p. Sinclair* [1991] 3 P.L.R. 60).

The Class does not override a condition imposed on a planning permission excluding the benefits of the 1972 Order, nor does it override a planning agreement restricting use of premises: *R. v. Tunbridge Wells Borough Council, ex p. Blue Boys Developments Ltd.* [1990] 1 P.L.R. 55.

Part D

Class D1. Non-residential institutions

Any use not including a residential use—
(a) for the provision of any medical or health services except the use of premises attached to the residence of the consultant or practitioner,
(b) as a crêche, day nursery or day centre,
(c) for the provision of education,
(d) for the display of works of art (otherwise than for sale or hire),
(e) as a museum,
(f) as a public library or public reading room,
(g) as a public hall or exhibition hall,
(h) for, or in connection with, public worship or religious instruction.

COMMENTARY

General Note

This class groups together classes XIII, XV and XVI of the 1972 Order, but with drafting improvements.

"Day centre" is defined by art. 2 as meaning:

> "premises which are visited during the day for social or recreational purposes or for the purposes of rehabilitation or occupational training, at which care is also provided."

See also the definition of "care" in art. 2.

Class D2. Assembly and leisure

Use as—
(a) a cinema,
(b) a concert hall,
(c) a bingo hall or casino,
(d) a dance hall,
(e) a swimming bath, skating rink, gymnasium or area for other indoor or outdoor sports or recreations, not involving motorised vehicles or firearms.

COMMENTARY

General Note

Theatres are now excluded from this class, which otherwise groups together classes XVII and XVIII of the 1972 Order, extended so as to include all indoor and outdoor sports except those involving motor sports and firearms.

See also appeal decision at [1988] J.P.L. 840.

THE TOWN AND COUNTRY PLANNING (GENERAL PERMITTED DEVELOPMENT) ORDER 1995

(S.I. 1995 No. 418)

Article

1. Citation, commencement and interpretation.
2. Application.
3. Permitted development.
4. Directions restricting permitted development.
5. Approval of Secretary of State for article 4(1) directions.
6. Notice and confirmation of article 4(2) directions.
7. Directions restricting permitted development under Class B of Part 22 or Class B of Part 23.
8. Directions.
9. Revocations.

SCHEDULE 1

Part

1. Article 1(4) land.
2. Article 1(5) land.
3. Article 1(6) land.

SCHEDULE 2

Permitted Development

Part

1. Development within the curtilage of a dwellinghouse.
2. Minor operations.
3. Changes of use.
4. Temporary buildings and uses.
5. Caravan sites.
6. Agricultural buildings and operations.
7. Forestry buildings and operations.
8. Industrial and warehouse development.
9. Repairs to unadopted streets and private ways.
10. Repairs to services.
11. Development under local or private Acts or orders.
12. Development by local authorities.
13. Development by local highway authorities.
14. Development by drainage bodies.
15. Development by the [Environment Agency].
16. Development by or on behalf of sewerage undertakers.

17. Development by statutory undertakers.
18. Aviation development.
19. Development ancillary to mining operations.
20. Coal mining development by the Coal Authority and licensed operators.
21. Waste tipping at a mine.
22. Mineral exploration.
23. Removal of material from mineral-working deposits.
24. Development by telecommunications code system operators.
25. Other telecommunications development.
26. Development by the Historic Buildings and Monuments Commission for England.
27. Use by members of certain recreational organisations.
28. Development at amusement parks.
29. Driver information systems.
30. Toll road facilities.
31. Demolition of buildings.
32. Schools, colleges, universities and hospitals.
33. Closed circuit television cameras.

SCHEDULE 3

STATUTORY INSTRUMENTS REVOKED

TOWN AND COUNTRY PLANNING (GENERAL PERMITTED DEVELOPMENT) ORDER 1995

Introductory Note

Origins of the General Development Orders

The first statutory power to make "development orders," both general and special, appears to have been conferred as long ago as 1919, by the Housing, Town Planning etc. Act 1919, s.45. That Act set out to strengthen and improve the powers conferred by the Housing, Town Planning etc. Act, 1909, which had given local authorities power to make planning schemes, which it was envisaged would proceed largely on the basis of consensus between landowners and "councils in whose districts signs of development are visible" (Local Government Board Circular dated December 31, 1909).

Under the 1909 Act, councils were to be able to enforce their schemes simply by removing, pulling down or altering any building which contravened the scheme (s.57), and although an owner could seek compensation for any injurious affect on property values caused by the making of a scheme, he could not claim in respect of any building erected after the date the local authority applied for consent to make a scheme (s.58(2)). Any building erected from then until the scheme was approved could be demolished by the local authority, and without any compensation liability, if it was not in accordance with the scheme as finally adopted.

Hence there was stalemate. A decision to apply for consent to make a scheme would freeze development in the area. The way chosen to get around it was to give the Local Government Board power to make development orders to permit the development of estates and buildings to proceed pending the adoption of the town planning scheme, subject to such conditions as may be prescribed by the order (1919 Act, s.45). Further, carrying out development in accordance with such an order was not to affect compensation entitlement.

The first such order, the Town Planning (General Interim Development) Order 1922 (S.R. & O. 1922 No. 927) did not itself grant permission for development. Instead, it created a regime for "interim" development control, which closely resembled the comprehensive development control introduced after the Second World War. Local authorities were empowered by the Order to grant permission, subject to such requirements as the authority might reasonably impose; and there was a right for aggrieved applicants to appeal to the Minister. The Minister of Health issued a memorandum in August 1922 (Dumsday, *Local Government Law and Legislation 1922,* p. 437) explaining that the purpose of the Order was to ensure that private development should not be arrested while a scheme was in the course of preparation, and it gave guidance on matters such as density, open space, building lines, character of buildings—and even the execution of agreements to secure developers' contributions towards the cost of streets to be constructed by the council. Within 5 months the Minister found it necessary to issue further guidance, this time in the form of a circular (Ministry of Health Circular 368; January 29, 1923), emphasising that "the presumption should always be in favour of the person who wishes to undertake development," and that it was "particularly desirable that no obstacles should be placed in the way of proposed development unless it is clearly detrimental to important local needs or interests." The Minister insisted that consent under the order "should be refused only if the development contravenes a definite proposal which the local authority intend to include in their town planning scheme, and this proposal is clearly of first importance; and he proposes to follow this course in deciding appeals which may be made to him under the Order."

The power to make orders was carried through unaltered to the Town Planning Act 1925, which was primarily a consolidating measure. Only 23 Orders were made by 1932. But with the Town and Country Planning Act 1932 came a new duty imposed on the Minister to make a general development order with respect to the interim development of land, with power to use it to permit the development of land either unconditionally or subject to any condition specified in the order. The new General Interim Development Order 1933 (No. 236) contained the first general grant of permission, limited to development which had parliamentary or ministerial approval, the maintenance or alteration of existing or permitted buildings, development in accordance with a town scheme that had progressed as far as being laid before both Houses of Parliament and certain development by statutory undertakers. But it still applied only to areas where there had been a resolution to prepare a scheme, and the discretionary powers of control came to an end once the scheme was in force.

The Town and Country Planning Act 1943 extended interim development control throughout the country: all land was deemed to be subject to a resolution to prepare a scheme, and this meant that the 1933 Order thereafter applied in all parts of the country except where a town scheme had finally been approved (thereby ironically giving wider development control powers to the authorities who had failed to finalise a scheme than to those who had).

After the Second World War, the Town and Country Planning (General Interim Development) Order 1946 (S.R. & O. 1946 No. 1621) superseded the 1933 Order, and also conferred permitted development rights. It was made under s.10 of 1932 Act.

Development Orders under the 1947 Act

But the 1946 Order was itself an interim measure. The basis of modern planning control was established in the Town and Country Planning Act 1947, which effectively took as its starting point the system of interim development control, and converted it into a permanent control system. It seems to have been for that reason that development orders remained part of the new system, but it is unlikely that it was ever envisaged that the general development order should carry the importance it does today. Because of the operation of the Parliamentary guillotine on the debates on the 1947 Act, there was no discussion of the function of development orders. But the Minister's view was set out in the notes on clauses to the 1947 Bill provided to Standing Committee members:

> "orders, being revocable, may relax or tighten restrictions in such a way as to encourage forms of development which are from time to time the most necessary or desirable. This is the answer to the criticism that the minister's power of control over development is too wide and comprehensive; he must initially be given a wide discretion in order that in operation the system may have the greatest degree of flexibility." (J. B. Cullingworth, *Peacetime History of Environmental Planning 1939–1969; Vol. IV: Land Values, Compensation and Betterment* H.M.S.O. 1980, p. 11)

Only limited advantage was taken of that flexibility by the first post-war General Development Order (1948 No. 958). It contained 21 classes of permitted development, most of which survive today, but which were then cast in narrow terms. The agricultural development class, for example, specified in some detail the types and dimensions of buildings that were permitted, and the Explanatory Memorandum issued by the Ministry made it clear that this was only for certain minor development required in connection with day-to-day working. Similarly, householder development included small buildings in the curtilage, but did not include extensions to existing dwellings.

That Order was replaced in 1950 by a substantially deregulatory measure, the Town and Country Planning General Development Order and Development Charge Applications Regulations 1950 (S.I. 1950 No. 728). It incorporated the provisions on planning applications that had previously been contained in separate regulations, and extended significantly the classes of permitted development. Householder development rights were broadened so as "to remove from the need to obtain express planning permission a number of minor operations which have so far occupied an amount of time and manpower out of all proportion to their importance to planning" (Ministry of Town and Country Planning Circular 87, 1950, para. 4).

Similarly, rights of agricultural development were widened, and recast in the form which lasted through into the 1977 Order. The Circular justified it thus:

> "farm and forestry buildings are erected only for essential purposes: experience has shown that the degrees of flexibility on siting is almost always governed by the purpose for which they are needed and the choice of materials is often limited by the cost as well as local tradition. For these reasons the Minister, while attaching the utmost importance to maintaining a good standard of siting and design, believes that the burden of work involved in the making of an express application for most new farm and forestry buildings is quite disproportionate to the value of the control. As an experiment he has therefore decided to give a general permission—outside certain areas of outstanding natural beauty—for farm buildings on areas of more than one acre and all forestry buildings and to rely, for the maintenance of decent standards, on the local planning authority to ensure that sound advice on practical methods of siting and building is readily available to farmers and on the farming community to make use of it wherever necessary. He is confident that farmers generally will respond to encouragement from local planning authorities to co-operate voluntarily in ensuring that the best local traditions are maintained . . ."

The 1950 Order also introduced outline planning permissions. The following General Development Orders have since been made prior to this Order, each successively revoking and replacing its predecessor:

Town and Country Planning General Development Order 1959 (S.I. No. 1286): amended by S.I. 1960 Nos. 283 and 1476.

Town and Country Planning General Development Order 1963 (S.I. No. 709): amended by S.I. 1964 No. 1239; 1965 No. 499; 1967 No. 1076; 1968 No. 1623; 1969 No. 276.

Town and Country Planning General Development Order 1973 (S.I. No. 31): amended by S.I. 1973 No. 273; 1974 No. 418; 1976 No. 301.

Town and Country Planning General Development Order 1977 (S.I. No. 289): amended by S.I. 1980 No. 1946; 1981 No. 245, and modified by 1981 No. 246 in specified areas; 1569; 1983 No. 1615; 1985 No. 1011 and 1981; 1986 No. 435 and modified by No. 1176; 1987 No. 765.

Town and Country Planning General Development Order 1988 (S.I. 1988 No. 1813).

Deregulation

When in 1977 the Labour Government sought to amend the Order so as to relax the limitations on the permitted development rights, it ran into spirited opposition in the Lords where a motion calling for the withdrawal of the amendments was passed, and the Government withdrew the proposals (H.L.Deb., Vol. 387, cols. 1793–1821, December 7, 1977). When the new Conservative regime introduced similar measures in 1981, they bowed to the strength of conservationist pressure by retaining the former tighter controls in national parks, conservation areas and areas of outstanding natural beauty. That differential regime, previously established by using a special development order for those areas which excluded the general rights, is maintained under the present order, but with all the rights now contained in the one Order. Those special areas have now become "article 1(5) land," and treated separately for many of the classes of permitted development rights.

The 1988 Order

The 1988 General Development Order marked a significant change in the content and presentation of permitted development rights. Until the 1988 Order, all the changes to it had been limited in nature and technical in effect, with redrafting and reappraisal kept to a minimum. The 1988 Order departed from that tradition. Following the major surgery that was carried out on the Town and Country Planning (Use Classes) Order in 1987, the order was completely redrafted and its layout improved, with an attempt made—particularly in the permitted development Classes in Schedule 2, to convert its language into comprehensible English. Inevitably, that did not always succeed, and the complexity of the task meant that the redrafting led to several unintended consequences which have had to be put right by subsequent amendments.

The *travaux preparatoires* for the 1988 Order started in 1981, when a consultation paper was issued proposing the abolition of the power of local highway authorities to direct refusal of planning applications. A major consultation paper was issued in 1984, proposing significant changes to update the provisions relating to telecommunications and agriculture. That paper also mooted extensions to existing rights for the Civil Aviation Authority, warehouse extensions and for consolidation with the special development orders affecting what is now article 1(5) land. Subsequently, a consultation letter was issued in January 1987 containing a redrafted version of Part 1 (householder development); and separate consultation exercises were undertaken on mineral rights.

Amendments to the 1977 Order in 1985 had already introduced new telecommunications and minerals classes, and new permitted development rights for warehouses, amusement parks and development by English Heritage; and further amendments were made in 1987 in implementation of the new Use Classes Order of that year. The Housing and Planning Act 1986 contained some minor statutory amendments to the 1971 Act and to the Local Government Act 1972 which allowed the proposed changes in highway authorities' powers, and the incorporation of the sensitive areas into the main Order (see further below). A comprehensive consultation paper, which contained the revised draft text of most of the new order was issued in February 1988, together with a draft Manual providing a commentary. The Manual was not eventually proceeded with, and instead the Secretaries of State issued a circular, DOE Circular 22/88 (W.O. 44/88) explaining the changes made by the Order and giving general policy advice.

Subsequent amending orders

The 1988 Order was amended once before it came into force on December 5, 1988, and again within five months of taking effect. The first amendment, by S.I. 1988 No. 2091, corrected a defect in the definition of permitted householder development in Sched. 2, Pt. 1. The second amending order, S.I. 1989 No. 603, further corrected that correction, and made other amendments to the order. It clarified the extent to which permitted development rights might be relied upon in relation to an existing use of land which was unlawful (art. 1(4)); it restored the rights of clay pigeon shooters to temporary permission under Pt. 4 of Sched. 2, and it brought the area of the Broads Authority (established by the Norfolk and Suffolk Broads Act 1988, with effect from April 1, 1989) within the definition of art. 1(5) land, to which a special regime of permitted development applies.

The Order was subsequently further amended by the following:

S.I. 1990 No. 457: substituted new Sched. 2, Part 16 (Development by or on behalf of sewerage undertakers) from March 31, 1990.

S.I. 1990 No. 2032: substituted new Class G in Sched. 2, Part 17 (Electricity undertakings) from November 12, 1990.

S.I. 1991 No. 1536, from July 31, 1991:

inserted new definition of article 1(7) land in art. 1 and Sched. 1;
amended Sched. 2, Part 1 (substituted Class H.1 and H.2, satellite antennae on or within the curtilage of a dwellinghouse);
Part 8 (new condition A.1A, industrial and warehouse development);
amended Part 17 (development by statutory undertakers);
amended Part 24 (code system operators);
amended Part 27 (telecommunications development) and inserted new Class B;
inserted new Part 29 (driver information systems);
amended standard forms 2 and 3 in Sched. 5.

S.I. 1991 No. 2268 inserted new Class A.2 and A.3 in Part 7 (forestry development).

S.I. 1991 No. 2805: various amendments to allow direct applications for "county matters"

new consultation requirements in art. 18.
new Part 6 in Sched. 2 (agricultural development).

S.I. 1992 No. 609: added new Part 30 (toll roads).

S.I. 1992 No. 658: deleted references to hazardous substances upon the implementation of the Planning (Hazardous Substances) Act 1990.

S.I. 1992 No. 1280: added new Part 31 (demolition of buildings).

S.I. 1992 No. 1493: various amendments relating to notification of, and publicity for, applications for planning permission; amendments to Parts 6 and 7 of Sched. 2 (agricultural and forestry operations).

S.I. 1992 No. 1563: amendments relating to enforcement, particularly certificates of established use or development, and breach of condition notices.

S.I. 1992 No. 2450: various amendments relating to mining development, and telecommunications code development.

S.I. 1994 No. 678: amendments relating to environmental assessment and telecommunications (Part 24).

S.I. 1994 No. 2595: amendments consequent upon coal mining privatisation under the Coal Industry Act 1994.

S.I. 1995 No. 298: amendments in order to subject permitted development rights to the Conservation (Natural Habitats, &c.) Regulations 1994 (S.I. 1994 No. 2716), to insert new Classes F and G in Part 3 of Sched. 2; to amend the definition of "protected building" in Part 6; and to insert new Part 32 (schools, colleges, universities and hospitals).

Function of the General Development Orders

The Secretary of State is required (1990 Act, s.59) to make a development order providing for the grant of planning permission, and an order may either grant permission itself or provide for the granting of permission by the local planning authority on an application made in accordance with the provisions of the order.

Up until now, one order has done both. But the 1995 reforms have seen the functions divided between two orders:

Town and Country Planning (General Permitted Development) Order 1995 (S.I. 1995 No. 418) (known as the "GPDO") which contains the provisions relating to permitted development rights; and

Town and Country Planning (General Development Procedure) Order 1995 (S.I. 1995 No. 419), (known as the "GDPO") which makes procedural provision for the grant of planning permission by local planning authorities (except for planning applications, which continue to be regulated by the Town and Country Planning (Applications) Regulations 1988.

Major changes in the 1995 Order

For the most part, the 1995 consolidation was confined to minor redrafting and clarification, but there were also four amendments of substance:

Environmental assessment: Article 3 was amended to remove permitted development rights from development requiring environmental assessment. Under the Town and Country Planning (Environmental Assessment and Permitted Development) Regulations 1995, prospective developers may apply to the local planning authority for an opinion as to whether development which would otherwise be permitted development requires an environmental assessment and therefore a planning application.

Closed circuit television (CCTV) cameras: new Part 33 extends permitted development rights to include the installation, alteration or replacement on shops, flats, houses and other buildings of CCTV cameras within specified limits on size and numbers. The new permitted development rights apply in all areas, including article 1(5) land, but not to listed buildings or scheduled monuments.

Dwelling-houses in conservation areas: a new art. 4(2) gives local planning authorities power to restrict specific permitted development rights in relation to dwellinghouses in conservation areas where the permitted development would front a highway, waterway or open space. Local planning authorities are not required to obtain the Secretary of State's approval, but have to notify residents and take account of local views before deciding whether to confirm an article 4(2) direction.

Demolition in conservation areas: directions under art. 4(2) may be used to withdraw permitted development rights for the demolition of a gate, fence, wall or other means of enclosure which (1) is within the curtilage of a dwellinghouse; and (2) is in a conservation area; and (3) fronts a highway, waterway or open space (Part 31, Class B).

Effect of European law

Rights under the General Development Orders were formerly unfettered, but have yielded in the past eight years to requirements under European law:

Environmental assessment: the requirements of the E.C. Directive on environmental assessment (85/337/EEC) are extended to permitted development rights by this Order, art. 3(10), which excludes certain descriptions of development which would, if they were the subject of a planning application, require environmental assessment. Under the Town and Country Planning (Environmental Assessment and Permitted development) Regulations 1995 (S.I. 1995 No. 417) a prospective developer may apply to the local planning authority for an opinion as to whether his development would be so excluded and, if so, whether it would constitute Schedule 1 or Schedule 2 development under the Town and Country Planning (Environmental Assessment) Regulations 1988 (S.I. 1988 No. 1199).

Habitats protection: this Order has effect subject to the requirements of the Conservation (Natural Habitats, &c.) Regulations 1994 (S.I. 1994 No. 2716), regs. 60 to 63 (see art. 3(1)).

Effect of the order

The order grants planning permission, in art. 3, for the classes of development set out in Sched. 2. It differs from the Town and Country Planning (Use Classes) Order 1987, in that under that Order certain changes of use are deemed not to constitute development at all, and hence not to require planning permission. This Order comes into effect where what is proposed does constitute development, and it then grants planning permission for it. This distinction was important under the 1947 Act which introduced it, because a development charge was levied on any enhancement in land values resulting from development (whether it had permission under the order or on an application) but use changes within the Use Classes Order were exempt.

Today the logic of the distinction is less obvious, but its practical significance is that the grant of permission under this order can be made subject to conditions, and it can be withdrawn (by a direction made under art. 4). Permitted development rights can also be withdrawn by a condition on a planning permission (see further the Commentary to art. 4).

The classification of permitted development rights is generally along three lines. First, rights are conferred in relation to certain types of existing use or building, such as dwellinghouses, industrial premises, warehouses, amusement parks and agricultural land. These rights, for the most part, relate to marginal development which is incidental to existing uses of land and they are subject to general conditions to prevent adverse impacts. But the permissions necessarily proceed on the basis of very high level abstractions which are not tailored to the circumstances of individual sites, and which inevitably cause some practical difficulties in operation. The permitted development rights are important not only in themselves, but also as establishing a baseline position in negotiations with the local planning authority for permission to carry out development exceeding the tolerances. The fact that a certain volume of development is permitted by the order without further permission is capable of being a material consideration, as representing a fall-back position, in determining such an application: see, *e.g. Burge v. Secretary of State for the Environment* [1988] J.P.L. 497 (note).

Second, rights are conferred on certain types of developers, such as local authorities, highway authorities, statutory undertakers, recreational groups, water authorities, airport operators and telecommunications operators. The justification for these special rights seems to be that the bodies have alternative controls (*e.g.* the recreational groups) or are providing public services (although they may be privately owned) and that there are often other forms of accountability to prevent abuse. Statutory undertakers, for example, can be urged to consult with local planning authorities and the public before exercising permitted development rights which are likely to have a significant effect (DOE Circular 9/95, Appendix B, para. 9); and telecommunications operators are subject to environmental conditions in the licences granted to them under the Telecommunications Act 1984.

The third category is that of rights which tie in with, and provide some limited expansion of, development rights conferred elsewhere, such as those under Pt. 3 of Sched. 2, which allow one-way movement between certain of the classes prescribed in the Use Classes Order, and Pts. 9 and 10 (repairs to unadopted streets and to services) which effectively extend the scope of the 1990 Act, ss.55(2)(b), (c).

Simplified planning zones

Development orders can be made only by the Secretary of State, but local planning authorities have power to grant general planning permissions in their areas by making simplified planning zones under ss.82 to 85 of the 1990 Act. The adoption or approval of an SPZ has effect to grant planning permission in relation to the zone, or any specified part of it, for development of any class specified in the scheme.

Cross references

The following general matters are further analysed in the General Notes to individual parts of the order as indicated:

- withdrawal of permitted development rights by direction (art. 4)
- withdrawal of permitted development rights by planning condition (art. 4)
- development contrary to existing planning condition (art. 4)
- lawful user as basis for reliance on permitted development rights (art. 2)
- effect of conditions and limitations (art. 3 and Sched. 2, Pts. 1 and 3).

Policy guidance

Detailed advice on the Order is contained in DOE Circular 9/95, *General Development Order Consolidation 1995.*

Citation, commencement and interpretation

1.—(1) This Order may be cited as the Town and Country Planning (General Permitted Development) Order 1995 and shall come into force on 3rd June 1995.

(2) In this Order, unless the context otherwise requires—

"the Act" means the Town and Country Planning Act 1990;

"the 1960 Act" means the Caravan Sites and Control of Development Act 1960;

"aerodrome" means an aerodrome as defined in article 106 of the Air Navigation Order 1989 (interpretation) which is—

(a) licensed under that Order,

(b) a Government aerodrome,

(c) one at which the manufacture, repair or maintenance of aircraft is carried out by a person carrying on business as a manufacturer or repairer of aircraft,

(d) one used by aircraft engaged in the public transport of passengers or cargo or in aerial work, or

(e) one identified to the Civil Aviation Authority before 1st March 1986 for inclusion in the UK Aerodrome Index,

and, for the purposes of this definition, the terms "aerial work", "Government aerodrome" and "public transport" have the meanings given in article 106;

"aqueduct" does not include an underground conduit;

"area of outstanding natural beauty" means an area designated as such by an order made by the Countryside Commission, as respects England, or the Countryside Council for Wales, as respects Wales, under section 87 of the National Parks and Access to the Countryside Act 1949 (designation of areas of outstanding natural beauty) as confirmed by the Secretary of State;

"building"—

(a) includes any structure or erection and, except in Parts 24, 25 and 33, and Class A of Part 31, of Schedule 2, includes any part of a building, as defined in this article; and

(b) does not include plant or machinery and, in Schedule 2, except in Class B of Part 31 and Part 33, does not include any gate, fence, wall or other means of enclosure;

"caravan" has the same meaning as for the purposes of Part I of the 1960 Act (caravan sites);

"caravan site" means land on which a caravan is stationed for the purpose of human habitation and land which is used in conjunction with land on which a caravan is so stationed;

"classified road" means a highway or proposed highway which—

(a) is a classified road or a principal road by virtue of section 12(1) of the Highways Act 1980 (general provision as to principal and classified roads); or

(b) is classified by the Secretary of State for the purposes of any enactment by virtue of section 12(3) of that Act;

"cubic content" means the cubic content of a structure or building measured externally;

"dwellinghouse" does not include a building containing one or more flats, or a flat contained within such a building;

"erection", in relation to buildings as defined in this article, includes extension, alteration, or re-erection;

"existing", in relation to any building or any plant or machinery or any use, means (except in the definition of "original") existing immediately before the carrying out, in relation to that building, plant, machinery or use, of development described in this Order;

"flat" means a separate and self-contained set of premises constructed or adapted for use for the purpose of a dwelling and forming part of a building from some other part of which it is divided horizontally;

"floor space" means the total floor space in a building or buildings;

"industrial process" means a process for or incidental to any of the following purposes—

- **(a) the making of any article or part of any article (including a ship or vessel, or a film, video or sound recording);**
- **(b) the altering, repairing, maintaining, ornamenting, finishing, cleaning, washing, packing, canning, adapting for sale, breaking up or demolition of any article; or**
- **(c) the getting, dressing or treatment of minerals in the course of any trade or business other than agriculture, and other than a process carried out on land used as a mine or adjacent to and occupied together with a mine;**

"land drainage" has the same meaning as in section 116 of the Land Drainage Act 1976, (interpretation);

"listed building" has the same meaning as in section 1 of the Planning (Listed Buildings and Conservation Areas) Act 1990 (listing of buildings of special architectural or historic interest);

"by local advertisement" means by publication of the notice in at least one newspaper circulating in the locality in which the area or, as the case may be, the whole or relevant part of the conservation area to which the direction relates is situated;

"machinery" includes any structure or erection in the nature of machinery;

"microwave" means that part of the radio spectrum above 1,000 MHz;

"microwave antenna" means a satellite antenna or a terrestrial microwave antenna;

"mine" means any site on which mining operations are carried out;

"mining operations" means the winning and working of minerals in, on or under land, whether by surface or underground working;

"notifiable pipe-line" means a pipe-line, as defined in section 65 of the Pipe-lines Act 1962 (meaning of pipe-line), which contains or is intended to contain a hazardous substance, as defined in regulation 2(1) of the Notification Regulations (interpretation), except—

- **(a) a pipe-line the construction of which has been authorised under section 1 of the Pipe-lines Act 1962 (cross-country pipe-lines not to be constructed without the Minister's authority); or**
- **(b) a pipe-line which contains or is intended to contain no hazardous substance other than—**
  - **(i) a flammable gas (as specified in item 1 of Part II of Schedule 1 to the Notification Regulations (classes of hazardous substances not specifically named in Part I)) at a pressure of less than 8 bars absolute; or**
  - **(ii) a liquid or mixture of liquids, as specified in item 4 of Part II of that Schedule;**

"Notification Regulations" means the Notification of Installations Handling Hazardous Substances Regulations 1982;

"original" means, in relation to a building existing on 1st July 1948, as existing on that date and, in relation to a building built on or after 1st July 1948, as so built;

"plant" includes any structure or erection in the nature of plant;

"private way" means a highway not maintainable at the public expense and any other way other than a highway;

"proposed highway" has the same meaning as in section 329 of the Highways Act 1980 (further provision as to interpretation);

"public service vehicle" means a public service vehicle within the meaning of section 1 of the Public Passenger Vehicles Act 1981 (definition of public service vehicles) or a tramcar or trolley vehicle within the meaning of section 192(1) of the Road Traffic Act 1988 (general interpretation);

"satellite antenna" means apparatus designed for transmitting microwave radio energy to satellites or receiving it from them, and includes any mountings or brackets attached to such apparatus;

"scheduled monument" has the same meaning as in section 1(11) of the Ancient Monuments and Archaeological Areas Act 1979 (schedule of monuments);

"by site display" means by the posting of the notice by firm affixture to some object, sited and displayed in such a way as to be easily visible and legible by members of the public;

"site of archaeological interest" means land which is included in the schedule of monuments compiled by the Secretary of State under section 1 of the Ancient Monuments and Archaeological Areas Act 1979 (schedule of monuments), or is within an area of land which is designated as an area of archaeological importance under section 33 of that Act (designation of areas of archaeological importance), or which is within a site registered in any record adopted by resolution by a county council and known as the County Sites and Monuments Record;

"site of special scientific interest" means land to which section 28(1) of the Wildlife and Countryside Act 1981 (areas of special scientific interest) applies;

"statutory undertaker" includes, in addition to any person mentioned in section 262(1) of the Act (meaning of statutory undertakers), the Post Office, the Civil Aviation Authority, the National Rivers Authority, any water undertaker, any public gas supplier, and any licence holder within the meaning of section 64(1) of the Electricity Act 1989 (interpretation etc. of Part 1);

"terrestrial microwave antenna" means apparatus designed for transmitting or receiving terrestrial microwave radio energy between two fixed points;

"trunk road" means a highway or proposed highway which is a trunk road by virtue of section 10(1) or 19 of the Highways Act 1980 (general provisions as to trunk roads, and certain special roads and other highways to become trunk roads) or any other enactment or any instrument made under any enactment;

"the Use Classes Order" means the Town and Country Planning (Use Classes) Order 1987

(3) Unless the context otherwise requires, any reference in this Order to the height of a building or of plant or machinery shall be construed as a reference to its height when measured from ground level; and for the purposes of this paragraph "ground level" means the level of the surface of the ground immediately adjacent to the building or plant or machinery in question or, where the level of the surface of the ground on which it is situated or is to be situated is not uniform, the level of the highest part of the surface of the ground adjacent to it.

(4) The land referred to elsewhere in this Order as article 1(4) land is the land described in Part I of Schedule 1 to this Order (land in listed counties).

(5) The land referred to elsewhere in this Order as article 1(5) land is the land described in Part 2 of Schedule 1 to this Order (National Parks, areas of outstanding natural beauty and conservation areas etc.).

(6) The land referred to elsewhere in this Order as article 1(6) land is the

land described in Part 3 of Schedule 1 to this Order (National Parks and adjoining land and the Broads).

COMMENTARY

DERIVATION

Town and Country Planning General Development Order 1988, art. 1, as amended:

(1) Art. 1(7) was added by the Town and Country Planning General Development (Amendment) Order 1991 (No. 1536), art. 2.
(2) The former definitions of "hazardous substance" and "notifiable quantity" were repealed, and the definition of "notifiable pipeline" substituted, by S.I. 1992 No. 658, from June 1, 1992.
(3) The definitions of "by local advertisement" and "by site display" were inserted by S.I. 1992 No. 1493.
(4) The definition of "existing" was amended, and former para. (4) (contravention of previous planning control) revoked, by S.I. 1992 No. 1563, from July 27, 1992.

GENERAL NOTE

General approach to interpretation

The highly technical and detailed nature of the Order is reflected in this complex definition article. Perhaps it always was so. Hence the observation of W. A. Leach on the 1950 Order: "It is evident as soon as art. 2 of the Order [interpretation] is reached that the Parliamentary draftsmen are losing their grip" ([1950] J.P.L. 473).

A general approach to interpretation was advanced by Goulding J. in *English Clays Lovering Pochin & Co. v. Plymouth Corporation* [1973] 2 All E.R. 730, at 735:

> "It is common ground that the Development Order is to be construed in what has sometimes been called in argument 'a broad or common sense manner,' at any rate in the manner appropriate, as counsel say, to a document framed for administrative purposes rather than as an instrument couched in conveyancing language. That has not prevented counsel on either side from spinning elaborate arguments worthy of a more complicated subject matter and drawn from other provisions of the Development Order itself, from other statutes or statutory instruments and from reported cases on different documents. While I greatly admire and acknowledge the thoroughness of counsel's endeavours, I do not find in the end that I can get any guidance from those illustrative arguments. It appears to me that, having considered all, I have to apply myself to the ordinary meaning of the language used by the Minister in making the Development Order ..."

The list of definitions contained in this article is not exhaustive. Expressions which make a single appearance in the Order are defined in the article or Part of the Schedule in which they appear, these are listed below. Moreover, all the definitions contained in the parent Act, the Town and Country Planning Act 1990 (see particularly the definition section, s.336) prevail for the purposes of the Order, except where a contrary intention appears (Interpretation Act 1978, s.11).

Cross-referenced definitions

Several of the definitions in this article draw upon definitions contained in other legislation. Full definitions and explanations are set out below:

"aerodrome"; "aerial work"; "Government aerodrome"; "public transport": under the Air Navigation Order 1985 (No. 1643), art. 96:

"aerodrome" means any area of land or water designed, equipped, set apart or commonly used for affording facilities for the landing and departure of aircraft and includes any area or space, whether on the ground, on the roof of a building or elsewhere, which is designed, equipped or set apart for affording facilities for the landing and departure of aircraft capable of descending or climbing vertically, but shall not include any area the use of which for affording facilities for the landing and departure of aircraft has been abandoned and has not been resumed.

"aerial work" means any purpose (other than public transport) for which an aircraft is flown if hire or reward is given or promised in respect of the flight or the purpose of the flight.

"Government aerodrome" means any aerodrome in the United Kingdom which is in the occupation of any Government department or visiting force.

"public transport": a detailed definition is provided by art. 96(5) of the Order, which provides principally that an aircraft in flight shall be deemed for the purposes of that Order to fly for the purposes of public transport if hire or reward is given or promised for the carriage of passengers or cargo in the aircraft on that flight or, with certain exceptions, if passengers or cargo are carried gratuitously.

"area of outstanding natural beauty:"

This is a designation made by the Countryside Commission under the National Parks and Access to the Countryside Act 1949, s.87, and confirmed by the Secretary of State.

"building": the definition is new. The definition in the 1988 Order read: "building" does not include plant or machinery, and in Schedule 2 to the order does not include any gate, fence, wall or other means of enclosure." The substituted definition makes it clear that "building" is to include part of a building for certain purposes only Parts 24 (telecommunications code:), 25 (other telecommunications development), 33 (closed circuit television cameras) and Part 31, Class A (demolition of buildings). Gates, fences, walls and other means of enclosure remain excluded, except for Part 31, Class B (demolition of buildings) and Part 33 (closed circuit television cameras).

"caravan": under the Caravan Sites and Control of Development Act 1960, s.29(1):

"caravan" means any structure designed or adapted for human habitation which is capable of being moved from one place to another (whether by being towed, or by being transported on a motor vehicle or trailer) and any motor vehicle so designed or adapted, but does not include:

(a) any railway rolling-stock which is for the time being on rails forming part of a railway system; or

(b) any tent

In *Backer v. Secretary of State for the Environment* [1983] J.P.L. 602; [1983] 1 W.L.R. 1485, the court held that a van which was capable of being lived in, because it had been fitted with a bed and a cooking stove, was not a caravan within this definition unless it had either been designed for human habitation or had been physically altered in some way for that purpose.

"classified road":

Under the Highways Act 1980, s.12(3), the Secretary of State for Transport has power to classify highways or proposed highways, for which local highway authorities are the highway authorities, in such manner as he may from time to time determine after consultation with the highway authorities concerned. By virtue of s.12(1), classifications made by him under earlier legislation continue under the 1990 Act. For practical purposes the category includes all A and B roads which are not trunk roads.

"drainage" includes defence against water (including sea water), irrigation, other than spray irrigation, and warping.

"land" includes water and any interests in land or water and any easement or right in, to, or over land or water.

"mine": *"mining operations"*:

In *English Clays Lovering Pochin & Co. v. Plymouth Corporation* [1974] 1 W.L.R. 742, the court held that the essential idea in the term "winning or working of minerals" is that of extracting or separation of raw material from the solid earth in which it occurs: see further the General Note to Sched. 2, Pt. 19.

"notifiable pipeline":

Pipelines Act 1962, s.65:

(1) In this Act "pipe-line" (except where the context otherwise requires) means a pipe (together with any apparatus and works associated therewith), or system of pipes (together with any apparatus and works associated therewith), for the conveyance of anything other than air, water, water vapour or steam, not being:

(a) a drain or sewer; or
(b) a pipe or system of pipes constituting or comprised in apparatus for heating or cooling or for domestic purposes; or
(c) a pipe or system of pipes on the site of any operations or works to which certain provisions of the Factories Act 1961 apply by virtue of s.127(1) (building operations and works of engineering construction) of that Act; or
(d) a pipe or system of pipes wholly situated within the boundaries of an agricultural unit and designed for use for purposes of agriculture; or
(e) a pipe or system of pipes wholly situated in premises used for the purposes of education or research; or
(f) a pneumatic dispatch-tube.

(2) For the purposes of the foregoing subsection, the following apparatus and works, and none other, shall be treated as being associated with a pipe, or system of pipes, namely:

(a) apparatus for inducing or facilitating the flow of any thing through the pipe or, as the case may be, through the system or part thereof;
(b) valves, valve chambers, manholes, inspection pits and similar works, being works annexed to, or incorporated in the course of, the pipe or system;
(c) apparatus for supplying energy for the operation of any such apparatus as is mentioned in paragraph (a) of this sub-section or of any such works as are mentioned in paragraph (b) thereof;
(d) apparatus for the transmission of information for the operation of the pipe or system;
(e) apparatus for affording cathodic protection to the pipe or system;
(f) a structure for the exclusive support of a part of the line or system.

"proposed highway":

Highways Act 1980, s.329:

"proposed highway" means land on which, in accordance with plans made by a highway authority, that authority are for the time being constructing or intending to construct a highway shown in the plans.

"site of archaeological interest": the definition was amended in the 1995 Order to refer to records "adopted by resolution" (instead of "kept") by a county council.

"statutory undertaker":
See the General Note to Sched. 2, Pt. 17.

"trunk road":
Under the Highways Act 1980 a road is a trunk road because it (a) was a trunk road under the Highways Act 1959 (1980 Act, s.10(1) or, (b) it is a special road provided by the Secretary of State for Transport which became a trunk road on the date specified in the scheme made under s.16 of the 1959 Act (1980 Act, s.19).

Other definitions elsewhere in the Order

Expressions which are separately defined elsewhere in this Order include the following:

"1984 Act": Sched. 2, Pt. 24, Class A.3
"active access": Sched. 2, Pt. 19, Class D.2; Pt. 20, Class F.1
"agricultural land": Sched. 2, Pt. 6, Class D.
"agricultural unit": Sched. 2, Pt. 6, Class A.3(2)
"amusement park": Sched. 2, Pt. 28, Class A.2
"ancillary mining land": Sched. 2, Pt. 19, Class D.2; Pt. 21, Class A.3
"antenna system": Sched. 2, Pt. 24, Class A.3
"booths or stalls": Sched. 2, Pt. 28, Class A.2
"building": Sched. 2, Pt. 6, Class A.3(2)
"building or monument": Sched. 2, Pt. 26, Class A.3
"camera": Sched. 2, Pt. 33, Class A.3
"coal related minerals": Sched. 2, Pt. 20, Class A.1
"coal industry activities": Sched. 2, Pt. 20, Class F.1
"colliery production activities": Sched. 2, Pt. 21, Class B.2
"construction of fishponds": Sched. 2, Pt. 6, Class C.2
"development ancillary to radio equipment housing": Sched. 2, Pt. 24, Class A.3
"development in accordance with a licence": Sched. 2, Pt. 24, Class A.3
"excluded demoliton": Sched. 2, Pt. 31, Clasa A.3
"facilities for the collection of tolls": Sched. 2, Pt. 30, Class A.3
"fish farming": Sched. 2, Pt. 6, Class D.1
"fishponds": Sched. 2, Pt. 6, Class C.2
"ground level": Sched. 2, Pt. 30, Class A.3; Pt. 33, Class A.3
"hazardous activity": art. 3(10)
"industrial building": Sched. 2, Pt. 8, Class E
"industrial land": Sched. 2, Pt. 8, Class B.2
"land controlled by an operator": Sched. 2, Pt. 24, Class A.3
"livestock": Sched. 2, Pt. 6, Class D.1
"mast": Sched. 2, Pt. 24, Class A.3
"mineral exploration": Sched. 2, Pt. 22, Class A.3 and B.3
"minerals": Sched. 2, Pt. 19, Class D.2
"normal and regular use": Sched. 2, Pt. 20, Class F.1
"notified site": art. 3(10)
"operational building": Sched. 2, Pt. 18, Class K
"painting": Sched. 2, Pt. 2, Class C.2
"prior approval of the mineral planning authority": Sched. 2, Pt. 19, Class D.2; Pt. 20, Class F.1
"protected building": Sched. 2, Pt. 6, Class A.3(2)
"purpose incidental to the enjoyment of a dwellinghouse": Sched. 2, Pt. 1, Class E.2
"purposes of agriculture": Sched. 2, Pt. 6, Class B.3
"recreational organisation": Sched. 2, Pt. 27, Class A.2
"registered business of fish farming or shellfish farming": Sched. 2, Pt. 6, Class C.2
"relevant obligation": Sched. 2, Pt. 31, Class A.3

"relevant scheme": Sched. 2, Pt. 21, Class B.2
"relevant airport operator": Sched. 2, Pt. 18, Class K
"relevant airport": Sched. 2, Pt. 18, Class K
"relevant period": Sched. 2, Pt. 24, Class A.3
"resulting building": Sched. 2, Pt. 1, Class I
"rooftop structure": Sched. 2, Pt. 30, Class A.3
"significant extension", "significant alteration": Sched. 2, Pt. 6, Class D.1; Pt. 7, Class A.3
"site": art. 3(10).
"site notice": Sched. 2, Pt. 31, Clas A.3
"stockpile": Sched. 2, Pt. 23, Class D
"structure": Sched. 2, Pt. 22, Class A.3 and B.3
"telecommunications system": Sched. 2, Pt. 24, Class A.3
"telecommunications code system operator": Sched. 2, Pt. 24, Class A.3
"telecommunications code": Sched. 2, Pt. 24, Class A.3
"telecommunications apparatus": Sched. 2, Pt. 24, Class A.3
"toll", "toll collection area", "toll collection booth", "toll order", "toll road": Sched. 2, Pt. 30, Class A.3
"unadopted street": Sched. 2, Pt. 9, Class A.1
"underground mine": Sched. 2, Pt. 19, Class D.2
"warehouse": Sched. 2, Pt. 8, Class E
"waste management scheme": Sched. 2, Pt. 21, Class A.3

Measuring height and ground level: para. (3)

Many of the tolerances of permitted development are defined in terms of height, and para. (3) provides a formula for assessing height. It was introduced in the Town and Country General Development (Amendment) Order 1981 (S.I. 1981 No. 245) in response to difficulties, following *Prengate Properties v. Secretary of State for the Environment* (1973) 25 P. & C.R. 311, in assessing what was the natural ground level from which to assess height when there was sloping land: see [1979] J.P.L. 491, where the Secretary of State upheld his inspector's ruling that where a wall was erected on top of a patio area which was already raised some two feet above the ground, the measurement should be from the natural ground area rather than of the wall alone. The formula in the order gives the benefit of doubt to the developer: height may be measured from the highest part of the surface of the ground adjoining the building.

But this formula applies only to a building. A building does not, for the purposes of Sched. 2 (except Parts 31 and 33), where all the height tolerances are prescribed, include any gate, fence, wall or other means of enclosure: see the definition in art. 1(2). Thus although Pt. 2 of that Schedule, which permits the erection of a gate, fence, wall, or other means of enclosure, uses the expressions "height" and "ground level," this definition does not apply.

Special regime for sensitive areas: paras. (5), (6)

When permitted development rights were extended in 1981, the old limits were retained in certain areas of environmental sensitivity. These were the National Parks, areas of outstanding natural beauty, and conservation areas. A subsequent amendment brought in areas specified under the Wildlife and Countryside Act 1981, s.41(3). Special protection was maintained for these areas by means of a special development order, but for convenience its provisions are now incorporated into this Order. These areas, as defined in Sched. 1, become "article 1(5) land," and different development tolerances are applied to them in Sched. 2, as follows:

Pt. 1 (householder development): Classes A.2, A.3; B.1 and E.1(f);
Pt. 8 (industrial development): Class A.1;

Pt. 17 (statutory undertakers): Class G (electricity)
Pt. 24 (telecommunications): Class A(1)(g): A.2(3)
Pt. 25 (other telecommunications development): Class A.1(g)

Similarly, when in 1950 the Minister decided to enlarge the scope of permitted agricultural development under what is now Pt. 6 of Sched. 2, he retained tighter controls within the National Parks and certain fringe areas by making a special development order which required that prior notice should be given to the local planning authority of proposed development, and allowing them to instruct the developer that it should not be undertaken without their prior approval of siting, design and external appearance (Town and Country Planning (Landscape Areas Special Development) Order 1950, subsequently replaced by Town and Country Planning (Agricultural and Forestry Development in National Parks, etc.) Special Development Order 1986).

This land, defined in Sched. 1, now "article 1(6) land," and the provisions as to prior approval now appear in Sched. 2, Pt. 6, Class A.2(2) (agricultural development) and Pt. 7, Class A.2 (forestry development).

The area of the Broads, as defined in the Norfolk and Suffolk Broads Act 1988, was also brought within the definitions of art. 1(5) land and art. 1(6) land, by S.I. 1989 No. 603.

Special protection is also provided by the exclusion of mineral exploration rights under Pt. 22 in any National Park, area of outstanding natural beauty, or site of archaeological or special scientific interest (Pt. 22, Class A.1(c)).

Application

2.—(1) This Order applies to all land in England and Wales, but where land is the subject of a special development order, whether made before or after the commencement of this Order, this Order shall apply to that land only to such extent and subject to such modifications as may be specified in the special development order.

(2) Nothing in this Order shall apply to any permission which is deemed to be granted under section 222 of the Act (planning permission not needed for advertisements complying with regulations).

COMMENTARY

DEFINITIONS

"advertisement": 1990 Act, s.336(1).
"land": 1990 Act, s.336(1).
"planning permission": 1990 Act, s.336(1).
"special development order": 1990 Act, s.58.

GENERAL NOTE

This order applies throughout England and Wales, but may be disapplied in any area by a special development order. That previously was the method used to establish a tighter regime in the sensitive areas that are now incorporated into the main order as arts. 1(5), 1(6) land, defined in Sched. 1.

The following special development orders have been made and remain unrevoked (though some conferred rights for a limited period which has since expired):

- Town and Country Planning (Ironstone Areas Special Development) Order 1950 (No. 1177)
- Town and Country Planning (Atomic Energy Establishments) Special Development Orders 1954 (No. 982) and 1957 (No. 806)
- Town and Country Planning (New Towns) Special Development Order 1977 (No. 665)
- Town and Country Planning (New Towns in Rural Wales) Special Development Order 1977 (No. 815)
- Town and Country Planning (Windscale and Calder Works) Special Development Order 1978 (No. 523)
- Town and Country Planning (Merseyside Urban Development Area) Special Development Order 1981 (No. 560)
- Town and Country Planning (London Docklands Urban Development Area) Special Development Order 1981 (No. 1082)
- Town and Country Planning (Vauxhall Cross) Special Development Order 1982 (No. 796)
- Town and Country Planning (Telecommunications Network) (Railway Operational Land) Special Development Order 1982 (No. 817)
- Town and Country Planning (NIREX) Special Development Order 1986 (No. 812)
- Town and Country Planning (Black Country Urban Development Area) Special Development Order 1987 (No. 1343)
- Town and Country Planning (Teeside Urban Development Area) Special Development Order 1987 (No. 1344)
- Town and Country Planning (Tyne and Wear Urban Development Area) Special Development Order 1987 (No. 1345)
- Town and Country Planning (Wolverhampton Urban Development Area) Special Development Order 1988 (No. 1400)

In the special development orders made for the new towns and urban development corporations, the approach has generally been to confer permitted development rights for development by the development corporation provided it is in accordance with general proposals previously approved by the Secretary of State, and provided prescribed consultation is carried out before commencement. Where an objection or representation made in the course of consultation is not withdrawn, the corporation is obliged to notify the Secretary of State and may not commence development until informed that he does not propose to give a direction requiring a formal planning application to be made.

Permitted development

3.—(1) Subject to the provisions of this Order and regulations 60 to 63 of the Conservation (Natural Habitats, &c.) Regulations 1994 (general development orders), planning permission is hereby granted for the classes of development described as permitted development in Schedule 2.

(2) Any permission granted by paragraph (1) is subject to any relevant exception, limitation or condition specified in Schedule 2.

(3) References in the following provisions of this Order to permission granted by Schedule 2 or by any Part, Class or paragraph of that Schedule are references to the permission granted by this article in relation to development described in that Schedule or that provision of that Schedule.

(4) Nothing in this Order permits development contrary to any condition imposed by any planning permission granted or deemed to be granted under Part III of the Act otherwise than by this Order.

(5) The permission granted by Schedule 2 shall not apply if—

(a)in the case of permission granted in connection with an existing building, the building operations involved in the construction of that building are unlawful;

(b) in the case of permission granted in connection with an existing use, that use is unlawful.

(6) The permission granted by Schedule 2 shall not, except in relation to development permitted by Parts 9, 11, 13 or 30, authorise any development which requires or involves the formation, laying out or material widening of a means of access to an existing highway which is a trunk road or classified road, or creates an obstruction to the view of persons using any highway used by vehicular traffic, so as to be likely to cause danger to such persons.

(7) Any development falling within Part 11 of Schedule 2 authorised by an Act or order subject to the grant of any consent or approval shall not be treated for the purposes of this Order as authorised unless and until that consent or approval is obtained, except where the Act was passed or the order made after 1st July 1948 and it contains provision to the contrary.

(8) Schedule 2 does not grant permission for the laying or construction of a notifiable pipe-line, except in the case of the laying or construction of a notifiable pipe-line by a public gas supplier in accordance with Class F of Part 17 of that Schedule.

(9) Except as provided in Part 31, Schedule 2 does not permit any development which requires or involves the demolition of a building, but in this paragraph "building" does not include part of a building.

(10) Subject to paragraph (12), development is not permitted by this Order if an application for planning permission for that development would be a Schedule 1 application or a Schedule 2 application within the meaning of the Town and Country Planning (Assessment of Environmental Effects) Regulations 1988 ("the Environmental Assessment Regulations") (descriptions of development).

(11) Where—

(a) the local planning authority have given an opinion under regulation 3 of the Town and Country Planning (Environmental Assessment and Permitted Development) Regulations 1995 ("the Permitted Development Regulations") (opinion as to need for environmental statement) that an application for particular development would be a Schedule 1 application or a Schedule 2 application within the meaning of the Environmental Assessment Regulations and the Secretary of State has issued no direction to the contrary under regulation 4 of the Permitted Development Regulations (directions by the Secretary of State); or

(b) the Secretary of State has given an opinion under regulation 5 of the Permitted Development Regulations (proposed development in

which a relevant planning authority has an interest) that an application for particular development would be a Schedule 1 application or a Schedule 2 application within the meaning of the Environmental Assessment Regulations,

the development to which that opinion relates shall be treated, for the purposes of paragraph (10), as development which is not permitted by this Order.

(12) Paragraph (10) does not apply to—

(a) development which comprises or forms part of a project serving national defence purposes;

(b) development which consists of the carrying out by a drainage body within the meaning of the Land Drainage Act 1991 of improvement works within the meaning of the Land Drainage Improvement Works (Assessment of Environmental Effects) Regulations 1988;

(c) development which consists of the installation of an electric line (within the meaning of Part I of the Electricity Act 1989 (electricity supply)) which replaces an existing line (as defined in regulation 2 of the Overhead Lines (Exemption) Regulations 1990 (interpretation)) and in respect of which consent under section 37 of that Act (consent required for overhead lines) is not required by virtue of regulation 3(1)(e) of those Regulations (exemptions from section 37(1) of the Electricity Act 1989): provided that, in the circumstances mentioned in paragraph (1)(a) or (b) of regulation 5 of those Regulations (further restrictions on the exemptions contained in regulation 3), the determination for the purposes of that regulation that there is not likely to be a significant adverse effect on the environment shall have been made otherwise than as mentioned in paragraph (2) of that regulation;

(d) development for which permission is granted by Part 7, Class D of Part 8, Part 11, Class B of Part 12, Class F(a) of Part 17, Class A or Class B of Part 20 or Class B of Part 21 of Schedule 2;

(e) development for which permission is granted by Class C or Class D of Part 20, Class A of Part 21 or Class B of Part 22 of Schedule 2 where the land in, on or under which the development is to be carried out is—

(i) in the case of Class C or Class D of Part 20, on the same authorised site,

(ii) in the case of Class A of Part 21, on the same premises or, as the case may be, the same ancillary mining land,

(iii) in the case of Class B of Part 22, on the same land or, as the case may be, on land adjoining that land,

as that in, on or under which development of any description permitted by the same Class has been carried out before 3rd June 1995;

(f) the completion of any development begun before 3rd June 1995.

COMMENTARY

DERIVATION

Town and Country Planning General Development Order 1988, as amended by S.I. 1992 No. 609, S.I. 1992 No. 658, S.I. 1992 No. 1280 and S.I. 1992 No. 1563.

DEFINITIONS

"building": art. 2(1).
"classified road": art. 2(1).
"development": 1990 Act, s.55.

"environmental statement": art. 1(2).
"Environmental Assessment Regulations": para. 10.
"planning permission": 1990 Act, s.336(1).
"Permitted Development Regulations": para. 11(a).
"public gas supplier": Gas Act 1986, s.7.
"trunk road": art. 2(1).

GENERAL NOTE

Introduction

This is the article that gives effect to the permitted development rights contained in Sched. 2. It is made by virtue of the 1990 Act, s.58, which allows the Secretary of State by a development order to provide for the granting of planning permission, and provides that the order may itself grant permission. This article therefore constitutes an express grant of planning permission by the Secretary of State. It follows that there is no right of appeal to the Secretary of State against any conditions, exceptions or limitations in Sched. 2. Instead, it will be necessary to obtain an express planning permission on the basis of an application to the local planning authority under Pt. III of the 1990 Act, although it may be possible to apply under s.73 for planning permission to carry out the development "without complying with conditions subject to which a previous planning permission was granted" (s.73(1)). There is nothing in the section limiting its effect to previous permissions granted on an application.

Conditions, exceptions and limitations

Conditions, exceptions and limitations are defined separately in Sched. 2 for each class of permitted development. In addition, this article prescribes several standard limitations.

The difference between condition, exception and limitation is important, although the distinction is somewhat fine. In essence, a *limitation* defines the permitted development. If development is undertaken in excess of the tolerances prescribed then, except for minor transgressions, it is outside the scope of the permission. The permission therefore is inapplicable, and none of the development has planning permission. An enforcement notice must be directed to the whole development, and may (though it need not) require its undoing in entirety. But where the development occurs in breach of a *condition*, only the breach of the condition constitutes a breach of planning control. Conditions are separately defined for each Part and Class in Sched. 2. But *exceptions* are not. For most purposes, an exception may be taken as equivalent to a limitation, because it forms part of the definition of the permitted development. But the use of the word "exceptions" in this article, introduced by the 1988 order, may have significant practical implications in some cases: see further the General Note to Sched. 2, Pt. 3.

General condition relating to habitats protection

The Conservation (Natural Habitats, &c.) Regulations 1994, reg. 60, impose a general condition on any planning permission granted by this Order (whether before or after the commencement of those Regulations) that development which:

(a) is likely to have a significant effect on a European site in Great Britain (either alone or in combination with other plans or projects), and
(b) is not directly concerned with or necessary to the management of the site,

should not be begun until the developer has received written notification of the approval of the local planning authority under reg. 62. The Regulations also provide a procedure whereby a developer may apply to the appropriate nature conservation body for their opinion whether his proposed development is likely to have such an effect (reg. 61); and a procedure for assessment by the local planning authority in cases where the proposed development is likely to have a significant effect on a European site (reg. 62).

Where such development had been begun but not completed before the commencement of those Regulations, it became unlawful for it to be continued until the developer had received written notification of the approval of the local planning authority, on an application made to them under reg. 62.

Exclusion of development requiring environmental assessment

Development permitted under this Order was formerly outside the requirements of the Town and Country Planning (Assessment of Environmental Effects) Regulations 1988 (S.I. 1988 No. 1199), which were made in order to transpose the requirements of the E.C. Directive on environmental assessment (85/337/EEC). The Government was reluctant to fetter the broad grants of planning permission conferred by the Order, and believed that the development permitted by the Order was generally of such minor character as not to warrant environmental assessment. A surrogate method of control was pursued in the case of afforestation through the financial schemes for grants and loans (see the Environmental Assessment (Afforestation) Regulations 1988 (S.I. 1988 No. 1207), and for land drainage through controls over drainage bodies (see Land Drainage Improvement Works (Assessment of Environmental Effects) Regulations 1988 (S.I. 1988 No. 1217)).

Other permitted development remained outside the requirements of environmental assessment. That changed with the 1995 Order. By virtue of para. (10), development is no longer permitted under this Order if an application for planning permission for that development would be a Schedule 1 application or a Schedule 2 application under the Town and Country Planning (Assessment of Environmental Effects) Regulations 1988. This is a matter which can be determined properly only by the local planning authority themselves, so a procedure is provided by the Town and Country Planning (Environmental Assessment and Permitted Development) Regulations 1995 (S.I. 1995 No. 417) for prospective developers to seek an opinion as to whether their proposed development is within either Schedule 1 or Schedule 2 to the 1988 Regulations. The procedure is similar to that prescribed by the 1988 Regulations themselves for developers to seek an opinion as to whether an environmental assessment will be required in connection with a planning application, and includes a right to appeal to the Secretary of State. If the authority or the Secretary of State give an opinion that an application for the proposed development would be within the 1988 Regulations, then it is to be treated as not being permitted development under this Order (para. (11)).

Guidance on the provisions is contained in DOE Circular 3/95, *Permitted Development and Environmental Assessment*, which suggests that, where a local planning authority becomes aware of a potential development that would otherwise benefit from permitted development rights and which might require environmental assessment, they should undertake informal discussions with the developer in order to avoid any delay in establishing the formal position (para. 6). They are advised that the new measures are not expected to result in a large number of developments requiring assessment, and that the great majority of developments carried out under permitted development rights are comparatively small-scale and unlikely to have significant effects on the environment (para. 8). The Appendix to the circular gives indicative criteria and thresholds for the types of development anticipated to be subject to the assessment requirements. The list includes: field drainage works; reclamation of land from the sea; surface storage of fossil fuels and natural gas; storage of petroleum, petro-chemical and chemical products; local authority roads; construction of harbours or marinas; long-distance aqueducts; waste water treatment plant and sites for depositing sewage sludge.

Several exceptions from the environmental assessment limitation are specified in para. (11):

(1) national defence works: these are exempted by art. 1(4) of the E.C. Directive ("projects serving national defence purposes are not covered by this Directive");

(2) drainage improvement works: these are covered by the Land Drainage Improvement Works (Assessment of Environmental Effects) Regulations 1988 (S.I. 1988 No. 1217);

(3) electricity lines: there is a limited exemption for cases where it has already been determined that there is not likely to be a significant adverse effect on the environment;

(4) development permitted by:

Part 7 (forestry): covered by the Environmental Assessment (Afforestation) Regulations 1988 (S.I. 1988 No. 1207);

Part 8, Class D (also Part 12, Class B; Part 20, Classes A and B; Part 21, Class B): projects begun before July 1, 1948);

Part 11 (development under local or private Act or order): outside E.C. Directive by virtue of art. 1(5). Nonetheless, environmental statements are now required in relation to such Acts and orders by virtue of Standing Order 27A.

(5) the completion of any development begun before June 3, 1995 (including certain cases of ancillary development under Parts 20, 21 and 22).

Lawful and unlawful uses

The general exclusion of unlawful uses was introduced in 1988, and in the original 1988 Order was initially ineptly drafted. Its purpose was clear. It was an attempt to deny permitted development rights where the qualifying use of land was unlawful. But it inadvertently went much further, because it assumed that a use was unlawful if it had no planning permission. Thus it proceeded inadvertently to exclude uses which never had planning permission because they never needed it, such as pre-1948 uses, uses which had changed under the Use Classes Order (which does not grant planning permission, but instead takes these use-changes outside development control) and changes of use to agricultural use. Indeed, if this provision had been given its literal interpretation, it would have destroyed altogether the permitted development rights under Pts. 6 and 7 for agricultural and forestry development.

It had long been unclear how far permitted development rights were available where the base use, or the works of construction of the building, were themselves unlawful. There was no difficulty where enforcement action was still possible against the original illegality, because further works or use changes could acquire no greater legitimacy. But where the starting use was immune from enforcement action, whether under the four-year rule, or as a pre-1964 established use, the position was unclear until amendments were made to the principal Act by the Planning and Compensation Act 1991, which now confer "lawfulness" on all immune uses.

The General Development Order 1977 did not impose any general limitation, but it did insist upon a prior lawful use in a number of specific instances: Classes VIII, XIX, XXVII, XXVIII and XXIX, and see *Brooks and Burton v. Secretary of State for the Environment* [1977] 1 W.L.R. 1294 where the Court of Appeal held that an established use was thereby excluded from Class VIII rights. Yet in *Young v. Secretary of State for the Environment* [1983] 2 A.C. 662, the Court of Appeal accepted that the Order could not be applied at all unless its provisions hinged upon a lawful use of land. Unfortunately, Watkins L.J. thought the point so clear that anything else was unarguable, and hence the full implications of the issue appear not to have been considered. In *Asghar v. Secretary of State for the Environment* [1988] J.P.L. 476, the question arose in the context of operational development under Class I of the First Schedule to the 1977 Order (householder development). The court held that the reference in that Class to development within the curtilage of a dwelling house had to be construed as applying only to land which was lawfully within the curtilage, and did not extend to land which had been added to the curtilage without planning permission.

But neither the pre-existing law, nor the new provisions of this article, touched on the case where it was an existing building, rather than a use, which was unlawful. Where a dwelling-house had been erected without planning permission, for example, or erected purportedly under a permission but with sufficient deviation from the approved plans so as to take it altogether outside the permission, the provisions of Part 1 (householder development) could only be disapplied by inserting the word "lawful" in front of "dwellinghouse" wherever it appeared. The problem was eventually resolved in 1992 when what is now art. 3(5) was inserted, excluding all permitted development rights under Sched. 2 in relation to buildings whose construction was illegal, and in relation to unlawful uses.

Lawful and unlawful uses under the 1995 Order

The position now is that:

(1) permitted development rights which are attached to specified uses of land can be relied upon only where that use is a lawful use. A use whose initiation was unlawful will become a lawful use once enforcement action can no longer be taken in respect of it (Act of 1990, s.191(2)), which is 10 years from the date of the breach (s.171B(3)), or four years in the case of change of use to use as a single dwellinghouse (s.171B(2)).

(2) permitted development rights under Sched. 2 which attach to buildings are not available where the building operations involved in the construction of that building are unlawful. Operations which were undertaken unlawfully will nonetheless become lawful operations once no enforcement action can be taken in respect of them (Act of 1990, s.191(2)), which is four years from the time of the substantial completion of the operations (s.171B(1)).

Use contrary to an enforcement notice

Where a particular use or operation on land is forbidden by an enforcement notice, permitted development rights under the Order do not override the notice (*Masefield v. Taylor* [1987] J.P.L. 721); but it is arguable that if the Order were amended so as to grant permission for the retention of the prohibited buildings or works, or the continuance of a prohibited use, the prohibition in the enforcement notice might cease to that extent to have effect, by virtue of the 1990 Act, s.180.

Exclusion of permitted development rights

Permitted development rights can be excluded by:

(1) a special development order: permitted development rights may be restricted or excluded by a special development order applicable to the land (art. 2(1));

(2) a direction under Article 4 or Article 7: permitted development rights under Sched. 2 may be withdrawn in relation to any development or any area by the local planning authority or the Secretary of State if satisfied that it is expedient to do so. Article 7 provides a special regime in relation to certain development permitted by Parts 22 and 23 (minerals).

(3) a planning condition: by virtue of para. (4), permitted development rights under this Order yield to a condition imposed upon an express grant of planning permission. In *East Barnet Urban District Council v. British Transport Commission* [1962] 2 Q.B. 484, the Divisional Court took the view (of the equivalent provision in the 1948 and 1950 Orders) that this covered a case where a specific permission had been granted subject to a condition, but had been followed by a general development order grant of unconditional permission. It did not mean that, in cases where planning permission was not required at all but had nonetheless been applied for and granted, that the development was subject to the conditions imposed by the local planning authority. This ruling was endorsed by the House of Lords in *Newbury District Council v. Secretary of State for the Environment* [1981] A.C. 578. Another case is where the local planning authority or Secretary of State, when granting permission for development not within the Order, imposes a condition restricting the exercise of permitted development rights. On this, DOE Circular 11/95, *The Use of Conditions in Planning Permissions* advises this should be an exceptional course, and that the Secretary of State "would regard such conditions as unreasonable unless there were clear evidence that the uses excluded would have serious adverse effects on amenity or the environment, that there were no other forms of control, and that the conditions would serve a clear planning purpose" (para. 87).

(4) an enforcement notice: where a particular use or operation on land is forbidden by an enforcement notice, permitted development rights under the Order do not override that prohibition (*Masefield v. Taylor* [1987] J.P.L. 721). However, if a subsequent amendment to the Order were to grant permission for the retention of the prohibited buildings or works, or the continuance of the prohibited use, the prohibition in the enforcement notice might cease to that extent to have effect by virtue of the 1990 Act, s.180.

The highways limitation (para. (6))

The highways limitation goes back as far as the Restriction of Ribbon Development Act 1935, which made it unlawful to construct, form or lay out any means of access to or from a classified road. The purpose was to allow highway authorities to control undesirable development along or near the frontages of roads. The limitation in para. (6) relates to:

(1) any access to trunk and classified roads; and

(2) access to any highway used by vehicular traffic where it creates an obstruction to the view of the persons using the highway so as to be likely to cause danger to such persons.

Since the limitation applies to all Sched. 2 development, apart from the Parts specified (Parts 9, 11, 13 and 30), it must apply to Pt. 2 of Sched. 2, which grants planning permission for the construction, laying out and construction of a means of access to a highway which is not a trunk road or a classified road, where that access is required in connection with development permitted by any class in Sched. 2 (excluding Class A of Pt. 2 itself, which relates to gates, fences, walls and other means of enclosure). Hence that Part does not authorise any obstructive or dangerous access.

There must, of course, be development requiring planning permission before there is any need to rely upon permitted development rights. The definition in the 1990 Act, s.336(1), of "engineering operations," which constitute development requiring permission for the purposes of the Act, includes "the formation or laying out of means of access to highways." But this requires some physical engineering operation: it does not extend to the simple removal of a hedge, or a removable fence, in order to obtain access. This is outside the scope of planning control altogether (see appeal decision at [1981] J.P.L. 380).

The approach has been adopted, in a planning appeal decision reported at [1995] J.P.L. 340, that the test of whether any development "*requires* the formation, laying out or material widening of a means of access" is not a matter for the subjective opinion of the developer, but for proper determination by the local planning authority or, an appeal or call-in, the Secretary of State.

Further highway limitations are imposed by various Parts of Sched. 2. Thus, permitted development rights under Pt. 6 (agriculture) may not be exercised within 25 metres of a trunk or classified road. Failure to keep within that boundary renders unlawful any development carried out in purported reliance on the Order: see, *e.g. Fayrewood Fish Farms v. Secretary of State for the Environment* [1984] J.P.L. 267.

Notifiable pipeline

Except for certain works by public gas suppliers under Part 17, Class F, notifiable pipelines are excluded altogether from permitted development rights. The appropriate procedure for obtaining planning permission for a notifiable pipeline is under the Pipelines Act 1962. An authorisation by the Secretary of State for Trade and Industry under that Act may, if it so provides, have effect under s.90 of the Town and Country Planning Act 1990 to grant planning permission.

Hazardous activities

Any development, the carrying out of which involved or was likely to involve a hazardous activity, was formerly outside permitted development rights. Moreover, where permitted development rights were exercised, a standard condition was imposed which prevented the use thereafter of the resulting development for any hazardous activity. These controls have now been superseded by the more specific controls under the Planning (Hazardous Substances) Act 1990.

Directions restricting permitted development

4.—(1) If the Secretary of State or the appropriate local planning authority is satisfied that it is expedient that development described in any Part, Class or paragraph in Schedule 2, other than Class B of Part 22 or Class B of Part 23, should not be carried out unless permission is granted for it on an application, he or they may give a direction under this paragraph that the permission granted by article 3 shall not apply to—

(a) all or any development of the Part, Class or paragraph in question in an area specified in the direction; or

(b) any particular development, falling within that Part, Class or paragraph, which is specified in the direction,

and the direction shall specify that it is made under this paragraph.

(2) If the appropriate local planning authority is satisfied that it is expedient that any particular development described in paragraph (5) below should not be carried out within the whole or any part of a conservation area unless permission is granted for it on an application, they may give a direction under this paragraph that the permission granted by article 3 shall not apply to all or any particular development of the Class in question within the whole or any part of the conservation area, and the direction shall specify the development and conservation area or part of that area to which it relates and that it is made under this paragraph.

(3) A direction under paragraph (1) or (2) shall not affect the carrying out of—

(a) development permitted by Part 11 authorised by an Act passed after 1st July 1948 or by an order requiring the approval of both Houses of Parliament approved after that date;

(b) any development in an emergency; or

(c) any development mentioned in Part 24, unless the direction specifically so provides.

(4) A direction given or having effect as if given under this article shall not, unless the direction so provides, affect the carrying out by a statutory undertaker of the following descriptions of development—

(a) the maintenance of bridges, buildings and railway stations;

(b) the alteration and maintenance of railway track, and the provision and maintenance of track equipment, including signal boxes, signalling apparatus and other appliances and works required in connection with the movement of traffic by rail;

(c) the maintenance of docks, harbours, quays, wharves, canals and towing paths;

(d) the provision and maintenance of mechanical apparatus or appliances (including signalling equipment) required for the purposes of shipping or in connection with the embarking, disembarking, loading, discharging or transport of passengers, livestock or goods at a dock, quay, harbour, bank, wharf or basin;

(e) any development required in connection with the improvement, maintenance or repair of watercourses or drainage works;

(f) the maintenance of buildings, runways, taxiways or aprons at an aerodrome;

(g) the provision, alteration and maintenance of equipment, apparatus and works at an aerodrome, required in connection with the movement of traffic by air (other than buildings, the construction, erection, reconstruction or alteration of which is permitted by Class A of Part 18 of Schedule 2).

(5) The development referred to in paragraph (2) is development described in—

(a) Class A of Part 1 of Schedule 2, consisting of the enlargement, improvement or other alteration of a dwellinghouse, where any part of

the enlargement, improvement or alteration would front a relevant location;

(b) Class C of Part 1 of that Schedule, where the alteration would be to a roof slope which fronts a relevant location;

(c) Class D of Part 1 of that Schedule, where the external door in question fronts a relevant location;

(d) Class E of Part 1 of that Schedule, where the building or enclosure, swimming or other pool to be provided would front a relevant location, or where the part of the building or enclosure maintained, improved or altered would front a relevant location;

(e) Class F of Part 1 of that Schedule, where the hard surface would front a relevant location;

(f) Class H of Part 1 of that Schedule, where the part of the building or other structure on which the satellite antenna is to be installed, altered or replaced fronts a relevant location;

(g) Part 1 of that Schedule, consisting of the erection, alteration or removal of a chimney on a dwellinghouse or on a building within the curtilage of a dwellinghouse;

(h) Class A of Part 2 of that Schedule, where the gate, fence, wall or other means of enclosure would be within the curtilage of a dwellinghouse and would front a relevant location;

(i) Class C of Part 2 of that Schedule, consisting of the painting of the exterior of any part, which fronts a relevant location, of—

(i) a dwellinghouse; or

(ii) any building or enclosure within the curtilage of a dwellinghouse;

(j) Class B of Part 31 of that Schedule, where the gate, fence, wall or other means of enclosure is within the curtilage of a dwellinghouse and fronts a relevant location.

(6) In this article and in articles 5 and 6—

"appropriate local planning authority" means—

(a) in relation to a conservation area in a non-metropolitan county, the county planning authority or the district planning authority; and

(b) in relation to any other area, the local planning authority whose function it would be to determine an application for planning permission for the development to which the direction relates or is proposed to relate;

"relevant location" means a highway, waterway or open space.

COMMENTARY

DEFINITIONS

"aerodrome": art 1(2).
"appropriate local planning authority": para. (6).
"building": art. 1(2).
"conservation area": 1990 Act, s.336(1).
"county planning authority": 1990 Act, s.1.
"development": 1990 Act, s.336(1).
"district planning authority": 1990 Act, s.1.
"local planning authority": 1990 Act, s.336(1).
"planning permission": 1990 Act, s.336.
"relevant location": para. (6).
"statutory undertaker": art. 1(2).

ALLOCATION OF FUNCTIONS

An article 4 direction may only be made by the Secretary of State or the "appropriate" authority, which is (art. 4(4)):

Conservation areas: the county planning authority have concurrent powers with the district authority.
Elsewhere: the local planning authority whose function it would be to determine an application for planning permission for the development to which the direction relates or is proposed to relate.

GENERAL NOTE

Introduction

By a direction made under this article, a local planning authority can restrict the scope of the permitted development rights in relation to defined areas. It is a power of pre-emption rather than prohibition: by withdrawing the deemed permission under this Order, its effect is to require an application to be made for express permission for development proposals. If that permission is refused, or granted subject to conditions other than those in the Order, the landowner is entitled under the 1990 Act, s.107 to claim compensation for abortive expenditure and any loss or damage caused by the loss of rights.

A new power was introduced by the 1995 Order, art. 4(2), to make directions, without the approval of the Secretary of State, in relation to dwellinghouses in conservation areas.

General and specific directions

A direction may relate to:

(a) permitted development in relation to any particular area, specified in the direction (a general direction); or
(b) any particular permitted development anywhere in the authority's area (a specific direction).

Thus "the planning authority may either ban all or any development or ban a specific development, that is to say, it can either sweep the board clean or be as extremely selective as it chooses" (*Thanet District Council v. Ninedrive* [1978] 1 All E.R. 703 at 711, *per* Walton J.). In the case of a general direction under art. 4(1)(a), the authority need not serve individual notice of the making of the direction if they think it impracticable because of the number of owners and occupiers of the land, or if it is difficult to identify or locate one or more of them (art. 5(12) and (14)). In *Spedeworth v. Secretary of State for the Environment* (1972) 116 S.J. 426, the Court of Appeal held that a direction withdrawing permitted development rights "except as a caravan site" was a general direction, and that individual service was not required.

Article 4(2) directions: dwellinghouses in conservation areas

The 1995 Order introduced a power for local planning authorities to make directions withdrawing permitted development rights specifically in relation to dwellinghouses in conservation areas. The permitted development which may be excluded includes the erection, alteration or removal of a chimney on a dwellinghouse, or on a building within the curtilage of a dwellinghouse.

It also includes any of the following rights for development which would front a highway, a waterway or open space. "Open space" is defined in the 1990 Act, s.336(1) as meaning "any land laid out as a public garden, or used for the purposes of public recreation, or land which is a disused burial ground".

(1) the enlargement, improvement or other alteration of a dwellinghouse (Part 1, Class A). Advice in DOE Circular 9/95, *General Development Order Consolidation 1995*, App. D, para. 17 explains that this power

could be used to exclude the erection of an extension if any part of it, such as a side wall, would front a highway, waterway or open space. It could not exclude permitted development rights for an extension lying wholly to the rear of the existing building. The circular urges that "The Secretaries of State are particularly concerned that the power to withdraw permitted development rights relating to extensions should be used exceptionally, and only where the character or appearance of a conservation area is likely to be threatened". It would be open to a local planning authority who wished to exclude rear extensions to make a direction under art. 4(1), and submit it to the Secretary of State for approval in the normal way.

(2) the alteration of a dwellinghouse roof (Part 1, Class C);
(3) the erection or construction of a porch outside any external door of a dwellinghouse (Part 1, Class D);
(4) the provision, within the curtilage of a dwellinghouse, of a building, enclosure, swimming or other pool required for a purpose incidental to the enjoyment of the dwellinghouse as such, or the maintenance, improvement or other alteration of such a building or enclosure (Part 1, Class E);
(5) the provision within the curtilage of a dwellinghouse of a hard surface for any purpose incidental to the enjoyment of the dwellinghouse as such (Part 1, Class F);
(6) the installation, alteration or replacement of a satellite antenna on a dwellinghouse or within its curtilage (Part 1, Class H);
(7) the erection or demolition of a gate, fence, wall or other means of enclosure within the curtilage of a dwellinghouse (Part 2, Class A); and
(8) the painting of a dwellinghouse or a building or enclosure within the curtilage of a dwellinghouse (Part 2, Class C).

Exclusions

Development within Class B of Pts. 22 and 23 (mineral exploration) is excluded from this power, and separate controls are established by art. 7.

Restrictions

(1) An art. 4 direction has no effect in respect of the carrying out of development authorised by Act of Parliament, or by a parliamentary order, approved by both Houses of Parliament after July 1, 1948 (art. 4(3)).
(2) Certain operations of statutory undertakers (art. 4(4)) are protected from inadvertent restriction, but it is clear (contrary to the suggestion in DOE Circular 9/95, *General Development Order Consolidation 1995*, Appendix B, para. 12) that a direction can exclude these operations if it so provides. It will, however, require the Secretary of State's approval (art. 5(3)). Compensation for such restrictions is calculated on the special basis provided for by the 1990 Act, ss.279 and 280.
(3) A direction is ineffective against any development undertaken in an emergency.
(4) Unless it provides otherwise, a direction is ineffective against Pt. 24 development (telecommunications).

Where development has already been undertaken: material change in use

The power to withdraw permission by making an art. 4 direction is entirely prospective. Under art. 4(1) and 4(2) the planning authority must be satisfied that it is expedient that the development "should not be carried out" without specific permission. It cannot, therefore, be used to withdraw permitted development rights in respect of development which already has been carried out.

The courts have confirmed the straightforward application of this principle to "once and for all" development, such as the making of a material change in the use of the land to a new permanent and continuous use (see, *e.g. Cole v. Somerset County Council* [1957] 1 Q.B. 23: change of use from a golf club to a caravan site under what is now Sched. 2, Pt. 5 of the Order). But the position is more complicated with discontinuous development under the permitted rights for temporary buildings and uses (Sched. 2, Pt. 4). In *South Bucks District Council v. Secretary of State for the Environment* [1989] 1 P.L.R. 69, C.A., reversing *Strandmill v. Secretary of State for the Environment* [1988] J.P.L. 491, the Court of Appeal rejected the High Court's view that the right to use land temporarily for any purpose for up to 14 days in any calendar year was implemented when the land was first put to such a use, and accordingly that use continued to have the benefit of the Order for the remainder of the permitted period for that calendar year. Instead, the Court of Appeal held that the permitted development under Pt. 4 is a change of use, and that there could be 28 such changes on each of the maximum 28 days per year. It followed that an art. 4 direction could have immediate effect to take away rights under that Part.

Where operational development has been undertaken

The position in relation to operational development is less clear. There are two possibilities:

(1) that the immunity for the whole development arises once the development has commenced;
(2) that immunity attaches only to so much of the development as has been completed at the time the order is made, so that the whole development is immune only when it is substantially completed.

The 1990 Act adopts the first model for the purposes of determining whether an express grant of planning permission has lapsed for non-implementation: all that is required is that the development process should have been begun by the carrying out of some physical works. The Act adopts the second model for the power under s.97 to revoke or modify an express planning permission, which is the closest analogy to an art. 4 direction. Under s.97(3)(a), planning permission relating to the carrying out of building or other operations may be revoked or modified "at any time before those operations have been completed," though without affecting any operations that have already been carried out.

The Minister's intention was that the same rule should be taken to apply to art. 4 directions. The General Development Order was deliberately amended in 1950, substituting the words "carried out" in art. 4 where previously it had referred to development that should not be "undertaken." The Circular (MTCP Circular 87, Appendix) explained that:

> "The effect of this change is to make it clear that a direction under Article 4 can be made *after* the development has been begun, provided it has not been completed. It would, of course, be necessary to rely on the powers of Section 26 [now s.102 of the 1990 Act: discontinuance orders] to provide for the removal of so much of the development as had been carried out when the direction came into force."

The arguments were rehearsed in a planning appeal reported at [1987] J.P.L. 663 where the appellants had dug a trench in preparation for the construction of fishing lakes. The inspector ruled that this constituted the commencement of permitted development, and that an art. 4 direction, though served swiftly by the authority, had been ineffective to remove the permission. He thus took a different view from that in the earlier circular, observing that:

"If it had been Parliament's intention that directions could have the effect of making GDO permission cease to apply after operations had been commenced in reliance on it, but before completion, it is likely that explicit provision would have been made to that effect, analogous to that made by section 45(4)(b) [now s.97(3) of the 1990 Act]."

That interpretation undermines the power of local planning authorities under this article, but the difference may in practice be narrow. If an art. 4 direction is ineffective to withdraw permission, an alternative power exists under s.102 to commence discontinuance proceedings. In both cases, the local planning authority is required to pay compensation for its intervention. The advantage of the use of art. 4 is that it may prove more effective as a pre-emptive remedy, and it may be (because it requires the making of an application for permission as a pre-condition to compensation entitlement) a better basis for negotiations leading to a grant of conditional permission, than s.102 proceedings.

When should an article 4 direction be used?

Advice on the use of art. 4 directions is contained in Appendix D to DOE Circular 9/95, which insists that, generally, permitted development rights should be withdrawn only in exceptional circumstances, and only where there is a real and specific threat. But there are some specific qualifications to that general rule:

(1) *agriculture and countryside*: the circular contemplates that use of the procedure may be appropriate where it is desirable that the siting and design of any building should be considered by the local planning authority before it is erected, or that control should be maintained over other developments which may harm the rural landscape. The Secretary of State takes the view that the limited Pt. 6 rights applicable to art. 1(6) land (see further the General Note to Sched. 2, Pt. 6) give local planning authorities in those areas sufficient control, and that an art. 4 direction would be justified only where because of the exceptional beauty of an area, or its topography, careful consideration needs to be given to the principle of allowing any development there. Directions covering whole National Parks or Areas of Outstanding Natural Beauty are likely to be approved only in exceptional circumstances.

(2) *subdivision of agricultural land*: the Secretary of State is willing to approve directions in these cases only where the development is likely to take place and would, if not controlled, seriously affect the attractiveness of the surrounding countryside.

(3) *conservation areas*: there are now two categories of case. First, where the local planning authority seeks to act under art. 4(2) to make a direction which does not require the approval of the Secretary of State. Advice on these powers is contained in DOE Circular 9/95, *General Development Order Consolidation 1995*, which observes (Appendix D, para. 16) that:

"An article 4(2) direction can be selective both between and within these types of development. Development relating to an individual type of architectural feature which is important to the character or appearance of the conservation area could be specified. Examples are windows, doors, quoins, fanlights, architraves, parapets, cornices, stonework etc. The Secretaries of State are concerned that local planning authorities should use these powers selectively and only in relation to development which is likely to threaten the character or appearance of a conservation area."

Second, for directions which go beyond the article 4(2) power, the Secretary of State's general approach is spelt out in PPG15, *Planning and the Historic Environment* (1994), para. 4.23, where he maintains the policy that permitted development rights should not be withdrawn without clear justification and that, wherever possible, residents in conservation areas should continue to enjoy the same freedom to undertake development as residents elsewhere. He does not consider that designation of a conservation area in itself automatically justifies making an article 4 direction, but he will generally be in favour of approving directions in conservation areas:

"where these are backed by a clear assessment of an area's special architectural and historic interest, where the importance to that special interest of the features in question is established, where the local planning authority can demonstrate support for the direction, and where the direction involves the minimum withdrawal of permitted development rights (in terms of both area and types of development) necessary to achieve its objective."

(4) *dwellinghouses*: DOE Circular 9/95, para. 9 insists that restrictions on householder development, beyond that applicable in conservation areas, should normally be made only where the dwelling itself is of particularly high quality.

(5) *telecommunications*: the circular advises that blanket directions excluding Pt. 24 rights (to achieve this a direction must, under art. 4(2)(c), specifically so provide), will not normally be approved because of the separate system of control under licences issued to individual operators, but that there may be special exceptions involving areas of special attractiveness particularly at risk.

Procedure: the need for Secretary of State's approval

There are three categories of art. 4 directions.

(1) those which do not require approval by the Secretary of State. This class includes:
   (a) directions relating to certain categories of permitted development rights in a conservation area (art. 4(2));
   (b) directions relating only to a listed building, or to a building which has been notified to the authority by the Secretary of State as a building of architectural or historic interest, or development within the curtilage of a listed building (art. 5(3));
   (c) directions whose effect is solely to cancel any previous direction (art. 5(1)).

   In the case of (a) and (b), a direction will require Secretary of State's approval if it purports to exclude permitted development rights of statutory undertakers.

(2) directions which are able to take effect from the time they are made by the local planning authority, but which lapse after six months if not approved by the Secretary of State, or earlier if disallowed by him. This category extends to directions relating only to development permitted by any of Pts. 1 to 4 or Pt. 31 of Sched. 2, if the relevant planning authority consider the development would be prejudicial to the proper planning of their area or constitute a threat to the amenities of their area (art. 5(4)). Given the purpose of art. 4 directions, and the Secretary of State's current policies on making them, that test is probably in practice equally applicable to the making of any art. 4 direction.

(3) all other directions, which require the Secretary of State's approval before taking effect.

In all cases, the language of the Order contemplates that the Order is *made* by the local planning authority, notwithstanding that in some cases it does not come into effect until approved by the Secretary of State. The Secretary of State has power himself to make an art. 4 direction (see art. 4(1)); and he has power also to make a special development order, with similar effect except as to liability to pay compensation.

Procedure: directions under article 4(2) not requiring approval

The procedure for article 4(2) directions is prescribed by art. 6. Notice of the direction must be given, as soon as practicable after it has been made, by publication in a local newspaper and by service on the owner and occupier of every dwellinghouse in the area covered by the direction. The requirement of individual service is relaxed, in any individual case, where it is difficult to identify or locate an owner or occupier; and in the general case, where the local planning authority consider that the number of owners or occupiers within the conservation area makes individual service impracticable (art. 6(4) and (5)).

A direction made under these provisions takes effect immediately notice of it is served on the owner or occupier, or where that requirement is relaxed, when it is published in a local newspaper (art. 6(3)). However, it expires after six months unless the authority confirm the direction beforehand (art. 6(7)). In deciding whether to confirm a direction, they are required to take into account any representations received by them within the period of at least 21 days specified in the public notice for that purpose. The Order confers no power upon the local planning authority to confirm the direction with variations, although the Secretary of State is entitled, when confirming an order, to make modifications to it (art. 5(1)). The Secretaries of State have advised authorities to pay particular attention to the views of occupiers and owners in the area covered by the direction (DOE Circular 9/95, *General Development Order Consolidation 1995* App. D para 20.)

The notice must (art. 6(2)):

(a) include a description of the development and the area covered by the direction and the effect of the direction;
(b) specify that the direction is made under art. 4(2);
(c) name the place where the direction and a map of the area which it covers may be inspected; and
(d) specify the period, covering at least 21 days, during which any representations on the direction may be made to the local planning authority.

Procedure: other directions not requiring approval

An Order relating solely to a listed or notified building (art. 5(3)) does not require the approval of the Secretary of State. Nor does it require confirmation by the local planning authority. It takes effect from the date on which notice is served on the occupier or, if there is no occupier, on the owner (art. 5(10)) (or, if substituted service is necessary under art. 5(12), then from the date of publication of the necessary notice: art. 5(15)).

Procedure: directions requiring approval

DOE Circular 9/95, *General Development Order Consolidation 1995*, Appendix D, advises that applications to the Secretary of State for approval of article 4(1) directions should be accompanied by two sealed copies and one unsealed copy of the direction and plan, and a full statement of the authority's reasons for making it. Authorities should include:

(a) a description of the site and/or area covered by the direction, and of the character of the surroundings;
(b) the grounds on which the authority consider that the direction is needed. Authorities should identify any known proposals to carry out

development which could damage an interest of acknowledged importance and address the harm which might arise from the exercise of permitted development rights, referring in particular to any rights exercisable for limited periods. The nature of the proposal should be stated and an explanation given of its likely effect;

(c) where the direction is not aimed at an immediate threat, the measures taken to inform those with an interest about the proposed direction and of any representations received;

(d) where a wide area direction is proposed, any special topographical features which make the area particularly vulnerable to damage should be stated, as well as (if applicable) the fact that the area is in a National Park or an area of outstanding natural beauty, etc.;

(e) where visual considerations are important, particularly where the direction would affect such areas as conservation areas, photographs of the site and its surroundings. Cases of urgency need not be delayed for this; and

(f) where there is urgency, the reasons for urgent treatment and the period within which a decision is needed.

Model directions

Model forms for directions under arts. 4(1) and 4(2) are reproduced in DOE Circular 9/95, *General Development Order Consolidation 1995*, App. D.

Service of notice of the Direction

There is no obligation on the authority to notify owners of their intention to make an art. 4 direction, and indeed prior notification might have the effect of inducing the owner to begin work in an attempt to pre-empt the process. Nor is the authority required to notify any person that a direction has been submitted to the Secretary of State for approval. Thus the application is effectively on an *ex parte* basis, and the owner or occupier of the land is unable to respond to any of the authority's arguments for making the direction. The Secretary of State has power subsequently to cancel a direction (art. 5(16)), however, and thus would be under an implied duty to take into account representations from an aggrieved owner or occupier of the land.

The authority are required to serve notice of any direction they make on the owner and occupier of every part of the land as soon as practicable after making it, and the notice does not take effect in respect of any part of the land until notice is served on the occupier (or, if there is no occupier, the owner): art. 5(10). If, however, the authority consider that individual service is impracticable because of the number of owners and occupiers, or because of difficulties in identifying or locating one or more of them, they may instead publish notice of the direction in one or more newspapers circulating in the locality. Despite the suggestion by the Lands Tribunal to the contrary in *Carter v. Windsor and Maidenhead Royal Borough Council* [1988] 3 P.L.R. 6, at 8, there has always been a requirement to notify owners once the direction has been made.

Fees for subsequent planning applications

No fee is payable for a planning application made in respect of what would have been permitted development had there been no art. 4 direction: Town and Country Planning (Fees for Applications and Deemed Applications) Regulations 1989 (S.I. 1989 No. 193), reg. 5. The exemption extends only to cases where the development would have been in one of the Parts of Sched. 2

to this Order, and it is solely because of the direction that the permitted development rights do not apply. In *Carter v. Windsor and Maidenhead Royal Borough Council* [1988] 3 P.L.R. 6, at 14, the Lands Tribunal, in assessing a compensation claim, relied on the fact that the local planning authority had acknowledged that no fee was payable for the planning applications whose refusal gave rise to the claim, as evidencing that the authority had accepted that the development would otherwise have been permitted.

Compensation

The withdrawal of permitted development rights by an art. 4 direction, as with the revocation or modification of an express planning permission, may give rise to liability to compensate. Any person interested in the land, or in any mineral in the land, may seek compensation for abortive expenditure, or other loss or damage directly attributable to the withdrawal of the permitted development rights (1990 Act, s.107, as applied by s.108). But the Act requires that a planning application should first have been made, and permission refused, or only granted subject to conditions other than those previously imposed by the development order (s.108(1)). Compensation may be claimed not only by fee simple owners and tenants, but also by persons with a contractual right to use the land (*Pennine Raceway v. Kirklees Metropolitan Council (No. 1)* [1983] Q.B. 382).

Special compensation provisions apply to statutory undertakers. Entitlement to compensation is conferred, and special methods for its calculation prescribed, by the Act of 1990, ss.279, 282.

Article 4 directions under earlier development orders

There is no express saving for directions made under earlier general development orders, as there was in the 1977 Order, art. 24(2), because they are now given continued effect by the Interpretation Act 1978, ss.17(2)(b) and 23.

Approval of Secretary of State for article 4(1) directions

5.—(1) Except in the cases specified in paragraphs (3) and (4), a direction by a local planning authority under article 4(1) requires the approval of the Secretary of State, who may approve the direction with or without modifications.

(2) On making a direction under article 4(1) or submitting such a direction to the Secretary of State for approval—

- **(a) a county planning authority shall give notice of it to any district planning authority in whose district the area to which the direction relates is situated; and**
- **(b) except in metropolitan districts, a district planning authority shall give notice of it to the county planning authority, if any.**

(3) Unless it affects the carrying out of development by a statutory undertaker as provided by article 4(4), the approval of the Secretary of State is not required for a direction which relates to—

- **(a) a listed building;**
- **(b) a building which is notified to the authority by the Secretary of State as a building of architectural or historic interest; or**
- **(c) development within the curtilage of a listed building,**

and does not relate to land of any other description.

(4) Subject to paragraph (6), the approval of the Secretary of State is not required for a direction made under article 4(1) relating only to development permitted by any of Parts 1 to 4 or Part 31 of Schedule 2, if the relevant authority consider the development would be prejudicial to the proper planning of their area or constitute a threat to the amenities of their area.

(5) A direction not requiring the Secretary of State's approval by virtue of paragraph (4) shall, unless disallowed or approved by the Secretary of State, expire at the end of six months from the date on which it was made.

(6) Paragraph (4) does not apply to a second or subsequent direction relating to the same development or to development of the same Class or any of the same Classes, in the same area or any part of that area as that to which the first direction relates or related.

(7) The local planning authority shall send a copy of any direction made by them to which paragraph (4) applies to the Secretary of State not later than the date on which notice of that direction is given in accordance with paragraph (10) or (12).

(8) The Secretary of State may give notice to the local planning authority that he has disallowed any such direction and the direction shall then cease to have effect.

(9) The local planning authority shall as soon as reasonably practicable give notice that a direction has been disallowed in the same manner as notice of the direction was given.

(10) Subject to paragraph (12), notice of any direction made under article 4(1) shall be served by the appropriate local planning authority on the owner and occupier of every part of the land within the area to which the direction relates as soon as practicable after the direction has been made or, where the direction is required to be approved by the Secretary of State, as soon as practicable after it has been so approved; and a direction shall come into force in respect of any part of the land within the area to which the direction relates on the date on which notice is so served on the occupier of that part, or, if there is no occupier, on the owner.

(11) If a direction to which paragraph (4) applies is approved by the Secretary of State within the period of six months referred to in paragraph (5), then (unless paragraph (12) applies) the authority who made the direction shall, as soon as practicable, serve notice of that approval on the owner and occupier of every part of the land within the area to which the direction

relates; and where the Secretary of State has approved the direction with modifications the notice shall indicate the effect of the modifications.

(12) Where in the case of a direction under article 4(1)(a) an authority consider that individual service in accordance with paragraph (10) or (11) is impracticable for the reasons set out in paragraph (14) they shall publish a notice of the direction, or of the approval, by local advertisement.

(13) A notice published pursuant to paragraph (12) shall contain a statement of the effect of the direction and of any modification made to it by the Secretary of State, and shall name a place or places where a copy of the direction, and of a map defining the area to which it relates, may be seen at all reasonable hours.

(14) The reasons referred to in paragraph (12) are that the number of owners and occupiers within the area to which the direction relates makes individual service impracticable, or that it is difficult to identify or locate one or more of them.

(15) Where notice of a direction has been published in accordance with paragraph (12), the direction shall come into force on the date on which the notice is first published.

(16) A local planning authority may, by making a subsequent direction and without the approval of the Secretary of State, cancel any direction made by them under article 4(1), and the Secretary of State may make a direction cancelling any direction under article 4(1) made by the local planning authority.

(17) Paragraphs (10) and (12) to (15) shall apply to any direction made under paragraph (16).

COMMENTARY

DERIVATION

Town and Country Planning General Development Order 1988, art. 5.

DEFINITIONS

"appropriate local planning authority": art. 4(6).
"county planning authority": 1990 Act, s.1.
"district planning authority": 1990 Act, s.1.
"land": 1990 Act, s.336.
"listed building": Planning (Listed Buildings and Conservation Areas Act 1990, s.1.
"owner": 1990 Act, s.336(1).
"statutory undertaker": art. 1(2).

GENERAL NOTE

See the General Note to art. 4.

Notice and confirmation of article 4(2) directions

6.—(1) Notice of any direction made under article 4(2) shall, as soon as practicable after the direction has been made, be given by the appropriate local planning authority—

(a) by local advertisement; and

(b) subject to paragraphs (4) and (5), by serving the notice on the owner and occupier of every dwellinghouse within the whole or the relevant part of the conservation area to which the direction relates.

(2) The notice referred to in paragraph (1) shall—

(a) include a description of the development and the conservation area or part of that area to which the direction relates, and a statement of the effect of the direction;

(b) specify that the direction is made under article 4(2) of this Order;

(c) name a place where a copy of the direction, and a copy of the map defining the conservation area or part of that area to which it relates, may be seen at all reasonable hours; and

(d) specify a period of at least 21 days, stating the date on which that period begins, within which any representations concerning the direction may be made to the local planning authority.

(3) The direction shall come into force in respect of any part of the land within the conservation area or part of that area to which it relates—

(a) on the date on which the notice is served on the occupier of that part of the land or, if there is no occupier, on the owner; or

(b) if paragraph (4) or (5) applies, on the date on which the notice is first published in accordance with paragraph (1)(a).

(4) The local planning authority need not serve notice on an owner or occupier in accordance with paragraph (1)(b) where they consider that individual service on that owner or occupier is impracticable because it is difficult to identify or locate him.

(5) The local planning authority need not serve any notice in accordance with paragraph (1)(b) where they consider that the number of owners or occupiers within the conservation area or part of that area to which the direction relates makes individual service impracticable.

(6) On making a direction under article 4(2)—

(a) a county planning authority shall give notice of it to any district planning authority in whose district the conservation area or part of that area to which the direction relates is situated; and

(b) except in metropolitan districts, a district planning authority shall give notice of it to the county planning authority, if any.

(7) A direction under article 4(2) shall expire at the end of six months from the date on which it was made unless confirmed by the appropriate local planning authority in accordance with paragraphs (8) and (9) before the end of that six month period.

(8) In deciding whether to confirm a direction made under article 4(2), the local planning authority shall take into account any representations received during the period specified in the notice referred to in paragraph (2)(d).

(9) The local planning authority shall not confirm the direction until a period of at least 28 days has elapsed following the latest date on which any notice relating to the direction was served or published.

(10) The appropriate local planning authority shall as soon as practicable give notice that a direction has been confirmed in the same manner as in paragraphs (1)(a) and (b) above.

COMMENTARY

Derivation

This article was new in the 1995 consolidation.

Definitions

"appropriate planning authority":
"conservation area": Planning (Listed Buildings and Conservation Areas) Act 1990, s.69.
"development": 1990 Act, s.55.
"local advertisement": art. 1(2).
"local planning authority": 1990 Act, s.1.
"owner": 1990 Act, s.336(1).

General Note

This article prescribes the procedures to be followed for the making of those article 4(2) directions which do not require the approval of the Secretary of State. See further the Commentary to art. 4.

Directions restricting permitted development under Class B of Part 22 or Class B of Part 23

7.—(1) If, on receipt of a notification from any person that he proposes to carry out development within Class B of Part 22 or Class B of Part 23 of Schedule 2, a mineral planning authority are satisfied as mentioned in paragraph (2) below, they may, within a period of 21 days beginning with the receipt of the notification, direct that the permission granted by article 3 of this Order shall not apply to the development, or to such part of the development as is specified in the direction.

(2) The mineral planning authority may make a direction under this article if they are satisfied that it is expedient that the development, or any part of it, should not be carried out unless permission for it is granted on an application because—

(a) the land on which the development is to be carried out is within—

(i) a National Park,

(ii) an area of outstanding natural beauty,

(iii) a site of archaeological interest, and the operation to be carried out is not one described in the Schedule to the Areas of Archaeological Importance (Notification of Operations) (Exemption) Order 1984 (exempt operations),

(iv) a site of special scientific interest, or

(v) the Broads;

(b) the development, either taken by itself or taken in conjunction with other development which is already being carried out in the area or in respect of which notification has been given in pursuance of the provisions of Class B of Part 22 or Class B of Part 23, would cause serious detriment to the amenity of the area in which it is to be carried out or would adversely affect the setting of a building shown as Grade I in the list of buildings of special architectural or historic interest compiled by the Secretary of State under section 1 of the Planning (Listed Buildings and Conservation Areas) Act 1990 (listing of buildings of special architectural or historic interest);

(c) the development would constitute a serious nuisance to the inhabitants of a nearby residential building, hospital or school; or

(d) the development would endanger aircraft using a nearby aerodrome.

(3) A direction made under this article shall contain a statement as to the day on which (if it is not disallowed under paragraph (5) below) it will come into force, which shall be 29 days from the date on which notice of it is sent to the Secretary of State in accordance with paragraph (4) below.

(4) As soon as is reasonably practicable a copy of a direction under this article shall be sent by the mineral planning authority to the Secretary of State and to the person who gave notice of the proposal to carry out development.

(5) The Secretary of State may, at any time within a period of 28 days beginning with the date on which the direction is made, disallow the direction; and immediately upon receipt of notice in writing from the Secretary of State that he has disallowed the direction, the mineral planning authority shall give notice in writing to the person who gave notice of the proposal that he is authorised to proceed with the development.

COMMENTARY

DERIVATION

Town and Country Planning General Development Order 1988 (S.I. 1988 No. 1813), art. 6, introduced originally by S.I. 1985 No. 1981. The 1995 consolidation extended the provisions to land in the Broads (art. 7(2)(a)(v)).

DEFINITIONS

"aerodrome": art. 1(2).
"area of outstanding natural beauty": art. 1(2).
"development": 1990 Act, s.55.
"mineral planning authority": 1990 Act, s.1(4).
"National Park": art. 1(2).
"site of archaeological interest": art. 1(2).
"site of special scientific interest": art. 1(2).

GENERAL NOTE

This article establishes a different system of directions for development under Part 22, Class B (temporary rights of up to four months for mineral exploration) and Part 23, Class B (removal of material from mineral-working deposits other than a stockpile). Article 4 is excluded. Both of those classes confer permission only where the developer has given prior written notice to the mineral planning authority of its intention to carry out the development, together with the appropriate details. That notification triggers the powers of the authority under this article to issue, within 21 days, a direction excluding permitted development rights. The criteria by which they must act are specified in para. (2) and include the location of the land in a designated area (such as a National Park or the Broads) and the prospect of serious detriment to the amenity of the area or a serious nuisance to residents, or to a hospital or school.

Procedure

A direction must be sent, as soon as reasonably practicable, to the Secretary of State and to the person who gave notice, but it does not come into force until 29 days from notification to the Secretary of State. In the meantime, no development is permitted: the relevant rights under Pts. 22 and 23 are frozen for 28 days from the date the direction is sent to the Secretary of State. If the Secretary of State disallows the direction, permitted development rights arise from the time the mineral planning authority notify the developer of the decision. The Secretary of State has no power to disallow the direction beyond the 28-day period.

Directions

8. Any power conferred by this Order to give a direction includes power to cancel or vary the direction by a subsequent direction.

COMMENTARY

DERIVATION

Town and Country Planning General Development Order 1988 (S.I. 1988 No. 1813), art. 30 (unamended).

GENERAL NOTE

The powers conferred by this Order to make directions are those under arts. 4 and 7 (directions restricting permitted development).

Revocations

9. The statutory instruments specified in column 1 of Schedule 3 are hereby revoked to the extent specified in column 3.

COMMENTARY

General Note

This Order and the Town and Country Planning (General Development Procedure) Order 1995 (S.I. 1995 No. 419) between them revoke the whole of the Town and Country Planning General Development Order 1988 (S.I. 1988 No. 1813) and all subsequent amending orders.

SCHEDULE 1

Article 1

PART 1

ARTICLE 1(4) LAND

Land within the following counties—

Cleveland, Cornwall, Cumbria, Devon, Durham, Dyfed, Greater Manchester, Gwynedd, Humberside, Lancashire, Merseyside, Northumberland, North Yorkshire, South Yorkshire, Tyne and Wear, West Glamorgan, West Yorkshire.

PART 2

ARTICLE 1(5) LAND

Land within—

(a) a National Park;

(b) an area of outstanding natural beauty;

(c) an area designated as a conservation area under section 69 of the Planning (Listed Buildings and Conservation Areas) Act 1990 (designation of conservation areas);

(d) an area specified by the Secretary of State and the Minister of Agriculture, Fisheries and Food for the purposes of section 41(3) of the Wildlife and Countryside Act 1981 (enhancement and protection of the natural beauty and amenity of the countryside);

(e) the Broads.

PART 3

ARTICLE 1(6) LAND

Land within a National Park or within the following areas—

(a) In England, the Broads or land outside the boundaries of a National Park, which is within the parishes listed below—

in the district of Allerdale—

Blindcrake, Bothel and Threapland, Bridekirk, Brigham, Broughton, Broughton Moor, Camerton, Crosscanonby, Dean, Dearham, Gilcrux, Great Clifton, Greysouthen, Little Clifton, Loweswater, Oughterside and Allerby, Papcastle, Plumbland, Seaton, Winscales;

in the borough of Copeland—

Arlecdon and Frizington, Cleator Moor, Distington, Drigg and Carleton, Egremont, Gosforth, Haile, Irton with Santon, Lamplugh, Lowca, Lowside Quarter, Millom, Millom Without, Moresby, Parton, Ponsonby, St Bees, St Bridget's Beckermet, St John's Beckermet, Seascale, Weddicar;

in the district of Eden—

Ainstable, Asby, Bandleyside, Bolton, Brough, Brough Sowerby, Brougham, Castle Sowerby, Catterlen, Clifton, Cliburn, Crackenthorpe, Crosby Garrett, Crosby Ravensworth, Culgaith, Dacre, Dufton, Glassonby, Great Salkeld, Great Strickland, Greystoke, Hartley, Hesket, Hillbeck, Hunsonby, Hutton, Kaber, Kings Meaburn, Kirkby Stephen, Kirby Thore, Kirkoswald, Langwathby, Lazonby, Little Strickland, Long Marton, Lowther, Mallerstang, Milburn, Morland, Mungrisdale, Murton, Musgrave, Nateby, Newbiggin, Newby, Orton, Ousby, Ravenstonedale, Shap, Skelton, Sleagill, Sockbridge and Tirril, Soulby, Stainmore, Tebay, Temple Sowerby, Thrimby, Waitby, Warcop, Wharton, Winton, Yanwath and Eamont Bridge;

in the borough of High Peak—

Chapel-en-le-Frith, Charlesworth, Chinley Buxworth and Brownside, Chisworth, Green Fairfield, Hartington Upper Quarter, Hayfield, King Sterndale, Tintwistle, Wormhill;

in the district of South Lakeland—

Aldingham, Angerton, Arnside, Barbon, Beetham, Blawith and Subberthwaite, Broughton West, Burton, Casterton, Docker, Egton-with-Newland, Fawcett Forest, Firbank, Grayrigg, Helsington, Heversham, Hincaster, Holme, Hutton Roof, Killington, Kirkby Ireleth, Kirkby Lonsdale, Lambrigg, Levens, Lower Allithwaite, Lower Holker, Lowick, Lupton, Mansergh, Mansriggs, Middleton, Milnthorpe, Natland, New Hutton, Old Hutton and Holmescales, Osmotherley, Pennington, Preston Patrick, Preston Richard, Scalthwaiterigg, Sedgwick, Skelsmergh, Stainton, Strickland Ketel, Strickland Roger, Urswick, Whinfell, Whitwell and Selside;

in the district of West Derbyshire—

Aldwark, Birchover, Stanton; and

(b) In Wales, land outside the boundaries of a National Park which is—

(i) within the communities listed below—

in the borough of Aberconwy—

Caerhun, Dolgarrog;

in the borough of Arfon—

Betws Garmon, Bontnewydd, Llanberis, Llanddeiniolen, Llandwrog, Llanllyfni, Llanwnda, Waunfawr;

in the district of Meirionnydd—

Arthog, Corris, Llanfrothen, Penrhyndeudraeth; or

(ii) within the specified part of the communities listed below—

in the borough of Aberconwy, those parts of the following communities which were on 31st March 1974 within the former rural district of Nant Conway—

Conwy, Henryd, Llanddoged and Maenan, Llanrwst, Llansanffraid Glan Conwy;

in the borough of Arfon, those parts of the following communities which were on 31st March 1974 within the former rural district of Gwyrfai—

Caernarfon, Llandygai, Llanrug, Pentir, Y Felinheli;

in the district of Dwyfor, that part of the community of Porthmadog which was on 31st March 1974 within the former rural district of Deudraeth and those parts of

the following communities which were on that date within the former rural district of Gwyrfai—

Clynnog, Dolbenmaen, Llanaelhaearn;

in the district of Glyndwr, those parts of the following communities which were on 31st March 1974 within the former rural district of Penllyn—

Llandrillo, Llangwm;

in the district of Meirionnydd, those parts of the following communities which were on 31st March 1974 within the former rural district of Deudraeth—

Ffestiniog, Talsarnau;

and those parts of the following communities which were on that date within the former rural district of Dolgellau—

Barmouth, Mawddwy;

and that part of the community of Llandderfel which was on that date within the former rural district of Penllyn.

COMMENTARY

DERIVATION

Town and Country Planning General Development Order 1988 (S.I. 1988 No. 1813), Sched. 1, but with the amendment that what was under that Order "article 1(7) land" (introduced by S.I. 1991 No. 1536) is now "article 1(4) land": the numbering of the other two categories remains the same. The Norfolk and Suffolk Broads had been added to Parts 2 and 3 (Parts 1 and 2 in the 1988 Order) by S.I. 1989 No. 603.

DEFINITIONS

"area of outstanding natural beauty": art. 1(2); National Parks and Access to the Countryside Act 1949, s.87.

"the Broads": 1990 Act, s.336(1).

"conservation area": Planning Listed Buildings and Conservation Areas Act 1990, s.69

"land": 1990 Act, s.336(1)

"local planning authority": 1990 Act, s.1

"National Park": National Parks and Access to the Countryside Act 1949, s.5

GENERAL NOTE

This schedule defines so-called "article 1(4) land," "article 1(5) land," and "article 1(6) land" for which special stricter controls are maintained in the permitted development rights conferred by Sched. 2.

Article 1(4) land

In the counties listed in Part 1, permitted development rights for the installation of satellite antennae are restricted, under Part 1, Class H of Sched. 2, and Part 25, Class B of Sched. 2.

Article 1(5) land

"Article 1(5) land" includes the areas where the previous permitted development rights were retained intact in 1981 when they were relaxed elsewhere. These were the National Parks, areas of outstanding natural beauty, and conservation areas. A subsequent amendment brought in also areas specified under the Wildlife and Countryside Act 1981, s.41(3). Originally, this protection was maintained by means of a special development order, but for convenience its provisions were in 1988 incorporated into this Order. Different development tolerances are applied to them in Sched. 2, as follows:

Part 1 (householder development): Classes A.2, A.3, B.1 and E.1(f);
Part 8 (industrial development): Class A.1;
Part 17 (statutory undertakers): Class G (electricity);
Part 24 (telecommunications): Class A(1)(g): A.2(3);
Part 25 (other telecommunications development): Class A.1(g).

At one time, the reduced tolerances applied only to areas which had been designated before the special development order took effect, but now they become effective automatically upon designation. There is no provision for compensation for this loss of permitted development rights, which there would be if they had been removed instead by a direction made under art. 4 and planning permission was then refused.

Article 1(6) land

The categories of "article 1(6) land" are also a hangover from the introduction of a more liberal regime elsewhere. Agricultural permitted development under what is now Pt. 6 of Sched. 2, was relaxed in 1950, but the previous controls were retained within the National Parks and certain fringe areas, by a special development order which required that prior notice should be given to the local planning authority of proposed development, and allowing them to instruct the developer that it should not be undertaken without their prior approval of siting, design and external appearance (Town and Country Planning (Landscape Areas Special Development) Order 1950, subsequently replaced by Town and Country Planning (Agricultural and Forestry Development in National Parks, etc.) Special Development Order 1986 (S.I. 1986 No. 1176)).

The provisions as to prior approval now appear in Sched. 2, Pt. 6, Class A.2(2) (agricultural development) and Pt. 7, Class A.2 (forestry development). Under amendments made in 1992, the requirement of prior notification was extended to agricultural development on any land under Class A of Part 6 (agricultural units over 5 hectares); but the restriction to article 1(6) land was retained for development under Part 6, Class B (units of between 1 and 5 hectares) and for forestry development under Part 7.

Different protection is also provided by the exclusion of mineral exploration rights under Pt. 22, in any National Park area of outstanding natural beauty, or site of archaeological or special scientific interest (Pt. 22, Class A.1(c)).

SCHEDULE 2

Article 3

PART 1

DEVELOPMENT WITHIN THE CURTILAGE OF A DWELLINGHOUSE

Class A

Permitted development

A. The enlargement, improvement or other alteration of a dwellinghouse.

Development not permitted

A.1 Development is not permitted by Class A if—

(a) the cubic content of the resulting building would exceed the cubic content of the original dwellinghouse—

(i) in the case of a terrace house or in the case of a dwellinghouse on article 1(5) land, by more than 50 cubic metres or 10%, whichever is the greater,

(ii) in any other case, by more than 70 cubic metres or 15%, whichever is the greater,

(iii) in any case, by more than 115 cubic metres;

(b) the part of the building enlarged, improved or altered would exceed in height the highest part of the roof of the original dwellinghouse;

(c) the part of the building enlarged, improved or altered would be nearer to any highway which bounds the curtilage of the dwellinghouse than—

(i) the part of the original dwellinghouse nearest to that highway, or

(ii) any point 20 metres from that highway,

whichever is nearer to the highway;

(d) in the case of development other than the insertion, enlargement, improvement or other alteration of a window in an existing wall of a dwellinghouse, the part of the building enlarged, improved or altered would be within 2 metres of the boundary of the curtilage of the dwellinghouse and would exceed 4 metres in height;

(e) the total area of ground covered by buildings within the curtilage (other than the original dwellinghouse) would exceed 50% of the total area of the curtilage (excluding the ground area of the original dwellinghouse);

(f) it would consist of or include the installation, alteration or replacement of a satellite antenna;

(g) it would consist of or include the erection of a building within the curtilage of a listed building; or

(h) it would consist of or include an alteration to any part of the roof.

A.2 In the case of a dwellinghouse on any article 1(5) land, development is not permitted by Class A if it would consist of or include the cladding of any part of the exterior with stone, artificial stone, timber, plastic or tiles.

Interpretation of Class A

A.3 For the purposes of Class A—

(a) the erection within the curtilage of a dwellinghouse of any building with a cubic content greater than 10 cubic metres shall be treated as the enlargement of the dwellinghouse for all purposes (including calculating cubic content) where—

(i) the dwellinghouse is on article 1(5) land, or

(ii) in any other case, any part of that building would be within 5 metres of any part of the dwellinghouse;

(b) where any part of the dwellinghouse would be within 5 metres of an existing building within the same curtilage, that

building shall be treated. as forming part of the resulting building for the purpose of calculating the cubic content.

Class B

Permitted development

B. The enlargement of a dwellinghouse consisting of an addition or alteration to its roof.

Development not permitted

B.1 Development is not permitted by Class B if—

(a) any part of the dwellinghouse would, as a result of the works, exceed the height of the highest part of the existing roof;

(b) any part of the dwellinghouse would, as a result of the works, extend beyond the plane of any existing roof slope which fronts any highway;

(c) it would increase the cubic content of the dwellinghouse by more than 40 cubic metres, in the case of a terrace house, or 50 cubic metres in any other case;

(d) the cubic content of the resulting building would exceed the cubic content of the original dwellinghouse—

(i) in the case of a terrace house by more than 50 cubic metres or 10%, whichever is the greater,

(ii) in any other case, by more than 70 cubic metres or 15%, whichever is the greater, or

(iii) in any case, by more than 115 cubic metres; or

(e) the dwellinghouse is on article 1(5) land.

Class C

Permitted development

C. Any other alteration to the roof of a dwellinghouse.

Development not permitted

C.1 Development is not permitted by Class C if it would result in a material alteration to the shape of the dwellinghouse.

Class D

Permitted development

D. The erection or construction of a porch outside any external door of a dwellinghouse.

Development not perimitted

D.1 Development is not permitted by Class D if—

(a) the ground area (measured externally) of the structure would exceed 3 square metres;

(b) any part of the structure would be more than 3 metres above ground level; or

(c) any part of the structure would be within 2 metres of any boundary of the curtilage of the dwellinghouse with a highway.

Class E

Permitted development

E. The provision within the curtilage of a dwellinghouse of any building or enclosure, swimming or other pool required for a purpose incidental to the enjoyment of the dwellinghouse as such, or the maintenance, improvement or other alteration of such a building or enclosure.

Development not permitted

E.1 Development is not permitted by Class E if—

(a) it relates to a dwelling or a satellite antenna;

(b) any part of the building or enclosure to be constructed or provided would be nearer to any highway which bounds the curtilage than—

(i) the part of the original dwellinghouse nearest to that highway, or
(ii) any point 20 metres from that highway,
whichever is nearer to the highway;
(c) where the building to be constructed or provided would have a cubic content greater than 10 cubic metres, any part of it would be within 5 metres of any part of the dwellinghouse;
(d) the height of that building or enclosure would exceed—
(i) 4 metres, in the case of a building with a ridged roof; or
(ii) 3 metres, in any other case;
(e) the total area of ground covered by buildings or enclosures within the curtilage (other than the original dwellinghouse) would exceed 50% of the total area of the curtilage (excluding the ground area of the original dwellinghouse); or
(f) in the case of any article 1(5) land or land within the curtilage of a listed building, it would consist of the provision, alteration or improvement of a building with a cubic content greater than 10 cubic metres.

Interpretation of Class E

E.2 For the purposes of Class E—
"purpose incidental to the enjoyment of the dwellinghouse as such" includes the keeping of poultry, bees, pet animals, birds or other livestock for the domestic needs or personal enjoyment of the occupants of the dwellinghouse.

Class F

Permitted development

F. The provision within the curtilage of a dwellinghouse of a hard surface for any purpose incidental to the enjoyment of the dwellinghouse as such.

Class G

Permitted development

G. The erection or provision within the curtilage of a dwellinghouse of a container for the storage of oil for domestic heating.

Development not permitted

G.1 Development is not permitted by Class G if—
(a) the capacity of the container would exceed 3,500 litres;
(b) any part of the container would be more than 3 metres above ground level; or
(c) any part of the container would be nearer to any highway which bounds the curtilage than—
(i) the part of the original building nearest to that highway, or
(ii) any point 20 metres from that highway,
whichever is nearer to the highway.

Class H

Permitted development

H. The installation, alteration or replacement of a satellite antenna on a dwellinghouse or within the curtilage of a dwellinghouse.

Development not permitted

H.1 Development is not permitted by Class H if—
(a) the size of the antenna (excluding any projecting feed element, reinforcing rim, mountings and brackets) when measured in any dimension would exceed—
(i) 45 centimetres in the case of an antenna to be installed on a chimney;
(ii) 90 centimetres in the case of an antenna to be installed

on or within the curtilage of a dwellinghouse on article 1(4) land other than on a chimney;
(iii) 70 centimetres in any other case;
(b) the highest part of an antenna to be installed on a roof or a chimney would, when installed, exceed in height—
(i) in the case of an antenna to be installed on a roof, the highest part of the roof;
(ii) in the case of an antenna to be installed on a chimney, the highest part of the chimney;
(c) there is any other satellite antenna on the dwellinghouse or within its curtilage;
(d) in the case of article 1(5) land, it would consist of the installation of an antenna—
(i) on a chimney;
(ii) on a building which exceeds 15 metres in height;
(iii) on a wall or roof slope which fronts a waterway in the Broads or a highway elsewhere.

Conditions

H.2 Development is permitted by Class H subject to the following conditions—
(a) an antenna installed on a building shall, so far as practicable, be sited so as to minimise its effect on the external appearance of the building;
(b) an antenna no longer needed for the reception or transmission of microwave radio energy shall be removed as soon as reasonably practicable.

Interpretation of Part I

I. For the purposes of Part I—
"resulting building" means the dwellinghouse as enlarged, improved or altered, taking into account any enlargement, improvement or alteration to the original dwellinghouse, whether permitted by this Part or not; and
"terrace house" means a dwellinghouse situated in a row of three or more dwellinghouses used or designed for use as single dwellings, where—
(a) it shares a party wall with, or has a main wall adjoining the main wall of, the dwellinghouse on either side; or
(b) if it is at the end of a row, it shares a party wall with or has a main wall adjoining the main wall of a dwellinghouse which fulfils the requirements of sub-paragraph (a) above.

COMMENTARY

DERIVATION

Town and Country Planning General Development Order 1988 (S.I. 1988 No. 1813), Sched. 2, Pt. 1, as amended by S.I. 1989 No. 603; S.I. 1991 No. 1536. The only further amendment in the 1995 consolidation was in paragraph A.1(d) which formerly excluded development from the permitted development rights granted by Class A if the part of the building enlarged, improved or altered would be within 2 metres of the boundary of the curtilage of the dwellinghouse and would exceed 4 metres in height. This exclusion does not now apply to a window in an existing wall in that location.

DEFINITIONS

"article 1(5) land": Sched. 1.
"cubic content": art. 1(2).
"development": 1990 Act, s.55.
"dwellinghouse": art. 1(2).

"height": art. 1(3).
"listed building": 1990 Act, s.336(1).
"resulting building": Class I.
"satellite antenna": art. 1(2).
"terrace house": Class I.

GENERAL NOTE

Outline of Commentary

Introduction

This Part grants eight separate planning permissions for so-called "householder" development, *i.e.* development of, or within the curtilage of, a dwellinghouse. The tolerances of permitted development rights in some of the Classes are reduced in the sensitive areas (land falling within Sched. 1 as article 1(4) land), article 1(5) land or article 1(6) land), and for terrace houses.

What is a dwellinghouse?

"Dwellinghouse" is a concept both of design and use. There is no comprehensive definition of the expression in the Order. In *Gravesham Borough Council v. Secretary of State for the Environment* (1984) 47 P. & C.R. 142; [1983] J.P.L. 307 McCullough J. observed:

> "In using a simple word in common usage and leaving it undefined, Parliament realistically expected that, in the overwhelming majority of cases, there would be no difficulty at all in deciding whether a particular building was or was not a dwellinghouse."

The definition in art. 1(2) is only exclusive: a dwellinghouse does not include a building containing one or more flats, or a flat contained within such a building. A flat, in turn, is defined (art. 1(2)) as:

> "a separate and self-contained set of premises constructed for use for the purpose of a dwelling and forming part of a building from some other part of which it is divided horizontally."

Thus if a dwelling does not occupy all floors of the building, it constitutes a "flat" rather than a dwellinghouse, and attracts no permitted development rights under this Part. If it does, but there is another dwelling forming part of the same building with a vertical division between them, then it is a *semi-detached house or a terrace house*. It is a *terrace house* if three or more dwellings are joined by part walls, or have adjoining main walls (art. 1(2)). Reduced development tolerances apply to terrace houses under Class A and B.

But whatever the physical division, the building must still be a house for dwelling in. This characteristic was aptly captured by McCullough J. in *Gravesham Borough Council v. Secretary of State for the Environment* (1984) 47 P. & C.R. 143. [1983] J.P.L. 307, where he suggested that the common feature of all premises which could ordinarily be described as dwellinghouses was that they were buildings which ordinarily afford the facilities required for day to day private domestic existence. That characteristic was lacking in hotels, holiday camps, hostels, residential schools, and naval and military barracks. But it was present in houses which were used as second homes, or houses which were empty pending sale or because they were undergoing extensive repairs, or because they could not lawfully be used, or timeshare holiday cottages.

But there are some special exceptions:

(1) *premises used for human habitation but not constituting a dwellinghouse*: in *Gravesham Borough Council v. Secretary of State for the Environment* (1984) 47 P. & C.R. 142; [1983] J.P.L. 307, the Court upheld the finding of the Secretary of State that a small holiday chalet (20 feet by 17 feet) comprising a living room, kitchen and bedroom did constitute a dwellinghouse, notwithstanding that there was no bathroom or W.C., because it could reasonably be said to provide for the main activities of day to day existence. In *Backer v. Secretary of State for the Environment* (1984) 47 P. & C.R. 149; [1983] J.P.L. 167, the court (Mr David Widdicombe, Q.C. sitting as Deputy Judge) accepted that there was a distinction between "residential use" and "dwellinghouse," and that premises without basic facilities that were lived in whilst works were carried on for their conversion were not, during that period at least, a "dwellinghouse."

(2) *premises in mixed use*: premises with a dual purpose of residential and business use have been held not to constitute a dwellinghouse: see, *e.g. Scurlock v. Secretary of State for Wales* [1976] J.P.L. 431, where there was a three storey Georgian property which had the owner's estate agent's offices on the ground floor and her residence upstairs. The alternative analysis under the present Order would be that the upstairs accommodation constituted a flat (see the definition above) and that the building as a whole did not therefore constitute a dwellinghouse. This would allow the decision to be reconciled with *Wood v. Secretary of State for the Environment* [1973] 2 All E.R. 404, where a farmhouse which had pre-1948 use rights for the sale of agricultural produce was held nonetheless to be entitled to permitted development rights under the Order.

(3) *dwellinghouse constructed unlawfully, and premises with an unlawful dwellinghouse use*: art. 1(4) of the 1988 Order originally attempted to preclude reliance on the Order where the existing use was unlawful but it did not appear, even as redrafted in 1989, to extend to development under this Part. It merely excluded unlawful uses from references in the Order to a use of land for a specified purpose. But a "dwellinghouse" is not a concept solely of use. Where a dwellinghouse had been erected without planning permission, enforcement action could be taken in respect of it within four years of it being substantially completed. Such action could require the building to be demolished. Any further development that had been undertaken in purported reliance on this Part of the Order would thus be equally susceptible to enforcement action: it could not, by definition, stand without the dwellinghouse. But if the authority took no enforcement action in time, the dwellinghouse became immune: it might stay, although its erection was unlawful and, until there was a retrospective grant of planning permission, remained unlawful. The opportunity was therefore taken, when implementing the changes made to the enforcement rules by the Planning and Compensation Act 1991, to amend the

Order (now art. 3(5)) to provide that permitted development rights under Sched. 2 will not apply if, in the case of permission granted in connection with an existing dwellinghouse, the building operations involved in its construction are unlawful; nor in the case of permission granted in connection with an existing use, if that use is unlawful. There are therefore now two cases of unlawful development relevant to this Part:

(a) where the building operations involved in the construction of the dwellinghouse were unlawful;
(b) where the change of use to the existing dwellinghouse use was unlawful.

The operations or the use will become lawful with the passage of time if no enforcement action is taken in respect of the breach (s.191(2)). The requisite period is four years in both cases, unless the breach of planning control concerned involved a failure to comply with a planning condition rather than operational development (s.171B).

(4) *derelict buildings*: the High Court in *Trustees of the Earl of Lichfield's Estate v. Secretary of State for the Environment* [1985] J.P.L. 251 appears to have endorsed the view of the Secretary of State in a series of appeal decisions that, in order to benefit from rights under this Part, there must be a dwellinghouse in existence when the operations are being carried out. Although the building need not necessarily be a dwellinghouse actually in habitation at the time, there should at all times remain on the land a structure sufficiently intact as to reasonably support the description of a dwellinghouse and not merely the ruins of a dwelling. If there is insufficient structure to start with, then it will take more than the permitted works of enlargement, improvement or other alteration to turn it into one: see, *e.g. Sainty v. Minister of Housing and Local Government* (1964) 108 S.J. 118; (1964) 15 P. & C.R. 432; *Larkin v. Basildon District Council* [1980] J.P.L. 407. This requirement merges into the limitations on development under Class A: see further the General Note to that Class. But it is a freestanding requirement under the other classes.

(5) *dwellinghouse use abandoned*: where planning permission has been granted for the erection of a dwellinghouse (which by virtue of s.75(2) of the 1990 Act is deemed to include permission for its use as such), the doctrine of abandonment of rights is inapplicable (*Pioneer Aggregates (U.K.) v. Secretary of State for the Environment* [1985] A.C. 132). However, where the dwellinghouse existed before the introduction of comprehensive planning control in 1948, and was thus unaffected by the new legislation, the right to use it is capable of being abandoned (*White v. Secretary of State for the Environment* (1989) 58 P. & C.R. 281; [1989] 2 P.L.R. 29). Whether or not rights have been abandoned is a matter of drawing inferences from the fact of land having "remained unused for a considerable period of time, in such circumstances that a reasonable man might conclude that the previous use had been abandoned" (*Hartley v. Minister of Housing and Local Government* [1970] 1 Q.B. 413, 420 *per* Lord Denning M.R.). In some cases, but by no means all, the test will overlap with the preceding test: abandonment of a dwellinghouse use will be signalled by the extreme dereliction of the premises.

What is the curtilage?

(1) *general principles*

Many of the tolerances of permitted development in this Part are tied to the notion of the curtilage of the dwellinghouse concerned. It is the curtilage area and boundary which govern the tolerances under Class A, rather than the boundary of the land in the same ownership or occupation; and permitted development rights under all Classes are limited to the curtilage. It is not a difficult concept to apply to the straightforward case of a private dwelling-house with a small garden or outdoor area, and with no other associated land, but its application in other cases can be highly complex.

In *Dyer v. Dorset County Council* [1988] 3 W.L.R. 213, the Court of Appeal held that in the absence of any definition, "curtilage" bore its restricted and established meaning connoting a small area forming part or parcel with the house or building which it contained or to which it was attached. It was a matter of fact and degree. The Court found it impossible to accept that a house occupied by the applicant that was within but on the edge of the grounds of a college was within the curtilage of any relevant building. Nourse L.J. endorsed as "adequate for most present day purposes" the definition contained in the *Oxford English Dictionary*:

> "A small court, yard, garth, or piece of ground attached to a dwellinghouse, and forming one enclosure with it, or so regarded by the law; the area attached to and containing a dwellinghouse and its outbuildings."

He added that the kind of ground usually attached to a dwellinghouse would be a garden, and that the concept was not restricted to dwellinghouses: other buildings, such as factories or warehouses may have curtilages as well (as is recognised by the tolerances of permitted development in Pt. 8).

It need not be an area that is marked off or enclosed in any way: "it is enough that it serves the purpose of the house or building in some reasonably useful way" (*Sinclair-Lockhart's Trustees v. Central Land Board* (1950) 1 P. & C.R. 195; Scots Court of Session). In *Collins v. Secretary of State for the Environment* [1989] E.G.C.S. 15, the court upheld an inspector's findings that an area of rough grass, largely neglected, which lay beyond the well-cut lawns near a dwellinghouse, did not form part of its curtilage. Although it was in the same occupation, the land did not serve the dwellinghouse in some necessary or useful manner. Similarly, in *James v. Secretary of State for the Environment* [1991] 1 P.L.R. 58, the court upheld an inspector's finding that a tennis court that had been constructed at the end of a field some 100 metres from the dwellinghouse was not within its curtilage. The field was separate and distinct from the cultivated garden attached to the house, and the house and the tennis court did not have the appearance of being within the same enclosure. In *McAlpine v. Secretary of State for the Environment* [1994] E.G.C.S. 189 (Mr Nigel Macleod, Q.C. sitting as a Deputy Judge) the court upheld an enforcement notice requiring the removal of a swimming pool which had been constructed without express planning permission in the grounds of a substantial listed building. There was a formal garden at the rear of the house, and beyond that an extensive open grassed area which had been used by the appellant, as well as by his predecessors, for recreation as part of the garden since the 1960s. From a study of the authorities, the court identified three relevant characteristics of a curtilage: (a) it was confined to a small area about a building; (b) an intimate association with land which was undoubtedly within the curtilage was required in order to make the land under consideration part and parcel of that undoubted curtilage land; and (c) it was not necessary for there to be physical enclosure of that land which was within the curtilage, but the land in question at least needed to be regarded in law as part of one enclosure with the house. The inspector's analysis in that case is reported at (1993) 9 P.A.D. 166. But although the land need not be enclosed, communally shared land is unlikely to constitute the curtilage of any particular dwelling: see, *e.g.* the appeal decision [1988] J.P.L. 712 (amenity area shared by adjoining owners as a communal but private open space, but not part of the curtilage of any of the dwellings).

(2) *the curtilage and the planning unit*

This relationship between curtilage as ancillary land to the primary use of the dwellinghouse means that the curtilage boundary will also normally define the area of the planning unit. But the two are not necessarily the same. A curtilage relates to a building, and a planning unit to a use. The planning unit may be smaller: a building may have a single curtilage, even although it comprises more than one planning unit. For example, several functionally separate workshop and office uses may be contained in the same commercial building; or a building may have a dual use for residential and commercial purposes, as in *Scurlock* (*supra*). Land adjoining and held with such premises could constitute curtilage, although such premises would not qualify for permitted development rights under this Part.

Moreover, one building and its curtilage may fall within the curtilage of another building. In *Attorney-General, ex rel. Sutcliffe, Rouse and Hughes v. Calderdale Borough Council* (1982) 46 P. & C.R. 399; [1983] J.P.L. 310, the Court of Appeal held that a terrace of cottages which had been constructed as mill-workers' dwellings adjacent to, and linked by a bridge to, a mill which was now a listed building, was a structure within the curtilage of the mill for the purposes of listed building control under the 1971 Act, s.54(9) (now the Planning (Listed Buildings and Conservation Areas) Act 1990, Part I). The Court accepted that three factors had to be taken into account in determining what constituted the curtilage: (1) the physical layout of the building and structure; (2) their ownership, past and present; and (3) their use or function, past and present (though note the reservations expressed about some aspects of that ruling in the House of Lords in *Debenhams v. Westminster City Council* [1987] A.C. 396).

Equally, the planning unit may be bigger. In the *Collins* case (above), for example, the area of rough land beyond the curtilage may well have been within the same planning unit, so that it could have been used for purposes ancillary to the primary residential use of the unit in accordance with the usual principles, even although the specific "curtilage" rights under the Act (s.55(2)(d)) and this Part of the Order were inapplicable.

It follows that where the curtilage does coincide with the planning unit, planning permission will normally be necessary for the appropriation of further adjoining land into the curtilage: see, *e.g. Sampson's Executors v. Nottinghamshire County Council* [1949] 2 K.B. 439; *Stephens v. Cuckfield Rural District Council* [1960] 2 Q.B. 373. Thus where other land has been unlawfully appropriated to the curtilage, there can be no reliance upon Part 1 rights, because the use of that land for the purposes of curtilage for a dwellinghouse is unlawful (art. 1(4)), unless and until the period for taking enforcement action (10 years under the 1990 Act, s.171B(3)) has expired without such action being taken.

Development tolerances: conditions, exceptions and limitations

Permitted development rights under all Parts of the Schedule are limited by supplementary definitions. Each Part establishes rights within specified tolerances, such as maximum cubic capacity, and maximum site coverage; and in some cases prescribes exceptions and imposes conditions. Effect is given to these by art. 3(2), which provides that permitted development rights are granted "subject to any relevant, exception, limitation or condition." But the effect of each may be different.

(1) *conditions*

A *condition*, for example, does not normally affect the right to carry out the development, unless it is a condition precedent (such as a requirement that consent be obtained to something before development commences). If the condition is not complied with, the planning authority's remedy is to take enforcement action to secure compliance with it, not to take action against the development itself: *see, e.g. Clwyd County Council v. Secretary of State for Wales* [1982] J.P.L. 696 *(sub nom Welsh Aggregates v. Secretary of State for Wales* [1983] J.P.L. 50 (C.A.); *Oakimber v. Elmbridge Borough Council* [1992] J.P.L. 48; *F.G. Whitley & Sons v. Secretary of State for Wales* [1992] 3 P.L.R. 72).

(2) *exceptions*

Where development is specified in an exception it is *ex hypothesi* outside the permission granted by the Order.

(3) *limitations*

With limitations, the analysis is more complex because of confusion as to what a limitation actually is, in light of the power under s.172 to take enforcement action directly against a breach of a limitation, in the same way as for breach of condition. This provision, introduced in 1959 to cope with the problem of time limitations such as the 28-day temporary use right under Part 4 following *Cater v. Essex County Council* [1960] 1 Q.B. 424 (see further Grant, *Urban Planning Law*, 182, 355–356, 389), gave rise to the argument that where development undertaken in purported reliance on the Order actually exceeded the prescribed tolerances, only the excess was unlawful. That submission was rejected by both the Divisional Court and the Court of Appeal in *Garland v. Minister of Housing and Local Government* (1968) 20 P. & C.R. 93 (followed in *Rochdale Metropolitan Borough Council v. Simmonds* [1981] J.P.L. 191 and *Copeland Borough Council v. Secretary of State for the Environment* (1976) 31 P. & C.R. 403), where it was held that, apart from time-limits, the specified limits to permitted development should not be regarded as "limitations" but as part of the definition of the permitted development. An extension had been built which exceeded the tolerances under this Part by some 25 per cent and it was held to be entirely outside permitted development rights. In the words of Lord Denning M.R. (at p. 102), "this is not a permission subject to a limitation, but is a permission." Widgery L.J. insisted that (p. 104):

> "the limit of cubic capacity prescribed by column (1) [now Class A.1(a)] does not limit or restrict development which would otherwise be authorised, but is part of the definition of the permitted development itself."

Thus, as with an express planning permission, development which departs materially from the development specified in the Order is undertaken without the benefit of that planning permission. The permission embraces any immaterial variations (*Lever (Finance) Ltd v. Westminster City Council* [1971] 1 Q.B. 222), and this later ruling may now provide a better way of accommodating Lord Denning's suggestion in *Garland* (at p. 102) that a "trifling excess" might be treated as only an excess over a limitation, and should not involve having to treat the whole development as unauthorised.

The effect of *Garland* is therefore to restrict the meaning of "limitation" in the Order to time limitations. In that context it means that the authority need not determine before taking enforcement action whether a particular use complained of was unlawful from the time it commenced, or only upon the expiry of the temporary use rights under Part 4. In all other cases, material excess over development tolerances is something more than a mere breach of limitation: the whole development becomes unauthorised. A later decision of the Court of Appeal, in *Cynon Valley Borough Council v. Secretary of State for Wales* [1986] J.P.L. 760; (1986) 53 P. & C.R. 68, causes some difficulties with this doctrine, however, because the Court ruled that, for the purposes of s.23(8) of the 1971 Act (now s.57(3) of the 1990 Act), development tolerances in Part 3 of the Order did constitute "limitations." What was then Class III of the 1977 Order allowed change from a fish and chip shop to use as a shop for any purpose *except for the sale of hot food*: the Court of Appeal held that this was a limitation, and that the owner was therefore entitled subsequently to resume the "normal" use of the premises under s.23(8) (now s.57(3)). Although the Court referred to *Garland* and *Rochdale*, it restricted their application to the validity of enforcement notices.

But there are great difficulties with this part of the Court's ruling, not least that it would convert the one-way rights conferred by Pt. 3 of this Order to reversible rights (see further the General Note to Pt. 3). Moreover, the Court failed to indicate how the previous use of the land in that case could be said to be its "normal" use, when there had been a five year period in which it had been used for another use. Indeed, the reference in s.57(3) to the "use of land which (apart from its use in accordance with [planning permission granted subject to limitations by a development order]) is the normal use of that land" suggests that the draftsman had in mind only the temporary use rights subject to time limitations under Part 4. The *Cynon* decision may therefore need to be regarded with some caution: as discussed in the General Note to Part 3, it may be that the redrafting of the Order in 1988 has in any event overridden this aspect of the decision altogether.

(4) *Enforcement action where development exceeds tolerances*

It follows from the *Garland* analysis that work undertaken prior to the time that the tolerance is breached may be permitted development, but it will lose that permission if it continues to the point where it materially exceeds the specified limits. If the work falls into two separate operations, it may be possible as a matter of fact and degree to accept that the first did constitute permitted development, and that only the second constituted an excess. Moreover, the enforcement provisions have been amended since the *Garland* case. Where development has been undertaken in purported reliance on the Order, but exceeds the tolerances, the local planning authority now has discretion not to require total demolition, but only the taking of such steps as will make the development comply with the terms of the relevant permission including any conditions and limitations (1990 Act, s.173(4)(a)). But this is a matter for their discretion (or for the Secretary of State on appeal) and to comply with s.173(1) the enforcement notice must still accurately identify the breach as one involving development without permission, rather than a breach of a limitation.

Class A: enlargement, improvement or other alteration of a dwelling-house

(1) *relationship to the 1990 Act*

The categories of enlargement, improvement or other alteration, all overlap, and the permitted development rights under this Class interact with the 1990 Act, s.55(2)(a), which provides that the following should not be taken to involve development at all:

> "the carrying out of any works for the maintenance, improvement or other alteration of any building, being works which affect only the interior of the building or which do not materially affect the external appearance of the building and (in either case) are not works for making good war damage or works begun after December 5, 1968 for the alteration of a building by providing additional space therein below ground."

Thus, provided the works amount to no more than maintenance, improvement or other alteration, and do not materially affect the external appearance of the building, permission is not required at all. Where they go beyond that, permission may be granted by this Order. Thus, works of maintenance will normally not require planning permission at all (though repainting may materially affect external appearance and take the works outside the Act: see further the General Note to Pt. 2). This Part goes further than the Act by conferring specific rights for defined works, including "enlargement," whether or not they will materially affect the external appearance of the building; but they apply only to dwellinghouses. Class E of this Part confers parallel rights of maintenance, improvement and other alteration of buildings and enclosures in the curtilage of a dwellinghouse, and Pt. 8 confers similar rights for industrial buildings and warehouses. The relationship between s.55(2)(a) and this Part is well illustrated by *Bradford Metropolitan District Council v. Secretary of State for the Environment* (1977) 35 P. & C.R. 387, where the court held that the application of stone cladding to the front elevation of a dwellinghouse could be an improvement or other alteration, but that since it would materially affect the external appearance it was outside s.55(2)(a): it was, however, permitted development within this Part (though it is now excluded in the sensitive areas defined in Sched. 1, Pt. I).

(2) *rebuilding*

The Act falls short of conferring rights to reconstruct a building: as a matter of fact and degree the demolition of the original building down to foundation level and its reconstruction is likely to go beyond its maintenance or improvement (see, *e.g. Street v. Essex County Council* (1965) 193 E.G. 537); and similarly the conversion of a dilapidated and ramshackle building into a more substantial and permanent structure (see, *e.g Hewlett v. Secretary of State for the Environment* [1983] J.P.L. 105 (McNeil J.); [1985] J.P.L. 404, C.A.).

"Enlargement, improvement or other alteration" does not include complete rebuilding either. In the case of a largely derelict building, there may be difficulty in crossing the first hurdle of demonstrating that it is still a "dwellinghouse" attracting permitted development rights: see above. But even where there is an existing dwellinghouse, this Part does not authorise its demolition and rebuilding. In *Sainty v. Minister of Housing and Local Government* (1964) 15 P. & C.R. 432, the court rejected the submission that this Part would allow a proposal to demolish two old cottages and replace them with two new houses of different design and on slightly different foundations. But Lord Parker C.J. accepted that it might permit the demolition of one wall, so as to put in a damp course, and its re-erection, and that it might even be possible to arrive at a new erection of the whole, in stages over time; but this would be very rare, because it would have to be over a sufficiently long period to be able to say that each stage was a work of improvement rather than of rebuilding. That view was endorsed by the Court of Appeal in *Hewlett v. Secretary of State for the Environment* [1985] J.P.L. 404 where Sir John Donaldson M.R. observed (in the context of s.22(2)(a) of the 1971 Act, now s.55(2)(a) of the principal Act) that:

> "it was very difficult to think how you could rebuild by stages in such a way as to produce what was in effect a new building and still be able to maintain that it was merely the old building in an improved form unless, as was pointed out in argument, there was a very substantial separation between the stages—a century or so was suggested."

Certainly the period involved in *Larkin v. Basildon District Council* [1980] J.P.L. 407 was insufficient: there, the appellant had rebuilt two external walls, having been advised that planning permission was not required; but subsequently, and as a separate stage, proceeded to rebuild a further two. The court upheld an enforcement notice requiring him to demolish all the external walls, accepting the Secretary of State's view that the works had constituted a single operation and that the original building had virtually ceased to exist. Thus the works were not within s.55(2)(a) of the Act, since they went beyond maintenance, improvement or other alteration; and because they constituted the construction of a new dwelling they did not fall within this Part of the Order. See also the appeal decision at [1987] J.P.L. 147 where only the floor and part of the substructure of the building were original, and the inspector ruled that the identity of the former chalet building had been lost.

(3) *change of use*

Planning permission under this Part does not extend to the sub-division of residential premises. Under s.55(3) there is deemed to be a material change in the use of the building, and of each part involved, if a single dwellinghouse comes to be used as two or more separate dwellinghouses. Thus sub-division of residential premises constitutes development and there are no permitted development rights under this Part: see, *e.g.* the appeal decision at [1988] J.P.L. 128. Moreover, rights under this Part are limited to works to existing dwellinghouses, and do not extend to the construction of a new dwelling: see the observations of Bridge J. in *Garland v. Minister of Housing and Local Government* (1968) 20 P. & C.R. 93 and 96.

(4) *the development tolerances*

The general effect of the development tolerances is discussed above. Each of them is now analysed individually.

(a) cubic content

This tolerance relates principally to extensions, but it also extends to outbuildings within five metres of the dwellinghouse. The measurement of cubic content is to be undertaken externally (art. 1(2)), and the base for measurement is the "original dwellinghouse." That is, in relation to a building existing before July 1, 1948, the building as it existed on that date; and, in relation to one built subsequently, as so built (art. 1(2)). An integral garage will be part of a dwellinghouse "as so built," but not a free standing garage, even if within the five metre zone of class A.3(c): see planning appeal decision at [1992] J.P.L. 88. It follows that any post-1948 extension counts against the tolerances specified in this limitation, whether it was constructed in reliance on this Part (or its predecessors), or without requisite planning permission but now immune from enforcement and therefore lawful (see, *e.g.* appeal decision at [1970] J.P.L. 351) or in accordance with an express grant of planning permission (see the definition of "resulting building" in Class I, and *Dawson v. Secretary of State for the Environment and London Borough of Barnet* [1983] J.P.L. 544 on the corresponding provisions of the 1977 Order). Loft extensions are separately dealt with (Class B) but remain within the same cubic capacity rules.

Where the extension would bring the dwellinghouse within five metres of any existing building (of whatever size), in the same curtilage that building is required by Class A.3(b) to be treated in effect as if it were part of the extension in calculating its cubic capacity: See, *e.g.* the decision at [1992] J.P.L. 88.

There is a separate grant of permission for ancillary buildings in the curtilage under Class E below, but that Class excludes any building exceeding 10 cubic metres in cubic content if it would encroach within five metres of any part of the dwellinghouse. Such a building instead falls within this Class, by virtue of Class A.3(a), and is treated as if it were an extension. In the sensitive areas (article 1(5) land) there is no permission under Class E for curtilage buildings exceeding 10 cubic metres, and thus all such buildings on article 1(5) land are treated as dwellinghouse extensions under this Class (see Class A.3(a)). This has the somewhat surprising effect that the erection of a new curtilage building is required to be treated as an enlargement of the dwellinghouse for all purposes (Class A.3(a)), including its use. Thus, where a curtilage building is not intended for residential accommodation as part of the dwellinghouse, but for incidental purposes such as a summerhouse, it can still qualify as the "enlargement of the dwellinghouse" under these rules if it falls within the tolerances. Hence a summerhouse or a greenhouse on article 1(5) land many fall outside the 10 cubic metre tolerance under Class E as an incidental building, yet be entitled under Class A.3 to a tolerance calculated against the cubic content of the original dwellinghouse of up to 50 cubic metres. Moreover, the building need not have a use incidental to the use of the dwellinghouse: see the appeal decision reported at [1995] J.P.L. 165, and discussion in the Practical Points columns at [1994] J.P.L. 298 and [1995] J.P.L. 559. Nor is there permission under Class E for buildings exceeding 10 cubic metres in the curtilage of listed buildings, but they are not brought within this Class either (Class A.1(g)) and thus remain outside permitted development rights.

In order to count against the cubic capacity tolerances, the development concerned must have the effect of enclosing some space. In an appeal decision at [1987] J.P.L. 735, the Secretary of State took the view that the erection of balcony railings around the edge of the roof of a ground floor extension did not have that effect, and that they, together with patio doors provided to open out onto the balcony, constituted permitted development as improvements or other alteration of the dwellinghouse. It follows that such an unenclosed area equally could not be taken into account in calculating the cubic capacity of the "original dwellinghouse." But a point will be reached where, even although the area remains largely open, there is sufficient by way of enclosure to bring it within the calculation of cubic capacity (see, *e.g.* appeal decision at [1983] J.P.L. 67: volume of open space below a first floor extension, bounded only by the brick piers supporting the extension, regarded as part of the dwellinghouse for this purpose).

Any extension constructed under this permission enjoys permission for use for dwellinghouse purposes by virtue of the 1990 Act, s.75(2), and where an existing dwellinghouse enjoys some non-residential use-rights, these will extend also to the extension (*Wood v. Secretary of State for the Environment* [1973] 2 All E.R. 404, 409).

(b) height of the building enlarged, improved or altered

The height of the highest part of the original dwellinghouse (see the note to para. (a) above) sets the upper limit for permitted development under this Part. Any part of the development within two metres of the curtilage boundary must not exceed four metres in height (para. (d) below). Roof alterations or additions resulting from enlargement of the dwellinghouse (principally loft extensions) are governed by the same height restriction (though not by the curtilage boundary restriction) under Class B. There is no specific height restriction on other roof alterations (Class C), but anything exceeding the original height would be at risk of breaching the requirement in that Class that there should be no material alteration to the shape of the dwellinghouse.

(c) proximity to highway

This limitation is a revised version of that which appeared in the 1977 Order, which required that the altered building should not project beyond "the forward most part of any wall which fronts on a highway." The current rule adapts and clarifies the interpretation placed on the old in *North West*

Leicestershire District Council v. Secretary of State for the Environment and Lees (*Barry J. and Margaret*) (1983) 46 P. & C.R. 154; [1982] J.P.L. 777 (and see appeal decisions at [1982] J.P.L. 531; [1983] J.P.L. 750). Where the original house is at an angle to the highway, or has two fronting walls at different distances from it (as with an L-shaped house), the rule allows infilling to occur up to the line parallel with the highway drawn from the closest point to it of the original dwellinghouse. It also gets away from the debate as to what constitutes "fronting" on to a highway (although this test is retained for roof alterations under Class B) by limiting the requirement to highways bounding the curtilage, and to dwellinghouses within 20 metres of the highway. But it does not define the point to which the measurement should be made, unlike Pt. 6 (agricultural development) which restricts development to within 25 metres of the *metalled portion* of a trunk or classified road. In the absence of a definition for this Class, that may well provide a useful starting point as indicating that it should be the nearest boundary rather than the central point of the highway which is relevant. A highway is not defined, even for the purposes of the Highways Act 1980, but in accordance with common usage includes not only a made-up road but any way over which members of the public have the right to pass and repass, including a footpath. There are difficulties in applying the rule in a case where the highway does not immediately bound the curtilage; for example, where there is a strip of amenity land in between. But where the amenity land lies between footpath and carriageway, it will presumably be the footpath which sets the line.

The "part of the original dwellinghouse nearest the highway" sets the line for the new development. It does not include a separate curtilage building such as a garage (appeal decision at [1979] J.P.L. 336) unless it is an integral garage (appeal decisions at [1985] J.P.L. 199; 501). The application of stone cladding is not normally precluded by this provision (although it is excluded altogether in the sensitive areas by Class A.2), because it would rarely project forward beyond the window sills or eaves of the dwellinghouse (*Bradford Metropolitan District Council v. Secretary of State for the Environment* (1978) 35 P. & C.R. 387; [1978] J.P.L. 177). The 1977 Order referred to "the forward most part of any wall" of the dwellinghouse, but "wall" was omitted from the 1988 Order and that change was carried into the present Order, suggesting that the building line is now projected forward as far as the eaves.

(d) distance from curtilage boundary

This provision has an unhappy history. It started with the decision of the High Court (Mr. David Widdicombe, Q.C., sitting as Deputy Judge) in *Wandsworth London Borough Council v. Secretary of State for the Environment and Khan* [1988] J.P.L. 483 which gave a literal, but nonetheless extraordinary, interpretation to the wording of the 1977 Order, which had required that no part of the building (as so enlarged, improved or altered) which lay within a distance of two metres from any boundary of the curtilage of the dwellinghouse should have, as a result of the development, a height exceeding four metres. The court held that where such a part of the dwellinghouse already exceeded four metres in height before the development was carried out, the limitation did not apply. Hence it only applied where the excessive height was the result of the development. Thus, an owner could erect metal railings on the roof of a rear extension if it was already over four metres, but not if it was not and the railings brought it up to a height exceeding that limit.

The first draft of the 1988 Order attempted to overcome this absurdity by referring instead to "the resulting building," and defining it as including the whole building, including the rear extension. But this meant that all semi-detached and terraced houses which were already over four metres, stood immediately to lose all permitted development rights for rear extensions, because the original building already encroached within two metres of the curtilage. By including it in the "resulting building," all further works were excluded, whether or not any of the works were within the two metre boundary strip. The 1988 Order was therefore amended immediately before coming into force, by S.I. 1988 No. 2091, so as to make it clear that the limitation applied only where the works affected some part of the dwelling (whether original or as altered) which was within two metres of the curtilage, that part would be increased in height thereby, and would exceed four metres in height.

But the substituted provisions also proved difficult to apply in practice, because they were based on the concept of the "resulting building," which was the dwellinghouse as enlarged, improved or altered. And so a further amendment was made by S.I. 1989 No. 603, to simplify the provisions and to impose a four metre height limitation only on the part of the building which was being enlarged, improved or altered, and only if it would be within two metres of the curtilage boundary. A further amendment was made by the 1995 consolidation, which restricted the limitation to development other than the insertion, enlargement, improvement or other alteration of a window in an existing wall of a dwellinghouse.

Height is to be measured from ground level, meaning the level of the surface of the ground immediately adjacent (or, if it is not uniform, the level at its highest adjacent part): art. 1(3), and see the General Note to that article.

(e) ground area

This restriction prevents any enlargement being undertaken where there is a restricted area of open curtilage. It requires first a calculation of the total curtilage area (excluding the original dwellinghouse), then a calculation of the proportion of that area which is covered by other buildings. If it exceeds 50 per cent, no permitted development rights arise under this Part; if it is less, then permitted development may be undertaken provided the 50 per cent limit is not breached.

These rules tie in with those governing the erection of other buildings in the curtilage (Class E.1(e)).

(f) satellite antennae

Permission for installation of a single satellite antenna on, or within the curtilage of, a dwellinghouse, is conferred separately by Class H of this Part, and so is excluded from Class A. Similarly, dwellinghouses are excluded from rights under Pt. 25 for installation of microwave antennae on buildings.

(g) curtilage of listed buildings

Permitted development rights under Class A do not extend to the erection of a building in the curtilage of a listed building. Rights to erect buildings in the curtilage are conferred by Class E, except for any building exceeding 10 cubic metres which would be within five metres of the dwellinghouse itself. That is outside Class E (see Class E(1)(c)), and instead is deemed to constitute an enlargement of the dwellinghouse and hence is permitted (if at all) by Class A. The exclusion of listed buildings from this permission under Class A ties in with Class E.1(f), which excludes from that Class the provision, alteration or improvement of any building exceeding 10 cubic metres in the curtilage of a listed building. A building or structure within the curtilage of a listed building is treated as part of the building for the purposes of listed building control, provided it forms part of the land and has done so since before July 1, 1948 (s.54(9)).

There is no general exclusion of permitted development rights for the enlargement, improvement or other alteration of dwellinghouses which are listed buildings (but note the exclusion of development in the curtilage under Pt. 1, Class E.1(f) and Pt. 2 Class A.1(g)). But any such works, where they would affect the character of a listed building, will require listed building consent under the (Planning Listed Buildings and Conservation Areas) Act, 1990. Moreover, they may without that consent constitute acts causing damage to a listed building (s.9): the only works excepted from that offence are those authorised by listed building consent or by a planning permission granted on an application (s.9(2)), thereby excluding permission under this Order.

(h) roof alterations

Roof alterations are outside this Class and treated separately in their own Classes (Classes B and C).

(5) *withdrawal of rights by article 4(2) direction*

Permitted development rights under this Class can be withdrawn by the local planning authority under an article 4(2) direction, (which does not require confirmation by the Secretary of State) where (a) the land is in a conservation area; and (b) the enlargement, improvement or other alteration of a dwellinghouse would front a highway, waterway or open space: see further the Commentary to art. 4.

(6) *withdrawal of rights by planning condition*

A local planning authority may, when granting planning permission for the erection of a single dwellinghouse, or for a residential estate, restrict by planning condition the exercise of permitted development rights under this Part. Although stressing that this should occur only in exceptional circumstances, DOE Circular 11/95, *The Use of Conditions in Planning Permissions*, para. 88 suggests that an appropriate case might arise where it was necessary "to avoid overdevelopment by extensions to dwellinghouses in an area of housing at exceptionally high density". Model conditions restricting rights under this Order are reproduced in Appendix A to that Circular, at paras. 50 to 52.

Class A 2: cladding

Cladding is generally within the scope of permitted development, but the rights do not extend to:

(1) buildings other than dwellinghouses (see, *e.g.* appeal decision at [1985] J.P.L. 736; old person's home);
(2) cladding which projects forward of the part of the original dwelling nearest to the highway (see further the note to para. (c) above);
(3) cladding of the prescribed types (stone, artificial stone, timber, plastic or tiles) in the sensitive areas (article 1(5) land). But the list is incomplete, and other forms of cladding, such as rendering, brick, artificial brick, glass or aluminium—possibly less attractive than those specified—may be applied in those areas without further permission provided they are within the limitations discussed above. The application of pebbledash does not fall within the list of excluded cladding: *Tower Hamlets London Borough Council v. Secretary of State for the Environment and Nolan* [1994] J.P.L. 1112. (Mr. D. Keene, Q.C. sitting as Deputy Judge).

Class B: roof enlargements

(1) *general principles*

All extensions involving roof alterations fall within this separate Class rather than Class A. They do not constitute permitted development in National Parks, areas of outstanding natural beauty, the Broads or conservation areas, and they qualify elsewhere only if they do not project beyond the plane of any existing roof slope fronting a highway. They are governed by height and cubic capacity restrictions similar to those in Class A, except that there is no provision corresponding to Class A.3(b), which requires aggregation with any curtilage building within five metres of the existing building for calculating the cubic content of the resulting building. This may mean that a larger volume may be created as a result of a roof alteration than by a Class A extension where there are curtilage buildings within five metres.

The construction of parapet walls around a flat roof was held in *Richmond upon Thames London Borough Council v. Secretary of State for the Environment* [1991] 2 P.L.R. 107 to amount to an enlargement of the dwellinghouse under this Class, rather than an alteration under Class A, notwithstanding that the "enlargement" was a matter of external appearance rather than of creating additional useful enclosed accommodation for the occupier. The court took the view that the test of external appearance was the correct approach because planning restrictions should relate to external appearances—on what is apparent in the neighbourhood of the building—rather than on internal arrangements, and because the Order provides for measurement to be undertaken by external rather than internal dimensions. In a planning appeal decision reported at [1995] J.P.L. 450 the Secretary of State ruled that a roof alteration involving the removal of a flat roof from a rear extension, and its replacement by a pitched roof which then connected into the main roof, was permitted development within Class B. It did not fall within Class C, because there would be a material alteration to the shape of the dwellinghouse; nor Class A, because it involved works for the enlargement of the dwellinghouse. The view was taken that the works would not exceed in size, design and scale what might reasonably be regarded, as a matter of fact and degree, as an addition or alteration to the roof of the dwellinghouse. They were within the prescribed limitations, and, following the *Richmond*, case, they would therefore fall within Class B.

(2) *the height restriction (para. B.1(a))*

In *Hammersmith and Fulham London Borough Council v. Secretary of State for the Environment* [1994] J.P.L. 957 (Mr. D. Keene, Q.C. sitting as Deputy Judge) the court took the view that, given that this part of the Order was directed to householders up and down the country, a straightforward interpretation was to be preferred. On the face of it, "the existing roof" referred to the roof of the house as a whole, and not just that of the flat roof extension. If one were to take the latter approach, there would be extremely difficult arguments in relation to some houses, especially Victorian or Edwardian houses, with quite complex roof structures. There was therefore no reason to cut down the scope of the words in para. B.1(a), which should be taken as referring to the highest part of the roof of the dwellinghouse as a whole. Thus, where wrought iron railings had been installed around the perimeter of a flat roof extension, about one metre high and surmounted by a wooden trellis, also around one metre high, the works constituted permitted development under Class B and were not excluded by para. B.1(a).

(3) *where the roof plane fronts a highway (para. B.1(b))*

Development is restricted where the roof plane fronts a highway. Even a rear wall can "front" on to a highway, but a highway some distance away cannot be "fronted" onto (see appeal decision at [1982] J.P.L. 53, where the nearest highway was some 33 metres from the house).

The restriction on development fronting a highway means that dormer-type windows are generally limited to side and rear elevations (see, *e.g.* the Secretary of State's decision issued in November 1988 in anticipation of the 1988 Order, ref. APP/G/88/A1205/1). Non-dormer windows, such as flat windows, may front a highway, and are permitted under this Class if they constitute an alteration comprised in works of enlargement of the dwellinghouse, and under Class C if they do not. A limited projection beyond the roof slope may be permitted for a flat window (see further under para. (c) below).

Class C: other roof alterations

(1) *general principles*

This permission has no height limitation, but anything exceeding the height of the original dwelling would run the risk of breaching the requirement that the shape of the original dwellinghouse should not be altered, provided there was also a material alteration in the external appearance of the dwellinghouse such as to take the works outside s.55(2)(a) of the 1990 Act. It was intended that it should allow the replacement of a roof irrespective of the materials used (replacement using original or similar materials would normally not constitute development at all by virtue of s.55(2)(a)), and the insertion of rooflights: DOE Circular 22/88, para. 55 (since cancelled). The Secretary of State has ruled in a planning appeal that this Class would cover the provision of non-dormer windows in the roof of front and rear elevations of a house (APP/G/88/A1205/1). A flat window may presumably under this Class project beyond the front plane of an existing roof slope fronting a highway provided the degree of projection is not sufficient to constitute a material alteration to the shape of the dwellinghouse.

(2) *withdrawal of rights by article 4(2) direction*

Permitted development rights under this Class can be withdrawn by the local planning authority under an article 4(2) direction, (which does not require confirmation by the Secretary of State) where (a) the land is in a conservation area; and (b) the alteration would be to a roof slope which fronts a highway, waterway or open space: see further the Commentary to art. 4.

Class D: porches

(1) *general principles*

This is a minor development right. It is not governed by the cubic capacity requirements of Classes A and B but instead by reference to ground area, and thus may be undertaken even where those rights have already been used up; but since any area enclosed would not form part of the "original dwellinghouse," it would score against any subsequent exercise of permitted development rights under those classes.

The boundary with a highway referred to in Class D.1(c) includes a footpath (see further the note to Class A, para. (c) above).

(2) *withdrawal of rights by article 4(2) direction*

Permitted development rights under this Class can be withdrawn by the local planning authority under an article 4(2) direction, (which does not require confirmation by the Secretary of State) where (a) the land is in a conversation area; and (b) the external door in question fronts a highway, waterway or open space: see further the Commentary to art. 4.

Class E: building within the curtilage

(1) *general principles*

The Act itself (s.55(2)(d)) confers the right to *use* any buildings or other land within the curtilage of a dwellinghouse for any purpose incidental to the enjoyment of the dwellinghouse as such. This covers not only the use of buildings, but also other incidental activities not in themselves constituting development, such as the storage of a touring caravan, or a canal narrow boat (appeal decision at [1988] J.P.L. 283), but not commercial vehicles (see, *e.g.* [1978] J.P.L. 200; [1988] J.P.L. 202).

This Class goes beyond the 1990 Act and authorises operational development involved in the *provision* of such buildings, and their maintenance, improvement or other alteration. By virtue of the definition in art. 1(2), "building" does not here include any plant or machinery, although it does include the provision of a septic tank (see, *e.g.* appeal decisions at [1967] J.P.L. 669; [1968] J.P.L. 46; [1969] J.P.L. 50). Nor, in this Schedule, does it normally include any "gate, fence, wall or other means of enclosure," but any enclosure is here permitted where it is required for a purpose incidental to the enjoyment of the dwellinghouse; and a separate right is granted by Pt. 2 for such enclosures, but subject to different limitations. In particular, the maximum height of an enclosure under Pt. 2 is 1 metre (adjoining a highway) or 2 metres (elsewhere). Under this Class the maximum height is 3 metres.

(2) *purposes incidental to the enjoyment of the dwellinghouse*

There is often some difficulty in assessing what constitutes a purpose incidental to the enjoyment of the dwellinghouse. Two principles have emerged. First, that something which is "incidental" cannot itself be a dwellinghouse; nor, therefore, can it be something for the provision of a primary dwellinghouse purpose, such as a bedroom or kitchen. In an appeal decision reported at [1987] J.P.L. 144, the Secretary of State rejected the argument that a granny annex which was separate from the dwelling would fall within this Class:

> "...the view is taken that for a proposal to qualify as permitted development under the provisions of Class [E of Pt. 1] of the GDO, it should not include any accommodation that could be regarded as adding to or extending the normal living accommodation of the dwellinghouse. Additions to the normal, basic, domestic living accommodation of a dwellinghouse, such as bedrooms, which are normally to be expected as part and parcel of any dwelling's normal facilities, are not regarded, as a matter of fact and degree, as being 'incidental' to the enjoyment of the dwellinghouse as such for the purposes of Class [E]; they are an integral part of the ordinary residential use as a dwellinghouse (see [1983] J.P.L. 683). The view is taken that the word 'incidental,' on the other hand, means something occurring together with something else and being subordinate to it. Accordingly, a purpose which is incidental to the enjoyment of a dwellinghouse is distinct from activities which constitute actually living in a dwellinghouse. Incidental purposes are regarded as being those connected with the running of the dwellinghouse or with the domestic or leisure activities of the persons living in it, rather than with the use as ordinary living accommodation."

But this distinction between primary purposes and incidental purposes relates only to the justification for providing the building in the first place. It does not govern subsequent changes in use, and in this respect the fact that s.55(2)(d) refers only to "incidental" uses is irrelevant. A building in the curtilage may be put to any use which is either a primary residential use or incidental to such a use. In the words of the Secretary of State in an appeal decision at [1987] J.P.L. 144:

> "... the Department's present view is that the use of an existing building in the garden of a dwellinghouse for the provision of additional bedroom accommodation is not now to be regarded as being 'incidental'
> to the enjoyment of the dwellinghouse as such for the purpose of s.22(2)(d) [now s.55(2)(d) of the 1990 Act]: it merely constitutes an integral part of the main use of the planning unit as a single dwellinghouse and, provided that the planning unit remains in single family occupation, does not therefore involve any material change of use of the land; in those circumstances it is now considered that there is therefore no need to rely on s.22(2)(d)."

It is, however, a matter of fact and degree for the decision maker as to what is the appropriate planning unit for these purposes: *Uttlesford District Council v. Secretary of State for the Environment* [1992] J.P.L. 171.

Secondly, a "purpose incidental to the enjoyment of the dwellinghouse as such" is a broad concept. Although the building must be "required" for the incidental purpose, it is a matter primarily for the occupier to determine what incidental purposes he proposes to enjoy. Whilst a purely commercial purpose would be outside the scope of the permission, a wide range of recreational purposes is within it. Under Class E.2, the keeping of livestock is included, and recreational ponies would appear to fall within that definition, thus permitting the erection of stabling and other required facilities within the permitted tolerances. So too recreational facilities, such as swimming pools (now expressly included) and games rooms (see, *e.g.* appeal decision reported at [1987] J.P.L. 733, where a games room to house a billiard table was held to satisfy this requirement, though on the facts it was not within the prescribed tolerances). In *Emin v. Secretary of State for the Environment* [1989] E.G.C.S. 16, the High Court held that an inspector was wrong in concluding that archery was not a possible incidental purpose, although it was primarily an outdoor sport. The Court accepted that since it could, as the appellant contended, be a hobby and be practised in a building, such a building was capable of being required for a purpose incidental to the enjoyment of the dwellinghouse. The Court held that the inspector was also wrong to have considered that the proposed buildings (for archery, billiards and pottery) could not reasonably be said to be required for a use reasonably incidental to the enjoyment of the dwellinghouse as such, because they would provide more accommodation for secondary activities than the dwellinghouse provided for primary activities. It was held that this was not part of the test as to what buildings fell within this Class.

However, the test must retain an element of "objective reasonableness" (*Wallington v. Secretary of State for Wales* (1990) 62 P. & C.R. 150, and the Court of Appeal in *Croydon London Borough Council v. Gladden* [1994] 1 P.L.R. 30 was unanimous in holding that no one could regard it as reasonable to keep a large wooden replica of a Spitfire in the curtilage of a dwellinghouse as something incidental to the enjoyment of the dwellinghouse as such. That, after all, had not actually been its actual purpose:

> "Indeed, it is plain that it was put there solely for the purpose of teasing the local planning authority. That is no doubt good sport and not unlawful provided the defendant does not infringe planning control..." (*per* Stuart-Smith L.J. at 37).

In *Peche d'or Investments v. Secretary of State for the Environment* [1995] J.P.L. B63 the High Court held that an inspector had been wrong to rule, as a matter of law, that a curtilage building containing a study or music room, a passage hall, and W.C. and shower facilities, was outside this class. The court stressed that it must be a matter of fact and degree in each case.

(3) *limitations and exceptions to Class E*

The Class adopts limitations similar to those applicable to Class A:
(a) separate permission for a satellite antenna appears in Class H;
(b) adjacency to highway (see the note to Class A.1(c) above);
(c) cubic content exceeding 10 cubic metres: this is designed to correspond with Class A.3, requiring buildings exceeding this capacity and within five metres of the dwellinghouse to be treated as an enlargement under that Class rather than as freestanding buildings under this Class;
(d) height: the height is to be measured from ground level (see further art. 1(3) and the General Note to that article);
(e) ground area: this ties in with Class A.1(e), and permits cumulative development under the two Classes only up to 50 per cent of the curtilage not covered by the original dwellinghouse;
(f) article 1(5) land and curtilages of listed buildings: this restriction excludes not only the provision of buildings exceeding 10 cubic metres in the curtilage, but also the alteration or improvement of any building already there. Thus where such works involving building or engineering operations would materially affect the external appearance of such a building, taking them outside s.55(2)(a), express planning permission would be required. The result is that there is tighter control over curtilage buildings than over the dwellinghouses themselves. Curtilage buildings are included in the listing only if they formed part of the land before July 1, 1948 (Town and Country Planning (Listed Buildings and Conservation Areas) Act 1990, s.1(8)).

Moreover, rights under Pt. 2, Class A (gates, fences, walls and other means of enclosure) are not permitted development within the curtilage of a listed building, nor is any gate, fence, wall or other means of enclosure surrounding a listed building.

Class F: provision of hard surfaces

(1) *general principles*

This right is conferred in broad terms. It does not specify any purpose to which the hard standing may be put. It is not limited to vehicle hardstandings, and may therefore be relied upon for the construction of patio areas, and for tennis courts (though rights to erect fencing would be limited to those under Pt. 2, and limited to two metres, unless it could be established that the fencing was itself required for a purpose incidental to the enjoyment of the dwellinghouse and thus qualified for three metres under Pt. 1, Class E); and perhaps even for a helicopter landing pad. There are no limitations as to area, and it is conceivable that the hard surfacing of the entire curtilage could be for a purpose incidental to the enjoyment of the dwellinghouse.

(2) *withdrawal of rights by article 4(2) direction*

Permitted development rights under this Class can be withdrawn by the local planning authority under an article 4(2) direction, (which does not require confirmation by the Secretary of State) where (a) the land is in a conservation area; and (b) the hard surface would front a highway, waterway or open space: see further the Commentary to art. 4.

Class G: heating oil tank

The explanation for this separate permission for oil storage tanks appears to be that they fall outside Class E as not constituting a "building." Under the Building Regulations 1985 such a tank may not be enclosed in a building. The permission does not extend to tanks for the storage of liquid gas.

Class H: satellite antenna

(1) *general principles*

This Class (introduced in 1991) grants planning permission for a single (notwithstanding the potential availability of more than one channel using incompatible antennae) satellite antenna, not exceeding 90 cm in any dimension, on a dwellinghouse or within its curtilage. "Satellite antenna" means (art. 1(2)):

> "apparatus designed for transmitting microwave radio energy to satellites or receiving it from them, and includes any mountings or brackets attached to such apparatus."

Permission to erect a satellite antenna is also granted by Pt. 24 (limited to telecommunications code system operators) and Pt. 25, which allows the erection of one antenna, on a tall building (15 metres or more) other than a dwellinghouse (not in the sensitive areas), but requires that it should be sited, so far as practicable, so as to minimise its effect on the external appearance of the building. Pt. 25 is the appropriate permission in the case of a block of flats, which would be outside the present permission because it would not constitute a dwellinghouse.

(2) *withdrawal of rights by article 4(2) direction*

Permitted development rights under this Class can be withdrawn by the local planning authority under an article 4(2) direction, (which does not require confirmation by the Secretary of State) where (a) the land is in a conservation area; and (b) the part of the building or other structure on which the satellite antenna is to be installed, altered or replaced fronts a highway, waterway or open space: see further the Commentary to art. 4.

PART 2

MINOR OPERATIONS

Class A

Permitted development — **A. The erection, construction, maintenance, improvement or alteration of a gate, fence, wall or other means of enclosure.**

Development not permitted — **A.1 Development is not permitted by Class A if—**

(a) the height of any gate, fence, wall or means of enclosure erected or constructed adjacent to a highway used by vehicular traffic would, after the carrying out of the development, exceed one metre above ground level;

(b) the height of any other gate, fence, wall or means of enclosure erected or constructed would exceed two metres above ground level;

(c) the height of any gate, fence, wall or other means of enclosure maintained, improved or altered would, as a result of the development, exceed its former height or the height referred to in sub-paragraph (a) or (b) as the height appropriate to it if erected or constructed, whichever is the greater; or

(d) it would involve development within the curtilage of, or to a gate, fence, wall or other means of enclosure surrounding, a listed building.

Class B

Permitted development — **B. The formation, laying out and construction of a means of access to a highway which is not a trunk road or a classified road, where that access is required in connection with development permitted by any Class in this Schedule (other than by Class A of this Part).**

Class C

Permitted development — **C. The painting of the exterior of any building or work.**

Development not permitted — **C.1 Development is not permitted by Class C where the painting is for the purpose of advertisement, announcement or direction.**

Interpretation of Class C — **C.2 In Class C, "painting" includes any application of colour.**

COMMENTARY

Definitions

"classified road": art. 1(2).
"development": 1990 Act, s.55.
"height": art. 1(3).
"listed building": Listed Buildings Act 1990, s.1.
"painting": Class C.2.
"trunk road": art. 1(2).

General Note

Introduction

This Part grants planning permission for minor operations in relations to walls and enclosures, and means of access. There is some overlap with Pt. 1, which permits the erection of buildings and enclosures, but is limited to dwellinghouse curtilages. Rights under this Part are not so limited.

Class A: gates, fences, walls or other means of enclosure

(1) *general principles*

In order to satisfy the requirements of this Class, the wall must have some function of enclosure. In *Prengate Properties v. Secretary of State for the Environment* [1973] J.P.L. 313; (1973) 25 P. & C.R. 311 (and see also *South Oxfordshire District Council v. Secretary of State for the Environment* (1986) 52 P. & C.R. 1; [1986] J.P.L. 435) Lord Widgery C.J. stated that the permission:

> "would not extend to someone who places a free standing wall in the middle of his garden in circumstances in which the wall neither encloses nor plays any part in the enclosure of anything."

Provided a wall did enclose something, it would not lose that quality if it were also a structural or retaining wall. In *Prengate*, the court accepted that there might be cases where such a wall was erected as part of a larger engineering operation and that, following *Garland v. Minister of Housing and Local Government* (1968) 20 P. & C.R. 93, if the whole operation was not permitted then neither, despite this permission, would the part (although in that case the enforcement notice was quashed because at the time it was served, the wall had an enclosing function and the owner's intention to incorporate it some time in the future into a larger engineering operation was inconclusive).

The words "or other means of enclosure" are governed by the *ejusdem generis* rule, so that to satisfy the test the means of enclosure must be similar to a gate, fence or wall. In *Ewen Developments Ltd v. Secretary of State for the Environment* [1980] J.P.L. 404, the court was unable to find that an inspector had misdirected himself in ruling that the construction of a number of earth embankments was not permitted by this Class, notwithstanding that they did enclose land. In *Wycombe District Council v. Secretary of State for the Environment* [1994] E.G.C.S. 61 the court held that a "means of enclosure" must provide some way of closing in an area, so that it became enclosed. This necessarily imported the character of surrounding the area: it need not be a perfect surrounding, and it would be a matter of fact and degree whether any gaps in the structure took it outside the essential character of enclosure.

(2) *maximum height where adjacent to highway*

The maximum height permitted is 2 metres, except where it is adjacent to a highway. The Order uses the expression "adjacent" in place of the word "abutting," which caused some difficulties under earlier Orders. But it is similar to the interpretation which had been adopted previously, particularly in right of the decision in *Simmonds v. Secretary of State for the Environment and Rochdale Metropolitan District Council* [1981] J.P.L. 509, where the court declined to rule that "abut" meant actually to "touch." It was therefore sufficient that a fence be adjacent to a highway in order to trigger the lower height limit. See also the appeal decision at [1988] J.P.L. 198 where a wall which was sited very close to a footway was held to be outside this Class.

The Order prescribes no method for measuring height where the land is uneven. The special formula in art. 1(3), which allows the measurement to be made from the highest adjacent ground level, applies only to buildings, plant and machinery. By virtue of art. 1(2), a building does not include, for the purposes of this Schedule, any gate, fence, wall or other means of enclosure. See further the General Note to art. 1(3). Any excess of 2 metres will take the whole wall outside the permission (see (1993) 8 P.A.D. 304).

(3) *demolition*

By virtue of Pt 31, Class B, any building operation consisting of the demolition of the whole or any part of any gate, fence, wall or other means of enclosure is permitted development.

(4) *withdrawal of rights by planning condition*

A local planning authority may, when granting planning permission for the erection of a single dwellinghouse, or for a residential estate, restrict by planning condition the exercise of permitted development rights under this Part. Although stressing that this should occur only in exceptional circumstances, DOE Circular 11/95, *The Use of Conditions in Planning Permissions*, Annex, para. 88 suggests that an appropriate case might be where it was desired "to preserve an exceptionally attractive open plan estate free of fences". A suggested model condition to that effect is reproduced in Appendix A to that Circular, at para. 51.

Class B: means of access to a highway

This Part does not permit operations in respect of any means of access to a trunk road or classified road. In relation to any other road it is subject to the requirement of art. 3(6), which excludes permission under the Order for any development which requires or involves the formation, laying out or material widening of a means of access to any highway used by vehicular traffic where it creates an obstruction to the view of the persons using the highway so as to be likely to cause danger to such persons. The Order grants no permission for such development, so that rights under this Class, which authorise only access required in connection with development permitted by the Order, do not arise.

There must, of course, be development requiring planning permission before there is any need to rely upon permitted development rights. The definition in the 1990 Act, s.336(1), of "engineering operations," which constitute development requiring permission for the purposes of the Act, includes "the formation or laying out of means of access to highways." But this requires some physical engineering operation: it does not extend to the simple removal of a hedge, or of a removable fence, in order to obtain access. This is outside the scope of planning control altogether (see appeal decision at [1981] J.P.L. 380).

In an appeal decision at [1988] J.P.L. 787, the view was taken that planning permission was not required for the proposed erection of a brick wall and gates not exceeding 1 metre in height to facilitate a re-positioning of an existing access and formation of a new access. Neither the removal of the existing fence nor the proposed erection of a wall and gates amounted to the creation of an access. Although gates would provide a means of entry to and egress from the premises, it was not thought that they provided something by way of an access which was not there before. The permitted development rights under this Class were not restricted to one access for any particular site.

Class C: painting of the exterior of any building or work

In *Windsor and Maidenhead Royal Borough Council v. Secretary of State for the Environment* (1988) 86 L.G.R. 402; [1988] J.P.L. 410; [1988] 2 P.L.R. 17, the High Court (Mann J.) held that the painting or repainting of a building was capable of amounting to a building operation within the broad definition in the 1971 Act, s.290(1) [now s.55(1A) of the 1990 Act] as "operations normally undertaken by a person carrying on business as a builder." Hence, it constituted development requiring planning permission. Except where it is removed by a planning condition or an art. 4 direction, a general permission is granted by this Class. But listed building consent might also be required under the Listed Buildings Act 1990 in the case of the painting or repainting of a listed building, because such works were capable of constituting an "alteration" affecting the character of a building as a building of special architectural or historic interest.

PART 3

CHANGES OF USE

Class A

Permitted development — **A. Development consisting of a change of the use of a building to a use falling within Class A1 (shops) of the Schedule to the Use Classes Order from a use falling within Class A3 (food and drink) of that Schedule or from a use for the sale, or display for sale, of motor vehicles.**

Class B

Permitted development — **B. Development consisting of a change of the use of a building—**

(a) to a use for any purpose falling within Class B1 (business) of the Schedule to the Use Classes Order from any use falling within Class B2 (general industrial) or B8 (storage and distribution) of that Schedule;

(b) to a use for any purpose falling within Class B8 (storage and distribution) of that Schedule from any use falling within Class B1 (business) or B2 (general industrial).

Development not permitted — **B.1 Development is not permitted by Class B where the change is to or from a use falling within Class B8 of that Schedule, if the change of use relates to more than 235 square metres of floor space in the building.**

Class C

Permitted development — **C. Development consisting of a change of use to a use falling within Class A2 (financial and professional services) of the Schedule to the Use Classes Order from a use falling within Class A3 (food and drink) of that Schedule.**

Class D

Permitted development — **D. Development consisting of a change of use of any premises with a display window at ground floor level to a use falling within Class A1 (shops) of the Schedule to the Use Classes Order from a use falling within Class A2 (financial and professional services) of that Schedule.**

Class E

Permitted development — **E. Development consisting of a change of the use of a building or other land from a use permitted by planning permission granted on an application, to another use which that permission would have specifically authorised when it was granted.**

Development not permitted — **E.1 Development is not permitted by Class E if—**

(a) the application for planning permission referred to was made before the 5th December 1988;
(b) it would be carried out more than 10 years after the grant of planning permission; or
(c) it would result in the breach of any condition, limitation or specification contained in that planning permission in relation to the use in question.

Class F

Permitted development

F. Development consisting of a change of the use of a building—

(a) to a mixed use for any purpose within Class A1 (shops) of the Schedule to the Use Classes Order and as a single flat, from a use for any purpose within Class A1 of that Schedule;
(b) to a mixed use for any purpose within Class A2 (financial and professional services) of the Schedule to the Use Classes Order and as a single flat, from a use for any purpose within Class A2 of that Schedule;
(c) where that building has a display window at ground floor level, to a mixed use for any purpose within Class A1 (shops) of the Schedule to the Use Classes Order and as a single flat, from a use for any purpose within Class A2 (financial and professional services) of that Schedule.

Conditions

F.1 Development permitted by Class F is subject to the following conditions—

(a) some or all of the parts of the building used for any purposes within Class A1 or Class A2, as the case may be, of the Schedule to the Use Classes Order shall be situated on a floor below the part of the building used as a single flat;
(b) where the development consists of a change of use of any building with a display window at ground floor level, the ground floor shall not be used in whole or in part as the single flat;
(c) the single flat shall not be used otherwise than as a dwelling (whether or not as a sole or main residence)—
   (i) by a single person or by people living together as a family, or
   (ii) by not more than six residents living together as a single household (including a household where care is provided for residents).

Interpretation of Class F

F.2 For the purposes of Class F—
"care" means personal care for people in need of such care by reason of old age, disablement, past or present dependence on alcohol or drugs or past or present mental disorder.

Class G

Permitted development

G. Development consisting of a change of the use of a building—

(a) to a use for any purpose within Class A1 (shops) of the Schedule to the Use Classes Order from a mixed use for any purpose within Class A1 of that Schedule and as a single flat;
(b) to a use for any purpose within Class A2 (financial and professional services) of the Schedule to

the Use Classes Order from a mixed use for any purpose within Class A2 of that Schedule and as a single flat;

(c) where that building has a display window at ground floor level, to a use for any purpose within Class A1 (shops) of the Schedule to the Use Classes Order from a mixed use for any purpose within Class A2 (financial and professional services) of that Schedule and as a single flat.

Development not permitted

G.1 Development is not permitted by Class G unless the part of the building used as a single flat was immediately prior to being so used used for any purpose within Class A1 or Class A2 of the Schedule to the Use Classes Order.

COMMENTARY

DERIVATION

Town and Country Planning General Development Order 1988 (S.I. 1988 No. 1813). New Classes F and G were added from March 9, 1995 by S.I. 1995 No. 298.

DEFINITIONS

"building": art. 1(2).
"care": Class F.2.
"development": 1990 Act, s.55.
"land": 1990 Act, s.336(1).
"Use Classes Order": art. 1(2).

GENERAL NOTE

This Part grants permission for two categories of change of use: changes between classes of use defined in the Town and Country Planning (Use Classes) Order 1987, and changes between alternative uses permitted in a flexible planning permission.

Use Classes Order

The Use Classes Order has a different technical basis from this Order. It proceeds from the fact that the principal Act includes "material change in use" in its definition of development which requires planning permission, but also allows the Secretary of State to loosen the tight control that would otherwise exist by prescribing classes of use within which changes may be made. Such changes are then deemed not to constitute development at all. The instrument by which this is done is the Use Classes Order, which defines certain types of use at relatively high levels of abstraction, such as shops and offices, and allows landowners to switch between uses without attracting planning control, provided they still remain within the same class. The scope of the Use Classes Order was greatly expanded in 1987, when, for example, office uses were for the first time put into the same class as light industrial use and research and development. Changes between those uses are now outside the scope of ordinary planning control, although in certain cases the rights under the Use Classes Order may be restricted by planning condition.

This Part of the General Permitted Development Order then builds on to the structure provided by the Use Classes Order, by granting permission to move between certain classes of the Use Classes Order. It needs to be emphasised that permission may not necessarily be required for this. The first question is whether any given use-change actually constitutes a material change in use. Moving from a use in one class to a use in another does not automatically mean that there has been a material change in use constituting development. Nor does moving from or to a use which is *sui generis*, and outside the Use Classes Order altogether. The Use Classes Order becomes relevant only once it is clear that the change would otherwise constitute a material change in use. For example, an office building houses two firms of solicitors. On the ground floor, a firm which provides services principally to visiting members of the public, and is within Class A2. On the upper floors, a commercial firm whose business is within Class B1. The firms then merge. There is a new planning unit comprising the premises as a whole, and their use as a whole falls within Class B2 (business). Thus the ground floor is now B1 rather than A2. If that constituted a material change in use, planning permission would be required and would not be granted by this Part. But there would be some difficulty in showing that there had been any material change when there was no change in the activity in the building as a whole and no material planning impact from the change.

Use changes permitted under this Order

The changes that are now permitted are summarised in the Table (below), which also indicates the history of each of the categories. The rights under Pt. 3 were extended in 1987 parallel with the new Use Classes Order of that year, and only two further changes were made by the 1988 Order. First, the right to switch from a professional or financial use within Class A2 to an A1 (shop) use, provided the premises have a display window at ground floor level. If that condition is satisfied, there is no limit on the size of the building whose use may be changed. But the practical limitation is that the existing use must be within A2 rather than B1 (general business use), and that it must therefore constitute the provision of services principally to visiting members of the public. This means that, in practice, units within A2 are generally smaller than those within B1.

The second change in the 1988 Order was the lifting of the limit of 235 square metres on use changes from general industrial (Class B2) to business use (Class B1). No such limit had previously been imposed on the pre-1987 right to switch from general to light industrial, and its imposition by the 1987 Use Classes Order appears to have been unintended.

The 1995 consolidation also embraced two new classes, F and G, which had been introduced earlier in 1995 by S.I. 1995 No. 298. They permit a change of use of a building from Class A1 (shops) or Class A2 (financial and professional services) of the Use Classes Order, to a mixed use for the purposes of either of those classes and as a single flat, and from such a mixed use to either of those classes (but a change of use of a building from Class A2 to Class A1 (except where premises have a display window at ground floor level) or from Class A1 to Class A2 is not permitted).

One-way use changes: the ratchet effect

Except for Classes E, F and G, the changes permitted by this Part are all designed as one-way movements only, and the underlying purpose is to permit changes to uses which are likely to be more desirable in planning terms. For example, permission is granted for change from sale of food and drink (Class A.3), to use as a shop for any purpose (except sale of hot food) (Class A.1); and for change from general industrial use (Class B2) to business use (Class B.1) or to storage and distribution (Class 8).

One consequence of this is that use rights may be inadvertently lost, if, for example, premises previously used for general industrial purposes are put to light industrial use (see, *e.g. Young v. Secretary of State for the Environment* [1983] 2 A.C. 662), even if all that has happened has been the installation of new equipment to prevent emissions (see appeal decision at [1978] J.P.L. 781).

But the decision for the Court of Appeal, in *Cynon Valley Borough Council v. Secretary of State for Wales* [1986] J.P.L. 760; (1986) 53 P & C.R. 68, causes some difficulties with this doctrine. There, the Court ruled that, the development tolerances in this Part of the Order constituted "limitations" for the purpose of s.23(8) of the 1971 Act (now s.57(3) of the 1990 Act), which provides that:

> "Where by a development order planning permission to develop land has been granted subject to limitations, planning permission is not required for the use of that land which (apart from its use in accordance with that permission) is the normal use of that land ..."

On that basis the Court held that the ratchet effect of this Part was, after all, reversible. The 1977 Order (Class III of Sched. 1) granted planning permission to change from use as a fish and chip shop to use as a shop for any purpose *except for the sale of hot food*: the Court of Appeal held that this was a limitation, and that the owner was therefore entitled subsequently to resume the "normal" use of the premises under s.57(3).

The decision is difficult to reconcile with established authority on the meaning of the word "limitations" in relation to the Order (see further the discussion in the General Note to Sched. 2, above), and it is difficult also to reconcile with *Young v. Secretary of State for the Environment*, where it might equally have been argued that the general industrial use of the premises was its "normal" use, to which the owners could return under s.57(3), after a one-year flirtation with a light industrial use. In *Kingdon v. Minister of Housing and Local Government* [1968] 1 Q.B. 257, the court accepted counsel's submission that resumption to a "normal use" under s.23(2) of the 1971 Act (land in temporary use at appointed day: now s.57(7) and Sched. 4 of the 1990 Act) was possible only where "both the normal use and the temporary use exist in the sense that it can properly be said that the land has still a normal use for one purpose and a temporary use for another." It was for the site owner to prove that this situation had prevailed and continued to prevail.

Even if the decision is right, it is difficult to reconcile with the revised wording of the Order, which talks of permission being granted not only subject to conditions and limitations as the 1977 Order did, but "subject to any relevant *exception*, limitation or condition" (art. 3(2)) in construing this Order, the wording "except for the sale of hot food" would have to be considered as an *exception* rather than as a *limitation*, and that word did not appear in s.23(8).

Moreover, in the 1977 Order the exceptions were prescribed in Class III itself, whereas in this Order they are defined in terms of the Classes in the Use Classes Order, which contain their own relevant exceptions and limitations. For the reasoning in *Cynon Valley* to be carried through to this Order it would be necessary to show that permission under this Part was still granted subject to "limitations," even although they were now contained in a different statutory instrument and even although some of them are couched in the form of exceptions. Although it is not clear that the draftsmen set out to reverse the effect of *Cynon Valley*, that may well be the effect of the 1988 Order, where these changes first were made, in redrafting these provisions.

TABLE

USE CHANGES PERMITTED BY PART 3

FROM:	TO:	CLASS:
A1 (use for any purpose within that class)	mixed use within A1 and as a single flat	F(a)[1]
A1 and single flat in mixed use	A1	G(a)[2]
A2 (professional and financial)	A1 (shop) where premises have display window at ground floor level[3]	D
A2 and single flat in mixed use	A1 (where premises have display window at ground floor level)	G(c)[4]
A2 and single flat in mixed use	A2	G(b)[5]
Sale of motor vehicles (sui generis)[6]	A1 (shop)	A
A2 (use for any purpose in that class)	mixed use within A2 and as a single flat	F(b)[7]
A3 (food and drink)[8]	A1 (shop)	A
A3 (food and drink)[9]	A2 (financial and professional)	C
B1 (business)[10]	B8 (storage and distribution)	B(b)
B2 (general industrial)[11]	B1 (business)	B(a)
B2 (general industrial)[12]	B8 (storage and distribution)	B(b)
B8 (storage and distribution)[13]	B1 (business)	B(a)

[1] Introduced originally by S.I. 1995 No. 298. Subject to conditions requiring some or all of the retained Class A use to be situated on a floor below the part of the building used as a single flat; requiring the ground floor not to be used at all as a single flat if it has a display window; requiring the flat to be used as a dwelling by a single person, by people living together as a family or by up to six residents living together.

[2] Introduced by S.I. 1995 No. 298. Subject to condition that the change be a reversal of the immediately prior change of use.

[3] New permission in 1988 Order.

[4] Introduced by S.I. 1995 No. 298. Subject to condition that the change be a reversal of the immediately prior change of use.

[5] Introduced by S.I. 1995 No. 298. Subject to condition that the change be a reversal of the immediately prior change of use.

[6] Pre-1987 right to change to any shop use, from use for sale of motor vehicles. Recast by UCO 1987.

[7] Introduced originally by S.I. 1995 No. 298. Subject to conditions requiring some or all of the retained Class A use to be situated on a floor below the part of the building used as a single flat; requiring the ground floor not to be used at all as a single flat if it has a display window; requiring the flat to be used as a dwelling by a single person, by people living together as a family or by up to six residents living together.

[8] Right previously to change from use as shop for sale of hot food, to shop for any purpose: recast in 1987.

[9] Introduced by GDO 1988.

[10] Introduced in 1987: limited to change of use relating to not more than 235 square metres of floorspace in the building.

[11] Pre-1987 right to change from general industrial to light industrial; new Class B1 in 1987 combined light industrial with office, and the right to change to it from general industrial (now B2) was restricted to total floorspace not exceeding 235 square metres. That limitation now lifted altogether by 1988 GDO.

[12] Introduced in 1987: limited to change of use relating to not more than 235 square metres of floorspace in the building.

[13] Introduced in 1987: limited to change of use relating to not more than 235 square metres of floorspace in the building.

Flexible planning permissions

Class E is unrelated to the Use Classes Order. Its purpose is to make it easier for local planning authorities to grant flexible planning permissions; that is, permission which authorises alternative possible uses. In accordance with the usual time limits, the permission would lapse if one of the uses were not implemented within five years of grant. If it is so implemented, then Class E allows a change to another authorised use at any time up to 10 years from the date of grant, though only in accordance with any condition, limitation or specification relating to it in the permission. The advantage of these provisions is that they may allow land to be marketed with a clear planning profile that embraces a wider range of uses than normally available.

Some difficulties may arise from the way the right is drafted. For example, instead of the new use of the land being subject to the conditions imposed in the permission in the usual way, the right to switch to it arises only if such a condition is not breached. This may mean that the breach of planning control which the local planning authority might have to address with enforcement action could be the whole development (*i.e.*, the change of use) rather than merely the breach of condition. The restriction may therefore need to be read as applicable solely to conditions which act as pre-conditions to switching to the new use, and not to conditions regulating the new use once implemented.

It is also unclear how far the flexible permission must arise from a flexible application: may, for example, an authority grant permission for more than one use when the application is for one only; and, where there is more than one specified in an application, how far are they free to pick and choose between them?

PART 4

TEMPORARY BUILDINGS AND USES

Class A

Permitted development

A. The provision on land of buildings, moveable structures, works, plant or machinery required temporarily in connection with and for the duration of operations being or to be carried out on, in, under or over that land or on land adjoining that land.

Development not permitted

A.1 Development is not permitted by Class A if—
- **(a) the operations referred to are mining operations, or**
- **(b) planning permission is required for those operations but is not granted or deemed to be granted.**

Conditions

A.2 Development is permitted by Class A subject to the conditions that, when the operations have been carried out—
- **(a) any building, structure, works, plant or machinery permitted by Class A shall be removed, and**
- **(b) any adjoining land on which development permitted by Class A has been carried out shall, as soon as reasonably practicable, be reinstated to its condition before that development was carried out.**

Class B

Permitted development

B. The use of any land for any purpose for not more than 28 days in total in any calendar year, of which not more than 14 days in total may be for the purposes referred to in paragraph B.2, and the provision on the land of any moveable structure for the purposes of the permitted use.

Development not permitted

B.1 Development is not permitted by Class B if—
- **(a) the land in question is a building or is within the curtilage of a building,**
- **(b) the use of the land is for a caravan site,**
- **(c) the land is, or is within, a site of special scientific interest and the use of the land is for—**
  - **(i) a purpose referred to in paragraph B.2(b) or other motor sports;**
  - **(ii) clay pigeon shooting; or**
  - **(iii) any war game,**

  or
- **(d) the use of the land is for the display of an advertisement.**

Interpretation of Class B

B.2 The purposes mentioned in Class B above are—
- **(a) the holding of a market;**
- **(b) motor car and motorcycle racing including trials of speed, and practising for these activities.**

B.3 In Class B, "war game" means an enacted, mock or imaginary battle conducted with weapons which are designed not to injure (including smoke bombs, or guns or grenades which fire or spray paint or are otherwise used to mark other participants), but excludes military activities or training exercises organised by or with the authority of the Secretary of State for Defence.

COMMENTARY

Derivation

Town and Country Planning General Development Order 1988 (S.I. 1988 No. 1813), Sched. 2, Pt. 4, as amended by S.I. 1991 No. 2805. A further amendment was effected by the 1995 consolidation, which inserted paragraph B.1(d) to provide that the temporary use of land for the display of an advertisement is not permitted development.

Definitions

"building": art. 1(2).
"caravan": art. 1(2).
"caravan site": 1(2).
"development": 1990 Act, s.55.
"land": 1990 Act, s.336(1).
"war game": Class B.3.

General Note

This Part grants permission for temporary buildings and for temporary uses, subject to exemptions and restrictions.

Class A: temporary buildings

Planning permission for operational development of land implies permission for carrying out all necessary operations. This permission extends that right to include the provision of buildings and other structures. Its principal effect is in relation to structures whose provision would itself amount to an engineering or building operation, but which will not form part of the development permitted; and in relation to land adjoining that which has planning permission, and which might not otherwise enjoy any incidental rights. The permission is temporary. In an appeal decision reported at (1993) 9 P.A.D. 182 the inspector upheld an enforcement notice requiring the removal of a builder's hut on scaffolding in the front garden of a house undergoing renovation, which had been there for two and a half years. In relation to moveable structures it may be that no permission is required, since no operational development is involved in their provision, and, provided their use is ancillary to the building operations being carried on, and is limited to that period, their provision does not constitute any material change in the use of the land. Separate permission is granted by Pt. 5 (by virtue of its reference to development within the Caravans Sites and Control of Development Act 1960, Sched. 1, para. 9) for the provision on-site (or on adjoining land) of a caravan site for construction workers.

The permission under this Part applies only where there is planning permission (including permission under this Order) for the works (Class A.1(b)), and it does not apply if that permission is only for material change in the use of land and not operational development (*Brown v. Hayes and Harlington Urban District Council* (1963) 107 S.J. 931). The permission is subject to conditions requiring the removal of any structures and the restoration of the land when the operations have been carried out (Class A.2).

Mining operations, which generally take place over a very much longer time-span than other development, are excepted from this permission, and are the subject instead of the special regime in Pts. 19 to 23.

Class B: temporary uses

This class permits the temporary use of open land for any purpose other than as a caravan site (which is separately provided for in Pt. 5). "Temporary", for most purposes, means for up to 28 days in any calendar year, but the period is reduced to 14 days for markets, motor racing and clay pigeon shooting.

It is not a single permission that is granted afresh each calendar year. Its effect is to allow up to 28 (or, as the case may be, 14) changes of use on each of the days permitted per year. Thus there is a grant of as many planning permissions as there are changes of use up to that level (*South Bucks District Council* v. *Secretary of State for the Environment* [1989] 1 P.L.R. 69; [1989] J.P.L. 351, C.A., reversing *Strandmill* v. *Secretary of State for the Environment and South Bucks District Council* [1988] J.P.L. 491; [1988] 2 P.L.R. 1). It follows that a local planning authority may at any time withdraw all or any future daily permissions by means of an article 4 direction with immediate effect, notwithstanding that there has already been some implementation of rights under this Part in the calendar year concerned.

Right to resume normal use

It is clearly the intention of the principal Act that no planning permission should be required to resume the normal use of the land after exploitation of the temporary rights under this Part. But that intention is not clearly expressed. The broadest right is that conferred by s.57(2), which applies where planning permission has been granted for a limited period and allows resumption, at the end of that period, of the use which was the normal use of the land *before the permission was granted.* Although there is no reason why that should not apply equally to this Part as to a time-limited permission granted on an application, the definition of "normal" use by reference to the period before the permission was granted raises problems. The permission under this Part has no clear date of grant: it may have been granted when the Order was made; or when these rights were first introduced by the 1950 GDO; or at the beginning of each calendar year; or on each day the rights are exploited.

These difficulties suggest that the more appropriate provision is s.57(3), which is designed solely for where planning permission is granted by a development order subject to limitations (which clearly includes time limitations under this Part): see further the analysis of this subsection in the General Note to Pt. 3 above. The "normal" use of the land in this case is its use other than in accordance with the development order permission.

In either case, resumption of an *unlawful* use is prohibited (see s.57(5) as qualifying s.57(2) and (3)), and thus exploitation of temporary rights under this Part, even for just one day, may destroy altogether any existing use rights the land enjoys, even if protected by an established use certificate or certificate of lawful existing use or development.

Temporary or permanent use?

The permission under this Part extends only to temporary use of land, but it has, ever since its inception, given rise to the practical problem of distinguishing between a temporary change of use and a permanent change. A temporary change of use is authorised up to the maximum number of days a year, and only constitutes unlawful development once those permissions have been used up and no other permission exists. But an unauthorised change of use which is intended to be permanent constitutes a breach of planning control from the start. The permission does not, therefore, offer a 14 or 28 day immunity period for all changes of use of open land. But much confusion was generated by a series of cases in the 1950s, culminating in *Cater v. Essex County Council* [1960] 1 Q.B. 424, where the courts insisted that the validity of an enforcement notice depended upon the local planning authority making the right allegation. The notice had to allege either that the change was without planning permission, or that it was in breach of the time-limited permission under this Part. That case-law was eventually over-ridden by the Town and Country Planning Act 1959, s.38 and the Caravan Sites and Control of Development Act 1960. In *Miller-Mead v. Minister of Housing and Local Government* [1963] 2 Q.B. 196, Lord Denning M.R. in the Court of Appeal expressed the view that not only had *Cater* been wrongly decided, but that the 1960 Act had overcome the technicalities.

It is now clear that if an authority are of the opinion that a change of use is intended to be permanent, then they are entitled to take enforcement action under s.172 of the 1990 Act, notwithstanding that the use has not yet been implemented for the full period allowed by this Part for temporary uses (see *e.g. Miller-Mead v. Minister of Housing and Local Government*; *Tidswell v. Secretary of State for the Environment* [1977] J.P.L. 104; *Stoke-on-Trent City Council v. W. & J. Wass Ltd. (No. 2)* [1992] 2 P.L.R. 22, 31). Under s.172 of the 1990 Act, it need only "appear" to the authority that unauthorised development has occurred, and the court in *Tidswell* accepted that for this purpose the authority are entitled to rely upon their own records as to whether planning permission has been granted. It is then a matter for the developer to establish in an appeal against the enforcement notice that he is within the permission under this Part, by bringing evidence to show that the use was temporary.

In *R. v. Rochester City Council, ex p. Hobday* [1989] 2 P.L.R. 38, where a site had been used for a market on seven days and the local planning authority apparently failed to consider whether it might be a change of a permanent character warranting immediate enforcement action, the authority resolved instead to issue an enforcement notice on the fifteenth day of user, when, they had been advised, it would be unlawful. The court held that such a course was not open to them: because they had not considered the possibility of a permanent change, it could not have "appeared to" the authority at the time of the resolution that there was a breach of planning control (although a subsequent resolution provided a fresh authorisation for enforcement action).

The planning unit

It is possible that an owner may seek to use up the full annual permission on one part of his land, and then shift to another part and start again. If the permission is read literally, then a move merely to an adjacent field would suffice. But it is likely that the courts would apply the familiar doctrine of the planning unit, and allow only the one exploitation of rights on the one unit. The planning unit will normally be the whole of the unit in the same occupation, but in the case of a business, including farming, which is carried out on different sites that are separated from each other by other land, each site may constitute a different planning unit: see, *e.g. Fuller v. Secretary of State for the Environment* [1987] J.P.L. 854; [1988] 1 P.L.R. 1, and the analysis in the General Note to Pt. 6 below.

Exclusions from Class B

(1) *land not within the curtilage of a building*

The permission extends only to open land. As to the meaning of "curtilage", see the General Note to Pt. 1 above.

(2) *caravans*

Use of land for a caravan site is excluded from this permission, and a limited permission is granted instead by Pt. 5 below. A separate permission for use of land by certain recreational organisations is given by Pt. 27.

The exclusion of caravans does not, however, exclude the use of land for camping for up to 28 days per year. The requirement under the Public Health Act 1936, s.269, to obtain a licence for camp sites is applicable only where the land is used for camping for more than 42 consecutive days at a time and on a more than 60 days in any period of 12 months. Where a use is outside these controls, there is no limit on the number of tents that may be stationed on the land. The Government once proposed that these provisions should be amended so as to bring all "28 day" sites within licensing control, whilst allowing existing operators to claim a licence as of right if they can show that the site has been in use at any time in the 3 years before the Bill is published (DOE Consultation Paper, *Proposed Legislation Unifying Tent and Caravan Site Licensing in England and Wales*, 1987). No further action has been taken on those proposals.

(3) *advertisements*
Paragraph B.1(d) was inserted to provide that the temporary use of land for the display of an advertisement is not permitted development. DOE Circular 9/95, *General Development Order Consolidation 1995* advises that this amendment removes a duplication. Any development involving the display of an advertisement, whether temporary or permanent, in accordance with the Town and Country Planning (Control of Advertisements) Regulations 1992 (S.I. 1992 No. 666), is granted deemed planning permission (but not advertisement consent) by section 222 of the 1990 Act.

(4) *war games*
The playing of war games in a site of specific scientific interest is excluded from Class B (B.1(c)(iii)).

(5) *clay pigeon shooting*
Clay pigeon shooting was originally excluded from the temporary use rights under this Part. In view of the concern that was expressed at this unexpected change, the Department of the Environment undertook to review the situation and issued a further consultation paper after the Order had come into force. The argument for restricting clay pigeon shooting rights to 14 days was its growing popularity and the noise it produced. But against that it would be restrictive, effectively reducing the frequency of meetings from fortnightly to monthly. Local environmental health officers already have powers to control noise nuisance.

In light of the responses to the consultation paper, the Secretary of State agreed in April 1989 to reinstate clay pigeon shooting as a 28-day permitted temporary use, and the necessary amendment to the Order was made by S.I. 1989 No. 603. It was accepted that the change from 28 to 14 days might have resulted in less control and safety, if it meant that shoots would simply shift to parcels of land for a further 14-day period. But in addition the Department agreed with the Clay Pigeon Shooting Association on a Code of Practice for the sport, approved under the Control of Pollution Act 1974, s.71. Although the Code has no direct legal effect, it is intended to assist local authorities and magistrates' courts in their exercise of functions under the 1974 Act, and it will help in assessing whether the best practicable means have been used to reduce noise emissions.

See also *Basingstoke and Deane Borough Council and Church* (1985) 1 P.A.D. 65, where a 28-day user condition was imposed on a grant of planning permission for use of ancillary structures to clay pigeon shooting.

The 14-day rule: markets

The fact that a market is held under a market franchise granted by the Crown will not extend to it Crown immunity from planning control (*Spook*

Erection v. Secretary of State for the Environment [1988] 3 W.L.R. 291; [1988] 2 All E.R. 667)

In *Fitzpatrick v. Secretary of State for the Environment* [1988] J.P.L. 564 (note) it was held that a car boot sale could be described as a market and thus limited to 14 days per year.

PART 5

CARAVAN SITES

Class A

Permitted development — **A. The use of land, other than a building, as a caravan site in the circumstances referred to in paragraph A.2.**

Condition — **A.1 Development is permitted by Class A subject to the condition that the use shall be discontinued when the circumstances specified in paragraph A.2 cease to exist, and all caravans on the site shall be removed as soon as reasonably practicable.**

Interpretation of Class A — **A.2 The circumstances mentioned in Class A are those specified in paragraphs 2 to 10 of Schedule 1 to the 1960 Act (cases where a caravan site licence is not required), but in relation to those mentioned in paragraph 10 do not include use for winter quarters.**

Class B

Permitted development — **B. Development required by the conditions of a site licence for the time being in force under the 1960 Act.**

COMMENTARY

Derivation

Town and Country Planning General Development Order 1988 (S.I. 1988 No. 1813), Sched. 2, Pt. 5 (unamended).

Definitions

"building": art. 1(2).
"caravan": art. 1(2).
"caravan site": art. 1(2).
"development": 1990 Act, s.55.
"land": 1990 Act, s.336(1).

General Note

Planning and licensing control over caravan and camping sites is particularly complex. Permanent caravan sites require both planning permission and a licence granted under the Caravan Sites and Control of Development Act 1960. Sched. 1 to that Act prescribes a number of exemptions from licensing control, and this Part then grants planning permission for some of those cases. It also grants planning permission (Class B) for any development required by the conditions of a site licence under the 1960 Act. Permanent tenting sites require a licence under the Public Health Act 1936, s.269, but no licence is required where the land is not used for camping for more than 42 consecutive days at a time, and on not more than 60 days in any twelve-month period. Moreover, it is possible for organisations to obtain exemption certificates under s.269, and planning permission for the use of land by exempted organisations is granted by Pt. 27 of this Order.

Proposals for legislative reform were outlined in a consultation paper issued by the Department of the Environment in 1987, *Proposed Legislation Unifying Tent and Caravan Site Licensing in England and Wales*, but have not been carried through. The Paper suggested that these were proposals which the Government would be prepared to support if contained in a Private Member's Bill, but that they would not introduce them as a Government Bill. The Paper proposed a single site licensing system for both tents and caravans, along the lines of legislation that was contained in an unsuccessful Private Member's Bill in 1983/84, but with some further refinements.

Circumstances in Class A.2: Sched. 1 to the 1960 Act

The following cases are within Sched. 1 to the 1960 Act:

para. 1—use within curtilage of a dwellinghouse: use of a caravan within the curtilage for purposes incidental to the enjoyment of the dwellinghouse falls within the primary use of the dwellinghouse, and does not require separate planning permission. This para. is therefore not included in those for which permission is granted by Class A.

para. 2—use by a person travelling with a caravan for one or two nights: land may be used as a caravan site for a single caravan for up to two nights, but subject to an annual limit of 28 days on that land or adjoining land.

para. 3—five acre holdings: up to three caravans are allowed without a site licence for up to 28 days a year on holdings of not less than 5 acres.

para. 4—exempted organisations: the Secretary of State for the Environment may grant a certificate of exemption under para. 12 of the Schedule to any organisation as to which he is satisfied that its objects include encouragement or promotion of recreational activities. Under para. 4, no site licence is then required if the use is for purposes of recreation and is under the supervision of the organisation.

para. 5—sites approved by exempted organisations: an exempted organisation may also certify caravan sites for use by its members for the purposes of recreation, for a period in each case of up to one year. Up to 5 caravans may then be stationed for the purposes of human habitation on the land without a site licence or (by virtue of this Part) planning permission.

para. 6—meetings organised by exempt organisations: such meetings for less than 5 days are outside controls.

paras. 7, 8—agricultural and forestry workers: the stationing of a caravan on agricultural land for purposes incidental to the agricultural use of the land, such as storage of food or as animal shelter, does not constitute the making of a material change in the use of the land and is thus outside development control (*Wealden District Council v. Secretary of State for the Environment and Day* (*Colin*) [1988] J.P.L. 268 (C.A.)). The effect of para. 7 and Class B of this Part is to grant planning permission for seasonal use of agricultural land as a caravan site for agricultural or forestry workers.

para. 9—building and engineering sites: this category covers caravans used on-site (or on adjoining land) for the accommodation of workers employed in carrying out building or engineering operations (provided they have planning permission where necessary).

para. 10—travelling showmen: use of land as a caravan site by a travelling showman who is a member of an organisation of travelling showmen which holds for the time being a certificate granted by the Secretary of State for the purposes of para. 10, and who is, at the time, travelling for the purposes of his business. Para. 10 also extends to winter quarters taken up by travelling showmen, but this is excluded from planning permission under this Part by Class A.2. In *Hammond v. Secretary of State for the Environment* [1988] 3 P.L.R. 90, the Court of Appeal held that travelling showmen, who go into winter quarters for some four months when fairs are not operating throughout the country as they do in summer, were not gypsies within the Caravan Sites Act 1968. The test under s.16, which excludes from the definition of "gypsies" any members of an organised group of travelling showmen, could not be applied on a time basis so as to include showmen during their four months winter period, but was confined solely to a quality assessment.

The Court of Appeal held in *Holmes v. Cooper* [1985] 1 W.L.R. 1060 that the exemption by virtue of para. 10 applies only where all the caravans on the site are used to accommodate travelling showmen who are on the site at the time when they are travelling for the purposes of their business. The fact that the caravans are predominantly used by travelling showmen is insufficient, and permanent residence by travelling showmen on the site did not qualify.

Policy advice

See DOE Circular 9/95, *General Development Order Consolidation 1995*, paras. 51 to 53; and DOE Circular 22/91, *Travelling Showpeople.*

PART 6

AGRICULTURAL BUILDINGS AND OPERATIONS

Class A Development on units of 5 hectares or more

Permitted development

A. The carrying out on agricultural land comprised in an agricultural unit of 5 hectares or more in area of—

(a) works for the erection, extension or alteration of a building; or

(b) any excavation or engineering operations,

which are reasonably necessary for the purposes of agriculture within that unit.

Development not permitted

A.1 Development is not permitted by Class A if—

(a) the development would be carried out on a separate parcel of land forming part of the unit which is less than 1 hectare in area;

(b) it would consist of, or include, the erection, extension or alteration of a dwelling;

(c) it would involve the provision of a building, structure or works not designed for agricultural purposes;

(d) the ground area which would be covered by—

(i) any works or structure (other than a fence) for accommodating livestock or any plant or machinery arising from engineering operations; or

(ii) any building erected or extended or altered by virtue of Class A,

would exceed 465 square metres, calculated as described in paragraph D.2 below;

(e) the height of any part of any building, structure or works within 3 kilometres of the perimeter of an aerodrome would exceed 3 metres;

(f) the height of any part of any building, structure or works not within 3 kilometres of the perimeter of an aerodrome would exceed 12 metres;

(g) any part of the development would be within 25 metres of a metalled part of a trunk road or classified road;

(h) it would consist of, or include, the erection or construction of, or the carrying out of any works to, a building, structure or an excavation used or to be used for the accommodation of livestock or for the storage of slurry or sewage sludge where the building, structure or excavation is, or would be, within 400 metres of the curtilage of a protected building; or

(i) it would involve excavations or engineering operations on or over article 1(6) land which are connected with fish farming.

Conditions

A.2(1) Development is permitted by Class A subject to the following conditions—

(a) where development is carried out within 400 metres of the curtilage of a protected building, any building, structure, excavation or works resulting from the development shall not be used for the accommodation of livestock except in the circumstances described in paragraph D.3 below or for the storage of slurry or sewage sludge;

(b) where the development involves—

(i) the extraction of any mineral from the land (including removal from any disused railway embankment); or

(ii) the removal of any mineral from a mineral-working deposit,

the mineral shall not be moved off the unit;

(c) waste materials shall not be brought on to the land from elsewhere for deposit except for use in works described in Class A(a) or in the provision of a hard surface and any materials so

brought shall be incorporated forthwith into the building or works in question.

(2) Subject to paragraph (3), development consisting of—

(a) the erection, extension or alteration of a building;

(b) the formation or alteration of a private way;

(c) the carrying out of excavations or the deposit of waste material (where the relevant area, as defined in paragraph D.4 below, exceeds 0.5 hectare); or

(d) the placing or assembly of a tank in any waters,

is permitted by Class A subject to the following conditions—

(i) the developer shall, before beginning the development, apply to the local planning authority for a determination as to whether the prior approval of the authority will be required to the siting, design and external appearance of the building, the siting and means of construction of the private way, the siting of the excavation or deposit or the siting and appearance of the tank, as the case may be;

(ii) the application shall be accompanied by a written description of the proposed development and of the materials to be used and a plan indicating the site together with any fee required to be paid;

(iii) the development shall not be begun before the occurrence of one of the following—

(aa) the receipt by the applicant from the local planning authority of a written notice of their determination that such prior approval is not required;

(bb) where the local planning authority give the applicant notice within 28 days following the date of receiving his application of their determination that such prior approval is required, the giving of such approval; or

(cc) the expiry of 28 days following the date on which the application was received by the local planning authority without the local planning authority making any determination as to whether such approval is required or notifying the applicant of their determination;

(iv) (aa) where the local planning authority give the applicant notice that such prior approval is required the applicant shall display a site notice by site display on or near the land on which the proposed development is to be carried out, leaving the notice in position for not less than 21 days in the period of 28 days from the date on which the local planning authority gave the notice to the applicant;

(bb) where the site notice is, without any fault or intention of the applicant, removed, obscured or defaced before the period of 21 days referred to in sub-paragraph (aa) has elapsed, he shall be treated as having complied with the requirements of that sub-paragraph if he has taken reasonable steps for protection of the notice and, if need be, its replacement;

(v) the development shall, except to the extent that the local planning authority otherwise agree in writing, be carried out—

(aa) where prior approval is required, in accordance with the details approved;

(bb) where prior approval is not required, in accordance with the details submitted with the application; and

(vi) the development shall be carried out—

(aa) where approval has been given by the local plan-

ning authority, within a period of five years from the date on which approval was given;

(bb) in any other case, within a period of five years from the date on which the local planning authority were given the information referred to in sub-paragraph (d)(ii).

(3) The conditions in paragraph (2) do not apply to the extension or alteration of a building if the building is not on article 1(6) land except in the case of a significant extension or a significant alteration.

(4) Development consisting of the significant extension or the significant alteration of a building may only be carried out once by virtue of Class A(a).

Class B Development on units of less than 5 hectares

Permitted development

B. The carrying out on agricultural land comprised in an agricultural unit of not less than 0.4 but less than 5 hectares in area of development consisting of—

(a) the extension or alteration of an agricultural building;

(b) the installation of additional or replacement plant or machinery:

(c) the provision, rearrangement or replacement of a sewer, main, pipe, cable or other apparatus;

(d) the provision, rearrangement or replacement of a private way;

(e) the provision of a hard surface;

(f) the deposit of waste; or

(g) the carrying out of any of the following operations in connection with fish farming, namely, repairing ponds and raceways; the installation of grading machinery, seration equipment or flow meters and any associated channel; the dredging of ponds; and the replacement of tanks and nets,

where the development is reasonably necessary for the purposes of agriculture within the unit.

Development not permitted

B.1 Development is not permitted by Class B if—

(a) the development would be carried out on a separate parcel of land forming part of the unit which is less than 0.4 hectare in area;

(b) the external appearance of the premises would be materially affected;

(c) any part of the development would be within 25 metres of a metalled part of a trunk road or classified road;

(d) it would consist of, or involve, the carrying out of any works to a building or structure used or to be used for the accommodation of livestock or the storage of slurry or sewage sludge where the building or structure is within 400 metres of the curtilage of a protected building; or

(e) it would relate to fish farming and would involve the placing or assembly of a tank on land or in any waters or the construction of a pond in which fish may be kept or an increase (otherwise than by the removal of silt) in the size of any tank or pond in which fish may be kept.

B.2 Development is not permitted by Class B(a) if—

(a) the height of any building would be increased;

(b) the cubic content of the original building would be increased by more than 10%;

(c) any part of any new building would be more than 30 metres from the original building;

(d) the development would involve the extension, alteration or provision of a dwelling;
(e) any part of the development would be carried out within 5 metres of any boundary of the unit; or
(f) the ground area of any building extended by virtue of Class B(a) would exceed 465 square metres.

B.3 Development is not permitted by Class B(b) if—
(a) the height of any additional plant or machinery within 3 kilometres of the perimeter of an aerodrome would exceed 3 metres;
(b) the height of any additional plant or machinery not within 3 kilometres of the perimeter of an aerodrome would exceed 12 metres;
(c) the height of any replacement plant or machinery would exceed that of the plant or machinery being replaced; or
(d) the area to be covered by the development would exceed 465 square metres calculated as described in paragraph D.2 below.

B.4 Development is not permitted by Class B(e) if the area to be covered by the development would exceed 465 square metres calculated as described in paragraph D.2 below.

Conditions

B.5 Development permitted by Class B and carried out within 400 metres of the curtilage of a protected building is subject to the condition that any building which is extended or altered, or any works resulting from the development, shall not be used for the accommodation of livestock except in the circumstances described in paragraph D.3 below or for the storage of slurry or sewage sludge.

B.6 Development consisting of the extension or alteration of a building situated on article 1(6) land or the provision, rearrangement or replacement of a private way on such land is permitted subject to—
(a) the condition that the developer shall, before beginning the development, apply to the local planning authority for a determination as to whether the prior approval of the authority will be required to the siting, design and external appearance of the building as extended or altered or the siting and means of construction of the private way; and
(b) the conditions set out in paragraphs A.2(2)(ii) to (vi) above.

B.7 Development is permitted by Class B(f) subject to the following conditions—
(a) that waste materials are not brought on to the land from elsewhere for deposit unless they are for use in works described in Class B(a), (d) or (e) and are incorporated forthwith into the building or works in question; and
(b) that the height of the surface of the land will not be materially increased by the deposit.

Class C Mineral working for agricultural purposes

Permitted development

C. The winning and working on land held or occupied with land used for the purposes of agriculture of any minerals reasonably necessary for agricultural purposes within the agricultural unit of which it forms part.

Development not permitted

C.1 Development is not permitted by Class C if any excavation would be made within 25 metres of a metalled part of a trunk road or classified road.

Condition

C.2 Development is permitted by Class C subject to the condition that no mineral extracted during the course of the operation shall be moved to any place outside the land from which it was extracted, except to land which is held or occupied with that land and is used for the purposes of agriculture.

Interpretation of Part 6

D.1 For the purposes of Part 6—
"agricultural land" means land which, before development permitted by this Part is carried out, is land in use for agriculture and which is so used for the purposes of a trade or business, and excludes any dwellinghouse or garden;
"agricultural unit" means agricultural land which is occupied as a unit for the purposes of agriculture, including—

- **(a) any dwelling or other building on that land occupied for the purpose of farming the land by the person who occupies the unit, or**
- **(b) any dwelling on that land occupied by a farmworker;**

"building" does not include anything resulting from engineering operations;
"fish farming" means the breeding, rearing or keeping of fish or shellfish (which includes any kind of crustacean and mollusc);
"livestock" includes fish or shellfish which are farmed;
"protected building" means any permanent building which is normally occupied by people or would be so occupied, if it were in use for purposes for which it is apt; but does not include—

- **(i) a building within the agricultural unit; or**
- **(ii) a dwelling or other building on another agricultural unit which is used for or in connection with agriculture;**

"significant extension" and "significant alteration" mean any extension or alteration of the building where the cubic content of the original building would be exceeded by more than 10% or the height of the building as extended or altered would exceed the height of the original building;
"slurry" means animal faeces and urine (whether or not water has been added for handling); and
"tank" includes any cage and any other structure for use in fish farming.

D.2 For the purposes of Part 6—

- **(a) an area calculated as described in this paragraph comprises the ground area which would be covered by the proposed development, together with the ground area of any building (other than a dwelling), or any structure, works, plant, machinery, ponds or tanks within the same unit which are being provided or have been provided within the preceding two years and any part of which would be within 90 metres of the proposed development;**
- **(b) 400 metres is to be measured along the ground.**

D.3 The circumstances referred to in paragraphs A.2(1)(a) and B.5 are—

- **(a) that no other suitable building or structure, 400 metres or more from the curtilage of a protected building, is available to accommodate the livestock; and**
- **(b) (i) that the need to accommodate the livestock arises from—**
  - **(aa) quarantine requirements; or**
  - **(bb) an emergency due to another building or structure in which the livestock could otherwise be accom-**

modated being unavailable because it has been damaged or destroyed by fire, flood or storm; or

(ii) in the case of animals normally kept out of doors, they require temporary accommodation in a building or other structure—

(aa) because they are sick or giving birth or newly born; or

(bb) to provide shelter against extreme weather conditions.

D.4 For the purposes of paragraph A.2(2)(c), the relevant area is the area of the proposed excavation or the area on which it is proposed to deposit waste together with the aggregate of the areas of all other excavations within the unit which have not been filled and of all other parts of the unit on or under which waste has been deposited and has not been removed.

D.5 In paragraph A.2(2)(iv), "site notice" means a notice containing—

(a) the name of the applicant,

(b) the address or location of the proposed development,

(c) a description of the proposed development and of the materials to be used,

(d) a statement that the prior approval of the authority will be required to the siting, design and external appearance of the building, the siting and means of construction of the private way, the siting of the excavation or deposit or the siting and appearance of the tank, as the case may be,

(e) the name and address of the local planning authority,

and which is signed and dated by or on behalf of the applicant.

D.6 For the purposes of Class B—

(a) the erection of any additional building within the curtilage of another building is to be treated as the extension of that building and the additional building is not to be treated as an original building;

(b) where two or more original buildings are within the same curtilage and are used for the same undertaking they are to be treated as a single original building in making any measurement in connection with the extension or alteration of either of them.

D.7 In Class C, "the purposes of agriculture" includes fertilising land used for the purposes of agriculture and the maintenance, improvement or alteration of any buildings, structures or works occupied or used for such purposes on land so used.

COMMENTARY

DERIVATION

Part 6 was substituted in the 1988 Order by the Town and Country Planning General Development (Amendment) (No. 3) Order 1991 (No. 2805), art. 9 and Schedule, from January 2, 1992. It had been previously amended with effect from the same date, by the Town and Country Planning General Development (Amendment) (No. 2) Order 1991 (No. 2268), but those amendments were overridden by the No. 3 Amendment Order. The definition of "protected building" was amended by S.I. 1995 No. 298 to exclude reference to buildings used for special industrial uses.

DEFINITIONS

"aerodrome": art. 1(2).
"agricultural land": Class D.1.
"agricultural unit": Class D.1.

"agriculture": 1990 Act, s.336(1).
"article 1(6) land": Sched. 1.
"building": art. 1(2); Class D.1; 1990 Act, s.336(1).
"development": 1990 Act, s.55.
"engineering operations": 1990 Act, s.336(1).
"fish farming": Class D.1.
"height": art. 1(3).
"land": 1990 Act, s.336.
"livestock": Class D.1.
"mining operations": art. 1(2).
"protected building": Class D.1.
"significant extension," "significant alteration": Class D.1.
"site notice": Class D.5.
"slurry": Class D.1.
"tank": Class D.1
"trunk or classified road": art. 1(2).

GENERAL NOTE

Outline of the commentary to Part 6

Background to Part 6

Classes A and B of Part 6 grant planning permission for general agricultural development (*i.e.*, development reasonably necessary for the purposes of agriculture within the agricultural unit). Formerly the Order granted a single permission, which applied to agricultural land over one acre (0.4 hectare). But following amendments made in 1992 the permission is divided. The Class A permission is now restricted to agricultural units of 5 hectares or more, and if the development is to be on a separate parcel within that unit, the parcel must be at least one hectare. The Class B permission is for smaller agricultural units, of between 0.4 and five hectares in area, and if the development is to be on a separate parcel, the parcel must be at least 0.4 hectare. Where Class A permits any building works or excavation or engineering operations (though with exceptions and conditions), Class B is limited to specified types of development.

The two Classes are mutually exclusive. Class B rights do not extend to agricultural units exceeding five hectares. Although the specific operations permitted by Class B are also, for the most part, within the more broadly defined test under Class A, it is against Class A rather than Class B that development on units over 5 hectares must be justified.

Development under both Classes is in certain cases subject to a requirement to give prior notification to the local planning authority, to enable them to determine whether their prior approval should be required to the siting, design and external appearance of the building or other development. This requirement was introduced by the 1992 amendments.

Further guidance and policy

Further advice on Pt. 6 rights is contained in PPG 7, *The Countryside and The Rural Economy* (1992).

General condition relating to protection of habitats

The Conservation (Natural Habitats, &c.) Regulations 1994, reg. 60, introduced a general condition, on any planning permission granted by the General Permitted Development Order (whether before or after the commencement of those Regulations), which has special significance to agricultural development. These Regulations require that development which:

(a) is likely to have a significant effect on (whether or not it comprises part of) a European site in Great Britain (either alone or in combination with other plans or projects), and

(b) is not directly concerned with or necessary to the management of the site,

should not be begun until the developer has received written notification of the approval of the local planning authority under reg. 62. The Regulations also provide a procedure whereby a developer may apply to the appropriate nature conservation body for their opinion whether his proposed development is likely to have such an effect (reg. 61); and a procedure for assessment by the local planning authority cases where the proposed development is likely to have a significant effect on a European site (reg. 62).

General exclusion of development otherwise requiring environmental assessment

Permitted development rights are not conferred by this Part to any development which would, if application were made for planning permission for it, require environmental assessment (art. 3(10)).

General principles

There are four principal tests in applying Class A or Class B: the first is whether permission is actually required in any event irrespective of this Part, the second relates to the nature of the land on which the development is to be carried out, the third is the functional relationship between the development and the use of the land, and the fourth relates to the physical limitations of the development which is permitted.

1. Agricultural activities not requiring permission

(1) the exemption under s.55

This Order confers a broad grant of permission for agricultural activities which would otherwise require express planning permission because they constitute "development" under the 1990 Act. But some types of agricultural activity need no permission at all, and for them the Order is irrelevant.

The 1990 Act, s.55(2)(e), provides that:

> "the use of any land for the purpose of agriculture or forestry (including afforestation) and the use for any of those purposes of any building occupied together with land so used"

does not constitute "development."

(2) changes between agricultural uses

It follows that there is no planning control involved when there is a change in the specific agricultural uses on a farm, such as when a barn used for housing livestock is used instead for the storage and maintenance of farm machinery used on the farm. Nor is development involved when land comes to be used more intensively than before, but still for an agricultural purpose; as where, for example, agricultural land is converted to use as allotments (*Crowborough Parish Council v. Secretary of State for the Environment* [1981] J.P.L. 281).

There is, however, a material change in use when all or part of the land is put over to a non-agricultural use. This may occur when a lawful ancillary use, such as a farm shop selling produce from the farm, breaks the ancillary link by selling produce imported from elsewhere (see, *e.g. Williams v. Minister of Housing and Local Government* (1967) 65 L.G.R. 495). But what if the produce comes from a different, physically separate farm, owned and occupied by the same farmer? This will normally depend upon how the appropriate planning unit is defined. If it includes both farms, then the retail use is ancillary to the primary use of the planning unit; but if each farm is a different unit (they may, for example, be many miles separate) then each is limited to such sales as are ancillary to its own agricultural uses. The complications arising from this analysis are considered further below.

(3) change from other use to agricultural use

The sub-section requires some translation, because the simple use of land or buildings does not constitute development in any event: that occurs only when there is a material change in use. So, in *McKellan v. Minister of Housing and Local Government* (1966) 198 E.G. 683, the court held that a broad interpretation should be given to the sub-section, and that it should be taken as authorising all changes of use from non-agricultural to agricultural use.

Hence, it is possible to change the use of any land to agricultural use without planning permission, whatever, its size, wherever its location and whatever its present use. Moreover, in *North Warwickshire Borough Council v. Secretary of State for the Environment* [1984] J.P.L. 434, the court held that, because of the definition of "land" in s.290(1) of the 1971 Act (now s.336(1) of the principal Act) as "including a building," the right also extended to buildings and was not limited to "any building occupied together with" agricultural land. Thus an intensive agricultural use may be introduced to an existing building in an urban area without need of planning permission (though subject to public health and nuisance controls). It does not follow, however, that it would then enjoy the further development rights under Pt. 6 of this Order. There are additional hurdles to clear, such as whether the area of the parcel of land involved is sufficient and whether the agricultural use is for the purposes of a trade or business: these are considered further below.

(4) placing structures on agricultural land

The breadth of s.55(2)(e) also means that structures may be placed on agricultural land for agricultural purposes without there being any "development", provided that no building or engineering works are involved. In order to attract control, it would be necessary to show that there had been a material change in the use of the land. But the act of placing a structure on the land does not itself involve a material change in use, notwithstanding that it may be inappropriate both in function and design for agricultural use. Thus a residential caravan placed in a field attracts no planning control so long as it is put to an agricultural or ancillary use (*Restormel Borough Council v. Secretary of State for the Environment* [1982] J.P.L. 785; *Wealden District Council v. Secretary of State for the Environment and Day (Colin)* [1988] J.P.L. 268, C.A.). It, may, for example, be used for shelter for animals on the land; or, to use some examples suggested by the Court of Appeal in the *Wealden* case (at

p. 277), to provide shelter for farmers or employees running "pick your own" ventures, storing and mixing feed, some related office work or the taking of shelter. The court rejected the submission that a residential caravan, because of its nature and ordinary use and associations, had to be regarded as incapable of being incidental to a primary agricultural use.

Additionally, permission is granted by Pt. 5 for the use of agricultural land as a caravan site for the seasonal accommodation of agricultural workers, by virtue of the Caravan Sites and Control of Development Act 1960, Sched. 1, para. 7.

(5) the consequence of the s.55 exemption

The rights conferred by s.55 fall entirely outside the scope of this Order which means that they are not restricted at all in the special environmental areas prescribed in either of the categories in Sched. 1 (art. 1(5) and art. 1(6) land); nor may they be taken away by an art. 4 direction; nor are they subject to the Habitats Regulations or the condition relating to environmental assessment.

2. Permission under Part 6: the nature of the land

The Class A permission is restricted to a parcel of land which:—
(1) is not less than 1 hectare in area
(2) is comprised in an agricultural unit of 5 hectares or more in area
(3) is in use for agriculture
(4) for the purpose of a trade or business

The Class B permission is restricted to a parcel of land which:
(1) is not less than 0.4 hectare in area
(2) is comprised in an agricultural unit of between 0.4 and 5 hectares in area
(3) is in use for agriculture
(4) for the purposes of a trade or business.
These requirements are analyzed in the following paragraphs.

(1) minimum parcel size

The Order specifies a minimum parcel size, which varies according to the size of the agricultural unit concerned. Previously, the 0.4 hectare minimum parcel size applied to all Part 6 development. Following the 1992 amendments, it applies only in the case of Class B development, which is applicable only where the agricultural unit is smaller than five hectares. For larger agricultural units the minimum parcel size is now 1 hectare. The purpose of these limitations is to prevent over-development on small parcels of agricultural land.

The rules on separate parcels of agricultural land have caused considerable difficulty in past versions of the Order. The 1988 Order permitted development on any agricultural land over 0.4 hectare, but required that area to be calculated without taking into account any separate parcels of land. That was an attempt to override one of the grounds of the decision in *Hancock v. Secretary of State for the Environment* [1987] J.P.L. 360, where Hodgson J. had indicated his view that a single piece of agricultural land could comprise a farmhouse and buildings plus garden totalling 1.1 acres situated in a village, together with 2 small fields (1.5 acres and 2.5 acres respectively) close by, and the remainder of the farm (six fields) about a third of a mile away. That decision was upheld on different grounds in the Court of Appeal (*sub-nom Tyack v. Secretary of State for Environment; Hancock v. Secretary of State for the Environment* [1988] 3 P.L.R. 78; [1989] J.P.L. 99), where the Court appears to have held that where component parts were separated by a substantial feature, they would probably not comprise a single piece of agricultural land, but it was a matter of fact and degree for the Secretary of State.

The 1992 amendments substituted a dual test: the parcel on which the development is to be carried out must be greater than one hectare, and the agricultural unit of which it forms part must exceed five hectares. Although the five hectares may include any dwelling occupied by the farmer of the unit (Class D.1 definition of "agricultural unit"), the minimum area of one hectare on which the development will take place must be calculated ignoring any dwellinghouse or garden (Class D.1 definition of "agricultural land"). This exclusion was first introduced by the 1988 Order, so as to override the other ground of the High Court decision in *Hancock v. Secretary of State for the Environment* [1987] J.P.L. 360, where the court held, following *Blackmore v. Butler* [1954] 2 Q.B. 171, that a farmhouse and its garden, occupied by a farmer and surrounded by farm buildings, was "land used for agriculture", and could be included in the calculation of the minimum size requirement. That ruling was upheld in the Court of Appeal, noted above; and further upheld by the House of Lords (*Tyack v. Secretary of State for the Environment* [1989] 1 W.L.R. 1392), where it was held that under the 1977 Order there was a strong, if not conclusive, indication that a dwellinghouse was excluded from the definition of agricultural land. Their Lordships noted, however, that under the 1988 Order dwellinghouses and gardens were now expressly excluded from the definition. That exclusion continues in the current Order.

(2) comprised in an agricultural unit

The purpose of this limitation is twofold. First, it excludes parcels of land which are put to agricultural use but which do not form part of a farming unit overall. A field might, for example, although itself in agricultural use, form part of a larger unit of occupation which is not agricultural. Thus where sheep are put to graze on open land within an industrial site to keep the grass down, Pt. 6 rights do not apply. Secondly, the agricultural unit is used to define functionally the extent of Pt. 6 rights, and this is discussed further below.

There is a reworded definition of "agricultural unit" contained in the order, as "agricultural land which is occupied as a unit for the purposes of agriculture", including dwellings (Class D). The 1977 order had simply incorporated the definition in the Agriculture Act 1947, s.109, which allowed the Minister to direct in specific cases that other land occupied by the same person but not in the same unit should be regarded as being in the same unit. That power seemed inappropriate to planning control, and has been discarded.

(3) in use for agriculture

To qualify for Pt. 6 rights under Class A and Class B, the land must be agricultural land, which means (Class D.1) that it must, before any development permitted by this Part is carried out, be land in use for agriculture and be so used for the purposes of a trade or business (see further below). This definition supersedes the definition contained in the Agriculture Act 1947, s.109, which had been applied by the 1977 Order. That definition allowed the Minister of Agriculture, Fisheries and Food (not, as the Court of Appeal may have assumed in *Fuller v. Secretary of State for the Environment* [1988] 1 P.L.R. 1, at 5, the Secretary of State for the Environment) to designate further land as agricultural land, although it had no present agricultural use.

3(a) "agriculture"

"Agriculture" is not defined by the Order, and thus the definition contained in s.336(1) of the 1990 Act prevails in the absence of any indication to the contrary:

> "agriculture" includes horticulture, fruit growing, seed growing, dairy farming, the breeding and keeping of livestock (including any creature kept for the production of food, wool, skins or fur, or for the purpose of its use in the farming of land), the use of land as grazing land, meadow land, osier land, market gardens and nursery grounds, and the use of land for woodlands where that use is ancillary to the farming of land for other agricultural purposes, and "agricultural" shall be construed accordingly.

The definition includes fox farming (since it involves the keeping of creatures for the production of skins or fur): see, *e.g. North Warwickshire Borough Council v. Secretary of State for the Environment* [1984] J.P.L. 434. But agricultural land that has been turned over to leisure plots is no longer agricultural (*Pittman v. Secretary of State for the Environment* [1988] J.P.L. 391; and see also *Canterbury County Council and Marty* (1985) 1 P.A.D. 374 where on the facts the use of leisure plots had remained agricultural because they had been used for rearing animals and taking crops, though the sites were too small to take advantage of permitted development rights under this Part).

(3)(b) agricultural dwelling houses

A dwellinghouse and its garden will normally be in residential use, not agricultural, and Pt. 6 rights under Class A and Class B will not therefore apply so as to allow agricultural development in the garden. It is conceivable, however, that a dwelling lawfully erected on farm land could be turned over to agricultural use, and it may be on this basis that the Court of Appeal in *Tyack v. Secretary of State for the Environment* [1988] E.G.C.S. 98 was prepared to hold that the Secretary of State had erred in finding that a house and garden were incapable of being agricultural land, and that whether they were was a matter of fact and degree in each case. However, the test now laid down by the definition in Class D.1 of "agricultural land" qualifying for Class A rights, in referring to "dwellinghouse or garden", implies that regard should be had to both the design and use, rather than simply actual use on its own. Hence the fact that a dwellinghouse had come to be used for agricultural purposes might not be sufficient to bring it outside the exclusion in that definition if it still had the physical characteristics of a dwellinghouse.

There is a possible further argument, to the effect that farm houses could generally be regarded as having an agricultural use, as ancillary to the primary agricultural use of the farm. But that would be to imply that a material change of use requiring planning permission occurred whenever such a house was disposed of or occupied separately from the agricultural use, without the need for any agricultural occupancy conditions; and that construction seems insupportable.

(3)(c) "agriculture" or "horsiculture": planning law's ponies

When it comes to animals, the Order has no regard to the nature of the creature but only to its function. Take the horse. Planning law knows only six horses:

- (i) *the working horse:* keeping and breeding them is an agricultural use (livestock bred or kept for the purpose of its use in the farming of land);
- (ii) *the racehorse:* keeping and breeding them is not an agricultural use of land because they are not livestock kept for agricultural production: *Belmont Farm Ltd v. Minister of Housing and Local Government* (1962) 13 P. & C.R. 417 (though he may graze: see (iv) below);
- (iii) *the recreational horse:* keeping them (as opposed to grazing them: see (iv) below) is not an agricultural use of land, so that there may be a

material change in the use of agricultural land when it is sub-divided into pony paddocks, when shelters are provided or when farm buildings are converted to livery use. The keeping of a recreational horse on agricultural land may mean that the land use has changed to a recreational use; or it may result in a mixed agricultural/recreational use. There is a suggestion in *South Oxfordshire District Council v. Secretary of State for the Environment* [1987] J.P.L. 868 that land may still be taken to be in agricultural use for Pt. 6 purposes where the agricultural use is mixed with another use, but the proposition is somewhat uncertain;

(iv) *the grazing horse:* the use of land as grazing land is an agricultural use, so that the use of land for *grazing* any of the above horses is agricultural; but not the use of the land for *keeping* them. There may be difficulties in telling the difference, but Donaldson L.J. in the Court of Appeal in *Sykes v. Secretary of State for the Environment* (1981) 42 P. & C.R. 19 stressed that regard should be had to what was the primary purpose for which the land was being used:

> "If horses were simply turned out on to the land with a view to feeding them from the land, clearly the land was being used for grazing. But if horses were being kept on the land and were being fed wholly or primarily by other means so that such grazing as they do was completely incidental and perhaps achieved merely because there were no convenient ways of stopping them doing it, then plainly the land was not being used for grazing but merely being used for keeping the animals...There was no difficulty in most cases in recognising whether the land was being used for grazing or for the keeping of non-agricultural horses. It was only if it was being used for the purpose of grazing that no planning permission was required."

It still does not follow that the grazing of ponies on land qualifies the land for exercise of Pt. 6 rights, however, because of the further requirement that the agricultural use should be for the purposes of a trade or business: see further below;

(v) *the residentially incidental horse:* the keeping of a horse within the curtilage of a dwelling-house may, though not an agricultural use, be incidental to the enjoyment of a dwelling-house and thus permitted by s.55(2)(d). Further, additional permitted development rights are conferred by Pt. 1, Class E in connection with such a use. That Class permits the provision of buildings and enclosures for "a purpose incidental to the enjoyment of the dwelling-house", which it defines as including the keeping of livestock for the personal enjoyment of the occupants of the dwelling-house. The 1977 Order excluded stables and looseboxes from that permission but the 1988 Order did not.

(vi) *horsemeat:* human consumption of horsemeat is common in other European countries, and the breeding and keeping of horses for food production would clearly constitute an agricultural use of land.

(4) for the purposes of a trade or business

Pt. 6 rights under both Class A and Class B do not apply where the agricultural use is purely recreational, such as where the keeping or breeding of a particular species is undertaken as a hobby. There is no direct authority bearing on the meaning of "trade or business" in the Order (in the definition of "agricultural land" in Class D.1), but in *South Oxfordshire District Council v. Secretary of State for the Environment* [1987] J.P.L. 868 the court found some assistance (though not decisive on the facts before it) in the decision of Gibson J. in *Customs and Excise Commissioners v. Fisher (Lord)* [1981] 2 All E.R. 147. In that case the court had to determine whether the expression "business, trade, profession and vocation" in s.45 of the Finance Act 1972, applied to a shoot in Norfolk. Gibson J. stated (p. 57):

> "It is clear, and there is much authority to support it, that 'business' is or may be in particular contexts a word of very wide meaning. Nevertheless, the ordinary meaning of the word 'business' in the context of this Act excludes, in my judgment, any activity which is *no more than* an activity for pleasure and social enjoyment.
>
> The primary meaning of all these words, 'business, trade, profession and vocation' is an occupation by which a person earns a living. It is clear that all ordinary businesses, trades, professions and vocations can be carried on with differences from this standard and norm in regularity or seriousness of application, in the pursuit or disregard of profit or earnings, and in the use or neglect of ordinary commercial principles of organisation ...
>
> Many people, however, carry on activities which are clearly 'business' but which have little to do with ordinary businesses or trades; thus a man may be a professional sportsman or make a business of his hobby, or make a trade of domestic hospitality. In this area, as it seems to me, the essential difference between what is 'business' or 'trade' and what is an activity for pleasure and social enjoyment may on occasions be difficult to discern or to prove, but no man, I believe, has any doubt that that essential difference is a real difference ..."

In *McKay v. Secretary of State for the Environment* [1989] 1 P.L.R. 7, the court held that profitability was not the test of whether an agricultural use was a trade or business. In *R. v. Sevenoaks District Council, ex p. Palley* [1995] J.P.L. 915 the court quashed decisions by the Council not to take enforcement action in respect of the erection of a greenhouse. The Council had insufficient material before it on which it could properly have concluded that the land was in use for agriculture for the purposes of a trade or business.

3. Permission under Classes A and B: the functional relationship between development and land

(1) development must be reasonably necessary

The 1977 Order permitted the carrying out of development "on agricultural land ... *requisite for the use of that land* for the purposes of agriculture". The 1988 Order substituted the test that the development must be "reasonably necessary for the purposes of agriculture within that unit," and that requirement is now carried across to both Class A and Class B.

That change gave effect to the interpretation given to the previous wording by the Court of Appeal in *Jones v. Metropolitan Borough of Stockport* [1984] J.P.L. 274 and the Scottish Court of Session in *Macpherson v. Secretary of State for Scotland* [1985] J.P.L. 788. In the *Jones* case the Court of Appeal took a broad view of "requisite", holding that there was no requirement that the building should be intended to accommodate an existing agricultural use on the land, so long as some agricultural use already existed (see also *Fayrewood Fish Farms Ltd v. Secretary of State for the Environment* [1984] J.P.L. 267: gravel extraction undertaken as part of engineering operation in establishment of a fish farm, now the subject of a separate regime; and *Clarke v. Secretary of State for the Environment* [1992] 1 P.L.R. 22: barn need not be justified solely by reference to existing use of land as a sheep unit). Nor, in the opinion of the Court, was there any requirement that the building to be provided should be subservient or ancillary to some activity carried out on the remainder of the land. However, the decision maker should take into account more than just the applicant's personal intentions: there may be a risk, especially on a small agricultural unit, that those intentions might change and that another owner might not carry on such intensive activity (*Broughton v. Secretary of State for the Environment* [1992] J.P.L. 550).

(2) for the purposes of agriculture within the agricultural unit

Under Class A and B, the "unit"—which is the whole agricultural unit of which the land forms part—rather than the particular parcel of land concerned, becomes the reference area for the development. An agricultural unit may be a farm that comprises more than a single area of land, perhaps a number of scattered fields. Applying the test in both Classes, before development may be undertaken pursuant to Pt. 6 on any of those parcels, it must itself have an existing agricultural use and be no smaller than one hectare (Class A) or 0.4 hectare (Class B). But once that test is satisfied, the question of whether the development is reasonably necessary can be assessed against the whole of the agricultural unit, and not the particular parcel where development is proposed. Thus, it may be reasonable to erect a storage facility on a particular part of the farm, although the produce to be stored there will be produced elsewhere in the agricultural unit; or to erect a building to provide a base for central maintenance of agricultural equipment.

(3) The relevance of the planning unit

Although Classes A and B now make it clear that the whole agricultural unit is the reference point for Pt. 6 rights, that unit is irrelevant for determining the quite different question of whether a material change of use has occurred on agricultural land. That question is determined in accordance with another reference point, the "planning unit."

The courts have adopted the view that the planning unit in any particular case may be something smaller than the agricultural unit. For example, in *Fuller v. Secretary of State for the Environment* [1987] J.P.L. 854, Q.B.D.; [1988] 1 P.L.R. 1 (C.A.), the appellant was a farmer with over 2,000 acres either owned or tenanted by him. One of the main areas of his unit was a large farm comprised of parcels of land that were more or less contiguous, and the next largest area was two miles distant. In addition, there were many other scattered areas. In an enforcement appeal the inspector suggested that the agricultural unit might be a more satisfactory means of determining planning issues than the planning unit. But the Secretary of State disagreed, and the High Court and Court of Appeal (in a reasoned judgment by Glidewell L.J. refusing leave to appeal) upheld his decision. The Secretary of State insisted that the agricultural unit and the planning unit were not the same, and that the agricultural unit there comprised a number of separate planning units. The scattered parcels of land could not be regarded as within the same planning unit "any more than, say, the similarly scattered retail outlets of a local chain of shops."

It followed that storage facilities on part of the agricultural holding could not be used to store grain grown on other parts of the farmer's land comprising separate planning units, although in the High Court the judge, Stuart Smith J., was moved to observe that it "seemed inconceivable that the local planning authority would seek to prevent him storing grain grown on other parts of his land." Similar sentiments surfaced in *Swinbank v. Secretary of State for the Environment* (1987) 55 P. & C.R. 371; [1987] J.P.L. 781 and led Mr David Widdicombe, Q.C. (sitting as Deputy Judge) to attempt to overcome the difficulties by holding that although, where two agricultural sites in the same ownership and occupation were too far apart to be regarded as the same planning unit, a use on one might be ancillary to the other: it was possible in law to have a use on one planning unit that was ancillary to the primary use of a different, planning unit. But the proposition is entirely at odds with the basic concept of the planning unit as a self-contained package of use-rights, and this analysis therefore looks unlikely to provide a path through the maze.

Against this background, the adoption by the 1988 GDO of the agricultural unit as the reference point for Pt. 6 rights added further complexity. It drew a clear line between erecting a new building, and changing the use of existing buildings. It meant that a farmer might erect on some part of his agricultural land a building intended to serve an ancillary agricultural purpose, such as the storage of grain, for the whole of his agricultural unit, notwithstanding that the farm might comprise more than one planning unit. The permission, though, extends not only to the erection of the building, but to its intended use. By virtue of the 1990 Act, s.75(2), the Pt. 6 permission is to be construed as "including permission to use the building for the purpose for which it is designed." But if the farmer instead puts an existing building to use for purposes which are not in themselves agricultural but are ancillary to the agricultural use of other planning units, express planning permission may be required.

4. Class A rights: Physical limitations on development

(1) *"works for the erection, extension or alteration of a building" (Class A(a))*

The meaning of a "building" for the purposes of this Part has to be pieced together from a variety of different sources. The 1990 Act, s.336(1) defines "building" as including any structure or erection, and any part of a building, but not as including any plant or machinery comprised in a building. Further, for the purposes of Pt. 6, a building does not include:

plant or machinery (art. 1(2)): all plant and machinery is excluded by this provision, and not merely that comprised in a building. But works for the erection, extension or alteration of plant or machinery may qualify separately for permission under this Part as an engineering operation, and "building" is defined for this Part as not including "anything resulting from engineering operations." (Class D.1);

any gate, fence, wall or other means of enclosure (art. 1(2)): permission is granted instead by Pt. 2 for the "erection, construction, maintenance, improvement or alteration of a gate, fence, wall or other means of enclosure," subject to the height limitations (1 metre if adjacent to a highway; otherwise 2 metres). This means that such operations on agricultural land are restricted by the Pt. 2 limitations rather than those under this Part, except to the extent that they involve engineering operations within this Part;

anything resulting from engineering operations (Class D.1): this does not limit the separate grant of planning permission for carrying out engineering operations, but it means that engineering projects (such as the construction of a reservoir) are not subject to the ground area exception in Class A.1(d); and it also narrows the definition of "protected building."

Further, Class A does not permit the erection, extension of alteration of a dwellinghouse, for which separate permitted development rights are applicable under Part 1 of Sched. 2.

As a result of the 1992 amendments, the right to extend or alter a building under Class A is restricted to just one "significant" alteration or extension (Class A.2(4)). This is one where the cubic content of the original building would be exceeded by more than 10 per cent., or the height of the building as extended or altered would exceed the height of the original building (Class D.1). As to the measurement of height under the Order, see art. 1(3) and the Commentary to that article. Any proposed "significant" extension or alteration is also subject to a requirement of prior notification to the local planning authority under Class A.2(2) to provide them with an opportunity to control its siting, design and external appearance.

(2) *"any excavation or engineering operations" (Class A(b))*

This separate permission for excavations and engineering operations was recast in 1988, and it is significant because such operations are not subject to the restrictions and exceptions in Class A that relate to buildings: a building does not include anything resulting from engineering operations (Class D.1). This reverses the decision in *South Oxfordshire District Council v. Secretary of State for the Environment* [1986] J.P.L. 435 where the court held that the Secretary of State had misdirected himself in not considering whether an embankment, which it was proposed should be constructed as part of engineering operations for an agricultural reservoir, should be considered a "building" and thus subject to the ground area restriction. Under the new formula, that question no longer arises.

The revised wording of the 1988 Order appears also to override the decision in *West Bowers Farm Products v. Essex County Council* [1985] J.P.L 857 (and see also the *South Oxfordshire* decision and *R. v. Surrey County Council, ex p. Monk* [1986] J.P.L. 828 on this point) where the Court of Appeal had insisted that the construction of an agricultural reservoir would involve two activities, each of them of substance. The extraction of a substantial volume of gravel could not be regarded merely as ancillary to engineering operations in the way that it might be if, for example, foundations were dug for a bridge or a building. It would constitute a separate mining operation, and was thus outside permitted development rights under the 1977 Order. But the issue of mineral extraction was tackled differently in the 1988 Order (following the line of amendments made in 1986 to the 1977 Order). Firstly, by the condition now in Class A.2(1)(b) which requires that where the development involves the removal of any mineral from the land (or from a disused railway embankment or mineral-working deposit), it may not be moved from the land without planning permission granted on an application. Secondly, permitted development rights for excavation are now separately conferred, so that it is no longer necessary to inquire whether an excavating activity is ancillary to a primary engineering operation.

The permission covers both engineering operations and excavation, but it does not extend to pure mining operations, for which a separate limited permission is granted by Class C. If minerals are excavated in the course of carrying out permitted development under this Class, they may not be moved off the land without express planning permission (Class A.2(1)(b)).

(3) *Exclusions and restrictions under Class A*

The following development is excluded from the Class A permission:

(*a*) *the erection, extension or alteration of a dwelling (Class A.1(b))*: dwelling-houses are excluded altogether from this Part, and the obvious temptation to erect a building that is called a barn but actually resembles a dwelling-house is met by the exclusion of buildings not designed for the purposes of agriculture (below): see, *e.g. Green v. Secretary of State for the Environment* [1985] J.P.L. 323 (plans for the appellant's calf-rearing building in course of erection bore remarkably close resemblance to a dwellinghouse); planning appeal decisions reported at (1994) 9 P.A.D. 587 (floor plan of agricultural storage building very similar to a two-bedroomed bungalow, with brick cavity construction and pitched roof); (1994) 10 P.A.D. 303 (non-horticultural greenhouse).

(*b*) *the provision of a building, structure or works not designed for agricultural purposes (Class A.1(c))*: in *Belmont Farm Ltd v. Minister of*

Housing and Local Government (1962) 13 P. & C.R. 417, the court held that a building "designed" for the purposes of agriculture meant one "designed for the purposes of agriculture in the sense of its physical appearance and layout", and on that test an aircraft hangar was not such a building. That decision was followed in *Harding v. Secretary of State for the Environment* [1984] J.P.L. 503, where the court distinguished the Court of Appeal's different approach in the context of s.33(2) of the 1971 Act in *Wilson v. West Sussex County Council* (1964) 14 P. & C.R. 301. The court in *Harding* accepted that "designed" related to appearance rather than function:

> "... the purpose was to secure that buildings in the countryside shall look like farm buildings and not like dwelling-houses or aircraft hangars, or something else. There was a reason why the draftsman had used the word 'designed' in [Pt. 6]."

Applying this test, the Secretary of State has ruled that a windmill (wind turbine) was not designed for the purposes of agriculture (appeal decision at [1987] J.P.L. 807). In *Clarke v. Secretary of State for the Environment* [1992] 3 P.L.R. 146 the Court of Appeal, applying the *Belmont* test, upheld an inspector's finding that a brick building with cavity walls was not an agricultural building (overruling the High Court which had found that finding "perverse");

(*c*) *ground area of buildings (Class A.1(d))*: the ground area restriction excludes outright any individual buildings or other structures exceeding 465 square metres, but it also requires all buildings within 90 metres of the proposed development which have been provided in the preceding two years to be included in the calculation (Class D.2). This has the curious result that it is possible to build several buildings of up to 465 square metres at any time, provided they are not grouped together; but if any part is within the 90 metre radius from another, express planning permission (or a two year delay) is necessary;

(*d*) *height (Class A.1(e) and (f))*: as to the measurement of height in relation to a building or of plant or machinery see art. 1(3), and the General Note to that article;

(*e*) *adjacency to trunk or classified road (Class A.1(g))*: if the 25 metre line is breached, the whole of the development is unauthorised and not merely the excess (*Fayrewood Fish Farms Ltd v. Secretary of State for the Environment* [1984] J.P.L. 267). The restriction does not limit access to unclassified roads, and where the formation, laying out or construction of such an access is required in connection with development permitted under this Part, planning permission is granted for it by Pt. 2, Class B;

(*f*) *livestock units, slurry and sludge storage, adjacent to protected buildings (Class A.1(h))*: this restriction establishes a special control over the location of intensive livestock units and sludge and slurry operation. Because of the difficulty in defining an intensive livestock building, the restriction applies to all buildings, structures or excavations used or to be used for accommodation of livestock, or for storage of slurry or sewage sludge. "Slurry" means (art. 1(2)) animal faeces and urine, whether or not water has been added for handling. No such building may be erected within 400 metres of a "protected building," and no other building erected under this Class which is within the 400 metre zone may be put to use for such purposes except in the limited cases specified in Class D.3. Previously there was a simple five-year ban, but the 1992 amendments converted that into a permanent restriction (Class A.2(1)(a)). In addition, PPG 7, *The Countryside and the Rural Economy* (1992), para. B3.3, advises local planning authorities to exercise particular care when considering planning applications for houses and other new "protected buildings" within 400 metres of existing livestock units, so as to minimise the potential for future problems of nuisance. The exclusion extends not only to the provision of such units, but also "the carrying out of any works to" such a unit. But that does not override the right under the 1990 Act, s.55(2)(a) to carry out any works for the maintenance, improvement or other alteration of any such building, provided the external appearance is not materially affected. The control applies only to facilities for slurry storage and no legal restrictions have yet been introduced over the spreading of slurry.

(g) *fish farming (Class A.1(i))*: excavations or engineering operations for the construction of fish farming facilities constitute permitted development under Class A, except on or over article 1(6) land (land in national parks and specified other areas: see Sched. 1, Part 2). However, permitted development rights are subject to the condition that no minerals extracted in the course of excavations may be moved off the agricultural unit (Class A.2(1)(b)).

(4) *Conditions on development under Class A*

(a) *livestock units*: see the note to Class A.1(f) above;

(b) *extraction of minerals*: the extraction of minerals is not prohibited, but minerals extracted in the course of building or engineering operations may not be moved from the land unless planning permission on an application has been granted for winning and working that mineral. Permission is granted by Class A for excavation, but not for any mining operations; but a separate permission is given by Class C. Minerals extracted under that permission may similarly not be exported from the agricultural unit;

(c) *deposit of waste*: this condition was introduced in 1985 to overcome the problem that the deposit of waste materials on agricultural land might, according to the intentions of the landowner, constitute either a material change of use from agriculture to waste disposal, requiring planning permission; or the carrying out of an engineering operation reasonably required for agriculture (such as filling in an unproductive gully) and be permitted development under this Part (see, *e.g. Northavon District Council v. Secretary of State for the Environment* (1980) 40 P. & C.R. 332; *Bilboe v. Secretary of State for the Environment* (1980) 39 P. & C.R. 495). Now the only waste that may be imported is in relation to Class A(a)—building works, and for the creation of a hard surface, where the material is incorporated forthwith into the building or works (Class A.2(1)(c)). But there is no restriction on the importing of other building material which does not constitute waste. The Order provides no definition of waste. But there may be some assistance to be drawn from the Environment Protection Act 1990, Sched. 2B (inserted by the Environment Act 1995, Sched. 22, paras. 88 and 95), which in turn reproduces Annex 1 to the Waste Directive (Council Directive 75/442/EEC, as amended by 91/156/EEC). The Schedule lists 16 categories of waste. Extensive guidance on implications of this legislation is contained in DOE Circular 11/94, *The Framework Directive on Waste*, Annexes 1 and 2.

The condition prohibiting the import of waste materials was considered in an appeal decision at [1988] J.P.L. 663, where imported clay soil had been deposited on the site. The local planning authority acknowledged that it was not refuse, so the issue was whether it nonetheless constituted waste. It was held that it did not, because it was clear that the sole intention had been to improve the agricultural quality of land. The soil had been spread and seeded. But in another appeal reported at [1989] J.P.L. 379, the inspector laid emphasis on the type and quality of the deposited material, and observed:

"Broken bricks, concrete rubble, and wood are in my opinion by-products of the building process which are generally unusable by the builder and are therefore removed from construction sites as waste material. Being interspersed with earthspoil, as is the case here, renders the brick and concrete rubble even more unusable to the builder. On the other hand, the fact that bricks and rubble are interspersed with soil would not, in my view, detract from the value of the material for the appellant's stated agricultural purpose, bearing in mind the considerable depth it would be below the proposed finished level of the fill.

As to the soil, it appears that building contractors had surplus excavated material they wanted to dispose of, they hired a haulage contractor to take it away, and he, finding a convenient disposal point at the appeal site tipped it there. The surplus excavated material is also a by-product of the building process, is of no value to the builder, and is waste as far as he is concerned. Whether the surplus material is excavated and loaded straight into lorries for disposal, or is excavated and loaded and stockpiled before loading onto lorries for disposal, is irrelevant in my view. There is no evidence that the building contractors who produced the surplus excavated material carried out any process of selection or quality control to ensure that the material was suitable for the appellant's purpose. The fact that the appellant finds it useful for his purpose does not alter my opinion that the material is imported waste."

Class A rights: control of siting, design and external appearance

(1) *Background*

Class A.2(2) incorporates requirements originally contained in the Town and Country Planning (Landscape Areas Special Development) Order 1950, subsequently replaced by the Town and Country Planning (Agricultural and Forestry Development in National Parks etc.) Special Development Order 1986. That Order extended the requirement to all "article 1(6) land," *i.e.* land in the National Parks and some fringe areas abutting National Parks defined in Sched. 1, Pt. 2. The 1992 amendments extended it to all agricultural land, so that the Class A permission is now qualified by the condition that the developer should give prior notice to the local planning authority of proposed development under this Class. They then have 28 days in which to notify him that it should not be begun without their prior approval to the siting, design and external appearance of the building. A similar condition is contained in Pt. 7 in relation to buildings and private ways for forestry purposes.

(2) *Extent of the prior notification requirement*

The prior notification requirement extends to:

(a) *the erection, extension or alteration of a building*: not all building works are caught by the requirement. It applies only to a "significant" extension or alteration (Class A.2(3)), which is one where the cubic content of the original building would be exceeded by more than 10 per cent., or the height of the building as extended or altered would exceed the height of the original building (Class D.1). As to the measurement of height under the Order, see art.1(3) and the Commentary to that article.

(b) *the formation or extension of a private way*: a private way is "a highway not maintained at the public expense and any other way other than a highway" (art. 1(1)). Reference to private ways was inadvertently omitted from the 1988 Order, and had subsequently to be restored to it by S.I. 1989 No. 603.

(c) *excavations or the deposit of waste material*: the formula is ambiguous. It could mean either (i) the carrying out of excavations, or the deposit of waste material; or (ii) the carrying out of excavations, or the deposit, of waste material. The former appears the more likely, since excavations of waste material on agricultural land would be a rare operation, and there is no readily discernible difference in terms of amenity between those excavations and any other excavations on agricultural land. However, the grouping together of excavations and waste disposal appears deliberate, and raises further ambiguities. Not all excavations and waste deposits are subject to the prior notification requirement. It applies only where the "relevant area" exceeds 0.5 hectares. However, there are two possible interpretations of the "relevant area," as defined by Class D.4, which requires the area of the proposed excavation or waste deposit to be aggregated with previous excavations and deposits. One approach would be to aggregate the area of a proposed excavation with that of previous excavations within the agricultural unit which have not been filled. If the total exceeds 0.5 hectares, no further excavation is permitted under Class A. The other approach would require that there should also be added "all other parts of the unit on or under which waste has been deposited and has not been removed." The language of Class D.4 suggests that the second approach is intended, notwithstanding that areas excluded from the first limb as being excavations that have been filled, will be brought back into the calculation under the second limb as being areas on or under which waste has been deposited. Excavations carried out by virtue of Class C (mineral working for agricultural purposes) would be added to the "relevant area," but further extraction under that Class is not governed by any territorial limit.

(d) *the placing or assembly of a tank in any waters*: following doubts as to whether these operations constituted "development" at all, the principal Act was amended by the Planning and Compensation Act 1991, which inserted new s.55(4A), under which the placing or assembly of a tank in inland waters for the purpose of fish farming there is deemed to involve engineering operations. Permission is granted by Class A for excavation and engineering operations reasonably necessary for the purposes of agriculture. It therefore includes:

   (a) excavation of land for fish farming, except for article 1(6) land (Class A.1(i)), and subject to the condition that no excavated minerals be moved off the agricultural unit (Class A.2(b));

   (b) the engineering operations that are deemed by s.55(4A) to occur in connection with the placing of a tank in any waters, subject to the requirement of prior notification to the local planning authority to allow them to exercise control over the siting and appearance of the tank; and

   (c) incidental building and engineering operations in connection with fish farming, and other works of repair and maintenance. For smaller agricultural units (between one and five hectares) a specific permission is granted under Class B for various minor operations in relation to fish farming (Class B.(g)), but it does not extend to the placing or assembly of a tank, the construction of a pond, or the increase in the size of any tank or pond (Class B.1(e)).

(3) *What prior notification involves*

Where the prior notification requirement applies, the exercise of permitted development rights under Class A is lawful only if application has been made to the local planning authority for a determination of whether they propose to exercise their power of prior approval, and they have either given written notification that they do not so propose, or granting approval; or 28 days has elapsed from the date the authority received the application without their making any such determination or notifying the applicant of their determination. Hence, the fact the applicant may not have received notification within the 28 days period is not enough in itself; a late notification of a determination made within the period will continue the suspension of permitted development rights pending the authority's approval. A fee is payable on such an application (set by the Town and Country Planning (Fees for Applications and Deemed Applications) Regulations 1989 (S.I. 1989 No. 193), reg. 11A, inserted by S.I. 1991 No. 2735, art. 3).

(4) *Handling applications*

The Secretary of State has urged that the controls be exercised selectively and efficiently. PPG7, *The Countryside and the Rural Economy* (1992), para. C6, advises:

> "Undue delays can have serious consequences for agricultural and forestry businesses, which are more dependent than most on seasonal and market considerations. The procedures adopted by authorities should be straightforward, simple, and easily understood. Delegation of decisions to officers will help to achieve prompt and efficient handling, and should be extended as far as possible. Authorities should use their discretion over consulting parish/community councils and other groups about particular proposals, having regard to the need to reach decisions within the required timescales. Requests for more time from consultees should not be used as a reason for requiring the submission of details."

The advice goes on to urge local planning authorities to prepare forms which developers can use to apply for determinations, to help to minimise the number of cases in which submission of details may be necessary; and suggests that where they do not propose to require further details, "it would be helpful and courteous to inform the developer as soon as possible, to avoid any unnecessary delay or uncertainty." (para. C7).

(5) *Criteria for control*

The Secretary of State has advised, in PPG7, *The Countryside and the Rural Economy*, that:

> "in operating these controls, local authorities should always have full regard to the operational needs of the agricultural and forestry industries; to the need to avoid imposing any unnecessary or excessively costly requirements; and to the normal considerations of reasonableness. However, they will also need to consider the effect of the development on the landscape in terms of visual amenity and the desirability of preserving ancient monuments and their settings, known archaeological sites, listed buildings and their settings, and sites of recognised nature conservation value. They should weigh these two sets of considerations. Long term conservation objectives will often be served best by ensuring that the rural economy, including farming and forestry which are prominent in the rural landscape, is able to function successfully." (para. C4)

(6) *Carrying out the development*

Where the authority do not require prior approval, the development is lawful only if it is carried out in accordance with the details provided to the local planning authority (Class A.2(2)(v)), and it must be carried out within five years from the date the details were provided (though see further below).

Where the authority do determine to exercise their power of approval, the permission under Class A assumes the character of an outline planning permission. Although the right to carry out the development is granted in principle, it is subject to the authority's approval of the siting, design and external construction of the building (or the siting and means of construction of the private way, or the siting of the excavation or deposit and appearance of the tank, as the case may be). The authority have no power to refuse approval on other grounds, such as a general objection to the carrying out of fish farming on the agricultural unit concerned. Nor does the Order confer power to impose conditions on approval: it is a power merely to approve or not approve the details submitted by the applicant.

Class B rights (units of between 0·4 and 5 hectares): physical limitations on development

Class B rights are confined to agricultural units between one and five hectares in area, and the parcel on which the development is to be undertaken must be at least 0.4 hectares. The rights conferred are:

(1) *Extension or alteration of agricultural buildings*

On the face of it, there is no permission under Class B to construct any building, merely to extend or alter an existing building (other than a dwelling: Class B.2(d)). However, by virtue of Class D.5, any building erected in the curtilage of an existing building is to be treated as an extension of that building and not as an original building. Hence the permission might be taken to authorise separate buildings in the curtilage of existing buildings, but that would be difficult to reconcile with the conditions below. The Class B permission is exercisable only if:

(a) the building's external appearance would not be materially altered (Class B.1(b)).

(b) the building is not used, or to be used, for the accommodation of livestock (which includes farmed fish or shellfish: Class D.1), or the storage of slurry or sewage sludge where the building is within 400 metres of a protected building.

(c) the height of the building would not be increased, nor its cubic capacity increased by more than 10 per cent, nor its dimensions increased to exceed 30 metres. Where two or more buildings within the same curtilage are used for the same undertaking they are to be treated as a single original building in making any measurement in connection with the extension or alteration of either of them (Class D.5(b)). The effect of this provision depends on whether the "undertaking" is the agricultural use of the unit as a whole, or the particular activity carried out in the building (*e.g.* storage of grain, maintenance of machinery, or keeping of livestock). The latter would seem to be indicated, since the lawful use of any agricultural buildings on the unit would normally have to be as part of the agricultural unit as a whole.

(d) the area of the building would not be increased to exceed 465 square metres, including aggregation with other buildings or works provided in the previous two years and within 90 metres (Class D.2); and subject to the aggregation of the floorspace of buildings in the same curtilage used for the same undertaking (see (c) above).

(e) any part of the development would be within five metres of the boundary of the unit: this requirement does not appear in Class A development, where the local planning authority is in any event able to exert control over the siting of, and significant extensions and alterations to, buildings. It reflects the prospect that, on the smaller units to which Class B rights extend, development up to unit boundaries is more likely.

(f) on article 1(6) land (land in or adjoining national parks) this right is subject to prior notification to the local planning authority, under the same regime as applies to all land under Class A (Class B.6).

(g) the building which is extended or altered is subject to a condition that it may not be used for the accommodation of livestock except in the circumstances in Class D.3, nor for the storage of slurry or sewage sludge (Class B.5).

(2) *Installation of additional or replacement plant and machinery*

This right is subject to height limits (12 metres, or three metres if within three kilometres of the perimeter of an aerodrome; but in any event no higher than the plant or machinery being replaced), and to a restriction on area covered (465 square metres, but aggregated with other development carried out in the preceding two years, under Class D.2).

(3) *Deposit of waste*

This right is confined to waste materials generated from the agricultural unit itself, and is subject to the condition that the height of the surface of the land should not be materially increased by the deposit. Waste materials may only be brought onto the land from elsewhere if they are for use in other permitted development, and are incorporated forthwith into those buildings or works (Class B.7).

Class C: winning and working of minerals

The minerals permission is limited to any minerals reasonably necessary for agricultural purposes within the agricultural unit, although this is broadly defined in Class D.6 to include fertilising land for the purposes of agriculture, and the maintenance, improvement or alteration of any buildings, structures or works occupied or used for agricultural purposes on agricultural land.

No mineral may be exported from the land from which it was extracted, except to land which is held or occupied with that land and used for agricultural purposes. The scope of this restriction is unclear, but it may be intended to embrace the relevant agriculture unit (defined in Class A.3(2) as agricultural land occupied as a unit for the purposes of agriculture) except for any non-agricultural components, such as a dwellinghouse.

Fish farming

Specific controls over fish farming were introduced in 1986 to forestall any possible abuse of permitted development rights by farmers using fish farming as a backdoor method of being able to extract minerals without express consent. They were formerly in Class C, which achieved this end by restricting rights to registered businesses of fish farming or shellfish farming, by restricting the "site" within which the operations would be carried out (although it was unclear whether this meant the particular parcel of land, or the area over which the operations were spread) and by restricting the depth and area of excavations permitted, on the basis of a rolling two-year allocation.

However, under the 1992 amendments fish farming is dealt with in Classes A and B, and no separate Class is allocated to it. Excavations for fish farming are permitted under Class A, but Class B rights are restricted to associated works. There is no longer a restriction to registered businesses.

Highways

By virtue of art. 3(6), the permission granted by this Part does not authorise any development which requires or involves the formation, laying out or material widening of a means for access to an existing highway which is a trunk or classified road, or creates an obstruction to the view of persons using any highway used by vehicular traffic, so as to be likely to cause danger to such persons. This prohibition is in addition to the limitation under Class A.1(g), that no development permitted in Class A should be within 25 metres of the metalled portion of a trunk or classified road (see above). But where the relevant road is not a trunk or classified road, neither restriction applies, and instead permission is granted by Pt. 2, Class B for the formation, laying out and construction of a means of access where it is required in connection with development permitted by the Order.

Powers of financial assistance

DOE Circular 9/95, *General Development Order Consolidation 1995*, para. 56, notes that National Park Authorities have powers under section 44 of the Wildlife and Countryside Act 1981 to give grants for purposes conducive to the conservation and enhancement of the natural beauty of the Parks, and advises that:

> "In general, such authorities should use their powers under Part 6 to influence and regulate the appearance of developments within the scope of that Part without the incentive of grant aid. Exceptionally, however, National Park Authorities may, when exercising their powers in accordance with section 44, consider that circumstances warrant their offering some measure of financial assistance to ensure that developers are not put to unreasonable extra expense in meeting planning requirements."

PART 7

FORESTRY BUILDINGS AND OPERATIONS

Class A

Permitted development

A. The carrying out on land used for the purposes of forestry, including afforestation, of development reasonably necessary for those purposes consisting of—

- **(a) works for the erection, extension or alteration of a building;**
- **(b) the formation, alteration or maintenance of private ways;**
- **(c) operations on that land, or on land held or occupied with that land, to obtain the materials required for the formation, alteration or maintenance of such ways;**
- **(d) other operations (not including engineering or mining operations).**

Development not permitted

A.1 Development is not permitted by Class A if—

- **(a) it would consist of or include the provision or alteration of a dwelling;**
- **(b) the height of any building or works within 3 kilometres of the perimeter of an aerodrome would exceed 3 metres in height; or**
- **(c) any part of the development would be within 25 metres of the metalled portion of a trunk road or classified road.**

A.2(1) Subject to paragraph (3), development consisting of the erection of a building or the extension or alteration of a building or the formation or alteration of a private way is permitted by Class A subject to the following conditions—

- **(a) the developer shall, before beginning the development, apply to the local planning authority for a determination as to whether the prior approval of the authority will be required to the siting, design and external appearance of the building or, as the case may be, the siting and means of construction of the private way;**
- **(b) the application shall be accompanied by a written description of the proposed development, the materials to be used and a plan indicating the site together with any fee required to be paid;**
- **(c) the development shall not be begun before the occurrence of one of the following—**
  - **(i) the receipt by the applicant from the local planning authority of a written notice of their determination that such prior approval is not required;**
  - **(ii) where the local planning authority give the applicant notice within 28 days following the date of receiving his application of their determination that such prior approval is required, the giving of such approval;**
  - **(iii) the expiry of 28 days following the date on which the application was received by the local planning authority without the local planning authority making any determination as to whether such approval is required or notifying the applicant of their determination;**
- **(d) (i) where the local planning authority give the applicant notice that such prior approval is required the applicant shall display a site notice by site display on or near the**

land on which the proposed development is to be carried out, leaving the notice in position for not less than 21 days in the period of 28 days from the date on which the local planning authority gave the notice to the applicant;

(ii) where the site notice is, without any fault or intention of the applicant, removed, obscured or defaced before the period of 21 days referred to in sub-paragraph (i) has elapsed, he shall be treated as having complied with the requirements of that sub-paragraph if he has taken reasonable steps for protection of the notice and, if need be, its replacement;

(e) the development shall, except to the extent that the local planning authority otherwise agree in writing, be carried out—

(i) where prior approval is required, in accordance with the details approved;

(ii) where prior approval is not required, in accordance with the details submitted with the application;

(f) the development shall be carried out—

(i) where approval has been given by the local planning authority within a period of five years from the date on which approval was given,

(ii) in any other case, within a period of five years from the date on which the local planning authority were given the information referred to in sub-paragraph (b).

(2) In the case of development consisting of the significant extension or the significant alteration of the building such development may be carried out only once.

(3) Paragraph (1) does not preclude the extension or alteration of a building if the building is not on article 1(6) land except in the case of a significant extension or a significant alteration.

Interpretation of Class A

A.3 For the purposes of Class A—

"significant extension" and "significant alteration" mean any extension or alteration of the building where the cubic content of the original building would be exceeded by more than 10% or the height of the building as extended or altered would exceed the height of the original building; and

"site notice" means a notice containing—

(a) the name of the applicant,

(b) the address or location of the proposed development,

(c) a description of the proposed development and of the materials to be used,

(d) a statement that the prior approval of the authority will be required to the siting, design and external appearance of the building or, as the case may be, the siting and means of construction of the private way,

(e) the name and address of the local planning authority,

and which is signed and dated by or on behalf of the applicant.

COMMENTARY

DERIVATION

Town and Country Planning General Development Order 1988 (S.I. 1988 No. 1813), Sched. 2, Pt. 7, as amended by S.I. 1991 No. 2268 and S.I. 1991 No. 2805.

DEFINITIONS

"article 1(6) land": art. 1(6) and Sched. 1, Pt. 3.
"building": art. 1(2).

"classified road": art. 1(2).
"development": 1990 Act, s.55.
"height": art. 1(3).
"land": 1990 Act, s.336(1).
"local planning authority": 1990 Act, s.1.
"mining operations": art. 1(2).
"private ways": art. 1(2).
"significant alteration", "significant extension": Class A.3.
"site notice": Class A.3.
"trunk road": art. 1(2).

GENERAL NOTE

This Part grants a permission for forestry development parallel to that for agricultural development under Pt. 6. By virtue of the 1990 Act, s.55(2)(e), the use of any land for the purposes of forestry, including afforestation, and the use for any of those purposes of any buildings occupied together with the land, does not involve development at all. But forestry is not an agricultural activity for the purposes of the 1990 Act, s.336(1) (except for ancillary woodlands use), and hence there is no overlap between this Part and Part 6.

A developer may carry out operations to obtain the materials required for the formation, maintenance or alteration of any private way. This may presumably involve extraction of minerals for the purpose, but there is no general right for minerals extraction under this Part and mining operations are expressly excluded from the "other operations" permitted by para. (d).

The 1992 amendments introduced a general requirement of prior notification to the local planning authority before exercising permitted development rights under this Part, except for extensions and alterations to buildings that are not "significant" as defined in Class A.3; and works not materially affecting a building's external appearance continue to enjoy the exemption from planning control conferred by the principal Act, s.55(2)(a). The prior notification requirement was previously confined to "Article 1(6) land" (*i.e.* land within or adjoining National Parks, as defined in Sched. 1 to the Order).

For a discussion of the scope and operation of the prior notification requirement, see the Commentary to Part 6.

Dwellings and caravans

Dwellinghouses are expressly excluded from this Part, and the Secretary of State has taken the view that a building capable of providing overnight accommodation may be sufficiently in the nature of a dwelling, rather than a shelter, to exclude it (appeal decision at [1971] J.P.L. 598). Permission is however granted by Pt. 5 for the use of forestry land as a caravan site for seasonal occupation by forestry workers (under the Caravan Sites and Control of Development Act 1960, Sched. 1, para. 8).

Highways

By virtue of art. 3(6), the permission granted by this Part does not authorise any development which requires or involves the formation, laying out or material widening of a means of access to an existing highway which is a trunk or classified road, or creates an obstruction to the view of persons using any highway used by vehicular traffic, so as to be likely to cause danger to such persons. This prohibition is in addition to the limitation under Class A.1(c) that no development permitted in Class A should be within 25 metres of the metalled portion of a trunk or classified road.

Powers of financial assistance

DOE Circular 9/95, *General Development Order Consolidation 1995*, para. 56, notes in connection with Pt. 7 (see para. 58) that National Park Authorities have powers under section 44 of the Wildlife and Countryside Act 1981 to give grants for purposes conducive to the conservation and enhancement of the natural beauty of the Parks, and advises that:

> "In general, such authorities should use their powers under Part 6 to influence and regulate the appearance of developments within the scope of that Part without the incentive of grant aid. Exceptionally, however, National Park Authorities may, when exercising their powers in accordance with section 44, consider that circumstances warrant their offering some measure of financial assistance to ensure that developers are not put to unreasonable extra expense in meeting planning requirements."

PART 8

INDUSTRIAL AND WAREHOUSE DEVELOPMENT

Class A

Permitted development — **A. The extension or alteration of an industrial building or a warehouse.**

Development not permitted

A.1 Development is not permitted by Class A if—

(a) the building as extended or altered is to be used for purposes other than those of the undertaking concerned;

(b) the building is to be used for a purpose other than—

(i) in the case of an industrial building, the carrying out of an industrial process or the provision of employee facilities;

(ii) in the case of a warehouse, storage or distribution or the provision of employee facilities;

(c) the height of the building as extended or altered would exceed the height of the original building;

(d) the cubic content of the original building would be exceeded by more than—

(i) 10%, in respect of development on any article 1(5) land, or

(ii) 25%, in any other case;

(e) the floor space of the original building would be exceeded by more than—

(i) 500 square metres in respect of development on any article 1(5) land, or

(ii) 1,000 square metres in any other case;

(f) the external appearance of the premises of the undertaking concerned would be materially affected;

(g) any part of the development would be carried out within 5 metres of any boundary of the curtilage of the premises; or

(h) the development would lead to a reduction in the space available for the parking or turning of vehicles.

Conditions

A.2 Development is permitted by Class A subject to the conditions that any building extended or altered—

(a) shall only be used—

(i) in the case of an industrial building, for the carrying out of an industrial process for the purposes of the undertaking or the provision of employee facilities;

(ii) in the case of a warehouse, for storage or distribution for the purposes of the undertaking or the provision of employee facilities;

(b) shall not be used to provide employee facilities between 7.00 p.m. and 6.30 a.m. for employees other than those present at the premises of the undertaking for the purpose of their employment;

(c) shall not be used to provide employee facilities if a notifiable quantity of a hazardous substance is present at the premises of the undertaking.

Interpretation of Class A

A.3 For the purposes of Class A—

(a) the erection of any additional building within the curtilage of another building (whether by virtue of Class A or otherwise) and used in connection with it is to be treated as the extension

of that building, and the additional building is not to be treated as an original building;

(b) where two or more original buildings are within the same curtilage and are used for the same undertaking, they are to be treated as a single original building in making any measurement;

(c) "employee facilities" means social, care or recreational facilities provided for employees of the undertaking, including creche facilities provided for the children of such employees.

Class B

Permitted development

B. Development carried out on industrial land for the purposes of an industrial process consisting of—

(a) the installation of additional or replacement plant or machinery,

(b) the provision, rearrangement or replacement of a sewer, main, pipe, cable or other apparatus, or

(c) the provision, rearrangement or replacement of a private way, private railway, siding or conveyor.

Development not permitted

B.1 Development described in Class B(a) is not permitted if—

(a) it would materially affect the external appearance of the premises of the undertaking concerned, or

(b) any plant or machinery would exceed a height of 15 metres above ground level or the height of anything replaced, whichever is the greater.

Interpretation of Class B

B.2 In Class B, "industrial land" means land used for the carrying out of an industrial process, including land used for the purposes of an industrial undertaking as a dock, harbour or quay, but does not include land in or adjacent to and occupied together with a mine.

Class C

Permitted development

C. The provision of a hard surface within the curtilage of an industrial building or warehouse to be used for the purpose of the undertaking concerned.

Class D

Permitted development

D. The deposit of waste material resulting from an industrial process on any land comprised in a site which was used for that purpose on 1st July 1948 whether or not the superficial area or the height of the deposit is extended as a result.

Development not permitted

D.1 Development is not permitted by Class D if—

(a) the waste material is or includes material resulting from the winning and working of minerals, or

(b) the use on 1st July 1948 was for the deposit of material resulting from the winning and working of minerals.

Interpretation of Part 8

E. For the purposes of Part 8, in Classes A and C—

"industrial building" means a building used for the carrying out of an industrial process and includes a building used for the carrying out of such a process on land used as a dock, harbour or quay for the purposes of an industrial undertaking but does not include a building on land in or adjacent to and occupied together with a mine; and

"warehouse" means a building used for any purpose within Class B8 (storage or distribution) of the Schedule to the Use Classes Order but does not include a building on land in or adjacent to and occupied together with a mine.

COMMENTARY

Derivation

Town and Country Planning General Development Order 1988 (S.I. 1988 No. 1813), Sched. 2, Pt. 8 as amended by S.I. 1991 No. 1536.

Definitions

"article 1(5) land": art. 1(5) and Sched. 1, Pt. 1.
"building": art. 1(2).
"development": 1990 Act, s.55.
"height": art. 1(3).
"industrial building": Class E.
"industrial land": Class B.2.
"industrial process": art. 1(2).
"land": 1990 Act, s.336(1).
"private way": art. 1(2).
"warehouse": Class E.

General Note

Background to Part 8

Permitted development rights under this Part were substantially recast in the 1988 Order. The rights were previously limited to "industrial undertakers," who were persons undertaking an "industrial process." Since 1988 the rights have attached instead to the use—industrial building or warehouse (Class A), industrial land use for an industrial purpose (Class B)—rather than the person carrying on the use. An industrial building is one used for an industrial process (Class E) which is (art. 1(2)):

"... a process for or incidental to any of the following purposes:
(a) the making of any article or part of any article (including a ship or vessel, or a film, video or sound recording);
(b) the altering, repairing, maintaining, ornamenting, finishing, cleaning, washing, packing, canning, adapting for sale, breaking up or demolition of any article; or
(c) the getting, dressing or treatment of minerals in the course of any trade or business other than agriculture, and other than a process carried out on land used as a mine or adjacent to and occupied together with a mine."

Permitted development rights for warehouses were introduced in 1985 (S.I. 1985 No. 1981). "Warehouse" is defined (Class E) as meaning "a building used for any purpose within Class B8 (storage or distribution) of the Schedule to the Use Classes Order" but excluding buildings at mines; and Class B8 itself specifies "use for storage or as a distribution centre."

There are four substantive classes: extension or alteration of buildings; incidental development on industrial land; creation of a hard surface and deposit of waste material.

Class A: Extension or alteration of buildings

This class extends to industrial buildings and warehouses, which were formerly in separate classes. It is limited to alteration and extension: there are no rights to provide new buildings in the curtilage, apart from the rights in

Class B to install plant and machinery, and any building provided pursuant to a planning permission is to be treated as an extension for the purpose of calculating the cubic capacity tolerances.

The limitations in Class A.1 relate to:

(1) *the developer's intention*: it must be intended, first, that the building will be used for the purposes of the undertaking (including, following the 1991 amendments, the provision of employee facilities), that is, for the developer's own purposes and not for occupation by others. But that limitation does not govern after-use, and in particular does not restrict rights under the Use Classes Order and Pt. 3 of Sched. 2 to this Order to switch between warehouse and industrial use, and to switch from a building within this Class to a use within Class B.1 (business class) of the Use Classes Order. Second, it must be intended that the building as extended or altered should be used only for an industrial process, or, in the case of a warehouse, for storage or distribution. That does not mean that an industrial process must actually be carried on in the extension: the important consideration is the primary use of the planning unit as a whole, which will normally be the whole unit of occupation. Thus a factory extension may be constructed in reliance upon this Part to be used solely for office use, or retail use, for example, provided the use is incidental to the primary industrial use of the premises.

(2) *height and cubic content*: the provisions parallel those for dwelling-house extensions under Pt. 1, including the special limitation for the sensitive areas defined in Sched. 1 (article 1(5) land). Cubic capacity tolerances are to be calculated against the "original building," which means (art. 1(2)), in relation to a building existing on July 1, 1948, as existing on that date; and, in relation to a building built on or after that date as so built. In particular, any additional building within the curtilage of another building and used in connection with it must be treated as an extension (*i.e.* as having already consumed permitted development rights) and not as part of the original building (*i.e.* not able to be aggregated for the purpose of calculating the 10 per cent. or 25 per cent. tolerance). An exception arises where there are two or more "original buildings" within the same curtilage and used for the same undertaking. In that case, the buildings are to be aggregated in making the necessary calculations. The only case in which this would arise would seem to be where the buildings all existed before 1948, or all were built contemporaneously or, perhaps, under the same planning permission. A building erected subsequently in the curtilage of another building is not otherwise to be treated as an "original building": Class A.2(1)(a).

The requirement that the external appearance of the "premises" of the undertaking should not be materially affected clearly extends further than merely the building which is being altered or extended, but the test is highly subjective: for an approach to interpretation, see the appeal decisions reported at [1983] J.P.L. 557 and [1987] J.P.L. 656.

(3) *the boundary of the curtilage*: as to the meaning of "curtilage," see the General Note to Pt. 1. It is the curtilage of the "premises" of the undertaking which is relevant, not that of the building which is being altered or extended. In an appeal decision at [1987] J.P.L. 656, the Secretary of State overruled his inspector's decision that where a building had no defined curtilage of its own and all occupiers shared service roads and common areas, then the relevant boundary was that of the industrial estate. The Secretary of State insisted that a service road could not be regarded as within the curtilage of the premises concerned.

(4) *car-parking*: prior to 1988 the requirement that car-parking and turning areas should not be reduced applied only to warehouses (Class XXVIII of the 1977 Order).

Class B: development on industrial land

This Class does not permit the construction of a building, but only the provision of industrial plant and machinery and certain apparatus and private railways and private ways. A private way is (art. 1(2)) "a highway not maintainable at the public expense and any other way other than a highway [sic]." A private conveyor may include a permanent gantry ([1971] J.P.L. 285).

The rights are exercisable only on industrial land, not in warehouse curtilages, and the expression is defined to include land used for an industrial process (see the definition in art. 1(2), set out above). Mining land is excluded (see further below), but industrial undertakings in docks, harbours and quays are expressly included. Thus this Class dovetails with the permitted development rights in those areas under Pt. 17, Class B, which are limited to development required for shipping and the movement of traffic.

Mining

Rights under Class B are not applicable to "land in or adjacent to and occupied together with a mine" (Class B.2), and a "warehouse" in Class A similarly does not include a building on land in or adjacent to and occupied together with a mine (see Class E). Instead, there are separate permitted development rights under Pt. 19, Class A.

But the present class is applicable where the process of "getting, dressing or treatment" of minerals is undertaken in the course of any trade or business other than agriculture, and other than at a mine (see the definition of "industrial process" in art. 1(2) set out above). Hence in *Welsh Aggregates v. Secretary of State for Wales* [1983] J.P.L. 50, C.A., it was held that the construction of a metalled road was incidental to the use of a quarry and thus within this Class, in that it would be quite impossible to work a limestone quarry unless there were a means of disposing of the limestone. It was submitted for the County that the work on the road-making had commenced before the actual work of quarrying, and hence there was no industrial process under way on the site to which it could have been incidental. This submission was rejected on the facts, the Court accepting that preliminary works at the quarry, such as removal of overburden and the clearing of the quarry floor, were essentially quarrying operations.

Class D: deposit of waste material resulting from an industrial process

Under Class D, development involving the deposit of waste material is permitted if it arises from an industrial process on any land comprised in a site which was used for that purpose prior to July 1, 1948. Development at a mine and the deposit of waste resulting from the winning and working of minerals is excluded. In *Kent County Council v. Secretary of State for the Environment* [1995] E.G.C.S. 130 the inspector had found that the depositing and processing of inert waste on the site had taken place since before 1945, and comprised principally contractor's waste from the demolition of walls and buildings and the breaking up of roads, driveways and paths. The County Council argued that it was nonetheless outside Class D, because the deposited material had not resulted from an industrial process. The court (Mr Nigel Macleod, Q.C., sitting as Deputy Judge) rejected this submission. It accepted that demolition was an industrial process for the purpose of the definition, as involving "the breaking up or demolition of any article", and that a building and its component parts were capable of amounting to an "article" for these purposes.

Highways

By virtue of art. 3(6), the permission granted by this Part does not authorise any development which requires or involves formation, laying out or material widening of a means of access to an existing highway which is a trunk or classified road, or creates an obstruction to the view of persons using any highway used by vehicular traffic, so as to be likely to cause danger to such persons.

PART 9

REPAIRS TO UNADOPTED STREETS AND PRIVATE WAYS

Class A

Permitted development	**A. The carrying out on land within the boundaries of an unadopted street or private way of works required for the maintenance or improvement of the street or way.**
Interpretation of Class A	**A.1 For the purposes of Class A—** **"unadopted street" means a street not being a highway maintainable at the public expense within the meaning of the Highways Act 1980.**

COMMENTARY

DERIVATION

Town and Country Planning General Development Order 1988 (S.I. 1988 No. 1813), Sched. 2, Pt. 9. The definition of "unadopted street" (Class A.1) has been shifted into this Part from art. 1(2).

DEFINITIONS

"land": 1990 Act, 2.336(1).
"private way": art. 1(2).
"unadopted street": art. 1(2).

GENERAL NOTE

Works by local highway authorities for maintenance and improvement of roads do not constitute development, by virtue of the 1990 Act, s.55(2)(b). This Part grants planning permission for such works, whoever undertakes them, in relation to unadopted streets and private ways, being in both cases ways or highways which are not maintainable at public expense (see the General Note to art. 1(2)).

The standard limitation on access to a highway under art. 3(6) does not extend to development under this Part.

PART 10

REPAIRS TO SERVICES

Class A

Permitted development	**The carrying out of any works for the purposes of inspecting, repairing or renewing any sewer, main, pipe, cable or other apparatus, including breaking open any land for that purpose.**

COMMENTARY

Derivation

Town and Country Planning General Development Order 1988 (S.I. 1988 No. 1813), Sched. 2, Pt. 10 (unamended).

Definitions

"land": 1990 Act, s.336(1).

General Note

Works for the purposes prescribed in this Part do not require planning permission if undertaken by local authorities and statutory undertakers, by virtue of the 1990 Act s.55(2)(c). This Part grants planning permission for cases where the works are to be carried out by others. For a detailed analysis, see the planning appeal reported at (1995) 10 P.A.D. 651, where the view was taken that this Part extended to the carrying out of works to drains and drainage channels, including works to clear and unblock a drain.

PART 11

DEVELOPMENT UNDER LOCAL OR PRIVATE ACTS OR ORDERS

Class A

Permitted development

A. Development authorised by—

(a) a local or private Act of Parliament,

(b) an order approved by both Houses of Parliament, or

(c) an order under section 14 or 16 of the Harbours Act 1964 (orders for securing harbour efficiency etc., and orders conferring powers for improvement, construction etc. of harbours)

which designates specifically the nature of the development authorised and the land upon which it may be carried out.

Condition

A.1 Development is not permitted by Class A if it consists of or includes—

(a) the erection, construction, alteration or extension of any building, bridge, aqueduct, pier or dam, or

(b) the formation, laying out or alteration of a means of access to any highway used by vehicular traffic,

unless the prior approval of the appropriate authority to the detailed plans and specifications is first obtained.

Prior approvals

A.2 The prior approval referred to in paragraph A.1 is not to be refused by the appropriate authority nor are conditions to be imposed unless they are satisfied that—

(a) the development (other than the provision of or works carried out to a dam) ought to be and could reasonably be carried out elsewhere on the land; or

(b) the design or external appearance of any building, bridge, aqueduct, pier or dam would injure the amenity of the neighbourhood and is reasonably capable of modification to avoid such injury.

Interpretation of Class A

A.3 In Class A, "appropriate authority" means—

(a) in Greater London or a metropolitan county, the local planning authority,

(b) in a National Park, outside a metropolitan county, the county planning authority,

(c) in any other case, the district planning authority.

COMMENTARY

DERIVATION

Town and Country Planning General Development Order 1988 (S.I. 1988 No. 1813), Sched. 2, Pt. 11 (unamended).

DEFINITIONS

"aqueduct": art. 1(2).
"appropriate authority": Class A.3.

"development": 1990 Act, s.55.
"land": 1990 Act, s.336.

General Note

This Part grants planning consent for development specifically authorised by a local or private Act of Parliament, or by certain Parliamentary Orders. Once it is established that a private or local Act does specifically authorise the development, the Act may need to be carefully construed to determine what development is actually authorised by it and how far ordinary planning control is thereby excluded (see, *e.g. Pyx Granite Co. v. Ministry of Housing and Local Government* [1960] A.C. 260 (quarrying operations under the Malvern Hills Act 1924)).

The permission resembles an outline permission, in that it does not authorise any building works, or means of access, without the prior approval of the local planning authority (county planning authority in a National Park outside a metropolitan county). But the grounds upon which that prior approval may be refused are limited to the location of the development on the site (where it ought to be and can reasonably be carried out elsewhere on the land) and its appearance (if it would injure the amenity of the neighbourhood and is reasonably capable of modification to avoid such injury). By virtue of art. 3(7), no development is to be treated as authorised under this Part unless or until the consent or approval is obtained (except in the case of a post-1948 Act making express provision to the contrary).

There is no condition requiring commencement of the development within any prescribed time, but it is now customary for a 10 year commencement requirement to be imposed by the private Act itself. Moreover, a private Act may grant a wider planning permission than that envisaged by this Part, and exclude the planning authority's approval powers wholly or in part, if the promoters can persuade Parliament that such a course is desirable.

The standard exception in art. 3(6) restricting development which requires or involves a means of access to a highway does not extend to development under this Part.

Private Bill procedure

> "Private legislation is legislation of a special kind for conferring particular powers or benefit on any person or body of persons... in excess of or in conflict with the general law" (*Erskine May*, p. 891)

At one time, private Bills seeking authority to the construction of works formed the major part of Parliamentary business. The *Report of the Joint Committee on Private Bill Procedure* (Session 1987–88; H.L. Paper 97, H.C. 625) para. 21 observed that:

> "Parliamentary approval was necessary because the works would interfere with private rights: they might, for example, require that land should be acquired compulsorily, or interfere with existing private rights of way, or of navigation; and without parliamentary approval they could not proceed."

But much has changed. Power has shifted from Parliament to the executive, and many of the objectives of the old Bills are now attainable through procedures which require ministerial, rather than Parliamentary, approval. Thus, the present use of private Bills is restricted to a somewhat anomalous assortment of cases where power has not been transferred out of Parliament. The most significant of these until recently was railway works. British Rail was for many years the biggest user of private Bills, and statutory authorisation gave it the ability to modify earlier enactments under which the existing railway network was constructed, to obtain immunity from private nuisance actions and to interfere with private rights for which no other authorisation was available (particularly for public highways, bridleways and footpaths, and navigable waters).

The Joint Committee was set up following widespread concern within and outside Parliament that the private Bill system might be open to abuse, and that promoters might be tempted to resort to it as a speedier route to planning permission than the usual public local inquiry. It was suggested that promoters might be tempted to bring into a major project some comparatively minor element, such as rail works, which would allow them to seek Parliamentary approval to the whole. The Committee considered, but rejected, the arguments for the repeal altogether of the corresponding Part of the 1977 G.D.O. and proceeded to recommend instead fundamental changes in the function of private legislation, principally:

(1) in principle, in cases where planning considerations are dominant, all works proposals for which private Bill approval is presently required should instead be authorised through non-parliamentary procedures involving the holding, if necessary, of a public local inquiry into objections;

(2) there should be an entirely new system of extra-parliamentary approval for rail works;

(3) in any remaining cases still requiring to go to Parliament, promoters should be required to prove that private legislation was necessary to secure the primary purpose of the Bill. If its primary purpose was to obtain planning permission, then the promoter should be required to obtain that in the usual way before going to Parliament. Private Bills were not, in the opinion of the Committee, an appropriate system for authorising works of purely local significance.

Those recommendations were accepted by the Government with some modifications (*Private Bills and New Procedures*, Cm. 1110 (1990)) and carried into effect by the Transport and Works Act 1992. An order made under that Act may include a grant of planning permission for the works, which has effect under s.90 of the 1990 Act.

Orders approved by both Houses of Parliament

This heading appears to include actions which require special parliamentary procedure (other than harbour revision orders which are specified separately), which are dealt with by Orders made under the Statutory Orders (Special Procedure) Act 1945 (*e.g.* taking of open space for development without supplying equally advantageous replacement land, under s.229 of the 1990 Act). Standing Orders of the House of Commons (*Private Business* 1984–85 H.C. 130; SO239A), anticipate that such an order may relate to the carrying out of works. A special procedure order must be submitted to Parliament, and if petitioned against must be referred to a joint committee of both Houses. It is not approved by formal resolution of both Houses: instead, if it is approved and reported by the joint committee without amendment, it takes effect on the date of the laying of the report unless a later date is specified in the instrument (s.6(1)). If amended, it then takes effect from a date set by the Minister, and if rejected, the order may not take effect unless confirmed by a public Act of Parliament.

A special development order, made under s.58 of the 1990 Act on a site-specific basis and with reference to a particular development proposal, would *prima facie* fall within this Part. But reliance on the permission conferred by this Part is in such a case unnecessary, because the special development order constitutes a grant of planning permission in its own right; and it may expressly exclude any provisions of this Order (see art. 2(1)).

Order under the Harbours Act 1964

A harbour revision order made under s.14 or s.16 of the Harbours Act 1964 may authorise the construction of works, where the Secretary of State is satisfied that the making of the order is desirable in the interests of securing the improvement, maintenance or management of the harbour in an efficient and economic manner. Such an order is first scrutinised informally in draft by the Department of Transport, and then formally published by the promoting Harbour Authority and advertised for six weeks. If objections are made which cannot be resolved, a public local inquiry must be held, and a report made to and considered by the Secretary of State for Transport. If objections are still maintained, the order becomes subject to special Parliamentary procedure. Harbour authorities (and prospective harbour authorities) are, uniquely, empowered to resort alternatively to private Bill procedure, and in view of possible delays under the procedure outlined above, many prefer to do so. They may have to do so if they seek powers going beyond those allowed in a harbour revision order; see further the *Memorandum* of the Leader of the House of Commons, Annex B, *Report of the Joint Committee on Private Bill Procedure* (1988) p. 174.

Planning permission granted by public Act

Planning permission may also be granted by a public general Act of Parliament, such as where the Government has promoted a hybrid Bill in relation to some major development project. The permission under this Part does not extend to projects authorised by public Acts, but such an Act may incorporate it by reference. Thus the Channel Tunnel Act 1987, s.9, itself granted planning permission for all authorised development by the Tunnel Concessionaires, and that development was required to be treated as not being development of a class for which planning permission was granted by the 1977 Order. It also granted planning permission for British Rail development and applied to it the provisions of the 1977 Order as if the development were authorised by a private Act.

Article 4 directions

So far as it relates to development authorised by an Act passed after July 1, 1948 (the commencement date of the Town and Country Planning Act 1947), or by an order approved by both Houses after that date, this permission cannot be withdrawn by an article 4 direction (art. 4(3)(a)). Harbour revision orders are not, however, excluded from art. 4.

Statutory undertakers and operational land

Where land has planning permission under this Part, and an interest is held in it by statutory undertakers for the purposes of their undertaking then it is operational land under the Act of 1990, s.262.

PART 12

DEVELOPMENT BY LOCAL AUTHORITIES

Class A

Permitted development	**A. The erection or construction and the maintenance, improvement or other alteration by a local authority or by an urban development corporation of—** **(a) any small ancillary building, works or equipment on land belonging to or maintained by them required for the purposes of any function exercised by them on that land otherwise than as statutory undertakers;** **(b) lamp standards, information kiosks, passenger shelters, public shelters and seats, telephone boxes, fire alarms, public drinking fountains, horse troughs, refuse bins or baskets, barriers for the control of people waiting to enter public service vehicles, and similar structures or works required in connection with the operation of any public service administered by them.**
Interpretation of Class A	**A.1 For the purposes of Class A—** **"urban development corporation" has the same meaning as in Part XVI of the Local Government, Planning and Land Act 1980 (urban development).** **A2. The reference in Class A to any small ancillary building, works or equipment is a reference to any ancillary building, works or equipment not exceeding 4 metres in height or 200 cubic metres in capacity.**

Class B

Permitted development	**B. The deposit by a local authority of waste material on any land comprised in a site which was used for that purpose on 1st July 1948 whether or not the superficial area or the height of the deposit is extended as a result.**
Development not permitted	**B.1 Development is not permitted by Class B if the waste material is or includes material resulting from the winning and working of minerals.**
Interpretation of Part 12	**C. For the purposes of Part 12—** **"local authority" includes a parish or community council.**

COMMENTARY

Derivation

Town and Country Planning General Development Order 1988 (S.I. 1988 No. 1813), Sched. 2, Pt. 12 (unamended except for the transfer from art. 1(2) of the definitions of "local authority" and "urban development corporation").

Definitions

"building": art. 1(2).
"land": 1990 Act, s.336(1).

"local authority": Class C.
"small ancillary buildings": Class A.2.
"statutory undertaker": 1990 Act, s.262.
"urban development corporation": Class A.1.

GENERAL NOTE

Class A: small ancillary buildings and facilities

Any ancillary building erected under this permission must not only be within the size and height limitations of para. A.1 (which were introduced by the 1988 Order), but also be required for any function exercised by the local authority on the land. Where the local authority hold the land as a statutory undertaker, this permission is excluded and the local authority may rely instead on the special rights under Pt. 17.

Other special local authority rights include:

(1) local highway authorities: road maintenance or improvement (1990 Act, s.55(2)(a)) does not constitute development, and permission is granted for incidental works on adjoining land (Pt. 13 of this Order);
(2) works for inspection, repair or renewal of sewers, mains, pipes, cables or other apparatus, including breaking open any street or other land for the purpose does not constitute development (1990 Act, s.55(2)(c)). Permission is in any event granted by Pt. 10 for these purposes, and is not limited to local authorities.

Class B: waste disposal

The deposit of refuse or waste material on land is deemed by the 1990 Act, s.55(3)(b) to involve a material change in the use of land. This is so, even where there are existing use rights, if the area or height of the deposit is extended. The method prescribed for calculation of height in art. 1(3) is limited to buildings, and hence is inapplicable to this Part.

This Class therefore grants permission to local authorities to continue to deposit waste on pre-1948 sites. It does not (unlike the 1990 Act) expressly include refuse, but the Order ventures no definition of "waste" and it may be that it is intended to include refuse (see further the discussion in relation to rights under Pt. 6 above). Mineral waste is excluded pursuant to a recommendation by the Stevens Committee in its Report, *Planning Control over Mineral Working* (HMSO, 1976), but see Pt. 21 as to waste tipping at mines.

PART 13

DEVELOPMENT BY LOCAL HIGHWAY AUTHORITIES

Class A

Permitted development — **A. The carrying out by a local highway authority on land outside but adjoining the boundary of an existing highway of works required for or incidental to the maintenance or improvement of the highway.**

COMMENTARY

DERIVATION

Town and Country Planning General Development Order 1988 (S.I. 1988 No. 1813), Sched. 2, Pt. 13 (unamended).

DEFINITIONS

"highway": 1990 Act, s.336(1).
"land": 1990 Act, s.336(1).
"local highway authority": 1990 Act, s.336(1).

GENERAL NOTE

This permission is complementary to the 1990 Act, s.55(2)(a), which provides that highway authority improvement and maintenance works do not constitute development if they are carried out on land within the boundaries of the road. This Part confers permission for necessary or incidental works outside but adjoining the road boundaries.

The standard limitation on access to a highway under art. 3(6) does not extend to development under this Part.

PART 14

DEVELOPMENT BY DRAINAGE BODIES

Class A

Permitted development

A. Development by a drainage body in, on or under any watercourse or land drainage works and required in connection with the improvement, maintenance or repair of that watercourse or those works.

Interpretation of Class A

A.1 For the purposes of Class A—
"drainage body" has the same meaning as in section 72(1) of the Land Drainage Act 1991 (interpretation) other than the [Environment Agency].

COMMENTARY

Derivation

Town and Country Planning General Development Order 1988 (S.I. 1988 No. 1813), Sched. 2, Pt. 14 (unamended apart from the updated reference to the Land Drainage Act 1991).

Definitions

"development": 1990 Act, s.336(1).
"drainage body": Class A.1.
"land drainage": art. 1(2).

General Note

This Part confers limited development rights on drainage bodies in connection with improvement, maintenance or repair of a watercourse or land drainage works. For the definition of "land drainage," see the General Note to art. 2.

The [Environment Agency] has separate permitted development rights for this type of development under Pt. 15, Class A(b).

"Drainage body" is defined by the Land Drainage Act 1991, s.72(1), as follows:

> "drainage body" means the [Environment Agency], an internal drainage board or any other body having power to make or maintain works for the drainage of land.

PART 15

DEVELOPMENT BY THE NATIONAL RIVERS AUTHORITY

Class A

Permitted development

A. Development by the [Environment Agency], for the purposes of their functions, consisting of—

(a) development not above ground level required in connection with conserving, redistributing or augmenting water resources,

(b) development in, on or under any watercourse or land drainage works and required in connection with the improvement, maintenance or repair of that watercourse or those works,

(c) the provision of a building, plant, machinery or apparatus in, on, over or under land for the purpose of survey or investigation,

(d) the maintenance, improvement or repair of works for measuring the flow in any watercourse or channel,

(e) any works authorised by or required in connection with an order made under section 73 of the Water Resources Act 1991 (power to make ordinary and emergency drought orders),

(f) any other development in, on, over or under their operational land, other than the provision of a building but including the extension or alteration of a building.

Development not permitted

A.1 Development is not permitted by Class A if—

(a) in the case of any Class A(a) development, it would include the construction of a reservoir,

(b) in the case of any class A(f) development, it would consist of or include the extension or alteration of a building so that—

(i) its design or external appearance would be materially affected,

(ii) the height of the original building would be exceeded, or the cubic content of the original building would be exceeded by more than 25%, or

(iii) the floor space of the original building would be exceeded by more than 1,000 square metres,

or

(c) in the case of any Class A(f) development, it would consist of the installation or erection of any plant or machinery exceeding 15 metres in height or the height of anything it replaces, whichever is the greater.

Condition

A.2 Development is permitted by Class A(c) subject to the condition that, on completion of the survey or investigation, or at the expiration of six months from the commencement of the development concerned, whichever is the sooner, all such operations shall cease and all such buildings, plant, machinery and apparatus shall be removed and the land restored as soon as reasonably practicable to its former condition (or to any other condition which may be agreed with the local planning authority).

COMMENTARY

DERIVATION

Town and Country Planning General Development Order 1988 (S.I. 1988 No. 1813), Sched. 2, Pt. 15, as amended by S.I. 1989 No. 1590.

DEFINITIONS

"building": art. 1(2).
"land": 1990 Act, s.336(1).
"operational land": 1990 Act, s.262.

GENERAL NOTE

This Part was considerably revised and updated in 1989 to extend the permitted development rights of the former water authorities, then newly transferred to the National Rivers Authority established by the Water Act 1989. It also now extends to development in connection with drought orders under the Water Resources Act 1991.

All functions of the National Rivers Authority were, from April 1, 1996, transferred to the Environment Agency (*Environment Act* 1995, section 3); and all references in subordinate legislation to the National Rivers Authority were amended to references to that Agency (*ibid.*, Sched. 22, para. 233).

Development rights under this Part are restricted to development carried by the Authority for their functions. The permission is not restricted to their operational land, except in the case of the general permission in Class A.(f) to carry out any development on operational land other than the provision of a building.

Permitted development rights are conferred upon sewerage undertakers by Pt. 16, and upon water undertakers by Pt. 17, Class E.

PART 16

DEVELOPMENT BY OR ON BEHALF OF SEWERAGE UNDERTAKERS

Class A

Permitted development

A. Development by or on behalf of a sewerage undertaker consisting of—

(a) development not above ground level required in connection with the provision, improvement, maintenance or repair of a sewer, outfall pipe, sludge main or associated apparatus;

(b) the provision of a building, plant, machinery or apparatus in, on, over or under land for the purpose of survey or investigation;

(c) the maintenance, improvement or repair of works for measuring the flow in any watercourse or channel;

(d) any works authorised by or required in connection with an order made under section 73 of the Water Resources Act 1991 (power to make ordinary and emergency drought orders);

(e) any other development in, on, over or under their operational land, other than the provision of a building but including the extension or alteration of a building.

Development not permitted

A.1 Development is not permitted by Class A(e) if—

(a) it would consist of or include the extension or alteration of a building so that—

(i) its design or external appearance would be materially affected;

(ii) the height of the original building would be exceeded, or the cubic content of the original building would be exceeded, by more than 25%; or

(iii) the floor space of the original building would be exceeded by more than 1,000 square metres;

or

(b) it would consist of the installation or erection of any plant or machinery exceeding 15 metres in height or the height of anything it replaces, whichever is the greater.

Condition

A.2 Development is permitted by Class A(b) subject to the condition that, on completion of the survey or investigation, or at the expiration of 6 months from the commencement of the development concerned, whichever is the sooner, all such operations shall cease and all such buildings, plant, machinery and apparatus shall be removed and the land restored as soon as reasonably practicable to its former condition (or to any other condition which may be agreed with the local planning authority).

Interpretation of Class A

A.3 For the purposes of Class A—

"associated apparatus", in relation to any sewer, main or pipe, means pumps, machinery or apparatus associated with the relevant sewer, main or pipe;

"sludge main" means a pipe or system of pipes (together with any pumps or other machinery or apparatus associated with it) for the conveyance of the residue of water or sewage treated in a water or sewage treatment works as the case may be, including final effluent or the products of the dewatering or incineration of such residue, or partly for any of those purposes and partly for the conveyance of trade effluent or its residue.

COMMENTARY

DERIVATION

Town and Country Planning General Development Order 1988 (S.I. 1988 No. 1813), Sched. 2, Pt. 16. The 1995 consolidation introduced Class A.3 (definitions).

DEFINITIONS

"associated apparatus": Class A.3.
"development": 1990 Act, s.55.
"sludge main": Class A.3.

GENERAL NOTE

This Part extends permitted development rights to development carried out by or on behalf of sewerage undertakers appointed under the Water Industry Act 1991. The following were appointed water and sewerage undertakers in 1989:

Anglian Water Services Ltd
Dwr Cymru Cyfyngedig
Northumbrian Water Ltd
North West Water Ltd
Severn Trent Water Ltd
Southern Water Services Ltd
South West Water Services Ltd
Thames Water Utilities Ltd
Wessex Water Services Ltd
Yorkshire Water Services Ltd

PART 17

DEVELOPMENT BY STATUTORY UNDERTAKERS

Class A Railway or light railway undertakings

Permitted development

A. Development by railway undertakers on their operational land, required in connection with the movement of traffic by rail.

Development not permitted

A.1 Development is not permitted by Class A if it consists of or includes —

(a) the construction of a railway,
(b) the construction or erection of a hotel, railway station or bridge, or
(c) the construction or erection otherwise than wholly within a railway station of—
(i) an office, residential or educational building, or a building used for an industrial process, or
(ii) a car park, shop, restaurant, garage, petrol filling station or other building or structure provided under transport legislation.

Interpretation of Class A

A.2 For the purposes of Class A, references to the construction or erection of any building or structure include references to the reconstruction or alteration of a building or structure where its design or external appearance would be materially affected.

Class B Dock, pier, harbour, water transport, canal or inland navigation undertakings

Permitted development

B. Development on operational land by statutory undertakers or their lessees in respect of dock, pier, harbour, water transport, or canal or inland navigation undertakings, required—

(a) for the purposes of shipping, or
(b) in connection with the embarking, disembarking, loading, discharging or transport of passengers, livestock or goods at a dock, pier or harbour, or with the movement of traffic by canal or inland navigation or by any railway forming part of the undertaking.

Development not permitted

B.1 Development is not permitted by Class B if it consists of or includes—

(a) the construction or erection of a hotel, or of a bridge or other building not required in connection with the handling of traffic,
(b) the construction or erection otherwise than wholly within the limits of a dock, pier or harbour of—
(i) an educational building, or
(ii) a car park, shop, restaurant, garage, petrol filling station or other building provided under transport legislation.

Interpretation of Class B

B.2 For the purposes of Class B, references to the construction or erection of any building or structure include references to the reconstruction or alteration of a building or structure where its design or external appearance would be materially affected, and the reference to operational land includes land designated by an order made under section 14 or 16 of the Harbours Act 1964 (orders for securing harbour efficiency etc., and orders conferring powers for improvement, construction etc. of harbours), and which has come into force, whether or not the order was subject to the provisions of the Statutory Orders (Special Procedure) Act 1945.

Class C Works to inland waterways

Permitted development

C. The improvement, maintenance or repair of an inland waterway (other than a commercial waterway or cruising waterway) to which section 104 of the Transport Act 1968 (classification of the Board's waterways) applies, and the repair or maintenance of a culvert, weir, lock, aqueduct, sluice, reservoir, let-off valve or other work used in connection with the control and operation of such a waterway.

Class D Dredgings

Permitted development

D. The use of any land by statutory undertakers in respect of dock, pier, harbour, water transport, canal or inland navigation undertakings for the spreading of any dredged material.

Class E Water or hydraulic power undertakings

Permitted development

E. Development for the purposes of their undertaking by statutory undertakers for the supply of water or hydraulic power consisting of—

(a) development not above ground level required in connection with the supply of water or for conserving, redistributing or augmenting water resources, or for the conveyance of water treatment sludge,

(b) development in, on or under any watercourse and required in connection with the improvement or maintenance of that watercourse,

(c) the provision of a building, plant, machinery or apparatus in, on, over or under land for the purpose of survey or investigation,

(d) the maintenance, improvement or repair of works for measuring the flow in any watercourse or channel,

(e) the installation in a water distribution system of a booster station, valve house, meter or switchgear house,

(f) any works authorised by or required in connection with an order made under section 73 of the Water Resources Act 1991 (power to make ordinary and emergency drought orders),

(g) any other development in, on, over or under operational land other than the provision of a building but including the extension or alteration of a building.

Development not permitted

E.1 Development is not permitted by Class E if—

(a) in the case of any Class E(a) development, it would include the construction of a reservoir,

(b) in the case of any Class E(e) development involving the installation of a station or house exceeding 29 cubic metres in capacity, that installation is carried out at or above ground level or under a highway used by vehicular traffic,

(c) in the case of any Class E(g) development, it would consist of or include the extension or alteration of a building so that—
  (i) its design or external appearance would be materially affected;
  (ii) the height of the original building would be exceeded, or the cubic content of the original building would be exceeded by more than 25%, or
  (iii) the floor space of the original building would be exceeded by more than 1,000 square metres, or

(d) in the case of any Class E(g) development, it would consist of the installation or erection of any plant or machinery exceeding 15 metres in height or the height of anything it replaces, whichever is the greater.

Condition

E.2 Development is permitted by Class E(c) subject to the condition that, on completion of the survey or investigation, or at the expiration of six months from the commencement of the development, whichever is the sooner, all such operations shall cease and all such buildings, plant, machinery and apparatus shall be removed and the land restored as soon as reasonably practicable to its former condition (or to any other condition which may be agreed with the local planning authority).

Class F Gas suppliers

Permitted development

F. Development by a public gas supplier required for the purposes of its undertaking consisting of—

(a) the laying underground of mains, pipes or other apparatus;

(b) the installation in a gas distribution system of apparatus for measuring, recording, controlling or varying the pressure, flow or volume of gas, and structures for housing such apparatus;

(c) the construction in any storage area or protective area specified in an order made under section 4 of the Gas Act 1965 (storage authorisation orders), of boreholes, and the erection or construction in any such area of any plant or machinery required in connection with the construction of such boreholes;

(d) the placing and storage on land of pipes and other apparatus to be included in a main or pipe which is being or is about to be laid or constructed in pursuance of planning permission granted or deemed to be granted under Part III of the Act (control over development);

(e) the erection on operational land of the public gas supplier of a building solely for the protection of plant or machinery;

(f) any other development carried out in, on, over or under the operational land of the public gas supplier.

Development not permitted

F.1 Development is not permitted by Class F if—

(a) in the case of any Class F(b) development involving the installation of a structure for housing apparatus exceeding 29 cubic metres in capacity, that installation would be carried out at or above ground level, or under a highway used by vehicular traffic,

(b) in the case of any Class F(c) development—
  (i) the borehole is shown in an order approved by the Sec-

retary of State for Trade and Industry for the purpose of section 4(6) of the Gas Act 1965; or
(ii) any plant or machinery would exceed 6 metres in height, or
(c) in the case of any Class F(e) development, the building would exceed 15 metres in height, or
(d) in the case of any Class F(f) development—
(i) it would consist of or include the erection of a building, or the reconstruction or alteration of a building where its design or external appearance would be materially affected;
(ii) it would involve the installation of plant or machinery exceeding 15 metres in height, or capable without the carrying out of additional works of being extended to a height exceeding 15 metres; or
(iii) it would consist of or include the replacement of any plant or machinery, by plant or machinery exceeding 15 metres in height or exceeding the height of the plant or machinery replaced, whichever is the greater.

Conditions

F.2 Development is permitted by Class F subject to the following conditions—
(a) in the case of any Class F(a) development, not less than eight weeks before the beginning of operations to lay a notifiable pipe-line, the public gas supplier shall give notice in writing to the local planning authority of its intention to carry out that development, identifying the land under which the pipe-line is to be laid,
(b) in the case of any Class F(d) development, on completion of the laying or construction of the main or pipe, or at the expiry of a period of nine months from the beginning of the development, whichever is the sooner, any pipes or other apparatus still stored on the land shall be removed and the land restored as soon as reasonably practicable to its condition before the development took place (or to any other condition which may be agreed with the local planning authority),
(c) in the case of any Class F(e) development, approval of the details of the design and external appearance of the building shall be obtained, before the development is begun, from—
(i) in Greater London or a metropolitan county, the local planning authority,
(ii) in a National Park, outside a metropolitan county, the county planning authority,
(iii) in any other case, the district planning authority.

Class G Electricity undertakings

Permitted development

G. Development by statutory undertakers for the generation, transmission or supply of electricity for the purposes of their undertaking consisting of—
(a) the installation or replacement in, on, over or under land of an electric line and the construction of shafts and tunnels and the installation or replacement of feeder or service pillars or transforming or switching stations or chambers reasonably necessary in connection with an electric line;
(b) the installation or replacement of any telecommunications line which connects any part of an electric line to any electrical plant or building, and the installation or replacement of any support for any such line;
(c) the sinking of boreholes to ascertain the nature of the subsoil and the installation of any plant or

machinery reasonably necessary in connection with such boreholes;

(d) the extension or alteration of buildings on operational land;

(e) the erection on operational land of the undertaking or a building solely for the protection of plant or machinery;

(f) any other development carried out in, on, over or under the operational land of the undertaking.

Development not permitted

G.1 Development is not permitted by Class G if—

(a) in the case of any Class G(a) development—

(i) it would consist of or include the installation or replacement of an electric line to which section 37(1) of the Electricity Act 1989 (consent required for overhead lines) applies; or

(ii) it would consist of or include the installation or replacement at or above ground level or under a highway used by vehicular traffic, of a chamber for housing apparatus and the chamber would exceed 29 cubic metres in capacity;

(b) in the case of any Class G(b) development—

(i) the development would take place in a National Park, an area of outstanding natural beauty, or a site of special scientific interest;

(ii) the height of any support would exceed 15 metres; or

(iii) the telecommunications line would exceed 1,000 metres in length;

(c) in the case of any Class G(d) development—

(i) the height of the original building would be exceeded;

(ii) the cubic content of the original building would be exceeded by more than 25% or, in the case of any building on article 1(5) land, by more than 10%, or

(iii) the floor space of the original building would be exceeded by more than 1,000 square metres or, in the case of any building on article 1(5) land, by more than 500 square metres;

(d) in the case of any Class G(e) development, the building would exceed 15 metres in height, or

(e) in the case of any Class G(f) development, it would consist of or include—

(i) the erection of a building, or the reconstruction or alteration of a building where its design or external appearance would be materially affected, or

(ii) the installation or erection by way of addition or replacement of any plant or machinery exceeding 15 metres in height or the height of any plant or machinery replaced, whichever is the greater.

Conditions

G.2 Development is permitted by Class G subject to the following conditions—

(a) in the case of any Class G(a) development consisting of or including the replacement of an existing electric line, compliance with any conditions contained in a planning permission relating to the height, design or position of the existing electric line which are capable of being applied to the replacement line;

(b) in the case of any Class G(a) development consisting of or including the installation of a temporary electric line providing a diversion for an existing electric line, on the ending of the diversion or at the end of a period of six months from the completion of the installation (whichever is the sooner) the temporary electric line shall be removed and the land on which any operations have been carried out to install that line shall be restored as soon as reasonably practicable to its condition before the installation took place;

(c) in the case of any Class G(c) development, on the completion of that development, or at the end of a period of six months from the beginning of that development (whichever is the sooner) any plant or machinery installed shall be removed and the land shall be restored as soon as reasonably practicable to its condition before the development took place;

(d) in the case of any Class G(e) development, approval of details of the design and external appearance of the buildings shall be obtained, before development is begun, from—

(i) in Greater London or a metropolitan county, the local planning authority,

(ii) in a National Park, outside a metropolitan county, the county planning authority,

(iii) in any other case, the district planning authority.

Interpretation of Class G

G.3 For the purposes of Class G(a), "electric line" has the meaning assigned to that term by section 64(1) of the Electricity Act 1989 (interpretation etc. of Part 1).

G.4 For the purposes of Class G(b), "electrical plant" has the meaning assigned to that term by the said section 64(1) and "telecommunications line" means a wire or cable (including its casing or coating) which forms part of a telecommunication apparatus within the meaning assigned to that term by paragraph 1 of Schedule 2 to the Telecommunications Act 1984 (the telecommunications code).

G.5 For the purposes of Class G(d), (e) and (f), the land of the holder of a licence under section 6(2) of the Electricity Act 1989 (licences authorising supply etc.) shall be treated as operational land if it would be operational land within section 263 of the Act (meaning of "operational land") if such licence holders were statutory undertakers for the purpose of that section.

Class H Tramway or road transport undertakings

Permitted development

H. Development required for the purposes of the carrying on of any tramway or road transport undertaking consisting of—

(a) the installation of posts, overhead wires, underground cables, feeder pillars or transformer boxes in, on, over or adjacent to a highway for the purpose of supplying current to public service vehicles;

(b) the installation of tramway tracks, and conduits, drains and pipes in connection with such tracks for the working of tramways;

(c) the installation of telephone cables and apparatus, huts, stop posts and signs required in connection with the operation of public service vehicles;

(d) the erection or construction and the maintenance, improvement or other alteration of passenger shelters and barriers for the control of people waiting to enter public service vehicles;

(e) any other development on operational land of the undertaking.

Development not permitted

H.1 Development is not permitted by Class H if it would consist of—

(a) in the case of any Class H(a) development, the installation of a structure exceeding 17 cubic metres in capacity,

(b) in the case of any Class H(e) development—

(i) the erection of a building or the reconstruction or alter-

ation of a building where its design or external appearance would be materially affected,

(ii) the installation or erection by way of addition or replacement of any plant or machinery which would exceed 15 metres in height or the height of any plant or machinery it replaces, whichever is the greater,

(iii) development, not wholly within a bus or tramway station, in pursuance of powers contained in transport legislation.

Class I Lighthouse undertakings

Permitted development

I. Development required for the purposes of the functions of a general or local lighthouse authority under the Merchant Shipping Act 1894 and any other statutory provision made with respect to a local lighthouse authority, or in the exercise by a local lighthouse authority of rights, powers or duties acquired by usage prior to the 1894 Act.

Development not permitted

I.1 Development is not permitted by Class I if it consists of or includes the erection of offices, or the reconstruction or alteration of offices where their design or external appearance would be materially affected.

Class J Post Office

Permitted development

J. Development required for the purposes of the Post Office consisting of—

(a) the installation of posting boxes or self-service machines,

(b) any other development carried out in, on, over or under the operational land of the undertaking.

Development not permitted

J.1 Development is not permitted by Class J if—

(a) it would consist of or include the erection of a building, or the reconstruction or alteration of a building where its design or external appearance would be materially affected, or

(b) it would consist of or include the installation or erection by way of addition or replacement of any plant or machinery which would exceed 15 metres in height or the height of any existing plant or machinery, whichever is the greater.

Interpretation of Part 17

K. For the purposes of Part 17—

"transport legislation" means section 14(1)(d) of the Transport Act 1962 (supplemental provisions relating to the Boards' powers) or section 10(1)(x) of the Transport Act 1968 (general powers of Passenger Transport Executive).

COMMENTARY

DERIVATION

Town and Country Planning General Development Order 1988 (S.I. 1988 No. 1813), Sched. 2 Pt. 17, as amended by S.I. 1990 No. 2032 and S.I. 1991 No. 1536. Amendments made in the 1995 consolidation include revised exceptions and conditions in Class G, and new Class K (interpretation).

DEFINITIONS

"building": art. 1(2).
"electric line": Class G.3.
"electrical plant": Class G.4.
"notifiable pipe-line": art. 1(2).
"operational land": 1990 Act, s.262 (and see Class G.5).
"statutory undertaker": art. 1(2).
"transport legislation": Class K.

GENERAL NOTE

Statutory undertakers

The class of statutory undertaker for the purposes of this Part includes (art. 1(2)):

(1) the Post Office;
(2) the Civil Aviation Authority (though permitted development rights are conferred not by this Part but by Pt. 18, Classes D-H);
(3) public gas suppliers under the Gas Act 1986, s.7, which provides:

> In this Act "public gas supplier" means any person who holds an authorisation under this section except where he is acting otherwise than for purposes connected with the supply of gas through pipes to premises in his authorised area (s.7(1));

(4) "persons authorised by any enactment to carry on any railway, light railway, tramway, road transport, water transport, canal, inland navigation, dock, harbour, pier or lighthouse undertaking, or any undertaking for the supply of electricity, hydraulic power or water" (1990 Act, s.262(1)).

Thus the category includes a variety of bodies carrying out functions of a public character under statutory powers. They need not be in public ownership, and the contemporary programme of privatisation has blurred the distinction between public and private ownership in the carrying on of statutory undertakings. A local authority may be a statutory undertaker for the purposes of some of its functions but not others. The statutory powers on which an undertaker relies may be conferred by public general Act, or by a local or private Act.

The following, though acting under statutory authority, are not statutory undertakers for the purposes of this Part:

Telecommunications code system operators: permitted development rights are conferred instead by Pt. 24, with additional telecommunications development rights under Pt. 25;

The Coal Authority and its licensees: permitted development rights are conferred instead by Pt. 20.

Operational land

Some of the permitted development rights under this Part are exercisable on any land, but others are restricted to the operational land of the undertaking. All rights under Classes A (rail) and B (docks, harbours etc.) are restricted to operational land. In Classes E, F, G, H and J there are particular development rights which are exercisable on any land, but followed up in each case by a broad residual right to carry out "any other development" (not including provision of new buildings in the case of Class E), exercisable only on operational land. There is also an extended definition of operational land in Class G.5.

Operational land, in relation to statutory undertakers, is defined by the 1990 Act, ss.263 as meaning:

"(a) land which is used for the purpose of carrying on their undertaking; and

(b) land in which as interest is held for that purpose,
not being land which, in respect of its nature and situation, is comparable rather with land in general than with land which is used, or in which interests are held, for the purpose of the carrying on of statutory undertakings."

Article 4 directions

A direction made under art. 4 is ineffective against certain operations (specified in art. 4(4)) carried out by statutory undertakers, unless it provides to the contrary. If any rights are removed by an art. 4 direction, a special compensation regime applies by virtue of s.279 of the 1990 Act. The right to compensation arises only where a decision has been made on an application under s.266 of the Act refusing permission or imposing conditions; but that section applies only to decisions made by the Secretary of State and the "appropriate Minister" on appeal or call-in, so that an adverse decision by a local planning authority alone is insufficient to activate the special compensation provisions. The special basis for assessment of compensation is prescribed in s.280.

Consultation and publicity for development proposals

Although planning permission is granted by this Part for development undertaken by statutory undertakers, the Secretary of State has asked that publicity should be given to some proposals before work commences. In DOE Circular 9/95, Appendix B, para. 8, statutory undertakers are asked to ensure that both local planning authorities and the public know of proposals for permitted development that are likely to affect them significantly, before the proposals are finalised. The circular acknowledges that it is impossible to give an exhaustive list of the kinds of development where this should be done, but stresses the need for local consultation and regular informal contact with planning authorities, with the object of establishing the kinds of development to be notified, and the areas the planning authorities consider important. Where a proposal is notified to an authority, adequate time should be allowed for them to consider whether it should be advertised, and to suggest ways in which the proposals might be amended to overcome any planning objections. It will also give local planning authorities an opportunity to consider whether to make an art. 4 direction, though it will have effect to withdraw certain permissions under this Part only if it specifically so provides (see above).

Class A: railway or light railway undertakings

The permitted development includes only incidental works required in connection with the movement of traffic by rail. This includes buildings and plant needed to handle traffic at rail terminals and the necessary storage of goods and loading and unloading facilities (see appeal decisions reported at [1967] J.P.L. 49), but not any unrelated industrial processes carried out on railway land for reasons only of convenience (see appeal decision reported at [1971] J.P.L. 412). Railway construction itself is not included, and will normally require specific authorisation by private Act of Parliament or, since 1992, by an order made under the Transport and Works Act 1992 (see the General Note to Pt. 11). Nor does the permission extend to any hotel, railway station or bridge; planning permission for these types of development may be obtained in the normal way, or it may be included in an order under the 1992

Act. Other types of development are permitted under para. (c) provided they are required in connection with the movement of traffic by rail and are wholly within a railway station. Rights under this Class are inapplicable where all rail traffic has ceased (see appeal decision at [1983] J.P.L. 616).

Class B: dock, pier, harbour, water transport, canal or inland navigation undertakings

The scope of this permission was examined in an appeal decision reported at [1987] J.P.L. 745, relating to the erection of a scrap shearer at Liverpool docks. The inspector took the view (which was accepted by the Secretaries of State although the appeal was determined on other technical grounds) that "for the purpose of shipping" in para. (a) suggested development "of which the immediate purpose is to facilitate the movement, guidance and docking of ships, such as lock gates, radar installations and winches at the quayside." Nor did the operation fall within para. (b), as being required in connection with shipping. The question to be asked was, why was the operation there? It was to process heavy metal scrap in a manner to meet the needs of the company's overseas' customers. The end product was in a form capable of ready handling by the company's stevedores, and acceptable to the shipping companies. But that was coincidental and fortuitous, and insufficient to bring the development within this class.

But a proposal which is outside permitted development rights in this Part may nonetheless come within Pt. 8, which authorises the extension or alteration of an industrial building, and certain associated development on industrial land. Industrial land is defined as including land used for the purposes of an industrial undertaking as a dock, harbour or quay (Pt. 8, Class B.2).

Dredgings

Permission is also granted by Class D to undertakers within this class for the use of any land for the spreading of any dredged material.

Class C: works to inland waterways

The Transport Act 1968, s.104 applies to inland waterways which are comprised in the undertaking of the British Waterways Board, and includes commercial waterways, waterways to be principally available for cruising, fishing and other recreational purposes, and the remainder. Commercial and cruising waterways are specifically excluded from permitted development rights under this Class of Pt. 17.

Class D: dredgings

The right to rely on the permission under this class is limited to the undertakers within Class D above, but the permission is not restricted to operational land nor to land owned by the undertakers or in the vicinity of their undertaking.

Class E: water or hydraulic power undertakings

Under the Water Resources Act 1991, s.73 (formerly the Drought Act 1976, ss.1, 2) orders may be made in exceptional drought circumstances and emergencies giving special powers to a water undertaker to take water from any source, to provide water, to limit water consumption and to suspend existing water control arrangements.

Class F: gas suppliers

Under the Gas Act 1965, s.4 (as amended by the Gas Act 1986), the Secretary of State for Trade and Industry may by an order (known as a "storage authorisation order") authorise the storage by a public gas supplier in natural porous strata underground of such kinds of gas (including natural gas) as, having regard to the safety of the public and the need to protect water resources, are in his opinion suitable for such storage. Under s.4(6), planning permission is deemed to be granted under s.90 of the Town and Country Planning Act 1990, for the following (so far as they constitute development requiring permission):

(a) the carrying out of construction of any surface works, boreholes or pipes associated with an underground gas storage which in a storage authorisation order are shown as approved by the Minister for the purposes of this subsection; or

(b) the bringing into use of an underground gas storage in accordance with a storage authorisation order.

Hence the development permitted by Class F(c) excludes any borehole shown in an approved order. It also excludes plant or machinery over 6 metres in height.

Class G: electricity undertakings

This Class grants a broad permission for electricity works carried out by electricity statutory undertakers, subject to the exceptions in Class G.1 and the conditions in Class G.2.

Class H: tramway or road transport undertakings

The construction of new tramway works was normally in the past authorised either under the Tramways Act 1870 or by private Act (and therefore attracting planning permission under Pt. 11). Nowadays, authorisation for new tramways works is under the Transport and Works Act 1992, which will carry with it the necessary planning permission as part of the authorisation. This Part permits ancillary works and equipment, subject to the exception in Class H.1.

Class I: lighthouse undertakings

Lighthouse undertakers are permitted to carry out development for the purposes of their undertaking, but not to provide offices.

Class J: post office

The installation of post boxes and self-service machines is permitted development wherever it is undertaken, and there is also a broader permission for any development (except certain building operations and high plant or machinery) carried out on operational land.

PART 18

AVIATION DEVELOPMENT

Class A Development at an airport

Permitted development

A. The carrying out on operational land by a relevant airport operator or its agent of development (including the erection or alteration of an operational building) in connection with the provision of services and facilities at a relevant airport.

Development not permitted

A.1 Development is not permitted by Class A if it would consist of or include—

(a) the construction or extension of a runway;
(b) the construction of a passenger terminal the floor space of which would exceed 500 square metres;
(c) the extension or alteration of a passenger terminal, where the floor space of the building as existing at 5th December 1988 or, if built after that date, of the building as built, would be exceeded by more than 15%;
(d) the erection of a building other than an operational building;
(e) the alteration or reconstruction of a building other than an operational building, where its design or external appearance would be materially affected.

Condition

A.2 Development is permitted by Class A subject to the condition that the relevant airport operator consults the local planning authority before carrying out any development, unless that development falls within the description in paragraph A.4.

Interpretation of Class A

A.3 For the purposes of paragraph A.1, floor space shall be calculated by external measurement and without taking account of the floor space in any pier or satellite.

A.4 Development falls within this paragraph if—

(a) it is urgently required for the efficient running of the airport, and
(b) it consists of the carrying out of works, or the erection or construction of a structure or of an ancillary building, or the placing on land of equipment, and the works, structure, building, or equipment do not exceed 4 metres in height or 200 cubic metres in capacity.

Class B Air navigation development at an airport

Permitted development

B. The carrying out on operational land within the perimeter of a relevant airport by a relevant airport operator or its agent of development in connection with—

(a) the provision of air traffic control services,
(b) the navigation of aircraft using the airport, or
(c) the monitoring of the movement of aircraft using the airport.

Class C Air navigation development near an airport

Permitted development

C. The carrying out on operational land outside but within 8 kilometres of the perimeter of a relevant airport, by a relevant airport operator or its agent, of development in connection with—

(a) the provision of air traffic control services,

(b) the navigation of aircraft using the airport, or
(c) the monitoring of the movement of aircraft using the airport.

Development not permitted C.1 Development is not permitted by Class C if—
(a) any building erected would be used for a purpose other than housing equipment used in connection with the provision of air traffic control services, with assisting the navigation of aircraft, or with monitoring the movement of aircraft using the airport;
(b) any building erected would exceed a height of 4 metres;
(c) it would consist of the installation or erection of any radar or radio mast, antenna or other apparatus which would exceed 15 metres in height, or, where an existing mast, antenna or apparatus is replaced, the height of that mast, antenna or apparatus, if greater.

Class D Development by Civil Aviation Authority within an airport

Permitted development **D. The carrying out by the Civil Aviation Authority or its agents, within the perimeter of an airport at which the Authority provides air traffic control services, of development in connection with—**
(a) the provision of air traffic control services,
(b) the navigation of aircraft using the airport, or
(c) the monitoring of the movement of aircraft using the airport.

Class E Development by the Civil Aviation Authority for air traffic control and navigation

Permitted development **E. The carrying out on operational land of the Civil Aviation Authority by the Authority or its agents of development in connection with—**
(a) the provision of air traffic control services,
(b) the navigation of aircraft, or
(c) monitoring the movement of aircraft.

Development not permitted E.1 Development is not permitted by Class E if—
(a) any building erected would be used for a purpose other than housing equipment used in connection with the provision of air traffic control services, assisting the navigation of aircraft or monitoring the movement of aircraft;
(b) any building erected would exceed a height of 4 metres; or
(c) it would consist of the installation or erection of any radar or radio mast antenna or other apparatus which would exceed 15 metres in height, or where an existing mast, antenna or apparatus is replaced, the height of that mast, antenna or apparatus, if greater.

Class F Development by the Civil Aviation Authority in an emergency

Permitted development **F. The use of land by or on behalf of the Civil Aviation Authority in an emergency to station moveable apparatus replacing unserviceable apparatus.**

Condition F.1 Development is permitted by Class F subject to the condition that on or before the expiry of a period of six months beginning with the date on which the use began the use shall cease, and any apparatus shall be removed, and the land shall be restored to its condition before the development took place, or to any other condition as may be agreed in writing between the local planning authority and the developer.

Class G Development by the Civil Aviation Authority for air traffic control etc.

Permitted development

G. The use of land by or on behalf of the Civil Aviation Authority to provide services and facilities in connection with—

(a) the provision of air traffic control services,

(b) the navigation of aircraft, or

(c) the monitoring of aircraft,

and the erection or placing of moveable structures on the land for the purpose of that use.

Condition

G.1 Development is permitted by Class G subject to the condition that, on or before the expiry of the period of six months beginning with the date on which the use began, the use shall cease, and any structure shall be removed, and the land shall be restored to its condition before the development took place, or to any other condition as may be agreed in writing between the local planning authority and the developer.

Class H Development by the Civil Aviation Authority for surveys etc.

Permitted development

H. The use of land by or on behalf of the Civil Aviation Authority for the stationing and operation of apparatus in connection with the carrying out of surveys or investigations.

Condition

H.1 Development is permitted by Class H subject to the condition that on or before the expiry of the period of six months beginning with the date on which the use began, the use shall cease, and any apparatus shall be removed, and the land shall be restored to its condition before the development took place, or to any other condition as may be agreed in writing between the local planning authority and the developer.

Class I Use of airport buildings managed by relevant airport operators

Permitted development

1. The use of buildings within the perimeter of an airport managed by a relevant airport operator for purposes connected with air transport services or other flying activities at that airport.

Interpretation of Part 18

J. For the purposes of Part 18—

"operational building" means a building, other than a hotel, required in connection with the movement or maintenance of aircraft, or with the embarking, disembarking, loading, discharge or transport of passengers, livestock or goods at a relevant airport;

"relevant airport" means an airport to which Part V of the Airports Act 1986 (status of certain airports as statutory undertakers etc.) applies; and

"relevant airport operator" means a relevant airport operator within the meaning of section 57 of the Airports Act 1986 (scope of Part V).

COMMENTARY

DERIVATION

Town and Country Planning General Development Order 1988 (S.I. 1988 No. 1813), Sched. 2, Pt. 18. Minor drafting amendments were made in the 1995 consolidation, including the subdivision of Class A.3 and renaming of Class J as Class I (which had not been used in the 1988 Order).

Definitions

"operational building": Class K.
"relevant airport": Class K.
"relevant airport operator": Class K.

General Note

This Part grants permission for development by:

(1) relevant airport operators, at and (Class C) within 8 kilometres of, relevant airports; and
(2) the Civil Aviation Authority in connection with air traffic control services, air navigation and monitoring services.

"Relevant" airports and operators

Pt. V of the Airports Act 1986 applies to all airports permitted under Pt. IV to levy airport charges (or for which an application is pending) and any airport owned or managed by any subsidiary of the CAA. However, it does not apply to any airport owned by the British Airports Authority, nor to any airport owned by a principal council, or by a metropolitan county passenger transport authority (or jointly so owned). A "relevant airport operator" means the airport operator in the case of an airport to which Pt. V applies (1986 Act, s.57(4)).

The Civil Aviation Authority

The CAA provides air traffic control services at Heathrow, Gatwick, Stansted, Birmingham, Cardiff and Manchester airports, and air navigational aids on other scattered sites. The permission under Class D allows the CAA to carry out development in connection with its operations at those airports.

PART 19

DEVELOPMENT ANCILLARY TO MINING OPERATIONS

Class A

Permitted development

A. The carrying out of operations for the erection, extension, rearrangement, replacement, repair or other alteration of any—

(a) plant or machinery,
(b) buildings,
(c) private ways or private railways or sidings, or
(d) sewers, mains, pipes, cables or other similar apparatus,

on land used as a mine.

Development not permitted

A.1 Development is not permitted by Class A—

(a) in relation to land at an underground mine—
  (i) on land which is not an approved site; or
  (ii) on land to which the description in paragraph D.1(b) applies, unless a plan of that land was deposited with the mineral planning authority before 5th June 1989;

(b) if the principal purpose of the development would be any purpose other than—
  (i) purposes in connection with the winning and working of minerals at that mine or of minerals brought to the surface at that mine; or
  (ii) the treatment, storage or removal from the mine of such minerals or waste materials derived from them;

(c) if the external appearance of the mine would be materially affected;

(d) if the height of any building, plant or machinery which is not in an excavation would exceed—
  (i) 15 metres above ground level; or
  (ii) the height of the building, plant or machinery, if any, which is being rearranged, replaced or repaired or otherwise altered,

whichever is the greater;

(e) if the height of any building, plant or machinery in an excavation would exceed—
  (i) 15 metres above the excavated ground level; or
  (ii) 15 metres above the lowest point of the unexcavated ground immediately adjacent to the excavation; or
  (iii) the height of the building, plant or machinery, if any, which is being rearranged, replaced or repaired or otherwise altered,

whichever is the greatest;

(f) if any building erected (other than a replacement building) would have a floor space exceeding 1,000 square metres; or

(g) if the cubic content of any replaced, extended or altered building would exceed by more than 25% the cubic content of the building replaced, extended or altered or the floor space would exceed by more than 1,000 square metres the floor space of that building.

Condition

A.2 Development is permitted by Class A subject to the condition that before the end of the period of 24 months from the date when the mining operations have permanently ceased, or any longer period which the mineral planning authority agree in writing—

(a) all buildings, plant and machinery permitted by Class A shall be removed from the land unless the mineral planning authority have otherwise agreed in writing; and

(b) the land shall be restored, so far as is practicable, to its condition before the development took place, or restored to such condition as may have been agreed in writing between the mineral planning authority and the developer.

Class B

Permitted development

B. The carrying out, on land used as a mine or on ancillary mining land, with the prior approval of the mineral planning authority, of operations for the erection, installation, extension, rearrangement, replacement, repair or other alteration of any—
- **(a) plant or machinery,**
- **(b) buildings, or**
- **(c) structures or erections.**

Development not permitted

B.1 Development is not permitted by Class B—
- (a) in relation to land at an underground mine—
  - (i) on land which is not an approved site; or
  - (ii) on land to which the description in paragraph D.1(b) applies, unless a plan of that land was deposited with the mineral planning authority before 5th June 1989;

  or
- (b) if the principal purpose of the development would be any purpose other than—
  - (i) purposes in connection with the operation of the mine,
  - (ii) the treatment, preparation for sale, consumption or utilization of minerals won or brought to the surface at that mine, or
  - (iii) the storage or removal from the mine of such minerals, their products or waste materials derived from them.

B.2 The prior approval referred to in Class B shall not be refused or granted subject to conditions unless the authority are satisfied that it is expedient to do so because—
- (a) the proposed development would injure the amenity of the neighbourhood and modifications can reasonably be made or conditions reasonably imposed in order to avoid or reduce that injury, or
- (b) the proposed development ought to be, and could reasonably be, sited elsewhere.

Condition

B.3 Development is permitted by Class B subject to the condition that before the end of the period of 24 months from the date when the mining operations have permanently ceased, or any longer period which the mineral planning authority agree in writing—
- (a) all buildings, plant, machinery, structures and erections permitted by Class B shall be removed from the land unless the mineral planning authority have otherwise agreed in writing; and
- (b) the land shall be restored, so far as is practicable, to its condition before the development took place or restored to such condition as may have been agreed in writing between the mineral planning authority and the developer.

Class C

Permitted development

C. The carrying out with the prior approval of the mineral planning authority of development required for the maintenance or safety of a mine or a disused mine or for the purposes of ensuring the safety of the surface of the

land at or adjacent to a mine or a disused mine.

Development not permitted

C.1 Development is not permitted by Class C if it is carried out by the Coal Authority or any licensed operator within the meaning of section 65 of the Coal Industry Act 1994 (interpretation).

Prior approvals

C.2(1) The prior approval of the mineral planning authority to development permitted by Class C is not required if—

(a) the external appearance of the mine or disused mine at or adjacent to which the development is to be carried out would not be materially affected;

(b) no building, plant, machinery, structure or erection—

(i) would exceed a height of 15 metres above ground level, or

(ii) where any building, plant, machinery, structure or erection is rearranged, replaced or repaired, would exceed a height of 15 metres above ground level or the height of what was rearranged, replaced or repaired, whichever is the greater,

and

(c) the development consists of the extension, alteration or replacement of an existing building, within the limits set out in paragraph (3).

(2) The approval referred to in Class C shall not be refused or granted subject to conditions unless the authority are satisfied that it is expedient to do so because—

(a) the proposed development would injure the amenity of the neighbourhood and modifications could reasonably be made or conditions reasonably imposed in order to avoid or reduce that injury, or

(b) the proposed development ought to be, and could reasonably be, sited elsewhere.

(3) The limits referred to in paragraph C.2(1)(c) are—

(a) that the cubic content of the building as extended, altered or replaced does not exceed that of the existing building by more than 25%, and

(b) that the floor space of the building as extended, altered or replaced does not exceed that of the existing building by more than 1,000 square metres.

Interpretation of Part 19

D.1 An area of land is an approved site for the purposes of Part 19 if—

(a) it is identified in a grant of planning permission or any instrument by virtue of which planning permission is deemed to be granted, as land which may be used for development described in this Part; or

(b) in any other case, it is land immediately adjoining an active access to an underground mine which, on 5th December 1988, was in use for the purposes of that mine, in connection with the purposes described in paragraph A.1(b)(i) or (ii) or paragraph B.1(b)(i) to (iii) above.

D.2 For the purposes of Part 19—

"active access" means a surface access to underground workings which is in normal and regular use for the transportation of minerals, materials, spoil or men;

"ancillary mining land" means land adjacent to and occupied together with a mine at which the winning and working of minerals is carried out in pursuance of planning permission granted or deemed to be granted under Part III of the Act (control over development);

"minerals" does not include any coal other than coal won or worked during the course of operations which are carried on exclusively for the purpose of exploring for coal or confined to the digging or carrying away of coal that it is necessary to dig or carry away in the course of activities carried on for purposes which do not include the getting of coal or any product of coal;

"the prior approval of the mineral planning authority" means prior written approval of that authority of detailed proposals for the siting, design and external appearance of the building, plant or machinery proposed to be erected, installed, extended or altered;
"underground mine" is a mine at which minerals are worked principally by underground methods.

COMMENTARY

Derivation

Town and Country Planning General Development Order 1988 (S.I. 1988 No. 1813), Sched. 2, Pt. 19, as amended by S.I. 1994 No. 2595.

Definitions

"active access": Class D.2.
"ancillary mining land": Class D.2.
"mine": art. 1(2).
"minerals": Class D.2.
"mining operations": art. 1(2).
"prior approval of the mineral planning authority": Class D.2 and see Class C.2.
"underground mine": Class D.2.

General Note

Detailed advice on this Part is contained in MPG5, *Minerals Planning and the General Development Order* (HMSO, 1988). The permitted development rights under this Part relate to the carrying out of development that is ancillary to mining operations, including the provision of certain buildings, plant and machinery at a mine (Class A), and, with the prior approval of the mineral planning authority, on ancillary mining land (Class B); and certain safety and maintenance works (with the prior approval of the mineral planning authority) at or adjacent to a mine or a disused mine (Class C).

"Mine," "mining operations"

The starting point is to determine what operations constitute "mining operations" (defined by art. 1(2) as "the winning and working of minerals in, on or under land, whether by surface or underground working"), and what land is to be regarded as a "mine" (defined by art. 1(2) as "any site on which mining operations are carried out"). In *English Clays Lovering Pochin & Co. v. Plymouth Corporation* [1974] 1 W.L.R. 742, the court held that the essential idea in the term "winning or working of minerals" is that of "extracting or separation of raw material from the solid earth in which it occurs." What is done afterwards may be called cleaning or dressing or treatment or refining or some other appropriate term, but is not within the ordinary meaning of the words "winning or working of minerals." That view was upheld in the Court of Appeal ([1974] 2 All E.R. 239 at 243) where Russell L.J. suggested that to "win" a mineral is to make it available or accessible to be removed from the land, and to "work" a mineral is (at least initially) to remove it from its position in the land. Thereafter, it may be that the processes of separation out are more aptly described as "treatment."

"Minerals" is defined by the 1990 Act, s.336(a) as including:

"all minerals and substances in or under land of a kind ordinarily worked for removal by underground or surface working, except that it does not include peat cut for purposes other than sale."

Minerals

In the 1988 Order, these provisions extended to coal won or worked by virtue of s.36 of the Coal Industry Nationalisation Act 1946, but not to any other coal. The intended effect of those provisions was to exclude British Coal and their licensees, because of their own permitted development rights under Pt. 20. That effect is maintained in this Order, despite the subsequent repeal of the 1946 Act, by the redefinition of "minerals" in Class D.2 which incorporates the distinction formerly drawn in the 1946 Act. In addition, licensees of the Coal Authority are specifically excluded from Class C.

Class A: operational development at mine

Class A grants permission for development actually at the mine (and within the "approved site"), and is narrower in its applicability than Class B which extends also to adjacent land. But under Class A the development may be undertaken without the prior approval of the mineral planning authority, and is therefore subject to restrictive limitations and exceptions.

Class B: operational development requiring prior approval at mine or on ancillary mining land

Development permitted under this Class overlaps with that under Class A, but this class permits development not only at the mine itself but also on "ancillary mining land" which is defined as land "adjacent to and occupied together with a mine at which the winning and working of minerals is carried out in pursuance of planning permission granted or deemed to be granted under Part III of the Act" (Class D.2). Thus, rights under this Class are not available where mineral working continues on the basis of existing use (*i.e.* pre-1948) rights without express planning permission. Because of special provisions affecting minerals (see further MPG5, para. 12) this is unlikely to be a significant group. Although the rights extend to surface development in connection with underground mines, this is dependent upon the mineral operators concerned depositing a plan of the approved site for permitted surface development within 6 months of the order coming into force.

There are three important limitations. First, that there must be prior written approval by the mineral planning authority of detailed proposals for the siting, design and external appearance of the proposed building, plant or machinery as erected, installed, extended or altered (Class D.2). Approval must be granted unconditionally unless the authority are satisfied that there would otherwise be avoidable injury to amenity, or the development ought to be and could reasonably be sited elsewhere (Class B.2).

Secondly, if the development is not on the site of the mine itself, it must be on adjacent land. Careful consideration was given to the meaning of "adjacent" in this context in *English Clays Lovering Pochin & Co. v. Plymouth Corporation*[1973] 2 All E.R. 730, 737, where Goulding J. said:

> "Seeing, therefore, that I have to determine what is land adjacent to a mine or quarry, with regard to the circumstances, I bear in mind as the determining factor that the phrase occurs in legislation dealing with town and country planning. I must ask, are the two areas under consideration properly to be considered adjacent, with planning considerations in mind? Town and country planning is concerned, of course, with the control of the neighbourhood in the public interest. It is concerned with amenities in the broadest sense, with the visual appearance

> of a neighbourhood, with the flow of traffic, with the density of population in relation to the essential services that are available and a proper balance between different types of land use, and other matters of the same kind. I do not intend to give an exhaustive list.
>
> . . .
>
> Then I ask myself why the Minister who made the General Development Order extended the general permission given by item 2 of class XVIII to work to be done on land in a quarry or mine adjacent and belonging to a quarry or mine but not to such work on land at a distance. The answer is plainly that an existing quarry or mine will already have had its effect on land in the vicinity, and therefore fresh building or other works erected either in the existing quarry or mine or on the adjacent and belonging land will merely be intensifying what has already occurred in that neighbourhood. But such an argument is not applicable to land at a greater distance."

On that basis, he declined to hold that a site was adjacent to a mine where it was two miles away at the nearest point to the two sites (4 miles from their respective centre points) and connected both physically (by a pipeline) and functionally (the two sites were used in the same process). That decision was upheld by the Court of Appeal ([1974] 1 W.L.R. 742) where Russell L.J. delivering the judgment of the Court added:

> " 'Adjacent' means close to or nearby or lying by: its significance or application in point of distance depends on the circumstances in which the word is used. The particular circumstances here are that the general development order is concerned with planning. It is easy to understand a general permission to erect buildings and plant, for purposes connected with operations at the site of a mine, *on* that site; or if not on that site (a word of somewhat loose import) very near to that site so that it would not appear to be other than a growth of the site; and this we believe to be the significance of the words 'adjacent to' in this paragraph of the general development order."

Thirdly, the development must be for a principal purpose that is in connection with the operation of the mine, for the treatment, preparation for sale, consumption or utilisation of minerals from the mine or the storage or removal of the minerals, their products or waste materials derived from them (Class B.1(b)). The wording of this limitation was significantly revised in 1988. Previously the permission was for the erection of plant "required in connection with the winning or working of minerals, . . . or which is required in connection with the treatment or disposal of such minerals." In *South Glamorgan County Council v. Hobbs* (*Quarries*) [1980] J.P.L. 35, the High Court held that those words did not encompass a ready-mixed concrete batching plant to be erected at a limestone quarry. The purpose of the plant was to produce concrete, and it was required neither for treatment nor disposal of minerals, but in connection with their utilisation. Such plant would now be within this Class, since its principal purpose (utilisation of minerals) would be within Class B.1(b).

Class C: works for maintenance or safety at used and disused mines

This permission did not extend to British Coal (which formerly had separate rights under Pt. 20) and does not now extend to licensees of the Coal Authority. Development is authorised only if it is within the limits prescribed by Class C.2(1), or it has the prior approval of the mineral planning authority. To this extent it resembles a grant of outline planning permission. The circumstances in which the authority may refuse approval, or impose conditions, are specified in Class C.2(3), but it would remain open to the authority to withdraw rights under this Part by an art. 4 direction in an appropriate case going beyond those circumstances. "Prior approval" means

(Class D.2) written approval of detailed proposals for the siting, design and external appearance of the proposed building, plant or machinery as erected, installed, extended or altered.

PART 20

COAL MINING DEVELOPMENT BY THE COAL AUTHORITY AND LICENSED OPERATORS

Class A

Permitted development

A. Development by a licensee of the Coal Authority, in a mine started before 1st July 1948, consisting of—

(a) the winning and working underground of coal or coal-related minerals in a designated seam area; or

(b) the carrying out of development underground which is required in order to gain access to and work coal or coal-related minerals in a designated seam area.

Conditions

A.1 Development is permitted by Class A subject to the following conditions—

(a) subject to sub-paragraph (b)—

(i) except in a case where there is an approved restoration scheme or mining operations have permanently ceased, the developer shall, before 31st December 1995 or before any later date which the mineral planning authority may agree in writing, apply to the mineral planning authority for approval of a restoration scheme;

(ii) where there is an approved restoration scheme, reinstatement, restoration and aftercare shall be carried out in accordance with that scheme;

(iii) if an approved restoration scheme does not specify the periods within which reinstatement, restoration or aftercare should be carried out, it shall be subject to conditions that;

(aa) reinstatement or restoration, if any, shall be carried out before the end of the period of 24 months from either the date when the mining operations have permanently ceased or the date when any application for approval of a restoration scheme under sub-paragraph (a)(i) has been finally determined, whichever is later, and

(bb) aftercare, if any, in respect of any part of a site, shall be carried out throughout the period of five years from either the date when any reinstatement or restoration in respect of that part is completed or the date when any application for approval of a restoration scheme under sub-paragraph (a)(i) has been finally determined, whichever is later;

(iv) where there is no approved restoration scheme—

(aa) all buildings, plant, machinery, structures and erections used at any time for or in connection with any previous coal-mining operations at that mine shall be removed from any land which is an authorised site unless the mineral planning authority have otherwise agreed in writing, and

(bb) that land shall, so far as practicable, be restored to its condition before any previous coal-mining operations at that mine took place or to such condition as may have been agreed in writing between the mineral planning authority and the developer,

before the end of the period specified in sub-paragraph (v);

(v) the period referred to in sub-paragraph (iv) is—

(aa) the period of 24 months from the date when the mining operations have permanently ceased or, if an application for approval of a restoration scheme has been made under sub-paragraph (a)(i) before that date, 24 months from the date when that application has been finally determined, whichever is later, or

(bb) any longer period which the mineral planning authority have agreed in writing;

(vi) for the purposes of sub-paragraph (a), an application for approval of a restoration scheme has been finally determined when the following conditions have been met—

(aa) any proceedings on the application, including any proceeding on or in consequence of an application under section 288 of the Act (proceedings for questioning the validity of certain orders, decisions and directions), have been determined, and

(bb) any time for appealing under section 78 (right to appeal against planning decisions and failure to take such decisions), or applying or further applying under section 288, of the Act (where there is a right to do so) has expired;

(b) sub-paragraph (a) shall not apply to land in respect of which there is an extant planning permission which—

(i) has been granted on an application under Part III of the Act, and

(ii) has been implemented.

Interpretation of Class A

A.2 For the purposes of Class A—

"a licensee of the Coal Authority" means any person who is for the time being authorised by a licence under Part II of the Coal Industry Act 1994 to carry on coal-mining operations to which section 25 of that Act (coal-mining operations to be licensed) applies;

"approved restoration scheme" means a restoration scheme which is approved when an application made under paragraph A.1(a)(i) is finally determined, as approved (with or without conditions), or as subsequently varied with the written approval of the mineral planning authority (with or without conditions);

"coal-related minerals" means minerals other than coal which are, or may be, won and worked by coal-mining operations;

"designated seam area" means land identified, in accordance with paragraph (a) of the definition of "seam plan", in a seam plan which was deposited with the mineral planning authority before 30th September 1993;

"previous coal-mining operations" has the same meaning as in section 54(3) of the Coal Industry Act 1994 (obligations to restore land affected by coal-mining operations) and references in Class A to the use of anything in connection with any such operations shall include references to its use for or in connection with activities carried on in association with, or for purposes connected with, the carrying on of those operations;

"restoration scheme" means a scheme which makes provision for the reinstatement, restoration or aftercare (or a combination of these) of any land which is an authorised site and has been used at any time for or in connection with any previous coal-mining operations at that mine; and

"seam plan" means a plan or plans on a scale of not less than 1 to 25,000 showing—

(a) land comprising the maximum extent of the coal seam or seams that could have been worked from shafts or drifts existing at a mine at 13th November 1992, without further development on an authorised site other than development permitted by Class B of Part 20 of Schedule 2 to the Town and Country Planning General Development Order 1988, as originally enacted;

(b) any active access used in connection with the land referred to in paragraph (a) of this definition;

(c) the National Grid lines and reference numbers shown on Ordnance Survey maps;

(d) a typical stratigraphic column showing the approximate depths of the coal seam referred to in paragraph (a) of this definition.

Class B

Permitted development

B. Development by a licensee of the British Coal Corporation, in a mine started before 1st July 1948, consisting of—

(a) the winning and working underground of coal or coal-related minerals in a designated seam area; or

(b) the carrying out of development underground which is required in order to gain access to and work coal or coal-related minerals in a designated seam area.

Interpretation of Class B

B.1 For the purposes of Class B—

"designated seam area" has the same meaning as in paragraph A.2 above;

"coal-related minerals" means minerals other than coal which can only be economically worked in association with the working of coal or which can only be economically brought to the surface by the use of a mine of coal; and

"a licensee of the British Coal Corporation" means any person who is for the time being authorised by virtue of section 25(3) of the Coal Industry Act 1994 (coal-mining operations to be licensed) to carry on coal-mining operations to which section 25 of that Act applies.

Class C

Permitted development

C. Any development required for the purposes of a mine which is carried out on an authorised site at that mine by a licensed operator, in connection with coal-mining operations.

Development not permitted

C.1 Development is not permitted by Class C if—

(a) the external appearance of the mine would be materially affected

(b) any building, plant or machinery, structure or erection or any deposit of minerals or waste—

(i) would exceed a height of 15 metres above ground level, or

(ii) where a building, plant or machinery would be rearranged, replaced or repaired, the resulting development would exceed a height of 15 metres above ground level or the height of what was rearranged, replaced or repaired, whichever is the greater;

(c) any building erected (other than a replacement building) would have a floor space exceeding 1,000 square metres;

(d) the cubic content of any replaced, extended or altered building would exceed by more than 25% the cubic content of the building replaced, extended or altered or the floor space would exceed by more than 1,000 square metres, the floor space of that building;

(e) it would be for the purpose of creating a new surface access to underground workings or of improving an existing access (which is not an active access) to underground workings; or

(f) it would be carried out on land to which the description in paragraph F.2(1)(b) applies, and a plan of that land had not been deposited with the mineral planning authority before 5th June 1989.

Conditions

C.2 Development is permitted by Class C subject to the condition that before the end of the period of 24 months from the date when the mining operations have permanently ceased, or any longer period which the mineral planning authority agree in writing—

(a) all buildings, plant, machinery, structures and erections and deposits of minerals or waste permitted by Class C shall be removed from the land unless the mineral planning authority have otherwise agreed in writing; and

(b) the land shall, so far as is practicable, be restored to its condition before the development took place or to such condition as may have been agreed in writing between the mineral planning authority and the developer.

Class D

Permitted development

D. Any development required for the purposes of a mine which is carried out on an authorised site at that mine by a licensed operator in connection with coal-mining operations and with the prior approval of the mineral planning authority.

Development not permitted

D.1 Development is not permitted by Class D if—

(a) it would be for the purpose of creating a new surface access or improving an existing access (which is not an active access) to underground workings; or

(b) it would be carried out on land to which the description in paragraph F.2(1)(b) applies, and a plan of that land had not been deposited with the mineral planning authority before 5th June 1989.

Condition

D.2 Development is permitted by Class D subject to the condition that before the end of the period of 24 months from the date when the mining operations have permanently ceased, or any longer period which the mineral planning authority agree in writing—

(a) all buildings, plant, machinery, structures and erections and deposits of minerals or waste permitted by Class D shall be removed from the land, unless the mineral planning authority have otherwise agreed in writing; and

(b) the land shall, so far as is practicable, be restored to its condition before the development took place or to such condition as may have been agreed in writing between the mineral planning authority and the developer.

Interpretation of Class D

D.3 The prior approval referred to in Class D shall not be refused or granted subject to conditions unless the authority are satisfied that it is expedient to do so because—

(a) the proposed development would injure the amenity of the neighbourhood and modifications could reasonably be made or conditions reasonably imposed in order to avoid or reduce that injury, or

(b) the proposed development ought to be, and could reasonably be, sited elsewhere.

Class E

Permitted development

E. The carrying out by the Coal Authority or a licensed operator, with the prior approval of the mineral planning authority, of development required for the maintenance

or safety of a mine or a disused mine or for the purposes of ensuring the safety of the surface of the land at or adjacent to a mine or a disused mine.

Prior approvals

E.1(1) The prior approval of the mineral planning authority to development permitted by Class E is not required if—

(a) the external appearance of the mine or disused mine at or adjacent to which the development is to be carried out would not be materially affected;

(b) no building, plant or machinery, structure or erection—

(i) would exceed a height of 15 metres above ground level, or

(ii) where any building, plant, machinery, structure or erection is rearranged, replaced or repaired, would exceed a height of 15 metres above ground level or the height of what was rearranged, replaced or repaired, whichever is the greater,

and

(c) the development consists of the extension, alteration or replacement of an existing building, within the limits set out in paragraph (3).

(2) The approval referred to in Class E shall not be refused or granted subject to conditions unless the authority are satisfied that it is expedient to do so because—

(a) the proposed development would injure the amenity of the neighbourhood and modifications could reasonably be made or conditions reasonably imposed in order to avoid or reduce that injury, or

(b) the proposed development ought to be, and could reasonably be, sited elsewhere.

(3) The limits referred to in paragraph E.1(1)(c) are—

(a) that the cubic content of the building as extended, altered or replaced does not exceed that of the existing building by more than 25%, and

(b) that the floor space of the building as extended, altered or replaced does not exceed that of the existing building by more than 1,000 square metres.

Interpretation of Part 20

F.1 For the purposes of Part 20—

"active access" means a surface access to underground workings which is in normal and regular use for the transportation of coal, materials, spoil or men;

"coal-mining operations" has the same meaning as in section 65 of the Coal Industry Act 1994 (interpretation) and references to any development or use in connection with coal-mining operations shall include references to development or use for or in connection with activities carried on in association with, or for purposes connected with, the carrying on of those operations;

"licensed operator" has the same meaning as in section 65 of the Coal Industry Act 1994;

"normal and regular use" means use other than intermittent visits to inspect and maintain the fabric of the mine or any plant or machinery; and

"prior approval of the mineral planning authority" means prior written approval of that authority of detailed proposals for the siting, design and external appearance of the proposed building, plant or machinery, structure or erection as erected, installed, extended or altered.

F.2(1) Subject to sub-paragraph (2), land is an authorised site for the purposes of Part 20 if—

(a) it is identified in a grant of planning permission or any instrument by virtue of which planning permission is deemed to be granted as land which may be used for development described in this Part; or

(b) in any other case, it is land immediately adjoining an active access which, on 5th December 1988, was in use for the purposes of that mine in connection with coal-mining operations.

(2) For the purposes of sub-paragraph (1), land is not to be regarded as in use in connection with coal-mining operations if—

(a) it is used for the permanent deposit of waste derived from the winning and working of minerals; or

(b) there is on, over or under it a railway, conveyor, aerial ropeway, roadway, overhead power line or pipe-line which is not itself surrounded by other land used for those purposes.

COMMENTARY

Derivation

Town and Country Planning General Development Order 1988 (S.I. 1988 No. 1813), Pt. 20, as amended by S.I. 1992 No. 2450 and S.I. 1994 No. 2595.

Definitions

"a licensee of the Coal Authority": Class A.2; Class B.1.
"active access": Class F.1.
"approved restoration scheme": Class A.2.
"building": art. 1(2).
"coal-mining operations": Class F.1.
"coal-related minerals": Class A.2; Class B.1.
"designated seam area": Class A.2.
"development": 1990 Act, s.55.
"licensed operator": Class F.1.
"normal and regular use": Class F.1.
"previous coal-mining operations": Class A.2.
"prior approval of the mineral planning authority": Class F.1.
"restoration scheme": Class A.2.
"seam plan": Class A.2.

General Note

Introduction

This Part grants rights for coal mining by the Coal Authority (established by the Coal Industry Act 1994) and its licensees, and for licensees of the former British Coal Corporation. Classes A and B relate to mines where mining operations commenced prior to the introduction of comprehensive planning control on July 1, 1948, and are restricted to areas designated in deposited seam plans. Class C permits any development required for mining purposes by an operator licenced by the former Corporation, at an authorised site, subject to limitations. Classes C and D are for the benefit of licensees of the Coal Authority as well licensees of the former Corporation in respect of ancillary development at an authorised site. Class E relates to safety and maintenance works at mines and disused mines. In some cases it requires the prior approval of the mineral planning authority.

Policy guidance

Advice on the original provisions is contained in MPG5, *Minerals Planning and the General Development Order* (1988), and in a Guidance note issued by the Department of the Environment in November 1994 which it is intended to incorporate into an MPG in due course.

Classes A and B: pre-1948 mines

These Classes preserve rights to mine coal and coal-related minerals in mines where mining started before the introduction of planning control in 1948. Following amendments to the Order in 1993, it became necessary, in order to protect these rights, for the operator to deposit with the mineral planning authority a seam plan showing a designated seam area. Permitted development rights under this Class are now restricted to development within that area.

Class A extends to licensees of the Coal Authority, and is subject to the requirements of Class A. 1 as to the execution of an approved scheme for the restoration of the land, unless the mine has the benefit of an extant planning permission which has been implemented (Class A.1(b)). In that case, it will be subject to the powers of the mineral planning authority to impose a restoration condition, either at the time the permission was granted, or subsequently using its powers under the 1990 Act, s.97 and Sched. 5. Where there is no approved restoration scheme, and mining operations have not permanently ceased, the operator must have applied to the mineral planning authority for approval of such a scheme by December 31, 1995 (or such later date as may have been agreed). Otherwise, the developer becomes subject to the requirements of Class A.1(a)(iv) as to the removal of plant and machinery and restoration to the condition of the land before any previous coal-mining operations at that mine took place (though the mineral planning authority have power to agree a different standard of restoration).

Class B extends only to licensees of the former British Coal Corporation, and does not include requirements as to restoration.

Class C: development required for mining purposes

This Class benefits licensed operators, both of the Coal Authority and the former British Coal Corporation, at authorised sites. It is solely for development in connection with coal mining operations. It is subject to various limitations, and also to the restoration condition in Class C.2.

Class D: other required development

This Class permits a range of surface development at authorised sites but requires the prior approval of the mineral planning authority.

Class E: maintenance and safety

Class E is similarly limited to the Coal Authority and licensed operators, and, except for the cases specified in Class E.1(1)(a), requires the prior approval of the mineral planning authority.

PART 21

WASTE TIPPING AT A MINE

Class A

Permitted development

A. The deposit, on premises used as a mine or on ancillary mining land already used for the purpose, of waste derived from the winning and working of minerals at that mine or from minerals brought to the surface at that mine, or from the treatment or the preparation for sale, consumption or utilization of minerals from the mine.

Development not permitted

A.1 Development is not permitted by Class A if—

(a) in the case of waste deposited in an excavation, waste would be deposited at a height above the level of the land adjoining the excavation, unless that is provided for in a waste management scheme or a relevant scheme;

(b) in any other case, the superficial area or height of the deposit (measured as at 21st October 1988) would be increased by more than 10%, unless such an increase is provided for in a waste management scheme or in a relevant scheme.

Conditions

A.2 Development is permitted by Class A subject to the following conditions—

(a) except in a case where a relevant scheme or a waste management scheme has already been approved by the mineral planning authority, the developer shall, if the mineral planning authority so require, within three months or such longer period as the authority may specify, submit a waste management scheme for that authority's approval;

(b) where a waste management scheme or a relevant scheme has been approved, the depositing of waste and all other activities in relation to that deposit shall be carried out in accordance with the scheme as approved.

Interpretation of Class A

A.3 For the purposes of Class A—

"ancillary mining land" means land adjacent to and occupied together with a mine at which the winning and working of minerals is carried out in pursuance of planning permission granted or deemed to be granted under Part III of the Act (control over development); and

"waste management scheme" means a scheme required by the mineral planning authority to be submitted for their approval in accordance with the condition in paragraph A.2(a) which makes provision for—

(a) the manner in which the depositing of waste (other than waste deposited on a site for use for filling any mineral excavation in the mine or on ancillary mining land in order to comply with the terms of any planning permission granted on an application or deemed to be granted under Part III of the Act) is to be carried out after the date of the approval of that scheme;

(b) where appropriate, the stripping and storage of the subsoil and topsoil;

(c) the restoration and aftercare of the site.

Class B

Permitted development

B. The deposit on land comprised in a site used for the deposit of waste materials or refuse on 1st July 1948 of waste resulting from coal-mining operations.

Development not permitted — **B.1 Development is not permitted by Class B unless it is in accordance with a relevant scheme approved by the mineral planning authority before 5th December 1988.**

Interpretation of Class B — **B.2 For the purposes of Class B—**
"coal-mining operations" has the same meaning as in section 65 of the Coal Industry Act 1994 (interpretation).

Interpretation of Part 21 — **C. For the purposes of Part 21—**
"relevant scheme" means a scheme, other than a waste management scheme, requiring approval by the mineral planning authority in accordance with a condition or limitation on any planning permission granted or deemed to be granted under Part III of the Act (control over development), for making provision for the manner in which the deposit of waste is to be carried out and for the carrying out of other activities in relation to that deposit.

COMMENTARY

DERIVATION

Town and Country Planning General Development Order 1988 (S.I. 1988 No. 1813), Sched. 2, Pt. 21, as amended by S.I. 1994 No. 2595.

DEFINITIONS

"ancillary mining land": Class A.3.
"coal mining operations": Class B.2.
"relevant scheme": Class C.
"waste management scheme": Class A.3.

GENERAL NOTE

Guidance on the scope of this Part is contained in MPG5, *Minerals Planning and the General Development Order*, paras. 27 and 28. It allows tipping of waste generated at the mine concerned or on ancillary mining land already used for tipping, but it does not allow the importing of waste from elsewhere, except for the continuance under Class B of pre-1948 rights for remote tipping that were preserved by the British Coal Corporation under schemes approved by the mineral planning authority before December 5, 1988.

PART 22

MINERAL EXPLORATION

Class A

Permitted development

A. Development on any land during a period not exceeding 28 consecutive days consisting of—

(a) the drilling of boreholes;

(b) the carrying out of seismic surveys; or

(c) the making of other excavations,

for the purpose of mineral exploration, and the provision or assembly on that land or adjoining land of any structure required in connection with any of those operations.

Development not permitted

A.1 Development is not permitted by Class A if—

(a) it consists of the drilling of boreholes for petroleum exploration;

(b) any operation would be carried out within 50 metres of any part of an occupied residential building or a building occupied as a hospital or school;

(c) any operation would be carried out within a National Park, an area of outstanding natural beauty, a site of archaeological interest or a site of special scientific interest;

(d) any explosive charge of more than 1 kilogram would be used;

(e) any excavation referred to in paragraph A(c) would exceed 10 metres in depth or 12 square metres in surface area;

(f) in the case described in paragraph A(c) more than 10 excavations would, as a result, be made within any area of 1 hectare within the land during any period of 24 months; or

(g) any structure assembled or provided would exceed 12 metres in height, or, where the structure would be within 3 kilometres of the perimeter of an aerodrome, 3 metres in height.

Conditions

A.2 Development is permitted by Class A subject to the following conditions—

(a) no operations shall be carried out between 6.00 p.m. and 7.00 a.m.;

(b) no trees on the land shall be removed, felled, lopped or topped and no other thing shall be done on the land likely to harm or damage any trees, unless the mineral planning authority have so agreed in writing;

(c) before any excavation (other than a borehole) is made, any topsoil and any subsoil shall be separately removed from the land to be excavated and stored separately from other excavated material and from each other;

(d) within a period of 28 days from the cessation of operations unless the mineral planning authority have agreed otherwise in writing—

(i) any structure permitted by Class A and any waste material arising from other development so permitted shall be removed from the land,

(ii) any borehole shall be adequately sealed,

(iii) any other excavation shall be filled with material from the site,

(iv) the surface of the land on which any operations have been carried out shall be levelled and any topsoil replaced as the uppermost layer, and

(v) the land shall, so far as is practicable, be restored to its condition before the development took place, including the carrying out of any necessary seeding and replanting.

Class B

Permitted development

B. Development on any land consisting of—
(a) the drilling of boreholes;
(b) the carrying out of seismic surveys; or
(c) the making of other excavations,
for the purposes of mineral exploration, and the provision or assembly on that land or on adjoining land of any structure required in connection with any of those operations.

Development not permitted

B.1 Development is not permitted by Class B if—
(a) it consists of the drilling of boreholes for petroleum exploration;
(b) the developer has not previously notified the mineral planning authority in writing of his intention to carry out the development (specifying the nature and location of the development);
(c) the relevant period has not elapsed;
(d) any explosive charge of more than 2 kilograms would be used;
(e) any excavation referred to in paragraph B(c) would exceed 10 metres in depth or 12 square metres in surface area; or
(f) any structure assembled or provided would exceed 12 metres in height.

Conditions

B.2 Development is permitted by Class B subject to the following conditions—
(a) the development shall be carried out in accordance with the details in the notification referred to in paragraph B.1(b), unless the mineral planning authority have otherwise agreed in writing;
(b) no trees on the land shall be removed, felled, lopped or topped and no other thing shall be done on the land likely to harm or damage any trees, unless specified in detail in the notification referred to in paragraph B.1(b) or the mineral planning authority have otherwise agreed in writing;
(c) before any excavation other than a borehole is made, any topsoil and any subsoil shall be separately removed from the land to be excavated and stored separately from other excavated material and from each other;
(d) within a period of 28 days from operations ceasing, unless the mineral planning authority have agreed otherwise in writing—
(i) any structure permitted by Class B and any waste material arising from other development so permitted shall be removed from the land,
(ii) any borehole shall be adequately sealed,
(iii) any other excavation shall be filled with material from the site,
(iv) the surface of the land shall be levelled and any topsoil replaced as the uppermost layer, and
(v) the land shall, so far as is practicable, be restored to its condition before the development took place, including the carrying out of any necessary seeding and replanting, and
(e) the development shall cease no later than a date six months after the elapse of the relevant period, unless the mineral planning authority have otherwise agreed in writing.

Interpretation of Class B

B.3 For the purposes of Class B—
"relevant period" means the period elapsing—
(a) where a direction is not issued under article 7, 28 days after the notification referred to in paragraph B.1(b) or, if earlier, on the date on which the mineral planning authority notify the developer in writing that they will not issue such a direction, or

(b) where a direction is issued under article 7, 28 days from the date on which notice of that decision is sent to the Secretary of State, or, if earlier, the date on which the mineral planning authority notify the developer that the Secretary of State has disallowed the direction.

Interpretation of Part 22

C. For the purposes of Part 22—
"mineral exploration" means ascertaining the presence, extent or quality of any deposit of a mineral with a view to exploiting that mineral; and
"structure" includes a building, plant or machinery.

COMMENTARY

Derivation

Town and Country Planning General Development Order 1988 (S.I. 1988 No. 1813), Sched. 2, Pt. 22.

Definitions

"aerodrome": art. 1(2).
"building": art. 1(2).
"development": 1990 Act, s.55.
"land": 1990 Act, s.336(1).
"mineral exploration": Class C.
"mineral planning authority": 1990 Act, s.1(4).
"structure": Class C.

General Note

This Part grants two separate permissions for mineral exploration.

Is planning permission required?

Not all works of mineral exploration will require planning permission. It might be difficult to argue that small scale exploratory works of short duration, such as exploration involving vibriosis techniques, constituted "development" within the 1990 Act. In *Bedfordshire County Council v. Central Electricity Generating Board* [1985] J.P.L. 48, the question arose whether certain exploratory works by the Nuclear Radioactive Waste Executive (Nirex) involving a process of preliminary sampling by means of bore holes constituted development. The High Court (Mr. P. Ashworth, Q.C. sitting as Deputy Judge), though required only to take a provisional view as a basis for issuing an interlocutory injunction, took the view that the proposals could not properly be considered alongside building, engineering and mining operations. It was to be a trifling matter, all over in two days, and no plant was to be erected on the site other than portable plant which would make a small hole to a shallow depth.

The scope of the permitted development

There are two Classes of permitted development for mineral exploration in this Part. The only difference between them on the face of the permission is the period for which they are exercisable: the first is a permission for up to 28 days; the other is for up to 42 days. The 28 days permission is narrowly confined in other ways as well; it is not available at all within 50 metres of occupied housing or hospitals, nor within any National Park, area of outstanding natural beauty or site of special scientific interest (conservation areas are omitted from this list), and explosive charges are limited to 1 kg (2 kg for the 42 day permission). To take advantage of the 42 day permission, a developer must previously notify the mineral planning authority of his intention to carry out the development, giving them the opportunity to negotiate improvements in the proposals if deemed necessary, against the backcloth of their power to make an art. 7 direction (see below).

Petroleum exploration is expressly excluded under both permissions: previously it had been assumed that the height limit of 4 metres would automatically exclude it, but improvements in technology in "micro-drilling" have since led to the production of oil and gas exploration rigs below this height (see further MPG5, *Minerals Planning and the General Development Order* 1988, para. 22).

Article 7 directions

The power to withdraw permission by an order under art. 4 does not apply to Class B of this Part. Instead, the special regime in art. 7 applies. If a mineral planning authority receive notification of proposed development they may within 21 days, if satisfied as required by art. 7(1), direct that the permission under Class B should not apply. This is an accelerated procedure. The prior approval of the Secretary of State is not required, but a copy of the direction must be sent to him. If he does not disallow it within 28 days of it being made, it comes into force on the 29th day. Use of this power may give a rise to liability to pay compensation (see further the General Note to art. 7).

PART 23

REMOVAL OF MATERIAL FROM MINERAL-WORKING DEPOSITS

Class A

Permitted development **A. The removal of material of any description from a stockpile.**

Class B

Permitted development **B. The removal of material of any description from a mineral-working deposit other than a stockpile.**

Development not permitted

B.1 Development is not permitted by Class B if—

(a) the developer has not previously notified the mineral planning authority in writing of his intention to carry out the development and supplied them with the appropriate details:

(b) the deposit covers a ground area exceeding 2 hectares, unless the deposit contains no mineral or other material which was deposited on the land more than 5 years before the development; or

(c) the deposit derives from the carrying out of any operations permitted under Part 6 of this Schedule or any Class in a previous development order which it replaces.

Conditions

B.2 Development is permitted by Class B subject to the following conditions—

(a) it shall be carried out in accordance with the details given in the notice sent to the mineral planning authority referred to in paragraph B.1(a) above, unless that authority have agreed otherwise in writing;

(b) if the mineral planning authority so require, the developer shall within a period of three months from the date of the requirement (or such other longer period as that authority may provide) submit to them for approval a scheme providing for the restoration and aftercare of the site;

(c) where such a scheme is required, the site shall be restored and aftercare shall be carried out in accordance with the provisions of the approved scheme;

(d) development shall not be commenced until the relevant period has elapsed.

Interpretation of Class B

B.3 For the purposes of Class B—

"appropriate details" means the nature of the development, the exact location of the mineral-working deposit from which the material would be removed, the proposed means of vehicular access to the site at which the development is to be carried out, and the earliest date at which any mineral presently contained in the deposit was deposited on the land; and

"relevant period" means the period elapsing—

(a) where a direction is not issued under article 7, 28 days after the notification referred to in paragraph B.1(a) or, if earlier, on the date on which the mineral planning authority notify the developer in writing that they will not issue such a direction; or

(b) where a direction is issued under article 7, 28 days from the date on which notice of that direction is sent to the Secretary of State, or, if earlier, the date on which the mineral planning authority notify the developer that the Secretary of State has disallowed the direction.

Interpretation of Part 23

C. For the purposes of Part 23—

"stockpile" means a mineral-working deposit consisting primarily of minerals which have been deposited for the purposes of their processing or sale.

COMMENTARY

DERIVATION

Town and Country Planning General Development Order 1988 (S.I. 1988 No. 1813), Sched. 2, Pt. 23.

DEFINITIONS

"appropriate details": Class B.3.
"development": 1990 Act, s.55.
"mineral working deposit": 1990 Act. s.336(1).
"relevant period": Class B.3.
"stockpile": Class C.

GENERAL NOTE

Until 1981, the extraction of minerals from a deposit on land did not generally constitute development requiring planning permission, because the view was taken that development occurred only when minerals were removed from "in" or "under" land, not from "on" land (see, *e.g.* appeal decisions at [1950] J.P.L. 437; [1952] J.P.L. 58, 165; [1981] J.P.L. 693). The Town and Country Planning (Minerals) Act 1981 then extended the scope of control by inserting a new subs. (3A) in s.22 of the 1971 Act so as to include removal of any material from a mineral working deposit, and the extraction of minerals from a disused railway embankment (now the 1990 Act, s.55(4)). "Mineral working deposit" is now defined (1990 Act, s.336(1)) as "any deposit of material remaining after minerals have been extracted from land or otherwise deriving from the carrying out of operations for the winning and working of minerals in, on or under land." Upon the coming into force of those provisions in 1986, the 1977 Order was amended to give effect to undertakings given by the Secretary of State that permission would be granted for some activities that the Act had brought within control.

Those provisions are carried through to this Part. Class A preserves the right to work a stockpile (minerals deposited for the purpose of processing or sale). Removal of minerals from other deposits is permitted under Class B, in accordance with the notification and other requirements of Class B.1, and the conditions in Class B.2.

Article 7 directions

The power to withdraw permission by an order under art. 4 does not apply to Class B of this Part. Instead, the special regime in art. 7 applies. If a mineral planning authority receive notification of proposed development they may, if satisfied as required by art. 7(2), direct that the permission under Class B should not apply.

PART 24

DEVELOPMENT BY TELECOMMUNICATIONS CODE SYSTEM OPERATORS

Class A

Permitted development

A. Development by or on behalf of a telecommunications code system operator for the purpose of the operator's telecommunication system in, on, over or under land controlled by that operator or in accordance with his licence, consisting of—

(a) the installation, alteration or replacement of any telecommunication apparatus,

(b) the use of land in an emergency for a period not exceeding six months to station and operate moveable telecommunication apparatus required for the replacement of unserviceable telecommunication apparatus, including the provision of moveable structures on the land for the purposes of that use, or

(c) development ancillary to radio equipment housing.

Development not permitted

A.1 Development is not permitted by Class A(a) if—

(a) in the case of the installation of apparatus (other than on a building or other structure) the apparatus, excluding any antenna, would exceed a height of 15 metres above ground level;

(b) in the case of the alteration or replacement of apparatus already installed (other than on a building or other structure), the apparatus, excluding any antenna, would when altered or replaced exceed the height of the existing apparatus or a height of 15 metres above ground level, whichever is the greater;

(c) in the case of the installation, alteration or replacement of apparatus on a building or other structure, the height of the apparatus (taken by itself) would exceed—

(i) 15 metres, where it is installed, or is to be installed, on a building or other structure which is 30 metres or more in height; or

(ii) 10 metres in any other case;

(d) in the case of the installation, alteration or replacement of apparatus on a building or other structure, the highest part of the apparatus when installed, altered or replaced would exceed the height of the highest part of the building or structure by more than—

(i) 10 metres, in the case of a building or structure which is 30 metres or more in height;

(ii) 8 metres, in the case of a building or structure which is more than 15 metres but less than 30 metres in height;

(iii) 6 metres in any other case;

(e) in the case of the installation, alteration or replacement of any apparatus other than—

(i) a mast,

(ii) an antenna,

(iii) a public call box,

(iv) any apparatus which does not project above the level of the surface of the ground, or

(v) radio equipment housing,

the ground or base area of the structure would exceed 1.5 square metres;

(f) in the case of the installation, alteration or replacement of an antenna on a building or structure (other than a mast) which

is less than 15 metres in height; on a mast located on such a building or structure; or, where the antenna is to be located below a height of 15 metres above ground level, on a building or structure (other than a mast) which is 15 metres or more in height—

(i) the antenna is to be located on a wall or roof slope facing a highway which is within 20 metres of the building or structure on which the antenna is to be located;

(ii) in the case of dish antennas, the size of any dish would exceed 0.9 metres or the aggregate size of all of the dishes would exceed 1.5 metres, when measured in any dimension;

(iii) in the case of antennas other than dish antennas, the development would result in the presence on the building or structure of more than two antenna systems; or

(iv) the building or structure is a listed building or a scheduled monument;

(g) in the case of the installation, alteration or replacement of an antenna on a building or structure (other than a mast) which is 15 metres or more in height, or on a mast located on such a building or structure, where the antenna is located at a height of 15 metres or above, measured from ground level—

(i) in the case of dish antennas, the size of any dish would exceed 1.3 metres or the aggregate size of all of the dishes would exceed 3.5 metres, when measured in any dimension;

(ii) in the case of antenna systems other than dish antennas, the development would result in the presence on the building or structure of more than three antenna systems; or

(iii) the building or structure is a listed building or a scheduled monument;

(h) in the case of development of any article 1(5) land, it would consist of—

(i) the installation or alteration of an antenna or of any apparatus which includes or is intended for the support of such an antenna; or

(ii) the replacement of such an antenna or such apparatus by an antenna or apparatus which differs from that which is being replaced,

unless the development is carried out in an emergency;

(i) it would consist of the installation, alteration or replacement of system apparatus within the meaning of section 8(6) of the Road Traffic (Driver Licensing and Information Systems) Act 1989 (definitions of driver information systems etc.);

(j) in the case of the installation of a mast, on a building or structure which is less than 15 metres in height, such a mast would be within 20 metres of a highway;

(k) in the case of the installation, alteration or replacement of radio equipment housing—

(i) the development is not ancillary to the use of any other telecommunication apparatus;

(ii) it would exceed 90 cubic metres or, if located on the roof of a building, it would exceed 30 cubic metres;

(iii) on any article 1(5) land, it would exceed 2 cubic metres, unless the development is carried out in an emergency;

or

(l) it would consist of the installation, alteration or replacement of any telecommunication apparatus on, or within the curtilage of, a dwellinghouse.

Conditions

A.2(1) Class A(a) and Class A(c) development is permitted subject to the condition that any antenna or supporting apparatus, radio equipment housing or development ancillary to radio equipment housing constructed, installed, altered or replaced on a building in accordance

with that permission shall, so far as is practicable, be sited so as to minimise its effect on the external appearance of the building.

(2) Class A(a) and Class A(c) development is permitted subject to the condition that any apparatus or structure provided in accordance with that permission shall be removed from the land, building or structure on which it is situated—

- **(a) if such development was carried out on any article 1(5) land in an emergency, at the expiry of the relevant period, or**
- **(b) in any other case, as soon as reasonably practicable after it is no longer required for telecommunication purposes,**

and such land, building or structure shall be restored to its condition before the development took place, or to any other condition as may be agreed in writing between the local planning authority and the developer.

(3) Class A(b) development is permitted subject to the condition that any apparatus or structure provided in accordance with that permission shall at the expiry of the relevant period be removed from the land and the land restored to its condition before the development took place.

(4) Class A development on—

- **(a) article 1(5) land (unless carried out in an emergency), or**
- **(b) any other land and consisting of the construction, installation, alteration or replacement of a mast or a public call box, or of radio equipment housing with a volume in excess of 2 cubic metres, or of development ancillary to radio equipment housing,**

is permitted subject to the following conditions—

- **(i) where the proposed development consists of the installation of a mast within 3 kilometres of the perimeter of an aerodrome, the developer shall notify the Civil Aviation Authority or the Secretary of State for Defence, as appropriate, of the proposal, before making the application required by sub-paragraph (ii);**
- **(ii) before beginning the development, the developer shall apply to the local planning authority for a determination as to whether the prior approval of the authority will be required to the siting and appearance of the development;**
- **(iii) the application shall be accompanied—**
  - **(aa) by a written description of the proposed development and a plan indicating its proposed location together with any fee required to be paid; and**
  - **(bb) where sub-paragraph (i) applies, by evidence that the Civil Aviation Authority or the Secretary of State for Defence, as the case may be, has been notified of the proposal;**
- **(iv) the development shall not be begun before the occurrence of one of the following—**
  - **(aa) the receipt by the applicant from the local planning authority of a written notice of their determination that such prior approval is not required;**
  - **(bb) where the local planning authority gives the applicant notice that such prior approval is required, the giving of such approval to the applicant within 28 days following the date on which they received his application; or**
  - **(cc) the expiry of 28 days following the date on which the local planning authority received the application, without the local planning authority making any determination as to whether such approval is required, notifying the applicant of their determination, or giving or refusing approval to the siting or appearance of the development;**
- **(v) the development shall, except to the extent that the**

local planning authority otherwise agree in writing, be carried out—

(aa) where prior approval has been given as mentioned in sub-paragraph (iv)(bb), in accordance with the details approved;

(bb) in any other case, in accordance with the details submitted with the application;

and

(vi) the development shall be begun—

(aa) where prior approval has been given as mentioned in sub-paragraph (iv)(bb), not later than the expiration of five years beginning with the date on which approval was given;

(bb) in any other case, not later than the expiration of five years beginning with the date on which the local planning authority were given the information referred to in sub-paragraph (iii).

(5) In a case of emergency, development on any article 1(5) land is permitted by Class A subject to the condition that the operator shall give written notice to the local planning authority of such development as soon as possible after the emergency begins.

Interpretation of Class A

A.3 For the purposes of Class A—

"antenna system" means a set of antennas installed on a building or structure and operated by a single telecommunications code system operator in accordance with his licence;

"development ancillary to radio equipment housing" means the construction, installation, alteration or replacement of structures, equipment or means of access which are ancillary to and reasonably required for the purposes of radio equipment housing;

"development in accordance with a licence" means development carried out by an operator in pursuance of a right conferred on that operator under the telecommunications code, and in accordance with any conditions, relating to the application of that code imposed by the terms of his licence;

"land controlled by an operator" means land occupied by the operator in right of a freehold interest or a leasehold interest under a lease granted for a term of not less than 10 years;

"mast" means a radio mast or a radio tower;

"relevant period" means a period which expires—

(i) six months from the commencement of the construction, installation, alteration or replacement of any apparatus or structure permitted by Class A(a) or Class A(c) or from the commencement of the use permitted by Class A(b), as the case may be, or

(ii) when the need for such apparatus, structure or use ceases,

whichever occurs first;

"telecommunication apparatus" means any apparatus falling within the definition of that term in paragraph 1 of Schedule 2 to the Telecommunications Act 1984 ("the 1984 Act") (the telecommunications code), and includes radio equipment housing;

"the telecommunications code" means the code contained in Schedule 2 to the 1984 Act;

"telecommunications code system operator" means a person who has been granted a licence under section 7 of the 1984 Act (power to license systems) which applies the telecommunications code to him in pursuance of section 10 of that Act (the telecommunications code); and

"telecommunication system" has the meaning assigned to that term by section 4(1) of the 1984 Act (meaning of "telecommunication system" and related expressions).

COMMENTARY

Derivation

Town and Country Planning General Development Order 1988 (S.I. 1988 No. 1813, Sched. 2, Pt. 24 as substituted by S.I. 1992 No. 2450, and amended by S.I. 1994 No. 678. In the 1995 consolidation, Clause A.2(2) is amended to provide that the land may alternatively be restored to "any other condition as may be agreed in writing between the local planning authority and the developer"; and Class A.2(4)(i) is amended to specify "within 3 kilometres of the perimeter of an aerodrome".

Definitions

"antenna system": Class A.3.
"article 1(5) land": art. 1(5) and Sched. 1, Pt. 1.
"building": art. 1(2) and 1990 Act, s.336(1). For this Part it includes part of a building.
"1984 Act" Class A. 3.
"development": 1990 Act, s.55.
"development ancillary to radio equipment housing": Class A.3.
"development in accordance with a licence": Class A.3.
"land": 1990 Act, s.336.
"land controlled by an operator": Class A.3.
"mast": Class A.3.
"relevant period": Class A.3.
"telecommunications apparatus": Class A.3 (and see below).
"telecommunications code": Class A.3 (and see below).
"telecommunications code system operator": Class A.3.
"telecommunication system": Class A.3 (and see below).

General Note

This Part grants permission for telecommunications development by licensed operators. It derives from Class XXIV of the 1977 Order, which was inserted in 1985, but was substantially redrafted and clarified in 1988, and again in 1992. It extends to development on land controlled by the operator, or development in accordance with his licence, in relation to telecommunications apparatus; and to the emergency use of land for up to 6 months to provide replacement moveable apparatus in place of unserviceable apparatus.

Where the operator undertakes development otherwise than on land controlled by him, the scope of his rights depends not only on this Part but also on the terms and conditions of his licence, and failure to comply with them renders the development unauthorised under this Part. A summary of planning-related code licence requirements is contained in Annex 2 to PPG 8, *Telecommunications* (1992), and a summary of permitted development rights for telecommunications development is in Annex 1.

Additional rights for telecommunications development by persons other than code operators are in Pt. 25.

Sensitive areas

Exercise of Pt. 24 rights is restricted on article 1(5) land (National Parks, areas of outstanding natural beauty, the Broads and conservation areas) by Class A.1(h) and A.2(4), so as to exclude installation or alteration of any microwave antenna otherwise than in an emergency, and to require that before other apparatus is installed on land controlled by the operator (*i.e.*, not in accordance with licence terms) the local planning authority should be given not less than four weeks prior written notice. The development does not then require their consent, but the notification enables them to make an art. 4 direction withdrawing permission should they see fit (see further below). In the case of apparatus to be installed on other land, licence conditions generally require prior notification to the local planning authority.

Class A.3: interpretation

The following expressions are defined by the Telecommunications Act 1984:

"telecommunications system" (s.4(1)):

(1) In this Act "telecommunications system" means a system for the conveyance, through the agency of electric, magnetic, electro-magnetic, electro-chemical or electro-chemical energy, of:

(a) speech, music and other sounds;
(b) visual images;
(c) signals serving for the impartation (whether as between persons and persons, things and things or persons and things) of any matter otherwise than in the form of sounds or visual images; or
(d) signals serving for the actuation or control of machinery of apparatus.

"telecommunications apparatus" (Sched. 2, para. 1):

"telecommunications apparatus" includes any apparatus falling within the definition of s.4(3) of this Act and any apparatus not so falling which is designed or adapted for use in connection with the running of a telecommunication system and, in particular:

(a) any line, that is to say, any wire, cable, tube, pipe or other similar thing (including its casing or coating) which is so designed or adapted; and
(b) any structure, pole or other thing in, on, by or form which any telecommunication apparatus is or may be installed, supported, carried or suspended;

and references to the installation of telecommunication apparatus shall be construed accordingly.

S.4(3) of the Act also provides:

"telecommunications apparatus" means (except where the extended definition in Sched. 2 to this Act applies) apparatus constructed or adapted for use:

(a) in transmitting or receiving anything falling within paras. (a) to (d) of sub. (1) above which is to be or has been conveyed by means of a telecommunication system; or
(b) in conveying, for the purposes of such a system, anything falling within those paragraphs.

Article 4 directions

No development rights conferred by this Part can be withdrawn by an art. 4 direction, unless the direction specifically so provides (art. 4(2)(c)). Such a direction requires the approval of the Secretary of State, and his policy is that blanket directions aimed at imposing full planning controls over a wide range of code operator development will not normally be approved: PPG 6, *Telecommunications* (1992), para. 19. The advice continues:

"But where a particular urban or rural location, *e.g.* a hill top site, seems likely to attract very obtrusive or inappropriate telecommunications development which would seriously threaten amenity, consideration

> will be given to directions submitted for approval. It will rarely be justified to withdraw permitted development rights unless there is a real and specific threat to the locality in which a development is to take place."

Withdrawal of permitted development rights may render the local planning authority liable to pay compensation under s.108.

The prior approval requirements

In *Tandridge District Council v. Telecom Securicor Cellular Radio Ltd* [1995] E.G.C.S. 121, the applicants notified the local planning authority of their proposals, but the site was not approved and they then submitted two copies of a drawing relating to a new location. The letter was not expressed to be an application, was not accompanied by a written description, and was not accompanied by a fee. The local planning authority responded that work was not to start until the applicants were informed that prior approval would not be required, or that approval was received. The authority then attempted, just before the expiry of the following 28-day period, to fax to the applicants a notification that prior approval would be required, and having failed in that attempt, telephoned them. The High Court held that the amended notification had not constituted a valid application, which should have been an application *de novo*, and been accompanied by the requisite fee. Also, under this Part, oral notice sufficed for the purpose of refusing approval to the siting and appearance of the installation in question. Only under condition A.2(iv)(a) was written notice required when the authority had decided that prior approval was not required.

PART 25

OTHER TELECOMMUNICATIONS DEVELOPMENT

Class A

Permitted development

A. The installation, alteration or replacement on any building or other structure of a height of 15 metres or more of a microwave antenna and any structure intended for the support of a microwave antenna.

Development not permitted

A.1 Development is not permitted by Class A if—

(a) the building is a dwellinghouse or the building or other structure is within the curtilage of a dwellinghouse;

(b) it would consist of development of a kind described in paragraph A of Part 24;

(c) the development would result in the presence on the building or structure of more than two microwave antennas;

(d) in the case of a satellite antenna, the size of the antenna, including its supporting structure but excluding any projecting feed element, would exceed 90 centimetres;

(e) in the case of a terrestrial microwave antenna—

(i) the size of the antenna, when measured in any dimension but excluding any projecting feed element, would exceed 1.3 metres; and

(ii) the highest part of the antenna or its supporting structure would be more than 3 metres higher than the highest part of the building or structure on which it is installed or is to be installed;

(f) it is on article 1(5) land; or

(g) it would consist of the installation, alteration or replacement of system apparatus within the meaning of section 8(6) of the Road Traffic (Driver Licensing and Information Systems) Act 1989 (definitions of driver information systems etc.).

Conditions

A.2 Development is permitted by Class A subject to the following conditions—

(a) the antenna shall, so far as is practicable, be sited so as to minimise its effect on the external appearance of the building or structure on which it is installed;

(b) an antenna no longer needed for the reception or transmission of microwave radio energy shall be removed from the building or structure as soon as reasonably practicable.

Class B

Permitted development

B. The installation, alteration or replacement on any building or other structure of a height of less than 15 metres of a satellite antenna.

Development not permitted

B.1 Development is not permitted by Class B if—

(a) the building is a dwellinghouse or the building or other structure is within the curtilage of a dwellinghouse;

(b) it would consist of development of a kind described in paragraph A of Part 24;

(c) it would consist of the installation, alteration or replacement of system apparatus within the meaning of section 8(6) of the Road Traffic (Driver Licensing and Information Systems) Act 1989 (definitions of driver information systems etc.);

(d) the size of the antenna (excluding any projecting feed element, reinforcing rim, mountings or brackets) when measured in any dimension would exceed—

(i) 90 centimetres in the case of an antenna to be installed on a building or structure on article 1(4) land;

(ii) 70 centimetres in any other case;

(e) the highest part of an antenna to be installed on a roof would, when installed, exceed in height the highest part of the roof;
(f) there is any other satellite antenna on the building or other structure on which the antenna is to be installed;
(g) it would consist of the installation of an antenna on a chimney;
(h) it would consist of the installation of an antenna on a wall or roof slope which fronts a waterway in the Broads, or a highway elsewhere.

Condition

B.2 Development is permitted by Class B subject to the following conditions—
(a) the antenna shall, so far as practicable, be sited so as to minimise its effect on the external appearance of the building or structure on which it is installed;
(b) an antenna no longer needed for the reception or transmission of microwave radio energy shall be removed from the building or structure as soon as reasonably practicable.

COMMENTARY

Derivation

Town and Country Planning General Development Order 1988 (S.I. 1988 No. 1813), Sched. 2, Pt. 25.

Definitions

"building": art. 1(2) and 1990 Act, s.336(1).
"development": 1990 Act, s.55.
"dwellinghouse": art. 1(2).
"microwave antenna": art. 1(2).
"satellite antenna": art. 1(2).

General Note

This Part is more limited than Pt. 24, but the rights are not restricted to telecommunication code operators. It grants permission for the installation, alteration or replacement of a microwave antenna (which includes both a satellite antenna and a terrestrial microwave antenna: art. 1(2)) on any building or other structure, to the extent that the works actually constitute development requiring permission. Dwellinghouses are excluded, and a separate permission limited to a single satellite antenna is instead granted by Pt. 1, Class H.

"Building" for the purposes of this Part includes part of a building (art. 1(2)).

PART 26

DEVELOPMENT BY THE HISTORIC BUILDINGS AND MONUMENTS COMMISSION FOR ENGLAND

Class A

Permitted development

A. Development by or on behalf of the Historic Buildings and Monuments Commission for England, consisting of—

(a) the maintenance, repair or restoration of any building or monument;

(b) the erection of screens, fences or covers designed or intended to protect or safeguard any building or monument; or

(c) the carrying out of works to stabilise ground conditions by any cliff, watercourse or the coastline;

where such works are required for the purposes of securing the preservation of any building or monument.

Development not permitted

A.1 Development is not permitted by Class A(a) if the works involve the extension of the building or monument.

Condition

A.2 Except for development also falling within Class A(a), Class A(b) development is permitted subject to the condition that any structure erected in accordance with that permission shall be removed at the expiry of a period of six months (or such longer period as the local planning authority may agree in writing) from the date on which work to erect the structure was begun.

Interpretation of Class A

A.3 For the purposes of Class A—

"building or monument" means any building or monument in the guardianship of the Historic Buildings and Monuments Commission for England or owned, controlled or managed by them.

COMMENTARY

DERIVATION

Town and Country Planning General Development Order 1988 (S.I. 1988 No. 1813), Sched. 2, Pt. 26 (unamended).

DEFINITIONS

"building or monument": Class A.3.
"development"; 1990 Act, s.55.

GENERAL NOTE

This Part gives permission to English Heritage to carry out minor works of development for the purposes of preservation of any buildings of which they are guardians, or which they own, control or manage.

PART 27

USE BY MEMBERS OF CERTAIN RECREATIONAL ORGANISATIONS

Class A

Permitted development	**A. The use of land by members of a recreational organisation for the purposes of recreation or instruction, and the erection or placing of tents on the land for the purposes of the use.**
Development not permitted	**A.1 Development is not permitted by Class A if the land is a building or is within the curtilage of a dwellinghouse.**
Interpretation of Class A	**A.2 For the purposes of Class A—** **"recreational organisation" means an organisation holding a certificate of exemption under section 269 of the Public Health Act 1936 (power of local authority to control use of moveable dwellings).**

COMMENTARY

DERIVATION

Town and Country Planning General Development Order 1988 (S.I. 1988 No. 1813), Sched. 2, Pt. 27 (unamended).

DEFINITIONS

"building": art. 1(2) 1990 Act, s.336(1).
"dwellinghouse": art. 1(2).
"recreational organisation": Class A.2.

GENERAL NOTE

This Part grants permission for use of land by members of certified recreational organisations for two purposes: for recreation or instruction, and for the placing of tents on the land. It is based directly on Class V of the 1948 Order, which was itself the outcome of lengthy negotiations between planning authorities and camping organisations. Planning authorities wanted there to be no permitted development rights, but for it to be left to their discretion whether to take any action in the relatively few cases where camping might do harm. Camping organisations argued that landowners would refuse them permission to camp for fear of enforcement action. The temporary use provisions (now in Pt. 4) satisfied neither side. The justification for the present provisions was explained by the Minister in a circular issued in 1948 as follows:

> "By Class V members of a number of well-known organisations which include camping among their activities are permitted, without limit of time, to use land for the purposes of recreation or instruction and to erect or place tents or caravans on the land. The safeguard to this, from the point of view of the Planning Authorities, is that these organisations lay down strict codes of rules for their members." (Circular 47 (1948), para. 7).

The system of controls over tenting and caravaning is complex, and proposals for rationalisation have been suggested by the Department of the Environment (see further the General Note to Pts. 4 and 5).

The organisations exempted under the 1936 Act and entitled to rely upon this Part are:

Boys' Brigade
Scout Association
Girl Guides
Salvation Army
Church Lads and Church Girls Brigade
National Council for the Y.M.C.A.
Army Cadet Force Association
Caravan Club
Camping and Caravaning Club
London Union of Youth Clubs

PART 28

DEVELOPMENT AT AMUSEMENT PARKS

Class A

Permitted Development

A. Development on land used as an amusement park consisting of—

(a) the erection of booths or stalls or the installation of plant or machinery to be used for or in connection with the entertainment of the public within the amusement park; or

(b) the extension, alteration or replacement of any existing booths or stalls, plant or machinery so used.

Development not permitted

A.1 Development is not permitted by Class A if—

(a) the plant or machinery would—

(i) if the land or pier is within 3 kilometres of the perimeter of an aerodrome, exceed a height of 25 metres or the height of the highest existing structure (whichever is the lesser), or

(ii) in any other case, exceed a height of 25 metres;

(b) in the case of an extension to an existing building or structure, that building or structure would as a result exceed 5 metres above ground level or the height of the roof of the existing building or structure, whichever is the greater, or

(c) in any other case, the height of the building or structure erected, extended, altered or replaced would exceed 5 metres above ground level.

Interpretation of Class A

A.2 For the purposes of Class A—

"amusement park" means an enclosed area of open land, or any part of a seaside pier, which is principally used (other than by way of a temporary use) as a funfair or otherwise for the purposes of providing public entertainment by means of mechanical amusements and side-shows; but, where part only of an enclosed area is commonly so used as a funfair or for such public entertainment only the part so used shall be regarded as an amusement park; and

"booths or stalls" includes buildings or structures similar to booths or stalls.

COMMENTARY

DERIVATION

Town and Country Planning General Development Order 1988 (S.I. 1988 No. 1813), Sched. 2, Pt. 28 (unamended).

DEFINITIONS

"aerodrome": art. 1(2).
"amusement parks": Class A.2.
"booths or stalls": Class A.2.
"development": 1990 Act, s.55.
"land": 1990 Act, s.336(1).

GENERAL NOTE

This Part permits development at existing amusement parks, but with the exceptions specified in Class A.1. An illustration of the effect of the exceptions is provided by the planning appeal decision in *Portsmouth City Council and Fun Acres Ltd* (1988) 3 P.A.D. 288, where a structure was held not to constitute permitted development because it exceeded 25 metres in height. Although the appellants stated that they proposed to substitute one not exceeding 25 metres height and thus within the Part if they lost the appeal, permission was refused.

PART 29

DRIVER INFORMATION SYSTEMS

Class A

Permitted development **A. The installation, alteration or replacement of system apparatus by or on behalf of a driver information system operator.**

Development not permitted **A.1 Development is not permitted by Class A if—**

(a) in the case of the installation, alteration or replacement of system apparatus other than on a building or other structure—

(i) the ground or base area of the system apparatus would exceed 1.5 square metres; or

(ii) the system apparatus would exceed a height of 15 metres above ground level;

(b) in the case of the installation, alteration or replacement of system apparatus on a building or other structure—

(i) the highest part of the apparatus when installed, altered, or replaced would exceed in height the highest part of the building or structure by more than 3 metres; or

(ii) the development would result in the presence on the building or structure of more than two microwave antennas.

Conditions **A.2 Development is permitted by Class A subject to the following conditions—**

(a) any system apparatus shall, so far as practicable, be sited so as to minimise its effect on the external appearance of any building or other structure on which it is installed;

(b) any system apparatus which is no longer needed for a driver information system shall be removed as soon as reasonably practicable.

Interpretation of Class A **A.3 For the purposes of Class A—**

"driver information system operator" means a person granted an operator's licence under section 10 of the Road Traffic (Driver Licensing and Information Systems) Act 1989 (operators' licences); and

"system apparatus" has the meaning assigned to that term by section 8(6) of that Act (definitions of driver information systems etc.).

COMMENTARY

Derivation

Town and Country Planning General Development Order 1988 (S.I. 1988 No. 1813), as inserted by S.I. 1991 No. 1536.

Definitions

"building": art. 1(2).
"development": 1990 Act, s.55.
"driver information system operator": Class A.3.
"system apparatus": Class A.3.

General Note

This Class permits the installation of special apparatus for driver information systems.

PART 30

TOLL ROAD FACILITIES

Class A

Permitted development

A. Development consisting of—

(a) the setting up and the maintenance, improvement or other alteration of facilities for the collection of tolls;

(b) the provision of a hard surface to be used for the parking of vehicles in connection with the use of such facilities.

Development not permitted

A.1 Development is not permitted by Class A if—

(a) it is not located within 100 metres (measured along the ground) of the boundary of a toll road;

(b) the height of any building or structure would exceed—

(i) 7.5 metres excluding any rooftop structure; or

(ii) 10 metres including any rooftop structure;

(c) the aggregate area of the floor space at or above ground level of any building or group of buildings within a toll collection area, excluding the floor space of any toll collection booth, would exceed 1,500 square metres.

Conditions

A.2 In the case of any article 1(5) land, development is permitted by Class A subject to the following conditions—

(a) the developer shall, before beginning the development, apply to the local planning authority for a determination as to whether the prior approval of the authority will be required to the siting, design and external appearance of the facilities for the collection of tolls;

(b) the application shall be accompanied by a written description, together with plans and elevations, of the proposed development and any fee required to be paid;

(c) the development shall not be begun before the occurrence of one of the following—

(i) the receipt by the applicant from the local planning authority of a written notice of their determination that such prior approval is not required;

(ii) where the local planning authority give the applicant notice within 28 days following the date of receiving his application of their determination that such prior approval is required, the giving of such approval; or

(iii) the expiry of 28 days following the date on which the application was received by the local planning authority without the local planning authority making any determination as to whether such approval is required or notifying the applicant of their determination;

(d) the development shall, except to the extent that the local planning authority otherwise agree in writing, be carried out—

(i) where prior approval is required, in accordance with the details approved;

(ii) where prior approval is not required, in accordance with the details submitted with the application;

and

(e) the development shall be carried out—

(i) where approval has been given by the local planning authority, within a period of five years from the date on which the approval was given;

(ii) in any other case, within a period of five years from the date on which the local planning authority were given the information referred to in sub-paragraph (b).

Interpretation of Class A

A.3 For the purposes of Class A—
"facilities for the collection of tolls" means such buildings, structures, or other facilities as are reasonably required for the purpose of or in connection with the collection of tolls in pursuance of a toll order;
"ground level" means the level of the surface of the ground immediately adjacent to the building or group of buildings in question or, where the level of the surface of the ground on which it is situated or is to be situated is not uniform, the level of the highest part of the surface of the ground adjacent to it;
"rooftop structure" means any apparatus or structure which is reasonably required to be located on and attached to the roof, being an apparatus or structure which is—

(a) so located for the provision of heating, ventilation, air conditioning, water, gas or electricity;
(b) lift machinery; or
(c) reasonably required for safety purposes;

"toll" means a toll which may be charged pursuant to a toll order;
"toll collection area" means an area of land where tolls are collected in pursuance of a toll order, and includes any facilities for the collection of tolls;
"toll collection booth" means any building or structure designed or adapted for the purpose of collecting tolls in pursuance of a toll order;
"toll order" has the same meaning as in Part I of the New Roads and Street Works Act 1991 (new roads in England and Wales); and
"toll road" means a road which is the subject of a toll order.

COMMENTARY

DERIVATION

Town and Country Planning General Development Order 1988 (S.I. 1988 No. 1813), Pt. 30, as inserted by S.I. 1992 No. 609.

DEFINITIONS

"development": 1990 Act, s.55.
"facilities for the collection of tolls": Class A.3.
"ground level": Class A.3.
"rooftop structure": Class A.3.
"toll": Class A.3.
"toll collection area": Class A.3.
"toll collection booth": Class A.3.
"toll order": Class A.3.
"toll road": Class A.3.

GENERAL NOTE

This Part was introduced following the enactment of the New Roads and Street Works Act 1991, which made provision for the construction of toll roads under a system of special concessions. This part grants permission for the setting up of toll collection facilities and the provision of ancillary hard surfaces for parking. Prior approval of the local planning authority may be required to the siting, design and external appearance of the facilities where they are to be provided on art. 1(5) land.

PART 31

DEMOLITION OF BUILDINGS

Class A

Permitted developments **A. Any building operation consisting of the demolition of a building.**

Development not permitted **A.1 Development is not permitted by Class A where—**

(a) the building has been rendered unsafe or otherwise uninhabitable by the action or inaction of any person having an interest in the land on which the building stands; and

(b) it is practicable to secure safety or health by works of repair or works for affording temporary support.

Conditions **A.2 Development is permitted by Class A subject to the following conditions—**

(a) where demolition is urgently necessary in the interests of safety or health and the measures immediately necessary in such interests are the demolition of the building the developer shall, as soon as reasonably practicable, give the local planning authority a written justification of the demolition;

(b) where the demolition does not fall within sub-paragraph (a) and is not excluded demolition—

(i) the developer shall, before beginning the development, apply to the local planning authority for a determination as to whether the prior approval of the authority will be required to the method of demolition and any proposed restoration of the site;

(ii) the application shall be accompanied by a written description of the proposed development, a statement that a notice has been posted in accordance with sub-paragraph (iii) and any fee required to be paid;

(iii) subject to sub-paragraph (iv), the applicant shall display a site notice by site display on or near the land on which the building to be demolished is sited and shall leave the notice in place for not less than 21 days in the period of 28 days beginning with the date on which the application was submitted to the local planning authority;

(iv) where the site notice is, without any fault or intention of the applicant, removed, obscured or defaced before the period of 21 days referred to in sub-paragraph (iii) has elapsed, he shall be treated as having complied with the requirements of that sub-paragraph if he has taken reasonable steps for protection of the notice and, if need be, its replacement;

(v) the development shall not be begun before the occurrence of one of the following—

(aa) the receipt by the applicant from the local planning authority of a written notice of their determination that such prior approval is not required;

(bb) where the local planning authority give the applicant notice within 28 days following the date of receiving his application of their determination that such prior approval is required, the giving of such approval; or

(cc) the expiry of 28 days following the date on which the application was received by the local planning authority without the local planning authority making any determination as to whether such approval is required or notifying the applicant of their determination;

(vi) the development shall, except to the extent that the

local planning authority otherwise agree in writing, be carried out—

(aa) where prior approval is required, in accordance with the details approved;

(bb) where prior approval is not required, in accordance with the details submitted with the application;

and

(vii) the development shall be carried out—

(aa) where approval has been given by the local planning authority, within a period of five years from the date on which approval was given;

(bb) in any other case, within a period of five years from the date on which the local planning authority were given the information referred to in sub-paragraph (ii).

Interpretation of Class A

A.3 For the purposes of Class A—

"excluded demolition" means demolition—

(a) on land which is the subject of a planning permission, for the redevelopment of the land, granted on an application or deemed to be granted under Part III of the Act (control over development),

(b) required or permitted to be carried out by or under any enactment, or

(c) required to be carried out by virtue of a relevant obligation;

"relevant obligation" means—

(a) an obligation arising under an agreement made under section 106 of the Act, as originally enacted (agreements regulating development or use of land);

(b) a planning obligation entered into under section 106 of the Act, as substituted by section 12 of the Planning and Compensation Act 1991 (planning obligations), or under section 299A of the Act (Crown planning obligations);

(c) an obligation arising under or under an agreement made under any provision corresponding to section 106 of the Act, as originally enacted or as substituted by the Planning and Compensation Act 1991, or to section 299A of the Act; and

"site notice" means a notice containing—

(a) the name of the applicant,

(b) a description, including the address, of the building or buildings which it is proposed be demolished,

(c) a statement that the applicant has applied to the local planning authority for a determination as to whether the prior approval of the authority will be required to the method of demolition and any proposed restoration of the site,

(d) the date on which the applicant proposes to carry out the demolition, and

(e) the name and address of the local planning authority,

and which is signed and dated by or on behalf of the applicant.

Class B

Permitted development

B. Any building operation consisting of the demolition of the whole or any part of any gate, fence, wall or other means of enclosure.

COMMENTARY

DERIVATION

Town and Country Planning General Development Order 1988 (S.I. 1988 No. 1813), Pt 31, as inserted by S.I. 1992 No. S.I. 1280. With the 1995 consolidation, Class A.2(b)(iii) is amended to refer to the display of a site notice "by site display", which is now defined in art. 1(2).

DEFINITIONS

"by site display": art. 1(2).
"building": art. 1(2), and see below.
"excluded development": Class A.3.
"relevant obligation": Class A.3.
"site notice": Class A.3.

GENERAL NOTE

Introduction

This Part is a component in the complex machinery that the Government introduced to address what was, initially, a relatively minor policy problem. This was the absence of planning control over demolition generally, because of the unwillingness of the House of Lords in *Coleshill and District Investment Co Ltd v. Minister of Housing and Local Government* [1969] 2 All E.R. 525 to find that it fell within the class of building, mining, engineering or other operations. The Court of Appeal in *Cambridge City Council v. Secretary of State for the Environment* [1992] 3 P.L.R. 4 overturned a brave attempt by a Deputy High Court judge to hold that substantial demolition works must constitute a building operation because it was an operation normally undertaken by a person carrying on business as a builder. The Court of Appeal would not necessarily have ruled that proposition out, but was of the opinion that the judge had made a finding of fact which he was not entitled to make.

The amendment of the 1990 Act

Under the 1990 Act, s.55(1A), inserted by the Planning and Compensation Act 1991 following the first instance judgment in the *Cambridge* case, demolition is now within the definition of "building operation". The amendments also empowered the Secretary of State to direct that the demolition of certain descriptions of building should not be taken to involve development (s.55(2)(g)). In accordance with that power, the Secretary of State has made the Town and Country Planning (Demolition—Description of Buildings) Direction 1995 (reproduced in DOE Circular 10/95, *Planning Controls over Demolition*, Appendix A). That Direction supersedes a Direction made in 1994 (which is reproduced as Appendix B to that Circular); which in turn superseded the second Direction made in 1992 (and contained in DOE Circular 26/92, *Planning Control over Demolition*), the first, issued in DOE Circular 16/92, *Planning Controls over Demolition*, having proved to be defective.

Under the 1995 Direction, the demolition of none of the following is to be taken to involve development of the land under the Town and Country Planning Act 1990, even if it involves acts which would, under the old law, have been construed by the courts as involving building or engineering operations:

(a) any building which is a listed building under the Planning (Listed Buildings and Conservation Areas) Act 1990: the justification for this category is the separate set of controls applicable under that Act;
(b) any building in a conservation area: similar, though more limited, controls apply under the Listed Buildings Act;
(c) scheduled monuments (for which there are controls under the Ancient Monuments and Archaeological Areas Act 1979);
(d) any other building than a dwellinghouse or a building adjoining a dwellinghouse;

(e) any building with a cubic content of less than 50 cubic metres measured externally;

(f) the whole or any part of any gate, fence, wall or other means of enclosure in a conservation area.

Parliament's intention in enacting the amendments to s.55 may have been to extend the scope of planning control over demolition, but it can be seen that the only buildings over which demolition control is now exercisable, irrespective of whether the operations involved are building or engineering operations, is dwellinghouses. Hence there has been a significant reduction in development control over demolition. The demolition of structures of such size or complexity that engineering operations were necessary, was formerly "development" by reason of those operations. Under the 1995 direction it is not to be taken to involve development at all.

Moreover, the extent to which control is exercisable over dwellinghouse demolition is further reduced by this Part, which grants permitted development rights for the demolition of dwellinghouses and buildings adjoining them (Class A) and for any building operation involving the demolition of any gate, fence, wall or other means of enclosure (Class B). Class B is unconditional; Class A is subject to a prior approval requirement (unless demolition is urgently necessary, in which case a written justification is required as soon as reasonably practicable thereafter).

Policy guidance

Advice on these provisions and the exercise of control under them is contained in DOE Circular 10/95, *Planning Controls over Demolition.*

Definition of building

For the purposes of Class A of this Part, the definition of building in art. 1(2) includes part of a building. Gates, fences, walls and other means of enclosure are excluded, except in Class B (demolition of buildings).

PART 32

SCHOOLS, COLLEGES, UNIVERSITIES AND HOSPITALS

Permitted development

A. The erection on the site of any school, college, university or hospital of any building required for use as part of, or for a purpose incidental to the use of, the school, college, university or hospital as such, as the case may be.

Development not permitted

A.1 Development is not permitted by Class A—

(a) unless—

(i) in the case of school, college or university buildings, the predominant use of the existing buildings on the site is for the provision of education, or

(ii) in the case of hospital buildings, the predominant use of the existing buildings on the site is for the provision of any medical or health services;

(b) where the cumulative total floor space of any buildings erected on a particular site (other than the original school, college, university or hospital buildings) would exceed 10% of the total floor space of the original school, college, university or hospital buildings on that site;

(c) where the cumulative total cubic content of buildings erected on a particular site (other than the original school, college, university or hospital buildings) would exceed 250 cubic metres;

(d) where any part of a building erected would be within 20 metres of the boundary of the site;

(e) where, as a result of the development, any land, used as a playing field immediately before the development took place, could no longer be so used.

Condition

A.2 Development is permitted by Class A subject to the condition that, in the case of any article 1(5) land, any materials used shall be of a similar appearance to those used for the original school, college, university or hospital buildings.

Interpretation of Class A

A.3 For the purposes of Class A—

"cumulative total floor space" or "cumulative total cubic content", as the case may be, of buildings erected, includes the total floor space or total cubic content of any existing buildings previously erected at any time under Class A; and

"original school, college, university or hospital buildings" means any school, college university or hospital buildings, as the case may be, other than any buildings erected at any time under Class A.

COMMENTARY

DERIVATION

Town and Country Planning General Development Order 1988 (S.I. 1988 No. 1813), Pt. 32, inserted by S.I. 1995 No. 298 from March 9, 1995.

DEFINITIONS

"building": art. 1(2).
"cumulative total floor space": Class A.3.
"original school, college, university or hospital building": Class A.3.

GENERAL NOTE

Introduction

This Class confers a narrow range of permitted development rights in respect of schools, colleges, universities and hospitals. It allows buildings to be erected or extended where the predominant use of buildings already on the site is for educational, health or medical services. Hence it does not apply in the case of sites where the predominant existing use is that of ancillary activities to these main purposes conducted elsewhere.

Playing fields

There is special protection for playing fields: the loss of any existing playing field takes the whole building or extension outside permitted development rights under this Part.

PART 33

CLOSED CIRCUIT TELEVISION CAMERAS

Class A

Permitted development

A. The installation, alteration or replacement on a building of a closed circuit television camera to be used for security purposes.

Development not permitted

A.1 Development is not permitted by Class A if—

(a) the building on which the camera would be installed, altered or replaced is a listed building or a scheduled monument;

(b) the dimensions of the camera including its housing exceed 75 centimetres by 25 centimetres by 25 centimetres;

(c) any part of the camera would, when installed, altered or replaced, be less than 250 centimetres above ground level;

(d) any part of the camera would, when installed, altered or replaced protrude from the surface of the building by more than one metre when measured from the surface of the building;

(e) any part of the camera would, when installed, altered or replaced, be in contact with the surface of the building at a point which is more than one metre from any other point of contact;

(f) any part of the camera would be less than 10 metres from any part of another camera installed on a building;

(g) the development would result in the presence of more than four cameras on the same side of the building; or

(h) the development would result in the presence of more than 16 cameras on the building.

Conditions

A.2 Development is permitted by Class A subject to the following conditions—

(a) the camera shall, so far as practicable, be sited so as to minimise its effect on the external appearance of the building on which it is situated;

(b) the camera shall be removed as soon as reasonably practicable after it is no longer required for security purposes.

Interpretation of Class A

A.3 For the purposes of Class A—

"camera", except in paragraph A.1(b), includes its housing, pan and tilt mechanism, infra red illuminator, receiver, mountings and brackets; and

"ground level" means the level of the surface of the ground immediately adjacent to the building or, where the level of the surface of the ground is not uniform, the level of the highest part of the surface of the ground adjacent to it.

COMMENTARY

DERIVATION

This Part was added by the 1995 consolidation.

DEFINITIONS

"building": art. 1(2).
"camera": Class A.3.
"development": 1990 Act, s.55.

"ground level": Class A.3.
"listed building": art. 1(2).
"scheduled monument": art. 1(2).

General Note

This Part grants permitted development rights in respect of the installation, alteration or replacement on shops, flats, houses and other buildings of closed circuit television cameras within specified limits on size and numbers. There are quantitative limits: up to four cameras are permitted on the same side of the building and up to 16 cameras on any one building, provided that they are at least 10 metres apart. In addition, each camera must be sited so as to minimise its effect on the external appearance of the building. Cameras must be removed once they are no longer required for security purposes.

These development rights apply in all areas, including article 1(5) land, but do not apply to listed buildings or scheduled monuments, where the installation of cameras is subject to listed building control and conservation area control under the Planning (Listed Buildings and Conservation Areas) Act 1990.

SCHEDULE 3

Article 9

STATUTORY INSTRUMENTS REVOKED

1 *Title of Instrument*	2 *Reference*	3 *Extent of Revocation*
The Town and Country Planning General Development Order 1988	S.I. 1988/1813	Paragraphs (3), (5), (6) and (7) of article 1 and articles 3, 4, 5 and 6 and Schedules 1 and 2
The Town and Country Planning General Development (Amendment) Order 1989	S.I. 1989/603	Paragraphs (2) to (8) of article 2
The Town and Country Planning General Development (Amendment) (No. 2) Order 1989	S.I. 1989/1590	Paragraphs (3) and (4) of article 2.
The Town and Country Planning General Development (Amendment) Order 1990	S.I. 1990/457	The whole Order to the extent not already revoked
The Town and Country Planning General Development (Amendment) (No. 2) Order 1990	S.I. 1990/2032	The whole Order
The Town and Country Planning General Development (Amendment) Order 1991	S.I. 1991/1536	The whole Order to the extent not already revoked
The Town and Country Planning General Development (Amendment) (No. 2) Order 1991	S.I. 1991/2268	The whole Order to the extent not already revoked
The Town and Country Planning General Development (Amendment) (No. 3) Order 1991	S.I. 1991/2805	Articles 8, 9 and 10 and the Schedule
The Town and Country Planning General Development (Amendment) Order 1992	S.I. 1992/609	The whole Order
The Town and Country Planning General Development (Amendment) (No. 2) Order 1992	S.I. 1992/658	Article 3
The Town and Country Planning General Development (Amendment) (No. 3) Order 1992	S.I. 1992/1280	The whole Order
The Town and Country Planning General Development (Amendment) (No. 4) Order 1992	S.I. 1992/1493	Articles 8, 9 and 12(2)
The Town and Country Planning General Development (Amendment) (No. 5) Order 1992	S.I. 1992/1563	Paragraph 2 of the Schedule
The Town and Country Planning General Development (Amendment) (No. 6) Order 1992	S.I. 1992/2450	Articles 2, 3, 4 and 6
The Town and Country Planning General Development (Amendment) Order 1994	S.I. 1994/678	Article 4
The Town and Country Planning General Development (Amendment) (No. 2) Order 1994	S.I. 1994/2595	Articles 4, 5 and 6 and paragraph (3) of article 7
The Town and Country Planning General Development (Amendment) Order 1995	S.I. 1995/298	The whole Order except article 3(1)

THE TOWN AND COUNTRY PLANNING (GENERAL DEVELOPMENT PROCEDURE) ORDER 1995

(S.I. 1995 No. 419)

Article

SCHEDULE 1

SCHEDULE 2

SCHEDULE 3

SCHEDULE 4

Certificate under article 24 of lawful use or development.

SCHEDULE 5

Statutory instruments revoked.

Citation, commencement and interpretation

1.—(1) This Order may be cited as the Town and Country Planning (General Development Procedure) Order 1995 and shall come into force on 3rd June 1995.

(2) In this Order, unless the context otherwise requires—

"the Act" means the Town and Country Planning Act 1990;

"building" includes any structure or erection, and any part of a building, as defined in this article, but does not include plant or machinery or any structure in the nature of plant or machinery;

"dwellinghouse" does not include a building containing one or more flats, or a flat contained within such a building;

"environmental information" and "environmental statement" have the same meanings respectively as in regulation 2 of the Town and Country Planning (Assessment of Environmental Effects) Regulations 1988 (interpretation);

"erection", in relation to buildings as defined in this article, includes extension, alteration, or re-erection;

"flat" means a separate and self-contained set of premises constructed or adapted for use for the purpose of a dwelling and forming part of a building from some other part of which it is divided horizontally;

"floor space" means the total floor space in a building or buildings;

"landscaping" means the treatment of land (other than buildings) being the site or part of the site in respect of which an outline planning permission is granted, for the purpose of enhancing or protecting the amenities of the site and the area in which it is situated and includes screening by fences, walls or other means, the planting of trees, hedges, shrubs or grass, the formation of banks, terraces or other earthworks, the laying out of gardens or courts, and the provision of other amenity features;

"by local advertisement" means by publication of the notice in a newspaper circulating in the locality in which the land to which the application relates is situated;

"mining operations" means the winning and working of minerals in, on or under land, whether by surface or underground working;

"outline planning permission" means a planning permission for the erection of a building, which is granted subject to a condition requiring the subsequent approval of the local planning authority with respect to one or more reserved matters;

"proposed highway" has the same meaning as in section 329 of the Highways Act 1980 (further provision as to interpretation);

"1988 Regulations" means the Town and Country Planning (Applications) Regulations 1988;

"reserved matters" in relation to an outline planning permission, or an application for such permission, means any of the following matters in respect of which details have not been given in the application, namely—

(a) siting,

(b) design,

(c) external appearance,

(d) means of access,

(e) the landscaping of the site;

"by site display" means by the posting of the notice by firm affixture to some object, sited and displayed in such a way as to be easily visible and legible by members of the public;

"special road" means a highway or proposed highway which is a special road in accordance with section 16 of the Highways Act 1980 (general provisions as to special roads);

"trunk road" means a highway or proposed highway which is a trunk road by virtue of sections 10(1) or 19 of the Highways Act 1980 (general provisions as to trunk roads, and certain special roads and other highways to become trunk roads) or any other enactment or any instrument made under any enactment.

COMMENTARY

General Note

General approach to interpretation

The highly technical and detailed nature of the Order is reflected in this complex definition article. Perhaps it always was so. Hence the observation of W. A. Leach on the 1950 Order: "It is evident as soon as art. 2 of the Order [interpretation] is reached that the Parliamentary draftsmen are losing their grip" ([1950] J.P.L. 473).

A general approach to interpretation was advanced by Goulding J. in *English Clays Lovering Pochin & Co. v. Plymouth Corporation* [1973] 2 All E.R. 730, at 735:

> "It is common ground that the Development Order is to be construed in what has sometimes been called in argument 'a broad or common sense manner,' at any rate in the manner appropriate, as counsel say, to a document framed for administrative purposes rather than as an instrument couched in conveyancing language. That has not prevented counsel on either side from spinning elaborate arguments worthy of a more complicated subject matter and drawn from other provisions of the Development Order itself, from other statutes or statutory instruments and from reported cases on different documents. While I greatly admire and acknowledge the thoroughness of counsel's endeavours, I do not find in the end that I can get any guidance from those illustrative arguments. It appears to me that, having considered all, I have to apply myself to the ordinary meaning of the language used by the Minister in making the Development Order ..."

The list of definitions contained in this article is not exhaustive. Expressions which make a single appearance in the Order are defined in the article or Part of the Schedule in which they appear, these are listed below. Moreover, all the definitions contained in the parent Act, the Town and Country Planning Act 1990 (see particularly the definition section, s.336) prevail for the purposes of the Order, except where a contrary intention appears (Interpretation Act 1978, s.11).

Cross-referenced definitions

Several of the definitions in this article draw upon definitions contained in other legislation. Full definitions and explanations are set out below:

"mine": "mining operations":

In *English Clays Lovering Pochin & Co. v. Plymouth Corporation* [1974] 1 W.L.R. 742, the court held that the essential idea in the term "winning or working of minerals" is that of extracting or separation of raw material from the solid earth in which it occurs: see further the General Note to the General Permitted Development Order 1995, Sched. 2, Pt. 19.

"proposed highway":

Highways Act 1980, s.329:

"proposed highway" means land on which, in accordance with plans made by a highway authority, that authority are for the time being constructing or intending to construct a highway shown in the plans.

"special road":

Under the Highways Act 1980, s.16, the Secretary of State for Transport may authorise a highway authority by means of a scheme under that section to provide, along a route prescribed by the scheme, a special road for the use of traffic of any class prescribed thereby.

"trunk road":

Under the Highways Act 1980 a road is a trunk road because it (a) was a trunk road under the Highways Act 1959 (1980 Act, s.10(1) or, (b) it is a special road provided by the Secretary of State for Transport which became a trunk road on the date specified in the scheme made under s.16 of the 1959 Act (1980 Act, s.19).

Definitions elsewhere in the Order

The following expressions are defined elsewhere in this Order:
"caravan": art. 10(2)
"classified road": art. 10(2)
"coal": art. 16(2)
"concessionaire": art. 10(2)
"consultee": art. 10(4)
"industrial process": art. 10(2)
"listed building": art. 10(2)
"network": art. 10(2)
"operator": art. 10(2)
"road subject to a concession": art. 10(2)
"schedule monument": art. 10(2)
"site of special scientific interest": art. 10(2)
"slurry": art. 10(2)
"street": art. 10(2)
"theatre": art. 10(2)
"toll order": art. 10(2)
"waste regulation authority": art. 10(2)

Application

2.—(1) This Order applies to all land in England and Wales, but where land is the subject of a special development order, whether made before or after the commencement of this Order, this Order shall apply to that land only to such extent and subject to such modifications as may be specified in the special development order.

(2) Nothing in this Order shall apply to any permission which is deemed to be granted under section 222 of the Act (planning permission not needed for advertisements complying with regulations).

COMMENTARY

DERIVATION

Town and Country Planning General Development Order 1988, art. 2.

DEFINITIONS

"advertisement": 1990 Act, s.336(1).
"land": 1990 Act, s.336(1).
"planning permission": 1990 Act, s.336(1).
"special development order": 1990 Act, s.58.

GENERAL NOTE

This order applies throughout England and Wales, but may be disapplied in any area by a special development order. That previously was the method used to establish a tighter regime in the sensitive areas that are now incorporated into the General Permitted Development Order 1995 as arts. 1(5) and 1(6) land, defined in Sched. 1.

The following special development orders have been made and remain unrepealed (though some related to a defined period which has now expired):

- Town and Country Planning (Ironstone Areas Special Development) Order 1950 (No. 1177)
- Town and Country Planning (Atomic Energy Establishments) Special Development Orders 1954 (No. 982) and 1957 (No. 806)
- Town and Country Planning (New Towns) Special Development Order 1977 (No. 665)
- Town and Country Planning (New Towns in Rural Wales) Special Development Order 1977 (No. 815)
- Town and Country Planning (Windscale and Calder Works) Special Development Order 1978 (No. 523)
- Town and Country Planning (Merseyside Urban Development Area) Special Development Order 1981 (No. 560)
- Town and Country Planning (London Docklands Urban Development Area) Special Development Order 1981 (No. 1082)
- Town and Country Planning (Vauxhall Cross) Special Development Order 1982 (No. 796)
- Town and Country Planning (Telecommunications Network) (Railway Operational Land) Special Development Order 1982 (No. 817)
- Town and Country Planning (NIREX) Special Development Order 1986 (No. 812)
- Town and Country Planning (Black Country Urban Development Area) Special Development Order 1987 (No. 1343)

Town and Country Planning (Teesside Urban Development Area) Special Development Order 1987 (No. 1344)
Town and Country Planning (Tyne and Wear Urban Development Area) Special Development Order 1987 (No. 1345)
Town and Country Planning (Wolverhampton Urban Development Area) Special Development Order 1988 (No. 1400)

In the special development orders made for the new towns and urban development corporations, the approach has generally been to confer permitted development rights for development by the development corporation provided it is in accordance with general proposals previously approved by the Secretary of State, and provided prescribed consultation is carried out before commencement. Where an objection or representation made in the course of consultation is not withdrawn, the corporation is obliged to notify the Secretary of State and may not commence development until informed that he does not propose to give a direction requiring a formal planning application to be made.

Applications for outline planning permission

3.—(1) Where an application is made to the local planning authority for outline planning permission, the authority may grant permission subject to a condition specifying reserved matters for the authority's subsequent approval.

(2) Where the authority who are to determine an application for outline planning permission are of the opinion that, in the circumstances of the case, the application ought not to be considered separately from all or any of the reserved matters, they shall within the period of one month beginning with the receipt of the application notify the applicant that they are unable to determine it unless further details are submitted, specifying the further details they require.

COMMENTARY

DERIVATION

Town and Country Planning General Development Order 1988, art. 7 (unamended).

DEFINITIONS

"outline planning permission": art. 1(2).
"reserved matters": art. 1(2).

GENERAL NOTE

Background

The idea of outline planning permissions was introduced by the 1950 General Development Order (arising from the informal practice of several planning authorities). It allows the planning authority to give a decision in principle, and to reserve details for subsequent approval. This requires a balance to be struck between the scope of the outline permission (which is the planning permission for all purposes of the Act: see *Hargreaves Transport v. Lynch* [1969] 1 W.L.R. 215; (1969) 20 P. & C.R. 143) and the detailed approval. The process is well explained in Circular 87 of the Ministry of Town and Country Planning, which accompanied the 1950 Order:

> "Since consideration at the approval stages is limited by the terms of the initial permission, it is essential that that permission should not take the form of a blank cheque, and, correspondingly, the authority must be furnished with sufficient information to enable them to form a proper judgment of what is proposed; there can be no question of entertaining propositions which are still in embryo. The application should indicate the character and approximate size of the building to be erected, and the use to which it is to be put (*e.g.*, 'a three-bedroomed house,' a 'two-storied factory for light industrial purposes with an aggregate floor-space of 30/35,000 square feet')."

Erection of a building

An outline planning permission as defined in art. 1(2) can be granted only for the erection of a building. But that is given an extended definition by the 1990 Act, s.336(1), which provides that:

"erection," in relation to buildings as defined in this subsection, includes extension, alteration and re-erection.

It may be argued that the definition does not carry across to this Order, because "building" is differently defined in art. 1(2); but the Order's definition is not different in kind but only narrower (it excludes certain structures from the definition in the Act) and this would not appear to affect the substantive sense of this extended definition of "erection."

Reserved matters

"Reserved matters" are defined by art. 1(2) as meaning "any of the following matters in respect of which details have not been given in the application, namely: (a) siting, (b) design, (c) external appearance, (d) means of access, (e) the landscaping of the site." The 1990 Act, s.336(1), defines "means of access" as including "any means of access, whether private or public, for vehicles or for foot passengers, and includes a street."

After the decision in *Chelmsford Corporation v. Secretary of State for the Environment* (1971) 22 P. & C.R. 880, where the court declined to hold that reserving the "layout" of the development for later approval empowered the authority to decide whether walls or fences for decorative purposes, and to protect privacy, should be provided, the Order was amended to allow authorities to reserve "landscaping" for subsequent approval. The word has deliberately been defined (art. 1(2)) in broad terms as meaning:

> "the treatment of land ... for the purpose of enhancing or protecting the amenities of the site and the area in which it is situated and includes screening by fences, walls or other means, the planting of trees, hedges, shrubs or grass, the formation of banks, terraces or other earthworks, the laying out of gardens or courts, and the provision of other amenity features."

As to applications for the approval of reserved matters, see the Commentary to art. 4.

Power to reserve approval of other matters

From the wording of this article, an authority may reserve matters for subsequent approval only where the application is an outline application, but that restriction is without prejudice to the inherent power to impose a condition reserving their subsequent approval to any component of the development (see, *e.g. Sutton London Borough Council v. Secretary of State for the Environment* (1975) 119 S.J. 321; (1975) 29 P. & C.R. 350, where the authority, on an application for full permission, had reserved approval of "the type and treatment of materials" to be used on the exterior of the building).

"Hybrid" applications

The critical difference between the formal outline procedure, and the inherent power of the planning authority to reserve matters by condition for subsequent approval, is that applicants have the right to insist upon an outline application in relation to any proposal to erect a building, and have a right of appeal against any exercise of the authority's power to require further information. Where details of a statutory reserved matter have been submitted in the outline application, the authority must deal with them at that stage. They are not "reserved matters," because those are by definition matters "in respect of which details have not been given in the application" (art. 1(2)). Thus the planning authority has no power to reserve them for subsequent approval, unless they have been submitted purely as illustrative material and thus are not part of the application; or the applicant agrees to amend the application so as to exclude them (see further, DOE Circular 11/95, Annex, para. 44). It follows also that the applicant is not bound by such materials in any subsequent submission of reserved matters for approval.

Requirement of further details

The power of the authority under para. (2) to require details of all or any reserved matters must be exercised within one month of the receipt of the application (though in the case of a county, whether it is receipt by them, or by the district authority with whom the application was lodged is not stated). The applicant may comply, or he may within six months of receiving the notice appeal to the Secretary of State (art. 23(2)(c)). The appeal is not, presumably, against the requirement to provide information, but is a substantive appeal as if planning permission had been refused. This was made clear in the 1977 Order (art. 6(2)) but was lost in the 1988 redrafting. It thus merely brings forward the date from which an appeal may be lodged from the eight week period specified in art. 23.

Applications for approval of reserved matters

4. An application for approval of reserved matters—

(a) shall be made in writing to the local planning authority and shall give sufficient information to enable the authority to identify the outline planning permission in respect of which it is made;

(b) shall include such particulars, and be accompanied by such plans and drawings, as are necessary to deal with the matters reserved in the outline planning permission; and

(c) except where the authority indicate that a lesser number is required, shall be accompanied by three copies of the application and the plans and drawings submitted with it.

COMMENTARY

DERIVATION

Town and Country Planning General Development Order 1988, art. 8 (unamended).

DEFINITIONS

"local planning authority": 1990 Act, s.1.
"outline planning permission": art. 1(2).
"reserved matters": art. 1(2).

GENERAL NOTE

An application for approval of reserved matters is not an application for planning permission, so the provisions as to ownership certificates (art. 6), publicity (art. 8) and consultation under art. 10 are all inapplicable (although under art. 12(1)(c) a county authority must consult the district before determining a reserved matters application relating to a county matter).

Although this article requires that the application be accompanied by particulars necessary to deal with the reserved matters, this requirement is directory, and the validity of the application is not therefore affected by a failure to supply all the necessary information at the time of the application (*Inverclyde District Council v. Secretary of State for Scotland*, 1982 S.L.T. 200).

Time limits for application

Application for approval of reserved matters must be made within three years of the grant of outline permission, or such other period as may have been specified in that permission (1990 Act, s.92(2)). The authority may specify different periods in relation to separate parts of the development so as to allow for phased implementation (s.92(5)). If the time limit is not met, the outline permission lapses, although it is open to an authority, if it so wishes, to treat a late application for reserved matter approval as a fresh application for full permission (see, *e.g. Cardiff Corporation v. Secretary of State for Wales* (1971) 115 S.J. 187).

In *Inverclyde District Council v. Secretary of State for Scotland*, 1982 S.L.T. 200, the House of Lords held (on the corresponding provisions of the Scottish legislation) that an application lodged within the prescribed time might still be amended after that time provided the amendment did not alter the whole character of the application, and did not bring in other reserved matters in respect of which an application should have been made in time. Authorities are exhorted by the Secretary of State to allow amendments, and not to deal at length with matters of detail (DOE Circular 9/95, para. 5).

Relationship to the outline permission

The reserved matters application must fall within the boundaries of the outline permission, and the reserved matters stage cannot be used to bring in matters completely outside the scope of the original permission. Thus in *Calcaria Construction Co. (York) v. Secretary of State for the Environment* (1974) 118 S.J. 421; (1974) 27 P. & C.R. 435, where outline permission had been granted for a warehouse, the court had little hesitation in upholding the Secretary of State's rejection of detailed proposals in which the development had become an out-of-town supermarket surrounded by a car-park for 992 cars. Similarly, there has been held to be a departure from the outline permission where a scheme approved in outline for a bungalow became a substantial house in the approval of reserved matters (*R. v. Castle Point District Council, ex p. Brooks* [1985] J.P.L. 473); and where outline permission for residential development of three five-storey blocks with garages, had changed to four four-storey blocks at detailed stage, with different parking and access arrangements (*Shemara v. Luton Corporation* (1967) 18 P. & C.R. 520). Although the number of residential units remained the same, the revised scheme was thought by the planning authority to be liable to prejudice the development of nearby sites. So too, if a new means of access, not sought at outline stage and therefore not reserved by the outline permission, is proposed in detailed plans, this would be a departure from the outline entitling the authority to refuse to approve the plans (*Chalgray v. Secretary of State for the Environment* (1976) 33 P. & C.R. 10).

In some cases it will be possible for the authority to overcome a departure from the terms of the outline permission by granting part approval only on the reserved matters application (see, *e.g. Inverclyde District Council v. Secretary of State for Scotland* 1982 S.L.T. 200).

But where an amendment has been made without off-site implications, such as the re-positioning of a private road, it would be unlikely to involve a departure from the outline permission (*Hamilton v. West Sussex County Council* [1958] 2 Q.B. 286; 9 P. & C.R. 279). Similarly, an applicant may omit a use which was included in the outline permission, particularly if that use was disadvantageous in planning terms, unless it was closely linked with other proposed uses, or there was a condition requiring all uses to be developed or none at all (*R. v. Hammersmith and Fulham London Borough Council, ex p. Greater London Council* (1985) 51 P. & C.R. 120).

The grant of outline permission constitutes commitment by the planning authority to the principle of the development, disentitling them to refuse approval to reserved matters on grounds going to the principle of the development (*Lewis Thirkwell v. Secretary of State for the Environment* [1978] J.P.L. 844; *Slough Borough Council v. Secretary of State for the Environment* [1995] E.G.C.S. 95).

Successive applications

Further applications may be lodged under the same outline permission, provided they are within the time limit, whether they follow an earlier refusal or offer an alternative to a scheme already approved (*Heron Corporation v. Manchester City Corporation* [1978] 1 W.L.R. 937; (1978) 37 P. & C.R. 44). Similarly, it is possible for separate applications to be made for piecemeal approval of reserved matters for separate parts of a development (*R. v. Secretary of State for the Environment, ex p. Percy Bilton Industrial Properties* (1975) 31 P. & C.R. 154; although the question of whether phased approval might be insisted upon by either party was expressly left open), or for different reserved matters (*Heron Corporation v. Manchester City Corporation* [1978] 1 W.L.R. 937; (1978) 37 P. & C.R. 44). But it would be possible for the authority in either case to withhold permission on planning grounds. They may consider, for example, that siting ought not to be considered separately from external design, or in the absence of a layout plan for the whole development.

Call-in by the Secretary of State

The High Court has held that an application for approval of reserved matters, as "an application ... for the approval of any local planning authority required under a development order" may be called in by the Secretary of State under s.77 of the 1990 Act; although the decision of the Secretary of State is not within the privative provisions of ss.284, 285 of that Act (see, *e.g. Turner v. Secretary of State for the Environment* (1973) 28 P. & C.R. 123). However, it is not clear that an application for reserved matters approval does pass that qualification, because the requirement to submit the application is imposed not by the development order, but by the planning permission itself.

[Applications in respect of Crown land

4A.—An application for planning permission made by virtue of section 299(2) of the Act shall be accompanied by—

(a) a statement that the application is made, by virtue of section 299(2) of the Act, in respect of Crown land; and

(b) where the application is made by a person authorised in writing by the appropriate authority, a copy of that authorisation.]

COMMENTARY

DERIVATION

Inserted as a modification by the Town and Country Planning (Crown Land Applications) Regulations 1995 (S.I. 1995 No. 1139), art. 2 and Sched. The article is in identical terms to that inserted in the Town and Country General Development Order 1988 (S.I. 1988 No. 1813) as art. 9A, by S.I. 1992 No. 2683.

DEFINITIONS

"appropriate authority": 1990 Act, s.293(2).
"Crown land": 1990 Act, s.293(1).
"land": 1990 Act, s.336(1).
"planning permission": 1990 Act, s.336(1).

GENERAL NOTE

Although the Town and Country Planning Act 1990 does not bind the Crown, s.299(2) enables the Crown to seek planning permission so as to enable Crown land to be disposed of with the benefit of permission. This article requires that an application purporting to be made under that section should identify that fact, and should be accompanied by proof of authorisation where necessary.

General provisions relating to applications

5.—(1) Any application made under regulation 3 of the 1988 Regulations (applications for planning permission) or article 4 above, shall be made—

(a) where the application relates to land in Greater London or a metropolitan county, to the local planning authority;

(b) where the application relates to land in neither Greater London nor a metropolitan county and—

(i) that land is in a National Park, or

(ii) the application relates to a county matter,

to the county planning authority;

(c) in any other case, to the district planning authority.

(2) When the local planning authority with whom an application has to be lodged receive—

(a) in the case of an application made under paragraph (1) of regulation 3 of the 1988 Regulations, the form of application required by that paragraph, together with the certificate or other documents required by article 7;

(b) in the case of an application made under regulation 3(3) of the 1988 Regulations, sufficient information to enable the authority to identify the previous grant of planning permission, together with the certificate or other documents required by article 7;

(c) in the case of an application made under article 4 above, the documents and information required by that article,

and the fee, if any, required to be paid in respect of the application, the authority shall as soon as is reasonably practicable, send to the applicant an acknowledgement of the application in the terms (or substantially in the terms) set out in Part 1 of Schedule 1 hereto.

(3) Where an application is made to a county planning authority in accordance with paragraph (1), that authority shall, as soon as practicable, send a copy of the application and of any accompanying plans and drawings to the district planning authority, if any.

(4) Where, after sending an acknowledgement as required by paragraph (2) of this article, the local planning authority consider that the application is invalid by reason of a failure to comply with the requirements of regulation 3 of the 1988 Regulations or article 4 above or any other statutory requirement, they shall as soon as reasonably practicable notify the applicant that his application is invalid.

(5) In this article, "county matter" has the meaning given to that expression in paragraph 1(1) of Schedule 1 to the Act (local planning authorities—distribution of functions).

COMMENTARY

DERIVATION

Town and Country Planning General Development Order 1988, art. 10, amended as respects cross-references to other provisions in this Order, and in relationship to unitary authorities established under the Local Government Act 1992.

DEFINITIONS

"county matter": para. (5).
"county planning authority": 1990 Act, s.1.
"district planning authority": 1990 Act, s.1.

"local planning authority": 1990 Act, s.1.

GENERAL NOTE

County matters

In Greater London and the metropolitan areas (Merseyside, West Midlands, Tyne and Wear, West Yorkshire, Greater Manchester, South Yorkshire) all planning applications are made to the London borough council or the metropolitan district council in whose area the land is. In the non-metropolitan counties, all planning applications had formerly to be made to the district planning authority, and, if they related to a "county matter," were forwarded to the county planning authority to be determined. Under amendments made from early 1992, however, all "county matter" applications are now made direct to the county planning authority. "County matters" are defined in the Town and Country Planning Act 1990, Sched. 1, para. 1.

In the urban development areas, except for Cardiff Bay, all functions of a local planning authority in relation to development control have been transferred by statutory instrument exclusively to the urban development corporations for the areas and planning applications are made direct to them as local planning authority.

In those parts of shire England where unitary authorities have been established under the Local Government Act 1992, and in Wales where unitary authorities replace the former two-tier structure from April 1, 1996, all planning applications are made to and determined by the unitary authority.

Action by the authority on receipt of application

The local planning authority may refuse to accept an application only if it is not valid. Provided it satisfies the criteria of this article, they must send an acknowledgement (para. (2)). If they subsequently take the view that an application is invalid, they must notify the applicant of that (para. (4)). An application does not become invalid merely because the cheque tendered in payment of the fee is dishonoured; instead, time ceases to run against the authority for the purposes of the eight week rule (see further the General Note to art. 23).

Notice of applications for planning permission

6.—(1) Subject to paragraph (2), an applicant for planning permission shall give requisite notice of the application to any person (other than the applicant) who on the prescribed date is an owner of the land to which the application relates, or a tenant,—

(a) by serving the notice on every such person whose name and address is known to him; and

(b) where he has taken reasonable steps to ascertain the names and addresses of every such person, but has been unable to do so, by local advertisement after the prescribed date.

(2) In the case of an application for planning permission for development consisting of the winning and working of minerals by underground operations, instead of giving notice in the manner provided for by paragraph (1), the applicant shall give requisite notice of the application to any person (other than the applicant) who on the prescribed date is an owner of any of the land to which the application relates, or a tenant,—

(a) by serving the notice on every such person whom the applicant knows to be such a person and whose name and address is known to him;

(b) by local advertisement after the prescribed date; and

(c) by site display in at least one place in every parish or community within which there is situated any part of the land to which the application relates, leaving the notice in position for not less than seven days in the period of 21 days immediately preceding the making of the application to the local planning authority.

(3) The notice required by paragraph (2)(c) shall (in addition to any other matters required to be contained in it) name a place within the area of the local planning authority to whom the application is made where a copy of the application for planning permission, and of all plans and other documents submitted with it, will be open to inspection by the public at all reasonable hours during such period as may be specified in the notice.

(4) Where the notice is, without any fault or intention of the applicant, removed, obscured or defaced before the period of seven days referred to in paragraph (2)(c) has elapsed, he shall be treated as having complied with the requirements of that paragraph if he has taken reasonable steps for protection of the notice and, if need be, its replacement.

(5)(a) The date prescribed for the purposes of section 65(2) of the Act (notice etc. of applications for planning permission), and the "prescribed date" for the purposes of this article, is the day 21 days before the date of the application;

(b) The applications prescribed for the purposes of paragraph (c) of the definition of "owner" in section 65(8) of the Act are minerals applications, and the minerals prescribed for the purposes of that paragraph are any minerals other than oil, gas, coal, gold or silver.

(6) In this article—

"minerals applications" mean applications for planning permission for development consisting of the winning and working of minerals;

"requisite notice" means notice in the appropriate form set out in Part 1 of Schedule 2 to this Order or in a form substantially to the like effect; and

"tenant" means the tenant of an agricultural holding any part of which is comprised in the land to which an application relates.

[(7) For the purposes of this article and the certificates required by article 7, where an application for planning permission is made by virtue of section 299(2) of the Act, the applicant shall be treated as an owner of the land and no account shall be taken of any Crown interest or Duchy interest in the land or in any mineral in the land.]

COMMENTARY

DERIVATION

Para. (7) was inserted as a modification by the Town and Country Planning (Crown Land Applications) Regulations 1995 (S.I. 1995 No. 1139), art. 2 and Sched. The article is in identical terms to that inserted in the Town and Country Planning General Development Order 1988 (S.I. 1988 No. 1813) by S.I. 1992 No. 2683.

DEFINITIONS

"appropriate authority": 1990 Act, s.293(2).
"Crown land": 1990 Act, s.293(1).
"land": 1990 Act, s.336(1).
"planning permission": 1990 Act, s.336(1).

Certificates in relation to notice of applications for planning permission

7.—(1) Where an application for planning permission is made, the applicant shall certify, in the appropriate form prescribed in Part 2 of Schedule 2 to this Order or in a form substantially to the like effect, that the requirements of article 6 have been satisfied.

(2) If an applicant has cause to rely on paragraph (4) of article 6, the certificate must state the relevant circumstances.

COMMENTARY

DERIVATION

Town and Country Planning General Development Order 1988, art. 12A, as substituted for the original art. 12 by the Town and Country Planning General Development (Amendment) (No. 4) Order 1992 (S.I. 1992 No. 1493), art. 3, from July 17, 1992.

DEFINITIONS

"planning permission": 1990 Act, s.336(1).

GENERAL NOTE

This article prescribes the form for certification, under art. 6, that the notification requirements of that article have been satisfied. In the case of a minerals application the applicant is required also to mount a site notice (art. 6(2)(c)). He is taken to have complied with that requirement even if the notice is, without any fault of his, removed, obscured or defaced, providing he has taken reasonable steps for its protection and, if need be, replacement (art. 6(4)). If he has cause to rely upon that provision, however, he is required to state the relevant circumstances in the certificate furnished in compliance with this article (para. (2)).

Publicity for applications for planning permission

8.—(1) An application for planning permission shall be publicised by the local planning authority to which the application is made in the manner prescribed by this article.

(2) In the case of an application for planning permission for development which—

(a) is the subject of an E.A. Schedule 1 or E.A. Schedule 2 application accompanied by an environmental statement;

(b) does not accord with the provisions of the development plan in force in the area in which the land to which the application relates is situated; or

(c) would affect a right of way to which Part III of the Wildlife and Countryside Act 1981 (public rights of way) applies,

the application shall be publicised in the manner specified in paragraph (3).

(3) An application falling within paragraph (2) ("a paragraph (2) application") shall be publicised by giving requisite notice—

(a) by site display in at least one place on or near the land to which the application relates for not less than 21 days, and

(b) by local advertisement.

(4) In the case of an application for planning permission which is not a paragraph (2) application, if the development proposed is major development the application shall be publicised by giving requisite notice—

(a) (i) by site display in at least one place on or near the land to which the application relates for not less than 21 days, or

(ii) by serving the notice on any adjoining owner or occupier, and

(b) by local advertisement.

(5) In a case to which neither paragraph (2) nor paragraph (4) applies, the application shall be publicised by giving requisite notice—

(a) by site display in at least one place on or near the land to which the application relates for not less than 21 days, or

(b) by serving the notice on any adjoining owner or occupier.

(6) Where the notice is, without any fault or intention of the local planning authority, removed, obscured or defaced before the period of 21 days referred to in paragraph (3)(a), (4)(a)(i) or (5)(a) has elapsed, the authority shall be treated as having complied with the requirements of the relevant paragraph if they have taken reasonable steps for protection of the notice and, if need be, its replacement.

(7) In this article—

"adjoining owner or occupier" means any owner or occupier of any land adjoining the land to which the application relates;

"E.A. Schedule 1 application" and "E.A. Schedule 2 application" have the same meanings as "Schedule 1 application" and "Schedule 2 application" respectively in regulation 2 of the Town and Country Planning (Assessment of Environmental Effects) Regulations 1988 (interpretation);

"major development" means development involving any one or more of the following—

(a) the winning and working of minerals or the use of land for mineral-working deposits;

(b) waste development;

(c) the provision of dwellinghouses where—

(i) the number of dwellinghouses to be provided is 10 or more; or

(ii) the development is to be carried out on a site having an area of 0.5 hectare or more and it is not known whether the development falls within paragraph (c)(i);

(d) the provision of a building or buildings where the floor space to be created by the development is 1,000 square metres or more; or

(e) development carried out on a site having an area of 1 hectare or more;

"requisite notice" means notice in the appropriate form set out in Schedule 3 to this Order or in a form substantially to the like effect;

"waste development" means any operational development designed to be used wholly or mainly for the purpose of, or a material change of use to, treating, storing, processing or disposing of refuse or waste materials.

COMMENTARY

DERIVATION

Town and Country Planning General Development Order 1988, art. 12B, as inserted by the Town and Country Planning General Development (Amendment) (No. 4) Order 1992 (S.I. 1992 No. 1493), art. 4, from July 17, 1992. The wording is identical to art. 12B, save for (a) the clarification of para. (6), and (b) deletion of a reference to the definition of "environmental statement" from para. (7).

DEFINITIONS

"adjoining owner or occupier": para. (7).
"development": 1990 Act, s.55.
"development plan": 1990 Act, s.336(1).
"E.A. Schedule 1 application"; "E.A. Schedule 2 application": para. (7).
"local advertisement": art. 1(2).
"major development": para. (7).
"owner": 1990 Act, s.65(8).
"planning permission": 1990 Act, s.336(1).
"requisite notice": para. (7).
"site display": art. 1(2).
"waste development": para. (7).

GENERAL NOTE

Introduction

This article gave effect to an undertaking given by the Government in the course of Parliamentary proceedings on the Planning and Compensation Act 1991, and reflected in the amendments made by that Act to s.71 of the principal Act, that all planning applications should receive publicity. Previously, that requirement applied only to particular applications, such as those for so-called "unneighbourly development," defined by the former art. 8 of this Order, and development plan departure applications. The courts had ruled that there was no general requirement to advertise applications, nor to notify neighbours, and that, although many local authorities had informal schemes for discretionary notification, these would not give rise to any legitimate expectation of notification: *R. v. Secretary of State for the Environment, ex p. Kent* [1988] J.P.L. 706; [1988] 3 P.L.R. 17 (upheld by the Court of Appeal, *The Times*, May 12, 1989).

All planning applications must be publicised by the local planning authority, either by a site notice or by notification to neighbours. In addition, an advertisement in a local newspaper is required in some cases. There are three categories of application for these purposes:

(1) the so-called "*paragraph (2) applications*":
   (a) where the application is accompanied by an environmental statement;
   (b) departures from the development plan;
   (c) development affecting a public right of way.

In each of these cases the local planning authority are required:
(a) to mount a site display on or near the land for at least 21 days prior to determining the application, and
(b) to publish a local advertisement.

(2) applications in respect of "*major development*":
(a) the winning and working of minerals or the use of land for mineral working deposits;
(b) all waste developments, meaning any development designed to be used wholly or mainly for the purpose or treating, storing, processing or disposing of refuse or waste materials;
(c) the provision of dwellinghouses where—
(i) the number of dwellinghouses to be provided is 10 or more; or
(ii) the development is to be carried out on a site having an area of 0.5 hectare or more and it is not known whether the development falls within paragraph (c)(i);
(d) the provision of a building or buildings where the floor space to be created by the development is 1,000 square metres or more; or
(e) development carried out on a site having an area of 1 hectare or more.

In each of these cases the local planning authority are required:
(a) either
(i) to mount a site display on or near the land for at least 21 days prior to determining the application, or
(ii) to serve the notice on any adjoining owner or occupier; and
(b) to publish a local advertisement.

(3) *all other applications*: for these, it is the responsibility of local planning authorities either:
(a) to mount a site display on or near the land for at least 21 days prior to determining the application, or
(b) to serve the notice on any adjoining owner or occupier.

They have also been asked, by DOE Circular 15/92 (W.O. 32/92), *Publicity for Planning Applications*, to decide, on a case by case basis, which developments falling outside the "major" category are likely to create a wider concern, and which may therefore warrant a newspaper advertisement in addition to a site notice or neighbour notification. The Circular offers the following list of such types of development:
(a) those affecting nearby property causing noise, smell, vibration, dust or other nuisance;
(b) attracting crowds, traffic and noise into a generally quiet area;
(c) causing activity and noise during unsocial hours;
(d) introducing significant change, for example particularly tall buildings;
(e) resulting in serious reduction or loss of light or privacy beyond adjacent properties;
(f) those affecting the setting of an ancient monument or archaeological site;
(g) proposals affecting trees subject to tree preservation orders.

Choice between site notice and neighbour notification

DOE Circular 15/92, *Publicity for Planning Applications* (paras. 7 to 11), suggests that neighbour notification may be the more appropriate method where interested parties are limited to those living in the immediate vicinity, and that site notices are likely to be more effective where there is doubt about who interested parties are, or because the development is likely to be of interest to more than immediate neighbours.

The form of the notice

The notice is prescribed by Sched. 2. The same notice is used for newspaper publication, site notices and neighbour notification, but a different model is prescribed in the case of planning applications accompanied by an environmental statement.

The site notice requirements

The local planning authority are required to post notice of the application in at least one place on or near the land, and to maintain it there for not less than 21 days. If it is removed, obscured or defaced during that time without fault or intention of the authority, they are not treated as having failed to meet this requirement so long as they have taken reasonable steps for its protection and, if need be, replacement (para. (6)).

Local advertisement

This is defined by art. 1(2) as meaning the publication of the notice in a newspaper circulating in the locality in which the land to which the application relates is situated. The form of notice is prescribed by Sched. 2. Provided the newspaper is one which circulates in the general locality, the courts will not insist on exhaustive coverage: see, *e.g. Wilson v. Secretary of State for the Environment* [1973] 1 W.L.R. 1083; *McMeecham v. Secretary of State for the Environment* (1974) 232 E.G. 201.

Service on neighbours

Local planning authorities are advised by DOE Circular 15/92, *Publicity for Planning Applications*, para. 8, that written communications should be addressed to the owner and/or the occupier of land adjoining the site.

Taking representations into account

The publicity and notification requirements are underpinned by art. 19 which requires the local planning authority to take into account any representations which have been made in response to them, and they are prohibited (by art. 20(5)) from determining an application for planning permission before the end of 21 days beginning with the date a site notice was first displayed or notice served, or 14 days from the date of publication of a requisite newspaper notice.

Development proposals of local planning authorities

This article applies also to applications for planning permission made by an interested planning authority (whether on its own or jointly with another party), but with references to "local planning authority" being construed as references to the interested planning authority concerned (Town and Country Planning General Regulations 1992 (S.I. 1992 No. 1492), reg. 7).

Notification to the Secretary of State

In the case of applications for development which constitutes a departure from the development plan, and for which the authority do not propose to refuse planning permission, there is a requirement also in certain cases for notification to the Secretary of State, by virtue of the Town and Country Planning (Development Plans and Consultation) Direction 1992 (Annex 3 to DOE Circular 19/92).

Appeals and call-ins

There is no requirement to undertake fresh publicity when an application is called-in or an appeal is lodged. If, however, the authority have failed to satisfy the requirements of this article at that time, the duty remains in force and they are required to inform the Secretary of State when they have carried it out (art. 9(2)).

The Crown

Development by the Crown does not formally attract planning control, but local planning authorities are advised by DOE Circular 15/92, para. 30 that notifications of intention under the special arrangements in DOE Circular 18/84 should receive the same publicity as if permission were required, except for cases involving matters of national security.

Other cases

Parallel publicity arrangements apply in respect of the notification requirements under Parts 6 and 7 of Sched. 2 to the General Permitted Development Order 1995 (agricultural and forestry development, notification of siting and design); and Part 31 (demolition). In these cases, however, the duty to post a site notice rests not with the local planning authority, but with the developer.

Applications for planning permission referred to the Secretary of State and appeals to the Secretary of State

9.—(1) Articles 6 and 7 apply to any appeal to the Secretary of State under section 78 of the Act (right to appeal against planning decisions and failure to take such decisions) as they apply to applications for planning permission.

(2) Subject to paragraph (3), if the local planning authority have failed to satisfy the requirements of article 8 in respect of an application for planning permission at the time the application is referred to the Secretary of State under section 77 of the Act (reference of applications to Secretary of State), or any appeal to the Secretary of State is made under section 78 of the Act, article 8 shall continue to apply, as if such referral or appeal to the Secretary of State had not been made.

(3) Where paragraph (2) applies, when the local planning authority have satisfied the requirements of article 8, they shall inform the Secretary of State that they have done so.

COMMENTARY

DERIVATION

Town and Country Planning General Development Order 1988, art. 12C, inserted by the Town and Country Planning General Development (Amendment) (No. 4) Order 1992 (S.I. 1992 No. 1493), art. 5. This article is in identical terms, save for amendments to cross-references.

DEFINITIONS

"local planning authority": 1990 Act, s.1.
"planning permission": 1990 Act, s.336(1).

GENERAL NOTE

This article: (1) requires that planning appeals should be notified to owners and tenants in the same way as planning applications; and (2) ensures that the local planning authority's publicity duties are not superseded when an application is called in, or an appeal is made to the Secretary of State. It does not, however, require fresh publicity to be given to an application upon it being called-in, or an appeal made. Such publicity is at the direction of the Secretary of State: see further the *Commentary* to s.78 of the principal Act.

Consultations before the grant of permission

10.—(1) Before granting planning permission for development which, in their opinion, falls within a category set out in the table below, a local planning authority shall consult the authority or person mentioned in relation to that category, except where—
(i) the local planning authority are the authority so mentioned;
(ii) the local planning authority are required to consult the authority so mentioned under articles 11 or 12; or
(iii) the authority or person so mentioned has advised the local planning authority that they do not wish to be consulted.

TABLE

Para	*Description of Development*	*Consultee*
(a)	**Development likely to affect land in Greater London or in a metropolitan county**	**The local planning authority concerned**
(b)	**Development likely to affect land in a non-metropolitan county, other than land in a National Park**	**The district planning authority concerned**
(c)	**Development likely to affect land in a National Park**	**The county planning authority concerned**
(d)	**Development within an area which has been notified to the local planning authority by the Health and Safety Executive for the purpose of this provision because of the presence within the vicinity of toxic, highly reactive, explosive or inflammable substances and which involves the provision of—** **(i) residential accommodation;** **(ii) more than 250 square metres of retail floor space;** **(iii) more than 500 square metres of office floor space; or** **(iv) more than 750 square metres of floor space to be used for an industrial process,** **or which is otherwise likely to result in a material increase in the number of persons working within or visiting the notified area**	**The Health and Safety Executive**
(e)	**Development likely to result in a material increase in the volume or a material change in the character of traffic—** **(i) entering or leaving a trunk road; or**	**In England, the Secretary of State for Transport and, in Wales, the Secretary of State for Wales**
	(ii) using a level crossing over a railway	**The operator of the network which includes or consists of the railway in question, and in England, the Secretary of State for Transport and, in Wales, the Secretary of State for Wales**
(f)	**Development likely to result in a material increase in the volume or a material change in the character of traffic entering or leaving a classified road or proposed highway**	**The local highway authority concerned**
(g)	**Development likely to prejudice the improvement or construction of a classified road or proposed highway**	**The local highway authority concerned**

Para	*Description of Development*	*Consultee*
(h)	**Development involving—** **(i) the formation, laying out or alteration of any means of access to a highway (other than a trunk road); or** **(ii) the construction of a highway or private means of access to premises affording access to a road in relation to which a toll order is in force**	**The local highway authority concerned** **The local highway authority concerned, and in the case of a road subject to a concession, the concessionaire**
(i)	**Development which consists of or includes the laying out or construction of a new street**	**The local highway authority**
(j)	**Development which involves the provision of a building or pipe-line in an area of coal working notified by the Coal Authority to the local planning authority**	**The Coal Authority**
(k)	**Development involving or including mining operations**	**[The Environment Agency]**
(l)	**Development within three kilometres of Windsor Castle, Windsor Great Park, or Windsor Home Park, or within 800 metres of any other royal palace or park, which might affect the amenities (including security) of that palace or park**	**The Secretary of State for National Heritage**
(m)	**Development of land in Greater London involving the demolition, in whole or part, or the material alteration of a listed building**	**The Historic Buildings and Monuments Commission for England**
(n)	**Development likely to affect the site of a scheduled monument**	**In England, the Historic Buildings and Monuments Commission for England, and, in Wales, the Secretary of State for Wales**
(o)	**Development likely to affect any garden or park of special historic interest which is registered in accordance with section 8C of the Historic Buildings and Ancient Monuments Act 1953 (register of gardens) and which is classified as Grade I or Grade II*.**	**The Historic Buildings and Monuments Commission for England**
(p)	**Development involving the carrying out of works or operations in the bed of or on the banks of a river or stream**	**[The Environment Agency]**
(q)	**Development for the purpose of refining or storing mineral oils and other derivatives**	**[The Environment Agency]**
(r)	**Development involving the use of land for the deposit of refuse or waste**	**[The Environment Agency]**
(s)	**Development relating to the retention, treatment or disposal of sewage, trade-waste, slurry or sludge (other than the laying of sewers, the construction of pumphouses in a line of sewers, the construction of septic tanks and cesspools serving single dwellinghouses or single caravans or single buildings in which not more than ten people will**	**[The Environment Agency]**

Para	*Description of Development*	*Consultee*
	normally reside, work or congregate, and works ancillary thereto)	
(t)	Development relating to the use of land as a cemetery	[The Environment Agency]
(u)	Development— (i) in or likely to affect a site of special scientific interest of which notification has been given, or has effect as if given, to the local planning authority by the Nature Conservancy Council for England or the Countryside Council for Wales, in accordance with section 28 of the Wildlife and Countryside Act 1981 (areas of special scientific interest); or (ii) within an area which has been notified to the local planning authority by the Nature Conservancy Council for England or the Countryside Council for Wales, and which is within two kilometres of a site of special scientific interest of which notification has been given or has effect as if given as aforesaid	The Council which gave, or is to be regarded as having given, the notice
(v)	Development involving any land on which there is a theatre	The Theatres Trust
(w)	Development which is not for agricultural purposes and is not in accordance with the provisions of a development plan and involves— (i) the loss of not less than 20 hectares of grades 1, 2 or 3a agricultural land which is for the time being used (or was last used) for agricultural purposes; or (ii) the loss of less than 20 hectares of grades 1, 2 or 3a agricultural land which is for the time being used (or was last used) for agricultural purposes, in circumstances in which the development is likely to lead to a further loss of agricultural land amounting cumulatively to 20 hectares or more	In England, the Minister of Agriculture, Fisheries and Food and, in Wales, the Secretary of State for Wales
(x)	Development within 250 metres of land which— (i) is or has, at any time in the 30 years before the relevant application, been used for the deposit of refuse or waste; and (ii) has been notified to the local planning authority by the waste regulation authority for the purposes of this provision	The waste regulation authority concerned
(y)	Development for the purposes of fish farming	[The Environment Agency]

(2) In the above table—

(a) in paragraph (d)(iv), "industrial process" means a process for or incidental to any of the following purposes—

(i) the making of any article or part of any article (including a ship or vessel, or a film, video or sound recording);

(ii) the altering, repairing, maintaining, ornamenting, finishing, cleaning, washing, packing, canning, adapting for sale, breaking up or demolition of any article; or

(iii) the getting, dressing or treatment of minerals in the course of any trade or business other than agriculture, and other than a process carried out on land used as a mine or adjacent to and occupied together with a mine (and in this sub-paragraph, "mine" means any site on which mining operations are carried out);

(b) in paragraph (e)(ii), "network" and "operator" have the same meaning as in Part I of the Railways Act 1993 (the provision of railway services);
(c) in paragraphs (f) and (g), "classified road" means a highway or proposed highway which—
(i) is a classified road or a principal road by virtue of section 12(1) of the Highways Act 1980 (general provision as to principal and classified roads); or
(ii) is classified for the purposes of any enactment by the Secretary of State by virtue of section 12(3) of that Act;
(d) in paragraph (h), "concessionaire", "road subject to a concession" and "toll order" have the same meaning as in Part I of the New Roads and Street Works Act 1991 (new roads in England and Wales);
(e) in paragraph (i), "street" has the same meaning as in section 48(1) of the New Roads and Street Works Act 1991 (streets, street works and undertakers), and "new street" includes a continuation of an existing street;
(f) in paragraph (m), "listed building" has the same meaning as in section 1 of the Planning (Listed Buildings and Conservation Areas) Act 1990 (listing of buildings of special architectural or historic interest);
(g) in paragraph (n), "scheduled monument" has the same meaning as in section 1(11) of the Ancient Monuments and Archaeological Areas Act 1979 (schedule of monuments);
(h) in paragraph (s), "slurry" means animal faeces and urine (whether or not water has been added for handling), and "caravan" has the same meaning as for the purposes of Part I of the Caravan Sites and Control of Development Act 1960 (caravan sites);
(i) in paragraph (u), "site of special scientific interest" means land to which section 28(1) of the Wildlife and Countryside Act 1981 (areas of special scientific interest) applies;
(j) in paragraph (v), "theatre" has the same meaning as in section 5 of the Theatres Trust Act 1976 (interpretation); and
(k) in paragraph (x), "waste regulation authority" has the same meaning as in section 30(1) of the Environmental Protection Act 1990 (authorities for purposes of Part II).

(3) The Secretary of State may give directions to a local planning authority requiring that authority to consult any person or body named in the directions, in any case or class of case specified in the directions.

(4) Where, by or under this article, a local planning authority are required to consult any person or body ("the consultee") before granting planning permission—
(a) they shall, unless an applicant has served a copy of an application for planning permission on the consultee, give notice of the application to the consultee; and
(b) they shall not determine the application until at least 14 days after the date on which notice is given under paragraph (a) or, if earlier, 14 days after the date of service of a copy of the application on the consultee by the applicant.

(5) The local planning authority shall, in determining the application, take into account any representations received from a consultee.

COMMENTARY

DERIVATION

Town and Country Planning General Development Order 1988 (S.I. 1988 No. 1813), art. 18, as amended by S.I. 1991 No. 2805 and S.I. 1992 No. 658.

Apart from several minor drafting, cross-referencing and updating references, the 1995 Order made three changes:

(1) the omission of the former requirements to consult the Secretary of State for Trade and Industry in relation to development for opencast mining (former para. (k));
(2) addition of requirements to consult on new streets (para. (i)) (which was previously in article 16(1) of the 1988 Order. References to new street byelaws—previously in article 16(1) and (2) of the GDO—are omitted from this Order. Although new street orders are extant, new street byelaws were abolished by section 81 of the Planning and Compensation Act 1991.
(3) a new requirement to consult on development affecting gardens and parks of historic interest (para. (o)).

References to the National Rivers Authority were amended to references to the Environment Agency by the *Environment Act 1995*, Sched. 22, para. 233, from April 1, 1996.

DEFINITIONS

"building": art. 1(2).
"caravan": para. (2).
"classified road": para. (2).
"concessionaire": para. (2).
"consultee": para. (4).
"county planning authority": 1990 Act, s.1.
"development": 1990 Act, s.55.
"development plan": 1990 Act, s.336.
"district planning authority": 1990 Act, s.1.
"industrial process": para. (2).
"listed building": para. (2).
"local highway authority": Highways Act 1980.
"mining operations": art. 1(2).
"National Park": art. 1(2).
"network": para. (2).
"operator": para. (2).
"road subject to a concession": para. (2).
"scheduled monument": para. (2).
"site of special scientific interest": para. (2).
"slurry": para. (2).
"street": para. (2).
"theatre": para. (2).
"toll order": para. (2).
"trunk road": art. 1(2).
"waste regulation authority": para. (2).

GENERAL NOTE

Introduction

This article imposes a duty on the local planning authority to consult before granting planning permission. It does not extend to other applications, such as for the approval of reserved matters, or for permission required under a planning condition. Nor does it impose any duty if the authority refuses permission.

Other consultation requirements

Other obligations on the local planning authority to consult are imposed by:

Article 11: relates to the requirement under the 1990 Act, Sched. 1, on the district planning authority to consult the county planning authority before determining applications.

Article 12: obligation on county planning authority to consult district planning authority on certain applications.

Article 13: procedure where parish or community council exercise right under 1990 Act, Sched. 1, para. 8(1), to be consulted by local planning authority.

Article 15: requirement to notify Secretary of State for Transport of certain applications affecting trunk roads.

Article 16: requirement to consult the Coal Authority, the Secretary of State for Trade and Industry and the Crown Estates Commissioners, of certain applications.

Other cases where the Secretary of State has requested local planning authorities to undertake consultation, but has not prescribed it as a requirement of the Order, are set out in the commentary below. The Secretary of State is also authorised to direct consultation in particular cases or classes of case, under para. (3); and consultation may also be imposed as a requirement of a direction issued under art. 14, restricting the grant of planning permission in certain cases.

The meaning of "consultation"

In *R. v. Secretary of State for Social Services, ex p. Association of Metropolitan Authorities* [1986] 1 W.L.R. 1; (1986) 130 S.J. 35; [1986] 1 All E.R. 164, Webster J. analysed the extent of the legal duty to consult, and observed:

> "... in any context the essence of consultation is the communication of a genuine invitation to give advice and a genuine consideration of that advice. In my view it must go without saying that to achieve consultation sufficient information must be supplied by the consulting party to the consulted party to enable it to tender helpful advice. Sufficient time must be given by the consulting to the consulted party to enable it to do that, and sufficient time must be available for such advice to be considered by the consulting party. Sufficient, in that context, does not mean ample, but at least enough to enable the relevant purpose to be fulfilled. By helpful advice, in this context, I mean sufficiently informed and considered information or advice about aspects of the form or substance of the proposals, or their implications for the consulted party, being aspects material to the implementation of the proposal as to which the Secretary of State might not be fully informed or advised and as to which the party consulted might have relevant information or advice to offer."

Advice on consultation under this article is contained in DOE Circular 9/95, Appendix B, para. 3. It urges local planning authorities to streamline the consultation process where possible, so as to avoid unnecessary delays. It suggests that where a body is frequently consulted, it may be useful to hold regular meetings with officers from that body to deal with a number of applications together; and that some consultees may find it useful to send an officer regularly to inspect new applications so as to indicate which will prove unobjectionable and which will need full comment. Prospective consultees may (para. (1)(iii)) notify the local planning authority that they do not wish to be consulted on all or any applications.

Direct notification by applicant

The 1988 Order introduced formal provision for an applicant to initiate the consultation process direct (though it did not go so far as to require direct application to the county in respect of county matter applications, which was subsequently introduced by the 1991 amendments). If an applicant serves a copy of his application direct on any consultee, the 14 day consultation period commences from then, rather than from when the local planning authority notify the consultee (para. (4)).

Environmental assessment: consultee's duty to provide information

Where there is a proposed application for planning permission for development which requires environmental assessment (as established by direction of the Secretary of State, or notification by or agreement with the prospective applicant), the local planning authority is required by the Town and Country Planning (Assessment of Environmental Effects) Regulations 1988 (No. 1199), reg. 8, to notify all the bodies with whom the authority would be required to consult under this article (or under any direction made under this article) of the name and address of the prospective applicant and of their duty under reg. 22 to make information available to him. They must also notify the prospective applicant of the names and addresses of those bodies. The purpose is to allow them to consult directly to determine whether the body has in its possession any information which he or they consider relevant to the preparation of an environmental statement, and, if they have, the body must make it available to him (excluding confidential information) (reg. 22). The body may make a reasonable charge for this service (reg. 20(2)).

Planning appeals following refusal or conditional permission

Where any authority or person consulted under this article does make representations, or expresses a view or issues a direction and there is a subsequent appeal to the Secretary of State against refusal or conditions imposed which will be dealt with by public local inquiry, the local planning authority is required to notify them of the inquiry and, "if they have not already done so, that person or body shall thereupon give the local planning authority a written statement of the reasons for making the direction, expressing the view or making the representations, as the case may be" (Town and Country Planning (Inquiries Procedure) Rules 1992 (No. 2038), r. 4(3); Town and Country Planning Appeals (Determination by Inspectors) (Inquiries Procedure) Rules 1992 (No. 2039), r. 4(3)).

If the appeal is to be determined by written representations, any consultees under this article who made representations are entitled to be notified of the appeal and to make further representations, by virtue of the Town and Country Planning (Appeals) (Written Representations) Regulations 1987 (S.I. 1987 No. 701), reg. 5.

Urban development corporations

The consultation obligations under this article do not extend to development permitted by special development order which is to be carried out by one of the urban development corporations to which all functions of the local planning authority in their area have been transferred. Instead, specific consultation requirements are prescribed by the individual special development orders for each corporation, modelled on the requirements of the 1977 Order. Under those orders, where a representation or objection is received from a consultee and not withdrawn, the corporation must refer it to the Secretary of State and not begin the development or grant the permission concerned until he notifies them that he does not intend to give a direction requiring an application for permission.

The specific consultation requirements contained in the Table
Paras (a), (b) and (c): consultation with planning authorities

These paragraphs relate to applications with cross-border implications. They do not require consultation with the other tier authority in the same area, because the scheme of Pt. III of the 1990 Act is to have only one authority designated as local planning authority in relation to any given area or category of development. County-district consultation is therefore separately required under arts. 19, 20.

Para. (d): hazardous substances

Local planning authorities are also requested to consult HSE on proposals for certain developments within specified distances of hazardous installations as notified by HSE under the Notification of Installations Handling Hazardous Substances Regulations (Circular 9/84). They were also formerly requested to consult on developments involving substances and quantities notifiable under the Control of Industrial Major Accident Hazard Regulations 1984 which were not covered by this article (see DOE Circular 22/88, Appendix C).

But both former para. (d) and that request were superseded upon the coming into force of the Planning (Hazardous Substances) Act 1990 on June 1, 1992.

Para. (e): Secretary of State for Transport and British Railways Board

The duty to consult the British Railways Board directly was introduced by the 1988 Order in order to speed up the process. It was previously the practice of the Secretary of State to consult the Board in these cases.

The duty to consult the Secretary of State on highways is in addition to the duty to notify him under art. 15 of applications for making or altering any access to a motorway or trunk road (where a speed limit of over 40 mph is in force), and any other development within 67 metres of any proposed trunk road, or trunk road which is to be improved. That article lays a formal basis for the making of directions under art. 14, by freezing the local planning authority's decision for up to 28 days. The Secretary of State would be equally entitled to make an art. 14 direction also upon being consulted under this article, but the consultation period is shorter.

"material increase in the volume ... of traffic"

The Secretaries of State have suggested that as a broad guide they would regard an increase in the order of five per cent. as being material in most cases, though where the capacity of the road is, or is near to being exceeded, a smaller percentage may well be material (PPG 13, para. 3).

Additional consultation: development in vicinity of motorway

In addition to the requirements of this article, the Secretaries of State have requested in PPG 13, *Transport*, that local planning authorities should consult Regional Offices of the Department of Transport, and in Wales the Welsh Office (Highways Directorate), wherever development is proposed of service facilities, such as refreshments, fuel or parking, partly or wholly within 400 metres of the boundary of a motorway; and also wherever development is proposed and the application area exceeds 5 acres, includes the provision of both fuel and refreshments, and lies within one kilometre of a motorway junction.

Paras. (f), (g) and (h): local highway authority

These provisions for consultation replace the former power of the local highway authority to direct refusal, or the imposition of conditions, on highways grounds. Any directions made under the former powers ceased to have effect except insofar as they related to applications made before December 5, 1988. A further effect of the 1988 Order was to reduce the consultation period on highways: local highways authorities formerly had 28 days in which to decide whether to make a direction, but now have the same 14 day consultation period as other consultees under this article.

But local highway authorities are still entitled, under the principal Act, Sched. 1, para. 3(5), to be sent by the district a copy of every planning application (other than county matter applications which are sent to them separately for determination), except to the extent that they waive this requirement. Consultation is also required, by art. 16, before the local planning authority grants planning permission for construction of a new street.

The change made by the 1988 Order means that district planning authorities need not automatically give effect to representations from the highways authority, and may indeed take and act on independent highways advice. DOE Circular 22/88, para. 12, advised that the weight to be attached to highways and traffic considerations was not intended to be diminished by this change, and that planning permission should not be granted for development likely to cause danger on the highway. If, however, the planning authority looked set to disregard highways representations, the local highway authority might in an exceptional case seek to support its representations by attempting to persuade the Secretary of State to call-in the application or (even more exceptionally) to revoke a permission.

The 1991 amendments introduced a further requirement to consult in the case of construction of access to a road for which a toll order is in force under the New Roads and Street Works Act 1991. Where the road is subject to a concession under that Act, the concessionaire must also be consulted.

Under the New Roads and Street Works Act 1991 the expressions used in this article are given the following meanings:

a "concessionaire" is a person who, in return for undertaking such obligations as may be specified in a concession agreement with respect to the design, construction, maintenance, operation or improvement of a special road, is appointed to enjoy the right to charge tolls in respect of the road (s.1(1)).

a "road subject to a concession" is a special road in relation to which a concession agreement is in force (s.1(2)).

a "toll order" is an order authorising the charging of tolls, which may be made in relation to a special road proposed to be provided by a highway authority (s.6(1)).

Para. (j): Coal Authority

A notification given under art. 18 of the 1988 Order is to be treated as if it had been made by the Coal Authority under this paragraph: art. 28(2).

Para. (l): Royal parks and palaces

The address for consultation is the Department of the Environment, Parks and Palaces Division, Room C11/17, 2 Marsham Street, London SW1P 3EP.

Paras. (m) and (n): listed buildings in London; scheduled monuments

The address of the Commission (aka English Heritage) is Fortress House, 23 Savile Row, London W1X 2HE.

Paras. (p), (q), (r), (s) and (t): the Environment Agency

Consultation with the Environment Agency is required where the application is for development involving or including mining operations (para. (j)) and also for deposit of refuse and waste. In England, the county planning authority will be responsible for undertaking that consultation.

Consultation with the Environment Agency is also requested by the Secretary of State (but not formally required under this Order) in the following cases:

Proposals which could lead to an increased industrial discharge into a river or estuary and in relation to development in areas at risk from flooding (DOE Circular 30/92; DOE Circular 9/95, Annex B, para. 17).

Para. (u): Nature Conservancy Council

This paragraph requires consultation with, in England, the Nature Conservancy Council for England (known as "English Nature"); and in Wales, the Countryside Council for Wales. The particular significance of this consultation requirement lies in the fact that a grant of planning permission may be taken as authorising an operation which is specified in the notification of the SSSI as one appearing to the NCC or CCW as being likely to damage the flora or fauna, or geological or physiographical features for which the SSSI was notified: the grant of planning permission constitutes a "reasonable excuse," under the Wildlife and Countryside Act 1981, s.28(8), in the event of prosecution under that section.

The requirements were strengthened by 1991 amendments. The NCC or CCW were formerly required to be notified only of applications for development *within* sites of special scientific interest. The 1991 amendment brings in also any area notified by the NCC or the Countryside Commission (in Wales, the CCW) which is within two kilometres of a designated site of special scientific interest.

Planning authorities have been urged to consult with the appropriate Council as soon as possible, and, if they are minded to grant permission against their advice, to inform the appropriate Council so that the Council may consider whether to ask the Secretary of State to call-in the application (PPG9, para. 30).

Further notification and consultation requirements in relation to SSSIs and other similar sites arise in relation to:

(1) the disposal of protected land by water and sewerage undertakers: see the Water Industry Act 1991, s.156;

(2) sites notified to the National Rivers Authority (or subsequently the Environment Agency) and to water and sewerage undertakers by the Nature Conservancy Council, the Countryside Council for Wales a National Park authority, or the Broads Authority under the Water Industry Act 1991, s.4 (formerly the Water Act 1989, s.9), as land of special interest which is potentially damageable by water industry operations;

(3) sites notified by Ministers in the Broads, where supplementary controls exist independently of planning control: see the Norfolk and Suffolk Broads Act 1988, s.5.

Para. (v): Theatres

By virtue of the Theatres Act 1976, s.5:

"Theatre" means any building or part of a building constructed wholly or mainly for the public performance of plays.

Para. (w): agricultural land

There was a significant reformulation of policy in relation to agricultural land in 1987, involving a shift of emphasis away from the need for preservation of agricultural land for production purposes. Previously local planning authorities were required to consult MAFF on applications not in accordance with the development plan and involving the loss of 10 acres or more of agricultural land. Advice on the protection of agricultural land from development is now contained in PPG7, paras. 2.5 and 2.6, and Annex A.

An authority may wish to consult MAFF on a non-statutory basis to obtain more information or technical advice, though PPG7 (Annex A, para. A16) insists that this should be confined to matters of technical detail and not relate to the merits of the application. Non-statutory consultation may also be undertaken in relation to applications involving agricultural development, but MAFF will charge for technical appraisals in relation to applications for agricultural dwellinghouses and the lifting of agricultural occupancy conditions (Annex A, para. A18).

Agricultural land classification

The following revised guidelines and criteria for agricultural land quality grading were brought into effect at the beginning of 1989.

Grade 1—excellent quality agricultural land

Land with no or very minor limitations to agricultural use. A very wide range of agricultural and horticultural crops can be grown and commonly includes top fruit, soft fruit, salad crops and winter harvested vegetables. Yields are high and less variable than on land of lower quality.

Grade 2—very good quality agricultural land

Land with minor limitations which affect crop yield, cultivation or harvesting. A wide range of agricultural and horticultural crops can usually be grown but on some land in the grade there may be reduced flexibility due to difficulties with the production of the more demanding crops such as winter harvested vegetables and arable root crops. The level of yield is generally high but may be low or more variable than Grade 1.

Grade 3—good to moderate quality agricultural land

Land with moderate limitations which affect the choice of crops, timing and type of cultivation, harvesting or the level of yield. Where more demanding crops are grown yields are generally lower or more variable than on land in Grades 1 and 2.

Sub-grade 3a—good quality agricultural land

Land capable of consistently producing moderate to high yields of a narrow range of arable crops, especially cereals, or moderate yields of a wide range of crops including cereals, grass, oilseed rape, potatoes, sugar beet and the less demanding horticultural crops.

Sub-grade 3b—moderate quality agricultural land

Land capable of producing moderate yields of a narrow range of crops, principally cereals and grass or lower yields of a wider range of crops or high yields of grass which can be grazed or harvested over most of the year.

Grade 4—poor quality agricultural land

Land with severe limitations which significantly restrict the range of crops and/or level of yields. It is mainly suited to grass with occasional arable crops (*e.g.* cereals and forage crops) the yields of which are variable. In moist climates, yields of grass may be moderate to high but there may be difficulties in utilisation. The grade also includes very droughty arable land.

Grade 5—very poor quality agricultural land
Land with very severe limitations which restrict use to permanent pasture or rough grazing, except for occasional pioneer forage crops.

Para. (x): landfill sites

The purpose of this consultation requirement is to deal with development proposals near landfill sites which are likely to emit gas. The onus is upon waste disposal authorities to identify the sites and to notify them to the local planning authority. DOE Circular 17/89, *Landfill Sites: Development Control*, para. 10, advises that the statutory consultation requirement is a minimum, and advises local planning authorities to consult also on any suspect sites outside the prescribed criteria. The Circular also provides advice on criteria for evaluating development proposals on or near landfill sites, and for applications for new landfill sites.

Para. (y): fish farming

This consultation requirement extends to any development in connection with fish farming, including the placing or assembly of a tank in inland waters for the purpose of fish farming, which is deemed by s.55(4A) of the Town and Country Planning Act 1990 (inserted by the Planning and Compensation Act 1991) to constitute development.

Other consultation requirements

In various circulars the Secretary of State has requested local planning authorities to consult on certain development proposals. The requests are now summarised in DOE Circular 9/95, Appendix C:

Consultee	*Criteria*
Regional Councils for Sport and Recreation	Proposals which could lead to the loss of sports facilities (PPG 17, "Sport and Recreation")
Environment Agency	Proposals which could lead to increased industrial discharge into a river or estuary and in relation to development in areas at risk from flooding (DOE Circular 30/92 (WO 68/92), "Development and Flood Risk")
Ministry of Agriculture, Fisheries and Food in England and, in Wales, the Welsh Office Agriculture Department	Where technical clarification is needed on agricultural land quality (Annex A of PPG 7)
Environment Agency (as successor to HM Inspectorate of Pollution)	Proposals sited within 500 metres (measured from the site boundary) of a process subject to Integrated Pollution Control under Part 1 of the Environmental Protection Act 1990, or subject to the Control of Industrial Air Pollution (Registration of Works) Regulations 1989 (SI 1989/318)
Local Authority Environmental Health Officers	Proposals sited within 250 metres (measured from the site boundary) of a process subject to Local Authority Air Pollution Control under Part 1 of the Environmental Protection Act 1990
Health and Safety Executive	Developments involving substances and quantities notifiable under the Control of Industrial Major Accident Hazard Regulations 1984 (SI 1984/1902) which do not require hazardous substances consent under the Planning (Hazardous Substances) Act 1990
Rights of way interests	Proposals for development affecting rights of way (DOE Circular 2/93 (WO 5/93), "Public Rights of Way")
Police Architectural Liaison Officers and, in the Metropolitan police service, Crime Prevention and Design Advisers	Planning applications where there is potential to reduce criminal activity through the adoption of appropriate measures at the design stage (DOE Circular 5/94 (WO 16/94), "Planning Out Crime")

Consultation with county planning authority

11. Where a district planning authority are required by paragraph 7 of Schedule 1 to the Act (local planning authorities—distribution of functions) to consult the county planning authority before determining an application for planning permission, they shall not determine the application until the expiry of at least 14 days after the date of the notice given to the county planning authority in accordance with sub-paragraph (6)(b) of that paragraph.

COMMENTARY

DERIVATION

Town and Country Planning General Development Order 1988, art. 19.

DEFINITIONS

"county planning authority": 1990 Act, s.1.
"district planning authority": 1990 Act, s.1.
"planning permission": 1990 Act, s.336(1).

GENERAL NOTE

Following local government re-organisation in 1974, county and district councils exercised overlapping functions in development control, and counties had broad powers of direction over decision-making by districts. The Local Government, Planning and Land Act 1980 reformed those arrangements, and restricted county jurisdiction to a limited range of "county matters" (see the General Note to art. 12). The matters which previously were also county matters were then converted into matters on which the county was merely to be consulted by the district. Consultation is required whether or not the district propose to grant permission.

The cases where consultation is required, now prescribed by the principal Act, Sched. 1, para. 7(1), break broadly into three categories. The first is applications involving conflict with policy; that is, where the proposed development "would materially conflict with or prejudice the implementation":

(i) of any policy or general proposal contained in an approved or submitted structure plan (or proposals for a structure plan or alteration); or

(ii) of any fundamental provision of an old style development plan still in force; or

(iii) of any proposal in a county local plan or alteration whether or not adopted or approved (provided the matter has received publicity under ss.39 or 40 of the 1990 Act).

The second category of applications comprises those relating to development of land "which would, by reason of its scale or nature or the location of the land, be of major importance for the implementation of the approved structure plan." Third, there is the "safeguarding" category. Here consultation is required where the site is one which the county have notified to the district as having minerals or (in England) waste disposal potential, or as being proposed for development by themselves. The consultation requirement extends to development of any land which would prejudice such a proposed use.

Consultation period

Under this article, the district planning authority may not proceed to determine the application for 14 days after notification to the county.

But by virtue of the principal Act, Sched. 1, paras. 4 and 7, they may determine it before the end of that period if they have received representations from the county or if the county have notified them that they do not propose to make any representations.

Applications relating to county matters

12.—(1) A county planning authority shall, before determining—

(a) an application for planning permission under Part III of the Act (control over development);

(b) an application for a certificate of lawful use or development under section 191 or 192 of the Act (certificates of lawfulness of existing or proposed use or development); or

(c) an application for approval of reserved matters,

give the district planning authority, if any, for the area in which the relevant land lies a period of at least 14 days, from the date of receipt of the application by the district authority, within which to make recommendations about the manner in which the application shall be determined; and shall take any such recommendations into account.

(2) A county planning authority shall—

(a) on determining an application of a kind mentioned in paragraph (1), as soon as reasonably practicable notify the district planning authority, if any, of the terms of their decision; or

(b) if any such application is referred to the Secretary of State, inform the district planning authority, if any, of the date when it was so referred and, when notified to them, of the terms of the decision.

COMMENTARY

DERIVATION

Town and Country Planning General Development Order 1988, art. 20.

Paras. (1)(b) and (c) had been substituted for the original paras. (1)(b), (c) and (d) in the 1988 Order by S.I. 1992 No. 1563 from July 27, 1992.

DEFINITIONS

"county planning authority": 1990 Act, s.1.
"established use certificate": 1990 Act, s.336(1).
"reserved matters": art. 1(2).

GENERAL NOTE

"County matters" are those planning applications over which county planning authorities (outside Greater London and the metropolitan areas) retain jurisdiction. The Local Government, Planning and Land Act 1980 restricted county involvement to two main areas: mineral related development and (except in Wales) waste disposal. "County matters" are defined in the Town and Country Planning Act 1990, Sched. 1, para. 1. Planning applications relating to county matters are now made direct to the county planning authority: art. 5(1)(b).

Applications requiring consultation under this article are not only planning applications for planning permission, but also applications for certificates of lawful use and applications for approval of reserved matters.

The 14 day consultation period was introduced by the 1988 Order: no period was previously prescribed.

Notice to parish and community councils

13.—(1) Where the council of a parish or community are given information in relation to an application pursuant to paragraph 8(1) of Schedule 1 to the Act (local planning authorities—distribution of functions), they shall, as soon as practicable, notify the local planning authority who are determining the application whether they propose to make any representations about the manner in which the application should be determined, and shall make any representations to that authority within 14 days of the notification to them of the application.

(2) A local planning authority shall not determine any application in respect of which a parish or community are required to be given information before—

(a) the council of the parish or community inform them that they do not propose to make any representations;

(b) representations are made by that council; or

(c) the period of 14 days mentioned in paragraph (1) has elapsed,

whichever shall first occur; and in determining the application the authority shall take into account any representations received from the council of the parish or community.

(3) The district planning authority (or, in a metropolitan county, the local planning authority) shall notify the council of the parish or community of the terms of the decision on any such application or, where the application is referred to the Secretary of State, of the date when it was so referred and, when notified to them, of the terms of his decision.

COMMENTARY

DERIVATION

Town and Country Planning General Development Order 1988, art. 21 as amended by the Town and Country Planning General Development (Amendment) (No. 3) Order 1991 (No. 2805).

DEFINITIONS

"development": 1990 Act ss.55, 336(1).
"district planning authority": 1990 Act, s.1.
"local planning authority": 1990 Act, s.1.

GENERAL NOTE

Consultation with parish and community councils

Parish and community councils are statutorily entitled to be notified of every planning application (and applications for approval of reserved matters) made in their area, except to the extent that they waive the requirement (principal Act, Sched. 1, para. 8). The district authority are required to inform the parish or community council in writing of the application, indicating the nature of the development and identifying the land to which it relates.

The Order establishes a two-stage procedure. The parish or community council is required as soon as practicable upon receiving information to notify the authority who are determining the application whether they propose to make any representations; and they must make their representations within 14 days of notification to them.

Planning appeal following refusal or conditional permission

If a parish or community council do make representations under these provisions, and an appeal follows, the council are entitled to appear at any inquiry into that appeal, by virtue of the Town and Country Planning (Inquiries Procedure) Rules 1992 (S.I. 1992 No. 2038), r. 11(1); Town and Country Planning Appeals (Determination by Inspectors) (Inquiries Procedure) Rules 1992 (S.I. 1992 No. 2039), r. 11(1). Moreover, they may be required to provide, unless they have already done so, a written statement of their reasons for expressing the view or making the representations (*ibid.* r. 4(3)).

If the appeal is to be determined by written representations, the council is entitled as a consultee to be notified of the appeal and to make further representations, by virtue of the Town and Country Planning (Appeals) (Written Representations) Regulations 1987 (S.I. 1987 No. 701), reg. 5.

Directions by the Secretary of State

14.—(1) The Secretary of State may give directions restricting the grant of permission by a local planning authority, either indefinitely or during such a period as may be specified in the directions, in respect of any development or in respect of development of any class so specified.

(2) The Secretary of State may give directions—

(a) that particular proposed development of a description set out in Schedule 1 or Schedule 2 to the Town and Country Planning (Assessment of Environmental Effects) Regulations 1988 (descriptions of development) is exempted from the application of those Regulations, in accordance with Article 2(3) of Council Directive 85/337/EEC;

(b) as to whether particular proposed development is or is not development in respect of which those Regulations require the consideration of environmental information (as defined in those Regulations) before planning permission can be granted; or

(c) that development of any class described in the direction is development in respect of which those Regulations require the consideration of such information before such permission can be granted.

(3) A local planning authority shall deal with applications for planning permission for development to which a direction given under this article applies in such manner as to give effect to the direction.

COMMENTARY

DERIVATION

Town and Country Planning General Development Order 1988, art. 14, as amended by S.I. 1994 No. 678.

DEFINITIONS

"development": 1990 Act, ss.55, 336(1).
"local planning authority": 1990 Act, s.1.
"planning permission": 1990 Act, s.290(1).

GENERAL NOTE

The Secretary of State's power to issue directions restricting the grant of planning permission is in practice exercised principally in the following cases:

(1) specific directions relating to applications with highway implications which have been notified to him under art. 15;

(2) specific directions relating to applications which the Secretary of State may wish to call-in under the 1990 Act, s.77. A direction may be made under this article to allow additional time for a decision to be taken on call-in, or prohibiting the local planning authority from granting permission;

(3) general directions relating to specified descriptions of development. Examples include:

   (a) the Aerodromes Direction 1992 (issued as Annex 2 to DOE Circular 2/92), which requires a local planning authority to consult with the Secretary of State for defence or the Civil Aviation Authority before granting planning permission for development in or adjacent to aerodromes for which a safe-guarding map has been furnished to the authority;

(b) the Shopping Development Direction (No. 2) 1993 (issued in DOE Circular 15/93, superseding that contained in PPG 6 (1993), which requires local planning authorities to notify the Secretary of State of any proposals for development involving specified amounts of gross retail floorspace before granting planning permission;

(4) individual directions relating to specific strategic sites. A direction has been made in respect of development within certain inner and outer zones round the Nuffield Radio Astronomy Laboratories at Jodrell Bank (following *Stringer v. Minister of Housing and Local Government* [1970] 1 W.L.R. 1281; 22 P. & C.R. 255). Safeguarding arrangements have also been made for land close to nuclear power stations, though these are not formally prescribed in a direction (see further MPG2, *Applications, Permissions and Conditions*, para. 28).

Power to make a direction under this article includes power to cancel it, or vary it, by a subsequent direction: art. 30.

Environmental assessment: para. (2)

Power to include these provisions in the Order was conferred by the Town and Country Planning (Assessment of Environmental Effects) Regulations 1988 (S.I. 1988 No. 1199), reg. 3. Their purpose is to allow the Secretary of State to determine conclusively whether any particular proposed development is exempt from environmental assessment requirements, or whether, if it is not exempt, environmental assessment is required. The power will normally be exercised where a developer applies to the Secretary of State for a direction, under regs. 5 or 6 of the Regulations, but the power is generally available and the Secretary of State has indicated that he may intervene where, for example, information submitted to him by other bodies or persons suggests the need for assessment (DOE Circular 15/88, para. 40).

The power conferred by art. 2(3) of the Directive is to exempt certain projects from the requirements of the Directive in exceptional circumstances.

Other powers of direction

Other powers of the Secretary of State under this order to issue directions to local planning authorities include the following:

—development plans directions (art. 14);

—directions requiring the authority to consult with any person or body named in the direction in any specified case or class of case (art. 10(3));

—directions requiring a local planning authority to provide information about planning applications, and how they have been dealt with.

Special provisions as to permission for development affecting certain existing and proposed highways

15.—(1) Where an application is made to a local planning authority for planning permission for development which consists of or includes—
(a) the formation, laying out or alteration of any access to or from any part of a trunk road which is either a special road or, if not a special road, a road subject to a speed limit exceeding 40 miles per hour; or
(b) any development of land within 67 metres (or such other distance as may be specified in a direction given by the Secretary of State under this article) from the middle of—
(i) any highway (other than a trunk road) which the Secretary of State has provided, or is authorised to provide, in pursuance of an order under Part II of the Highways Act 1980 (trunk roads, classified roads, metropolitan roads, special roads) and which has not for the time being been transferred to any other highway authority;
(ii) any highway which he proposes to improve under Part V of that Act (improvement of highways) and in respect of which notice has been given to the local planning authority;
(iii) any highway to which he proposes to carry out improvements in pursuance of an order under Part II of that Act; or
(iv) any highway which he proposes to construct, the route of which is shown on the development plan or in respect of which he has given notice in writing to the relevant local planning authority together with maps or plans sufficient to identify the route of the highway,

the local planning authority shall notify the Secretary of State by sending him a copy of the application and any accompanying plans and drawings.

(2) An application referred to in paragraph (1) above shall not be determined unless—
(a) the local planning authority receive a direction given under article 14 of this Order (and in accordance with the terms of that direction);
(b) they receive notification by or on behalf of the Secretary of State that he does not propose to give any such direction in respect of the development to which the application relates; or
(c) a period of 28 days (or such longer period as may be agreed in writing between the local planning authority and the Secretary of State) from the date when notification was given to the Secretary of State has elapsed without receipt of such a direction.

(3) The Secretary of State may, in respect of any case or any class or description of cases, give a direction specifying a different distance for the purposes of paragraph 1(b) above.

COMMENTARY

DERIVATION

Town and Country Planning General Development Order 1988, art. 15, as amended by the Town and Country Planning General Development (Amendment) (No. 3) Order 1991 (No. 2805).

DEFINITIONS

"development": 1990 Act, ss.55, 336(1).
"development plan": 1990 Act, s.336(1).

"district planning authority": 1990 Act, s.1.
"land": 1990 Act, s.336(1).
"local planning authority": 1990 Act, s.1.
"planning permission": 1990 Act, s.336(1).
"special road": art. 1(2).
"trunk road": art. 1(2).
"urban development corporation": art. 1(2).

General Note

Changes in highway consultation requirements

The highways regime was substantially altered by the 1988 Order. Previously, the local highway authority (the county council in the shire counties) had power to issue directions to the local planning authority requiring them to refuse planning permission, or impose conditions, on highways grounds. Until 1986, the local planning authority had no power to determine an application until it had received notification from the highway authority of a direction, or that it proposed not to issue a direction. But amendments introduced that year lifted the prohibition, and allowed the planning authority to proceed after 28 days if nothing had been heard from the local highway authority.

The 1988 Order lifted the local highway authority's control altogether, and replaced it with a right under what is now art. 10 of this Order to be consulted on certain categories of application. The Secretary of State also must be consulted on certain types of application under art. 10, but the present article establishes a separate regime under which some applications must be notified to the Secretary of State, and the local planning authority has no power to determine them until they receive a direction under art. 14, or notification that no direction is to be made, or the lapse of 28 days. Power under this article to make directions is limited to the Secretary of State, and relates only to trunk roads and motorways.

Secretary of State's power of direction

The Secretary of State for Transport (in Wales, the Secretary of State for Wales) retains power under this article to restrict the grant of planning permission for development of land requiring a new or altered access to trunk roads with a speed limit above 40 mph, and to motorways. Directions may also be given to safeguard the lines of proposed new roads, and realignments of existing roads. Guidance on the exercise of these powers is contained in Department of Transport Circular 4/88 (W.O. 42/88), *The Control of Development on Trunk Roads*.

Power to make a direction under this article includes power to cancel it, or vary it, by a subsequent direction (art. 27).

Additional consultation

In addition to the requirement to notify applications within 67 metres of a trunk road or motorway, local planning authorities are requested by the Secretaries of State to consult (with Regional Offices of the Department of Transport and in Wales the Welsh Office Highways Directorate) wherever development is proposed of service facilities such as refreshments, fuel or parking, partly or wholly within 400 metres of the boundary of a motorway; and also wherever development is proposed where the application area exceeds 5 acres, includes the provisions of both fuel and refreshments, and lies within 1 kilometre of a motorway junction (PPG13: *Transport* (1994), Annex A, para. 2).

Para. (3): power to specify a different distance

The power to specify a different distance, greater or less than 67 metres, was introduced by the 1988 Order. The distance of 67 metres is the contemporary equivalent of the *cordon sanitaire* of 220 yards that was originally introduced by the Restriction of Ribbon Development Act 1935, s.2(1)(b). That Act made it unlawful, except with permission of the highway authority, to put up any building (other than an agricultural building) within 220 feet of the middle of any classified road, or to make any new means of access to such a road; and it allowed the highway authority to specify a minimum width for a proposed highway of up to 160 feet (extendable in some cases by 20 foot steps to 440 feet) and to freeze development within the defined boundaries. The significance today of the *cordon* lies in its relationship with the compulsory purchase powers under the Highways Act 1980, s.249 and Sched. 18, which restrict compulsory acquisition to land lying within 220 yards (880 yards in limited cases) from the middle of a highway or proposed highway.

Notification of mineral applications

16.—(1) Where notice has been given for the purposes of this article to a mineral planning authority as respects land which is in their area and specified in the notice—

(a) by the Coal Authority that the land contains coal;

(b) by the Secretary of State for Trade and Industry that it contains gas or oil; or

(c) by the Crown Estates Commissioners that it contains silver or gold,

the mineral planning authority shall not determine any application for planning permission to win and work any mineral on that land, without first notifying the body or person who gave the notice that an application has been made.

(2) In this article, "coal" means coal other than that—

(a) won or worked during the course of operations which are carried on exclusively for the purpose of exploring for coal; or

(b) which it is necessary to dig or carry away in the course of activities carried on for purposes which do not include the getting of coal or any product of coal.

COMMENTARY

DERIVATION

Town and Country Planning General Development Order 1988, art. 13 as amended by the Town and Country Planning General Development (Amendment) (No. 2) Order 1994 (S.I. 1994 No. 2595).

DEFINITIONS

"coal": para. (2).
"land": 1990 Act, s.336(1).
"mineral planning authority": 1990 Act, s.1(4).

GENERAL NOTE

Where an application is made for planning permission for development consisting of the winning and working of minerals, the applicant is required not only to notify all owners of the land, but also to notify the owners of any minerals in the land. This requirement did not formerly apply to minerals already in state ownership and administered by formerly, the National Coal Board and now the Coal Authority (coal), the Department of Trade and Industry (oil and natural gas) and the Crown Estates Commission (silver and gold).

Under this article those bodies are now entitled to be notified by the mineral planning authority of all applications for permission to win and work any mineral, made in relation to land which the body concerned has specified in a notice to the authority as containing respectively coal, oil or gas, or silver or gold. These arrangements allow notification to be restricted to specific sites.

Prior notification

Notice already given under art. 13 of the 1988 Order is to be treated as if it had been given for the purposes of this article, by the Coal Authority on or after the date of this Order coming into force: art. 28(3).

Development not in accordance with the development plan

17. A local planning authority may in such cases and subject to such conditions as may be prescribed by directions given by the Secretary of State under this Order grant permission for development which does not accord with the provisions of the development plan in force in the area in which the land to which the application relates is situated.

COMMENTARY

Definitions

"development": 1990 Act, s.55.
"development plan": 1990 Act, s.336(1).
"local planning authority": 1990 Act, s.1.

General Note

Development plan directions

The Town and Country Planning (Development Plans and Consultation) Direction 1992 (Annex 3 to DOE Circular 19/92) has been made under this article, with effect from July 1992. It supersedes the separate Town and Country Planning (Development Plan) Directions issued for England and Wales in February 1992, which had in turn superseded directions issued in 1981. Formerly, the Directions imposed a requirement that the local planning authority should give publicity to applications for permission for development constituting a departure from the development plan, but those requirements have now been superseded by the general publicity arrangements now in force under s.71 of the Act and art. 8 of this Order.

The Direction does, however, require still that certain applications be notified to the Secretary of State. It applies to departure applications which the authority do not propose to refuse for:

(a) development which consists of or includes the provision of—
  (i) more than 150 houses or flats; or
  (ii) more than 10,000 square metres of retail floor space;
(b) development of land of an interested planning authority, or for the development of any land by such an authority, whether alone or jointly with any other person; or
(c) any other development which, by reason of its scale or nature or the location of the land, would significantly prejudice the implementation of the development plan's policies and proposals.

The authority are required to send to the Secretary of State—

  (i) a copy of the application (including copies of any accompanying plans and drawings);
  (ii) a copy of the requisite notice;
  (iii) a copy of any representations made to the authority in respect of the application;
  (iv) a statement of the issues involved in the decision and of any views expressed on the application by a government department or another local planning authority.

The effect of development plan directions

The continued appearance of this article in the Order is puzzling. It is made under the specific authorisation of the 1990 Act, s.74(1)(b), which provides that a development order may make provision:

> "(b) for authorising the local planning authority, in such cases and subject to such conditions as may be prescribed by the order, or by directions given by the Secretary of State thereunder, to grant planning permission for development which does not accord with the provisions of the development plan."

Such provision appeared first in the 1948 General Development Order, when it was intended that, although the development plan would not be legally binding in development control, it would rarely be departed from. The Minister advised authorities that, "It is anticipated that it will be used only for minor, but urgent, development which would not entail a major departure from the development plan such as would call for an amendment of the plan ... and which cannot await the normal quinquennial amendment ..." (*Town and Country Planning (General Development) Order 1948: Explanatory Memorandum*, (issued with Circular 47/1948), Part II.) Otherwise, it was assumed, the development plan would be followed closely. This was reflected in the power conferred on the Minister to reject an appeal without a hearing if the decision was one which the local planning authority was obliged to come to under the development plan: it was assumed that the Minister would simply uphold without further hearing the refusal of permission for development not in accordance with the plan (William Wood, *Planning and the Law* (1948) p. 69).

But there is a clear conflict in the practical operation of this provision. Although it purports to allow local planning authorities to grant permission for development which does not accord with the development plan if they comply with the requirements of a direction, no such special authorisation is actually required. Under s.70 of the 1990 Act, the provisions of the development plan constitute a material consideration in determining planning application so far as they are material to that application, but the authority is free to depart from them. Hence, the courts have held, any direction made under this article cannot be regarded as restricting the jurisdiction of authorities in determining applications (see, *e.g. Simpson v. Edinburgh Corporation* 1960 S.C. 313 at 319; *Co-operative Retail Services v. Taff-Ely Borough Council* (1981) 42 P. & C.R. 1, H.L. affirming; (1979) 39 P. & C.R. 223 (*per* Ormrod L.J. at 245–246 and Browne L.J. at 253–254); *R. v. Carlisle City Council, ex p. Cumbrian Cooperative Society* [1985] 2 E.G.L.R. 193; [1986] J.P.L. 206). In *R. v. St Edmundsbury Borough Council, ex p. Investors in Industry Commercial Properties* [1985] 1 W.L.R. 1157; (1985), 129 S.J. 623; [1985] 3 All E.R. 234; (1985) 51 P. & C.R. 251, Stocker J., in following the two cases cited, concluded that the requirements of a Direction made by the Secretary of State under this article were not mandatory but directory, and that failure by a local planning authority to comply with them did not render their decision void.

However, in *R. v. Doncaster Metropolitan Borough Council, ex p. British Railways Board* [1987] J.P.L. 444, Schiemann J. took a different view and quashed a grant of planning permission by a local planning authority to itself on the ground of failure to comply with the Direction. There is, however, no mention in the judgment of any of the above decisions, and it cannot therefore be regarded as having resolved the conflict conclusively.

Notice of reference of applications to the Secretary of State

18. On referring any application to the Secretary of State under section 77 of the Act (reference of applications to Secretary of State) pursuant to a direction in that behalf, a local planning authority shall serve on the applicant a notice—

(a) setting out the terms of the direction and any reasons given by the Secretary of State for issuing it;

(b) stating that the application has been referred to the Secretary of State; and

(c) containing a statement that the Secretary of State will, if the applicant so desires, afford to him an opportunity of appearing before and being heard by a person appointed by the Secretary of State for the purpose, and that the decision of the Secretary of State on the application will be final.

COMMENTARY

DERIVATION

Town and Country Planning General Development Order 1988, art. 22 (unamended).

DEFINITIONS

"local planning authority": 1990 Act, s.1.

GENERAL NOTE

Under the 1990 Act, s.77, the Secretary of State may call-in a planning application for determination by himself. This article imposes an obligation on the local planning authority to notify the applicant when this occurs. Once they have notified the applicant, under s.77 of the 1990 Act, the provisions of s.78 are deemed to apply as if the permission or approval had been refused by the local planning authority and as if notification of their decision had been received by the applicant at the end of the period prescribed by art. 20(2).

Representations to be taken into account

19.—(1) A local planning authority shall, in determining an application for planning permission, take into account any representations made, where any notice of the application has been—

(a) given by site display under article 6 or 8, within 21 days beginning with the date when the notice was first displayed by site display;

(b) served on—

(i) an owner of the land or a tenant of an agricultural holding under article 6, or

(ii) an adjoining owner or occupier under article 8,

within 21 days beginning with the date when the notice was served on that person, provided that the representations are made by any person who satisfies them that he is such an owner, tenant or occupier; or

(c) given by local advertisement under article 6 or 8, within 14 days beginning with the date on which the notice was published,

and the representations and periods in this article are representations and periods prescribed for the purposes of section 71(2)(a) of the Act (consultations in connection with determinations under section 70).

(2) A local planning authority shall give notice of their decision to every person who has made representations which they were required to take into account in accordance with paragraph (1)(b)(i), and such notice is notice prescribed for the purposes of section 71(2)(b) of the Act.

(3) Paragraphs (1) and (2) of this article apply to applications referred to the Secretary of State under section 77 of the Act (reference of applications to Secretary of State) and paragraphs (1)(b) and (2) apply to appeals to the Secretary of State made under section 78 of the Act (right to appeal against planning decisions and failure to take such decisions), as if the references to—

(a) a local planning authority were to the Secretary of State, and

(b) determining an application for planning permission were to determining such application or appeal, as the case may be.

COMMENTARY

DERIVATION

Town and Country Planning General Development Order 1988, art. 22A, inserted by the Town and Country Planning General Development (Amendment) (No. 4) Order 1992 (S.I. 1992 No. 1493).

DEFINITIONS

"local planning authority": 1990 Act, s.1.
"planning permission": 1990 Act, s.336(1).

GENERAL NOTE

This article reinforces the requirements for notification of planning applications to owners and agricultural tenants (art. 6), and publicity (art. 8) by requiring the local planning authority (and, on appeal or call-in, the Secretary of State: para. (3)) to take into account, in determining the application, any representations received within the prescribed period. They are also obliged to notify their decision to any owner or agricultural tenant who has made representations.

Time periods for decision

20.—(1) Subject to paragraph (5), where a valid application under article 4 or regulation 3 of the 1988 Regulations (applications for planning permission) has been received by a local planning authority, they shall within the period specified in paragraph (2) give the applicant notice of their decision or determination or notice that the application has been referred to the Secretary of State.

(2) The period specified in this paragraph is—

(a) a period of eight weeks beginning with the date when the application was received by a local planning authority;

(b) except where the applicant has already given notice of appeal to the Secretary of State, such extended period as may be agreed in writing between the applicant and the local planning authority by whom the application falls to be determined; or

(c) where a fee due in respect of an application has been paid by a cheque which is subsequently dishonoured, the appropriate period specified in (a) or (b) above calculated without regard to any time between the date when the authority sent the applicant written notice of the dishonouring of the cheque and the date when the authority are satisfied that they have received the full amount of the fee.

(3) For the purposes of this article, the date when the application was received shall be taken to be the date when each of the following events has occurred—

(a) the application form or application in writing has been lodged with the authority mentioned in article 5(1);

(b) any certificate or documents required by the Act or this Order has been lodged with that authority; and

(c) any fee required to be paid in respect of the application has been paid to that authority and, for this purpose, lodging a cheque for the amount of a fee is to be taken as payment.

(4) A local planning authority shall provide such information about applications made under article 4 or regulation 3 of the 1988 Regulations (including information as to the manner in which any such application has been dealt with) as the Secretary of State may by direction require; and any such direction may include provision as to the persons to be informed and the manner in which the information is to be provided.

(5) Subject to paragraph (6), a local planning authority shall not determine an application for planning permission, where any notice of the application has been—

(a) given by site display under article 6 or 8, before the end of the period of 21 days beginning with the date when the notice was first displayed by site display;

(b) served on—

(i) an owner of the land or a tenant of an agricultural holding under article 6, or

(ii) an adjoining owner or occupier under article 8.

before the end of the period of 21 days beginning with the date when the notice was served on that person;

(c) given by local advertisement under article 6 or 8, before the end of the period of 14 days beginning with the date on which the notice was published,

and the periods in this paragraph are periods prescribed for the purposes of section 71(1) of the Act (consultations in connection with determinations under section 70).

(6) Where, under paragraph (5), more than one of the prescribed periods applies, the local planning authority shall not determine the application before the end of the later or latest of such periods.

COMMENTARY

DERIVATION

Town and Country Planning General Development Order 1988, art. 23, as amended:

Paras. (5) and (6) were inserted by S.I. 1992 No. 1493 from July 17, 1992.

The words "or 9" were revoked by S.I. 1992 No. 1563 from July 27, 1992.

GENERAL NOTE

The eight-week rule

The general rule is that a local planning authority must determine a planning application within eight weeks of receiving it. The applicant may agree in writing to an extension of that period. The same rules apply where the application is made for consent, agreement or approval required by a planning condition (art. 21). In all cases, it is in practice more a target than a realistic prescription. The Government's current target is for local planning authorities to determine 80 per cent of planning applications within the eight week period, but in the year ending September 1993 only 41 planning authorities were actually meeting or surpassing that target. The proportion of all planning decisions made within eight weeks was 65 per cent (Department of the Environment, *Planning Performance Checklist 1993*, January 1994).

The applicant's remedy for failure to determine within the period is to appeal to the Secretary of State. Under s.78 of the 1990 Act, if the authority fail to give notice of their decision within the period as prescribed or agreed, it is treated as a deemed refusal at the end of the period, giving rise to a right of appeal under s.78. But a valid planning permission is still capable of being issued beyond the period (*James v. Minister of Housing and Local Government* [1968] A.C. 409; [1967] 1 W.L.R. 171; 18 P. & C.R. 165), and the Scottish courts have held that the local planning authority is not absolved from its duty to determine an application simply because the period has expired, and is compellable by mandamus (*Bovis Homes (Scotland) v. Inverclyde District Council* [1983] J.P.L. 171). The duty must cease, however, once an appeal is made to the Secretary of State, because then the duty to determine the application shifts to him. Once an applicant has given notice of appeal he cannot, under para. (2)(b), extend by agreement the period within which the authority may give a decision.

Calculating the period

The eight-week period begins with the date the application is received by a local planning authority. It need not be the authority which is to determine the application; thus time in a county matters application runs from the receipt of the application by the district, not when it is forwarded to the county.

When fees were introduced for planning applications in 1981, it was intended that failure to tender the correct amount on submitting an application, or the subsequent dishonouring of a cheque, should not render the application invalid. Instead, the eight-week decision period does not start to run until the fee has been paid (and lodging a cheque is taken to be payment: para. (3)(c)), and time stops running if a cheque is subsequently dishonoured (para. (2)(c)). Thus the processing of the application is not delayed, but the applicant has no right of appeal against an authority's failure to determine it unless and until the full fee is properly paid.

The Joint Study Group of the Association of County Councils and the Department of the Environment, *County Councils' Development Control Decisions* (HMSO, 1988) noted that many decisions were taken by counties in the ninth week after the application was made, but had not been forwarded by the districts until the second week. They recommended that applicants be required to send copies of applications direct to the county so as to expedite their decision, but the recommendation was not immediately accepted. They also accepted that the complexity of county matter applications indicated that a more realistic target time for county matters was 80 per cent within 13 weeks. However, as this sort of target was a matter for political judgment, the Group declined to make any firm recommendation.

However, the Order was in due course amended to require that all county matter applications must now be made directly to the county planning authority (see now art. 5(1)).

Environmental assessment

Where an application is subject to environmental assessment, the period of eight weeks specified in para. (2)(a) is extended to 16 weeks, and the date the application is deemed to have been received is to be fixed in accordance not only with the receipt of the items mentioned in para. (3) but also the requisite environmental statement and the documents required to accompany it: Town and Country Planning (Assessment of Environmental Effects) Regulations 1988 (S.I. 1988 No. 1199), reg. 16(2).

Applications made under planning condition

21. Where an application has been made to a local planning authority for any consent, agreement or approval required by a condition or limitation attached to a grant of planning permission (other than an application for approval of reserved matters or an application for approval under Part 24 of Schedule 2 to the Town and Country Planning (General Permitted Development) Order 1995 (development by telecommunications code system operators)) the authority shall give notice to the applicant of their decision on the application within a period of eight weeks from the date when the application was received by the authority, or such longer period as may be agreed by the applicant and the authority in writing.

COMMENTARY

DERIVATION

Town and Country Planning General Development Order 1988, art. 24, amended to include reference to development by telecommunications code system operators.

DEFINITIONS

"development": 1990 Act, ss.55, 336(1).
"local planning authority": 1990 Act, s.1.
"planning permission": 1990 Act, s.336(1).
"reserved matters": art. 1(2).

GENERAL NOTE

This article prescribes the period for decisions on applications for any consent, agreement or approval required by a condition or limitation attached to a grant of planning permission. It does not apply to an application for approval of reserved matters: such applications fall instead within art. 20 (as applications under art. 4). It applies not only to applications under planning permissions granted by local planning authorities or on appeal, or under a simplified planning zone scheme or enterprise zone scheme, but also to an application made under any condition or limitation contained in the General Permitted Development Order 1995, except where an alternative period is specifically prescribed.

Written notice of decision or determination relating to a planning application

22.—(1) When the local planning authority give notice of a decision or determination on an application for planning permission or for approval of reserved matters, and a permission or approval is granted subject to conditions or the application is refused, the notice shall—

(a)state clearly and precisely their full reasons for the refusal or for any condition imposed; and

(b) where the Secretary of State has given a direction restricting the grant of permission for the development for which application is made or where he or a Government Department has expressed the view that the permission should not be granted (either wholly or in part) or should be granted subject to conditions, give details of the direction or of the view expressed,

and shall be accompanied by a notification in the terms (or substantially in the terms) set out in Part 2 of Schedule 1 to this Order.

(2) Where—

(a) the applicant for planning permission has submitted an environmental statement; and

(b) the local planning authority have decided (having taken environmental information into consideration) to grant permission (whether unconditionally or subject to conditions),

the notice given to the applicant in accordance with article 20(1) shall include a statement that environmental information has been taken into consideration by the authority.

COMMENTARY

DERIVATION

Town and Country Planning General Development Order 1988, art. 25, as amended by S.I. 1992 No. 1563 and S.I. 1994 No. 678.

DEFINITIONS

"development": 1990 Act, ss.55, 336(1).
"environmental information": art. 1(2).
"environmental statement": art. 1(2).
"local planning authority": 1990 Act, s.1.
"planning permission": 1990 Act, s.336(1).
"reserved matters": art. 1(2).

GENERAL NOTE

This article imposes an obligation on the local planning authority to give reasons for its decision when imposing conditions on a planning permission, or refusing permission. The courts have held that failure to state any reasons does not invalidate a condition imposed on a planning permission, and even less so an enforcement notice served alleging non-compliance with the condition (*Brayhead (Ascot) v. Berkshire County Council* [1964] 2 Q.B. 303; [1964] 2 W.L.R. 507; 15 P. & C.R. 423).

The obligation to "state clearly and precisely their full reasons," is clearly intended to induce authorities to be both comprehensive and precise. Although failure to comply might not invalidate the authority's substantive decision, since the obligation does not form part of the decision-making process but relates only to notification, it would appear to be enforceable by application for judicial review. Hence, an aggrieved applicant need not proceed to appeal on the basis of an inadequate statement of reasons, but may seek an order requiring the authority to comply with the duty. Moreover, given that the duty is to provide the authority's "full" reasons, it may be difficult in practice (though not unlawful) for them to introduce further arguments against the development if the matter should go to appeal.

Appeals

23.—(1) An applicant who wishes to appeal to the Secretary of State under section 78 of the Act (right to appeal against planning decisions and failure to take such decisions) shall give notice of appeal to the Secretary of State by—

(a) serving on him, within the time limit specified in paragraph (2), a form obtained from him, together with such of the documents specified in paragraph (3) as are relevant to the appeal; and

(b) serving on the local planning authority a copy of the form mentioned in paragraph (a), as soon as reasonably practicable, together with a copy of any relevant documents mentioned in paragraph (3)(e).

(2) The time limit mentioned in paragraph (1) is six months from—

(a) the date of the notice of the decision or determination giving rise to the appeal;

(b) the expiry of the period specified in article 20 or, as the case may be, article 21; or

(c) in a case in which the authority have served a notice on the applicant in accordance with article 3(2) that they require further information, and he has not provided the information, the date of service of that notice,

or such longer period as the Secretary of State may, at any time, allow.

(3) The documents mentioned in paragraph (1) are—

(a) the application made to the local planning authority which has occasioned the appeal;

(b) all plans, drawings and documents sent to the authority in connection with the application;

(c) all correspondence with the authority relating to the application;

(d) any certificate provided to the authority under article 7;

(e) any other plans, documents or drawings relating to the application which were not sent to the authority;

(f) the notice of the decision or determination, if any;

(g) if the appeal relates to an application for approval of certain matters in accordance with a condition on a planning permission, the application for that permission, the plans submitted with that application and the planning permission granted.

COMMENTARY

DERIVATION

Town and Country Planning General Development Order 1988, art. 26, as amended by the Town and Country Planning General Development (Amendment) (No. 4) Order 1992 (S.I. 1992 No. 1493) and S.I. 1992 No. 1563.

GENERAL NOTE

The article prescribes the procedure for making appeals, and also makes provision for direct service of a notice of appeal on the local planning authority at the time it is lodged with the Secretary of State.

Certificate of lawful use or development

24.—(1) An application for a certificate under section 191(1) or 192(1) of the Act (certificates of lawfulness of existing or proposed use or development) shall be in writing and shall, in addition to specifying the land and describing the use, operations or other matter in question in accordance with those sections, include the following information—

(a) the paragraph of section 191(1) or, as the case may be, section 192(1), under which the application is made;

(b) in the case of an application under section 191(1), the date on which the use, operations or other matter began or, in the case of operations carried out without planning permission, the date on which the operations were substantially completed;

(c) in the case of an application under section 191(1)(a), the name of any use class specified in an order under section 55(2)(f) of the Act (meaning of "development") which the applicant considers applicable to the use existing at the date of the application;

(d) in the case of an application under section 191(1)(c), sufficient details of the planning permission to enable it to be identified;

(e) in the case of an application under section 192(1)(a), the use of the land at the date of the application (or, when the land is not in use at that date, the purpose for which it was last used) and the name of any use class specified in an order under section 55(2)(f) of the Act which the applicant considers applicable to the proposed use;

(f) the applicant's reasons, if any, for regarding the use, operations or other matter described in the application as lawful; and

(g) such other information as the applicant considers to be relevant to the application.

(2) An application to which paragraph (1) applies shall be accompanied by—

(a) a plan identifying the land to which the application relates;

(b) such evidence verifying the information included in the application as the applicant can provide; and

(c) a statement setting out the applicant's interest in the land, the name and address of any other person known to the applicant to have an interest in the land and whether any such other person has been notified of the application.

[(2A) Where, by virtue of section 299(2) of the Act, an application for a certificate under section 192(1) of the Act is made in respect of Crown land, it shall, in addition to the documents required by paragraph (2), be accompanied by—

(a)a statement that the application is made, by virtue of section 299(2) of the Act, in respect of Crown land; and

(b) where the application is made by a person authorised in writing by the appropriate authority, a copy of that authorisation.]

(3) Where such an application specifies two or more uses, operations or other matters, the plan which accompanies the application shall indicate to which part of the land each such use, operation or matter relates.

(4) Articles 5(1) and 20(4) shall apply to an application for a certificate to which paragraph (1) applies as they apply to an application for planning permission.

(5) When the local planning authority receive an application to which paragraph (1) applies and any fee required to be paid in respect of the application, they shall, as soon as reasonably practicable, send to the applicant an acknowledgement of the application in the terms (or substantially in the terms) set out in Part 1 of Schedule 1.

(6) Where, after sending an acknowledgement as required by paragraph (5), the local planning authority consider that the application is invalid by

reason of the failure to comply with the preceding paragraphs of this article or any other statutory requirement, they shall, as soon as practicable, notify the applicant that his application is invalid.

(7) The local planning authority may by notice in writing require the applicant to provide such further information as may be specified to enable them to deal with the application.

(8) The local planning authority shall give the applicant written notice of their decision within a period of eight weeks beginning with the date of receipt by the authority of the application and any fee required to be paid in respect of the application or, except where the applicant has already given notice of appeal to the Secretary of State, within such extended period as may be agreed upon in writing between the applicant and the authority.

(9) For the purpose of calculating the appropriate period specified in paragraph (8), where any fee required has been paid by a cheque which is subsequently dishonoured, the time between the date when the authority send the applicant written notice of the dishonouring of the cheque and the date when the authority receive the full amount of the fee shall not be taken into account.

(10) Where an application is refused, in whole or in part (including a case in which the authority modify the description of the use, operations or other matter in the application or substitute an alternative description for that description), the notice of decision shall state clearly and precisely the authority's full reasons for their decision and shall include a statement to the effect that if the applicant is aggrieved by the decision he may appeal to the Secretary of State under section 195 of the Act (appeals against refusal or failure to give decision on application).

(11) A certificate under section 191 or 192 of the Act shall be in the form set out in Schedule 4, or in a form substantially to the like effect.

(12) Where a local planning authority propose to revoke a certificate issued under section 191 or 192 of the Act in accordance with section 193(7) of the Act (certificates under sections 191 and 192: supplementary provisions), they shall, before they revoke the certificate, give notice of that proposal to—

(a) the owner of the land affected;

(b) the occupier of the land affected;

(c) any other person who will in their opinion be affected by the revocation; and

(d) in the case of a certificate issued by the Secretary of State under section 195 of the Act, the Secretary of State.

(13) A notice issued under paragraph (12) shall invite the person on whom the notice is served to make representations on the proposal to the authority within 14 days of service of the notice and the authority shall not revoke the certificate until all such periods allowed for making representations have expired.

(14) An authority shall give written notice of any revocation under section 193(7) of the Act to every person on whom notice of the proposed revocation was served under paragraph (12).

COMMENTARY

DERIVATION

Town and Country Planning General Development Order 1988, art. 26A, as inserted by S.I. 1992 No. 1563.

AMENDMENT

Para. (2A) was inserted as a modification by the Town and Country Planning (Crown Land Applications) Regulations 1995 (S.I. 1995 No. 1139), art. 2 and Sched.

DEFINITIONS

"appropriate authority": 1990 Act, s.293(2).
"Crown land": 1990 Act, s.293(1).
"land": 1990 Act, s.336(1).
"planning permission": 1990 Act, s.336(1).

GENERAL NOTE

This article prescribes the procedure for applications under the 1990 Act, ss.191 and 192, for certificates of lawful development. It also prescribes the form of certificates (para. (12)), and the procedure to be followed where the authority propose to revoke a certificate.

Register of applications

25.—(1) In this article and in article 26, "the local planning register authority" means—

(a) in Greater London or a metropolitan county, the local planning authority (and references to the area of the local planning register authority are, in this case, to the area of the local planning authority);

(b) in relation to land in a National Park (except in a metropolitan county), the county planning authority (and references to the area of the local planning register authority are, in this case, to the area of the county planning authority within a National Park);

(c) in relation to any other land, the district planning authority (and references to the area of the local planning register authority are, in this case, to the area of the district planning authority, other than any part of their area falling within a National Park).

(2) Each local planning register authority shall keep, in two parts, a register of every application for planning permission relating to their area.

(3) Part I of the register shall contain a copy of each such application, and a copy of any application for approval of reserved matters made in respect of an outline planning permission granted on such an application, made or sent to the local planning register authority and not finally disposed of, together with any accompanying plans and drawings.

(4) Part II of the register shall contain, in respect of every application for planning permission relating to the local planning register authority's area—

(a) a copy (which may be photographic) of the application and of plans and drawings submitted in relation thereto;

(b) particulars of any direction given under the Act or this Order in respect of the application;

(c) the decision, if any, of the local planning authority in respect of the application, including details of any conditions subject to which permission was granted, the date of such decision and the name of the local planning authority;

(d) the reference number, the date and effect of any decision of the Secretary of State in respect of the application, whether on appeal or on a reference under section 77 of the Act (reference of applications to Secretary of State);

(e) the date of any subsequent approval (whether approval of reserved matters or any other approval required) given in relation to the application.

(5) Where, on any appeal to the Secretary of State under section 174 of the Act (appeal against enforcement notices), the appellant is deemed to have made an application for planning permission and the Secretary of State has granted permission, the local planning register authority shall, on receipt of notification of the Secretary of State's decision, enter into Part II of the register referred to in paragraph (2) particulars of the development concerned, the land on which it was carried out, and the date and effect of the Secretary of State's decision.

(6) The register kept by the local planning register authority shall also contain the following information in respect of every application for a certificate under section 191 or 192 of the Act (certificates of lawfulness of existing or proposed use or development) relating to the authority's area—

(a) the name and address of the applicant;

(b) the date of the application;

(c) the address or location of the land to which the application relates;

(d) the description of the use, operations or other matter included in the application;

(e) the decision, if any, of the local planning authority in respect of the application and the date of such decision; and

(f) the reference number, date and effect of any decision of the Secretary of State on an appeal in respect of the application.

(7) The register shall contain the following information about simplified planning zone schemes in the area of the authority—

(a) brief particulars of any action taken by the authority or the Secretary of State in accordance with section 83 of or Schedule 7 to the Act (making of simplified planning zone schemes etc.) to establish or approve any simplified planning zone scheme, including the date of adoption or approval, the date on which the scheme or alteration becomes operative and the date on which it ceases to be operative;

(b) a copy of any simplified planning zone scheme, or alteration to an existing scheme, including any diagrams, illustrations, descriptive matter or any other prescribed material which has been made available for inspection under Schedule 7 to the Act;

(c) an index map showing the boundary of any operative or proposed simplified planning zone schemes, including alterations to existing schemes where appropriate, together with a reference to the entries in the register under sub-paragraph (a) and (b) above.

(8) To enable any person to trace any entry in the register, every register shall include an index together with a separate index of applications for development involving mining operations or the creation of mineral working deposits.

(9) Every entry in the register shall be made within 14 days of the receipt of an application, or of the giving or making of the relevant direction, decision or approval as the case may be.

(10) The register shall either be kept at the principal office of the local planning register authority or that part of the register which relates to land in part of that authority's area shall be kept at a place within or convenient to that part.

(11) For the purposes of paragraph (3) of this article, an application shall not be treated as finally disposed of unless—

(a) it has been decided by the authority (or the appropriate period allowed under article 20(2) of this Order has expired without their giving a decision) and the period of six months specified in article 23 of this Order has expired without any appeal having been made to the Secretary of State;

(b) if it has been referred to the Secretary of State under section 77 of the Act (reference of applications to Secretary of State) or an appeal has been made to the Secretary of State under section 78 of the Act (right to appeal against planning decisions and failure to take such decisions), the Secretary of State has issued his decision and the period of six weeks specified in section 288 of the Act (proceedings for questioning the validity of certain orders, decisions and directions) has expired without any application having been made to the High Court under that section;

(c) an application has been made to the High Court under section 288 of the Act and the matter has been finally determined, either by final dismissal of the application by a court or by the quashing of the Secretary of State's decision and the issue of a fresh decision (without a further application under the said section 288); or

(d) it has been withdrawn before being decided by the authority or the Secretary of State, as the case may be, or an appeal has been withdrawn before the Secretary of State has issued his decision.

COMMENTARY

DERIVATION

Town and Country Planning General Development Order 1988, art. 27, as amended by the Town and Country Planning General Development (Amendment) (No. 3) Order 1991 (No. 2805), art. 6 and S.I. 1992 No. 1563.

DEFINITIONS

"development": 1990 Act, ss.56, 336(1).
"district planning authority": 1990 Act, s.1.
"local planning authority": 1990 Act, s.1.
"local planning register authority": para. (1).
"mining operations": art. 1(2).
"National Park": art. 1(2).
"planning permission": 1990 Act, s.336(1).
"reserved matters": art. 1(2).
"simplified planning zone scheme": 1990 Act, s.336(1).

GENERAL NOTE

The planning register is a public record of all planning applications and decisions. It is required to be kept in two parts. Part I contains all pending planning applications, and applications for approval of reserved matters, together with copies of plans and drawings. This is the "live" part of the register. Part II contains all such applications which have been finally determined whether by the local planning authority or on reference or appeal to the Secretary of State. Material is retained in Part I until all proceedings on it have concluded (see para. (11)). Part II must contain details of any conditions imposed (though s.106 agreements or planning obligations need not be included). Separate registers are maintained under art. 26 for enforcement and stop notices, and breach of condition notices.

The registers are maintained in each area by the "local planning register authority", *i.e.* by the district planning authority in the shire counties, by the London boroughs and metropolitan districts in their areas, (except where all functions of a local planning authority have been transferred to an urban development corporation or housing action trust, who as local planning authority will maintain the register in their areas), and by the county council in a National Park (the two special Planning Boards themselves have the function in their areas).

Environmental assessment

By virtue of the Town and Country Planning (Assessment of Environmental Effects) Regulations 1988 (No. 1199), reg. 7, the following must also be placed on the planning register:

(1) a copy of any direction given by the Secretary of State as to whether any application on the register is, or is not, a Sched. 1 or 2 application, and any relevant opinion given pursuant to reg. 5;
(2) a copy of any notification by the local planning authority that they consider that an application cannot be granted unless an environmental statement is submitted;
(3) a copy of any direction made by the Secretary of State before application is made for planning permission for the development in question. In this case, the requirement is to keep the information available for public inspection along with the register (reg. 7(5)), but once an

application is received, a copy of the direction must be placed on the register (reg. 7(1)).

The deemed refusal by a local planning authority following their intimation to an applicant that environmental assessment is in their view required, and his failure to respond within three weeks, is to be treated (by virtue of reg. 9(3)) as a decision of the authority for the purposes of para. (4)(c).

Minerals applications

Minerals applications are included in the planning register, but the planning authority are required to maintain a separate index of applications for development involving mining operations or the creation of mineral working deposits (para. (8)). County mineral planning authorities have been advised also for administrative purposes to maintain their own registers of applications, decisions and conditions (MPG 5, *Minerals Planning and the General Development Order*, para. 7).

Simplified planning zones

Under para. (7), the planning register must also contain a copy of each simplified planning zone scheme operative in the authority's area, including any alterations, and any other material made available for inspection under Sched. 7. The Order also requires an index map to be maintained showing the boundary of any operative or proposed SPZ. Brief particulars of any action taken by the authority or the Secretary of State in accordance with s.82 or Sched. 7 to establish or approve any SPZ, including the date of adoption or approval, the date a scheme became operative and the date it ceases to be operative.

Certificates of lawfulness of use or development

The planning register is required by para. (6) to contain information relating to applications under ss.191 and 192 of the 1990 Act (certificates of lawfulness of existing or proposed use or development). The requirements of the 1988 Order, prior to its amendment in 1992, to maintain information in the register of applications under s.64 (to determine whether planning permission was required) and old s.192 (established use certificates) are kept in force by art. 28 of this Order.

The enforcement register

A separate register of enforcement notices and stop notices is required by art. 26. But where an appeal is made to the Secretary of State against an enforcement notice, and he grants planning permission on the deemed application, notice of his decision must be entered also in Part II of the planning applications register (para. (3)). The entry would then be removed from the enforcement register (art. 28(2)).

Register of enforcement and stop notices

26.—(1) Subject to paragraph (2) of this article, the register under section 188 of the Act (register of enforcement and stop notices) shall contain the following information with respect to every enforcement notice issued in relation to land in the area of the authority maintaining the register—

(a) the address of the land to which the notice relates or a plan by reference to which its situation can be ascertained;

(b) the name of the issuing authority;

(c) the date of issue of the notice;

(d) the date of service of copies of the notice;

(e) a statement or summary of the breach of planning control alleged and the requirements of the notice, including the period within which any required steps are to be taken;

(f) the date specified in the notice as the date on which it is to take effect;

(g) information on any postponement of the date specified as the date on which the notice will take effect by reason of section 175(4) of the Act (appeals: supplementary provisions) and the date of the final determination or withdrawal of any appeal;

(h) the date of service and, if applicable, of withdrawal of any stop notice referring to the enforcement notice, together with a statement or summary of the activity prohibited by any such stop notice;

(i) the date, if any, on which the local planning authority are satisfied that steps required by the notice for a purpose mentioned in section 173(4)(b) of the Act (remedying any injury to amenity) have been taken.

(2) That register shall also contain the following information with respect to every breach of condition notice served in relation to land in the area of the authority maintaining the register—

(a) the address of the land to which the notice relates or a plan by reference to which its situation can be ascertained;

(b) the name of the serving authority;

(c) the date of service of the notice;

(d) details of the relevant planning permission sufficient to enable it to be identified;

(e) a statement or summary of the condition which has not been complied with and the requirements of the notice, including the period allowed for compliance.

(3) All entries relating to an enforcement notice, stop notice or breach of condition notice shall be removed from the register if—

(a) in the case of an enforcement notice or stop notice, the relevant enforcement notice is quashed by the Secretary of State;

(b) in the case of a breach of condition notice, the notice is quashed by a court;

(c) in any case, the relevant notice is withdrawn.

(4) Every register shall include an index for enabling a person to trace any entry in the register by reference to the address of the land to which the notice relates.

(5) Where a county planning authority issue an enforcement notice or serve a stop notice or a breach of condition notice, they shall supply the information specified in paragraph (1) or (2) of this article, as the case may be, in relation to the notice to the district planning authority in whose area the land to which the notice relates is situated and shall inform that authority if the notice is withdrawn or the relevant enforcement notice or breach of condition notice is quashed.

(6) The information prescribed in paragraphs (1) and (2) of this article shall be entered in the register as soon as practicable and in any event within 14 days of the occurrence to which it relates, and information shall be so

supplied under paragraph (5) that entries may be made within the said period of 14 days.

(7) The register shall either be kept at the principal office of the local planning register authority or that part of the register which relates to land in part of that authority's area shall be kept at a place within or convenient to that part.

COMMENTARY

DERIVATION

Town and Country Planning General Development Order 1988, art. 28, as amended by S.I. 1992 No. 1563.

DEFINITIONS

"county planning authority": 1990 Act, s.1.
"district planning authority": 1990 Act, s.1.
"enforcement notice": 1990 Act, s.336(1).
"local planning register authority": para. (1).
"stop notice": 1990 Act, s.336(1).

GENERAL NOTE

The enforcement register is required to be kept separately from the planning applications register (art. 25), but it is maintained by the same authority. It is not maintained in two parts: material remains in the register unless and until the relevant notice is quashed by the Secretary of State or withdrawn.

The register is required to contain specified information relating to enforcement notices, stop notices and breach of condition notices.

Directions

27. Any power conferred by this Order to give a direction includes power to cancel or vary the direction by a subsequent direction.

COMMENTARY

The powers conferred by this Order to make directions are summarised in the Commentary to art. 14.

Revocations, transitionals and savings

28.—(1) Subject to paragraphs (2) to (5) of this article, the statutory instruments specified in Schedule 5 are revoked to the extent not already revoked.

(2) Where an area of coal working has been notified to the local planning authority for the purposes of paragraph (i) of the table in article 18 of the Town and Country Planning General Development Order 1988 (consultations before the grant of permission) before the date of the coming into force of this Order, such notification shall be treated as if it had been made for the purposes of paragraph (j) of the table in article 10 of this Order by the Coal Authority on or after that date; and, in relation to a particular application for planning permission made before 31st October 1994, the local planning authority are not required to consult the Coal Authority if they have already consulted the British Coal Corporation.

(3) Any notice given for the purposes of article 13 of the Town and Country Planning General Development Order 1988 (notification of mineral applications) before the date of the coming into force of this Order, shall be treated as if it had been given for the purposes of article 16 of this Order by the Coal Authority on or after that date; and, in relation to a particular application for planning permission made before 31st October 1994, the mineral planning authority are not required to notify the Coal Authority, before determining the application, if they have already notified the British Coal Corporation that that application has been made.

(4) The relevant provisions of the Town and Country Planning General Development Order 1988, in the form in which they were in force immediately before 27th July 1992, shall continue to apply with respect to applications made under section 64 of the Act (applications to determine whether planning permission required) before 27th July 1992.

(5) The relevant provisions of the Town and Country Planning General Development Order 1988, in the form in which they were in force immediately before 27th July 1992, shall continue to apply with respect to applications for established use certificates made under section 192 of the Act (applications for established use certificates), as originally enacted, before 27th July 1992.

COMMENTARY

GENERAL NOTE

This article makes transitional provision for notices given under the 1988 Order in respect of coal working, to have continuing effect for the purposes of arts. 10 and 13 of this Order. It also maintains in force the provisions of the 1988 Order as they stood prior to their amendment from July 27, 1992, in relation to:

(1) applications under s.64 of the 1990 Act for a determination as to whether planning permission was required: the principal relevant provisions of the 1988 Order were arts. 9 (relating to the content of such applications); 25(b) (written notice of decision) and 27(4) (planning register).

(2) applications for established use certificates: the principal relevant provisions of the 1988 Order was art. 29.

SCHEDULE 1

Articles 5, 22 and 24

PART 1

TOWN AND COUNTRY PLANNING ACT 1990

Letter to be sent by a local planning authority when they receive an application for planning permission or for a certificate of lawful use or development.

Thank you for your application dated . . . .

which I received on . . . .

I am still examining your application form and the accompanying plans and documents to see whether they comply with the law.*

If I find that your application is invalid because it does not comply with the statutory requirements then I shall write to you again as soon as I can.*

If, by ***(insert date at end of period of eight weeks beginning with the date when the application was received)*** **. . . . .**

- **you have not been told that your application is invalid; or**
- * **you have not been told that your fee cheque has been dishonoured; or**
- **you have not been given a decision in writing; or**
- **you have not agreed in writing to extend the period in which the decision may be given,**

then you can appeal to the Secretary of State for the Environment/Wales* under section 78/section 195* of the Town and Country Planning Act 1990. You should appeal within six months and you must use a form which you can get from the Planning Inspectorate at Tollgate House, Houlton Street, Bristol BS2 9DJ/Cathays Park, Cardiff CF1 3NQ*. This does not apply if your application has already been referred to the Secretary of State for the Environment/Wales*.

***delete where inappropriate**

PART 2

TOWN AND COUNTRY PLANNING ACT 1990

Notification to be sent to an applicant when a local planning authority refuse planning permission or grant it subject to conditions (*To be endorsed on notices of decision*)

Appeals to the Secretary of State

- **If you are aggrieved by the decision of your local planning authority to refuse permission for the proposed development or to grant it subject to conditions, then you can appeal to the Secretary of State for the Environment/Wales* under section 78 of the Town and Country Planning Act 1990.**
- **If you want to appeal, then you must do so within six months of the date of this notice, using a form which you can get from the Planning Inspectorate at Tollgate House, Houlton Street, Bristol BS2 9DJ/Cathays Park, Cardiff CF1 3NQ*.**
- **The Secretary of State can allow a longer period for giving notice of an appeal, but he will not normally be prepared to use this power unless there are special circumstances which excuse the delay in giving notice of appeal.**
- **The Secretary of State need not consider an appeal if it seems to him that the local planning authority could not have granted planning permission for the proposed development or could not have granted it without the conditions they imposed, having regard to the statutory requirements, to the provisions of any development order and to any directions given under a development order.**
- **In practice, the Secretary of State does not refuse to consider appeals solely because the local planning authority based their decision on a direction given by him.**

Purchase Notices

- **If either the local planning authority or the Secretary of State for the Environment/Wales* refuses permission to develop land or grants it subject to conditions, the owner may claim that he can neither put the land to a reasonably beneficial use in its existing state nor render the land capable of a reasonably beneficial use by the carrying out of any development which has been or would be permitted.**
- **In these circumstances, the owner may serve a purchase notice on the Council (District Council, London Borough Council or Common Council of the City of London) in whose area the land is situated. This notice will require the Council to purchase his interest in the land in accordance with the provisions of Part VI of the Town and Country Planning Act 1990.**

***delete where inappropriate**

SCHEDULE 2

Articles 6, 7 and 9

PART 1

Town and Country Planning (General Development Procedure) Order 1995

NOTICE UNDER ARTICLE 6 OF APPLICATION FOR PLANNING PERMISSION

(to be published in a newspaper or to be served on an owner* or a tenant**)

Proposed development at *(a)* ....

I give notice that *(b)* ....

is applying to the *(c)* .... **Council**

for planning permission to *(d)* ....

Any owner* of the land or tenant who wishes to make representations about this application should write to the Council at *(e)*** ....

by *(f)* ....

* **"owner" means a person having a freehold interest or a leasehold interest the unexpired term of which is not less than seven years, or, in the case of development consisting of the winning or working of minerals, a person entitled to an interest in a mineral in the land (other than oil, gas, coal, gold or silver).**

** **"tenant" means a tenant of an agricultural holding any part of which is comprised in the land.**

Signed ....

†On behalf of ....

Date ....

Statement of owners' rights

The grant of planning permission does not affect owners' rights to retain or dispose of their property, unless there is some provision to the contrary in an agreement or in a lease.

Statement of agricultural tenants' rights

The grant of planning permission for non-agricultural development may affect agricultural tenants' security of tenure.

†delete where inappropriate

Insert:

(a) **address or location of the proposed development**
(b) **applicant's name**
(c) **name of Council**
(d) **description of the proposed development**
(e) **address of the Council**
(f) **date giving a period of 21 days beginning with the date of service, or 14 days beginning with the date of publication, of the notice (as the case may be)**

Town and Country Planning (General Development Procedure) Order 1995

NOTICE UNDER ARTICLE 6 OF APPLICATION FOR PLANNING PERMISSION

(to be posted in the case of an application for planning permission for development consisting of the winning and working of minerals by underground operations (in addition to the service or publication of any other requisite notices in this Schedule))

Proposed development at *(a)* ....

I give notice that *(b)*..

is applying to the *(c)*.. Council

for planning permission to *(d)* ....

Members of the public may inspect copies of:

- **the application**
- **the plans**
- **and other documents submitted with it**

at *(e)* .... during

all reasonable hours until *(f)* ....

Anyone who wishes to make representations about this application should write to the Council

at *(g)* ....

.... by *(f)*..............................

Signed ....

†On behalf of ....

Date ....

†Delete where inappropriate

Insert:

(a) **address or location of the proposed development**
(b) **applicant's name**
(c) **name of Council**
(d) **description of the proposed development**
(e) **address at which the application may be inspected (the applicant is responsible for making the application available for inspection within the area of the local planning authority)**
(f) **date giving a period of 21 days, beginning with the date when the notice is posted**
(g) **address of Council**

Town and Country Planning (General Development Procedure) Order 1995

NOTICE UNDER ARTICLES 6 AND 9(1) OF APPEAL

(to be published in a newspaper or to be served on an owner* or a tenant**)

Proposed development at *(a)* . . . .

I give notice that *(b)*. . . . .

having applied to the *(c)* . . . . Council

to *(d)* . . . .

is appealing to the Secretary of State for the Environment/Secretary of State for Wales†

against the decision of the Council†

on the failure of the Council to give notice of a decision†

Any owner* of the land or tenant who wishes to make representations about this appeal should write to the Secretary of State for the Environment/Wales† at the Department of the Environment at Tollgate House, Houlton Street, Bristol BS2 9DJ/Welsh Office at Planning Division, Cathays Park, Cardiff CF1 3NQ†, by *(e)* . . . .**

* **"owner" means a person having a freehold interest or a leasehold interest the unexpired term of which is not less than seven years, or, in the case of development consisting of the winning or working of minerals, a person entitled to an interest in a mineral in the land (other than oil, gas, coal, gold or silver).**

** **"tenant" means a tenant of an agricultural holding any part of which is comprised in the land.**

Signed . . . .

†On behalf of . . . .

Date . . . .

Statement of owners' rights

The grant of planning permission does not affect owners' rights to retain or dispose of their property, unless there is some provision to the contrary in an agreement or in a lease.

Statement of agricultural tenants' rights

The grant of planning permission for non-agricultural development may affect agricultural tenants' security of tenure.

†delete where inappropriate

Insert:

(a) **address or location of the proposed development**
(b) **applicant's name**
(c) **name of Council**
(d) **description of the proposed development**
(e) **date giving a period of 21 days beginning with the date of service, or 14 days beginning with the date of publication, of the notice (as the case may be)**

Town and Country Planning (General Development Procedure) Order 1995

NOTICE UNDER ARTICLES 6 AND 9(1) OF APPEAL

(to be posted in the case of an application for planning permission for development consisting of the winning and working of minerals by underground operations (in addition to the service or publication of any other requisite notices in this Schedule))

Proposed development at *(a)* ....

I give notice that *(b)*..

having applied to the *(c)*.. Council

to *(d)*..

is appealing to the Secretary of State for the Environment/Secretary of State for Wales*

against the decision of the Council*

on the failure of the Council to give notice of a decision*

Members of the public may inspect copies of:

- **the application**
- **the plans**
- **and other documents submitted with it**

at *(e)*.. during

all reasonable hours until *(f)* ....

Anyone who wishes to make representations about this appeal should write to the Secretary of State for the Environment/Wales* at the Department of the Environment at Tollgate House, Houlton Street, Bristol BS2 9DJ/Welsh Office at Planning Division, Cathays Park, Cardiff CF1 3NQ* by *(f)* ....

..

Signed ....

***On behalf of ....**

Date ....

***delete where inappropriate**

Insert:
(a) **address or location of the proposed development**
(b) **applicant's name**
(c) **name of Council**
(d) **description of the proposed development**
(e) **address of Council**
(f) **date giving a period of 21 days, beginning with the date when the notice is posted**

PART 2

Town and Country Planning (General Development Procedure) Order 1995

CERTIFICATE UNDER ARTICLE 7

Certificate A(*a*)

I certify that:

on the day 21 days before the date of the accompanying application/appeal* nobody, except the applicant/appellant*, was the owner *(b)* of any part of the land to which the application/appeal* relates.

Signed . . . .

***On behalf of . . . .**

Date . . . .

***delete where inappropriate**

(*a*) This Certificate is for use with applications and appeals for planning permission (articles 7 and 9(1) of the Order). One of Certificates A, B, C or D (or the appropriate certificate in the case of certain minerals applications) must be completed, together with the Agricultural Holdings Certificate.

(*b*) "owner" means a person having a freehold interest or a leasehold interest the unexpired term of which is not less than seven years, or, in the case of development consisting of the winning and working of minerals, a person entitled to an interest in a mineral in the land (other than oil, gas, coal, gold or silver).

Town and Country Planning (General Development Procedure) Order 1995

CERTIFICATE UNDER ARTICLE 7

Certificate B(*a*)

I certify that:

I have/The applicant has/The appellant has* given the requisite notice to everyone else who, on the day 21 days before the date of the accompanying application/appeal*, was the owner *(b)* of any part of the land to which the application/appeal(*) relates, as listed below.

Owner's *(b)* name	Address at which notice was served	Date on which notice was served

Signed . . . .

***On behalf of** . . . .

Date . . . .

***delete where inappropriate**

(*a*) This Certificate is for use with applications and appeals for planning permission (articles 7 and 9(1) of the Order). One of Certificates A, B, C or D (or the appropriate certificate in the case of certain minerals applications) must be completed, together with the Agricultural Holdings Certificate.

(*b*) "owner" means a person having a freehold interest or a leasehold interest the unexpired term of which is not less than seven years, or, in the case of development consisting of the winning and working of minerals, a person entitled to an interest in a mineral in the land (other than oil, gas, coal, gold or silver).

Town and Country Planning (General Development Procedure) Order 1995

CERTIFICATE UNDER ARTICLE 7

Certificate C(*a*)

I certify that:

- **I/The applicant/The appellant* cannot issue a Certificate A or B in respect of the accompanying application/appeal*.**
- **I have/The applicant has/The appellant has* given the requisite notice to the persons specified below, being persons who on the day 21 days before the date of the application/appeal*, were owners *(b)* of any part of the land to which the application/appeal* relates.**

Owner's *(b)* name	Address at which notice was served	Date on which notice was served

- **I have/The applicant has/The appellant has* taken all reasonable steps open to me/him/her* to find out the names and addresses of the other owners *(b)* of the land, or of a part of it, but have/has* been unable to do so. These steps were as follows:**

  (c) . . . .

  . . . .

- **Notice of the application/appeal*, as attached to this Certificate, has been published in**

  the *(d)* . . . .

  . . . .

  on *(e)* . . . .

Signed . . . .

†On behalf of . . . .

Date . . . .

***delete where inappropriate**

(a) **This Certificate is for use with applications and appeals for planning permission (articles 7 and 9(1) of the Order). One of Certificates A, B, C or D (or the appropriate certificate in the case of certain minerals applications) must be completed, together with the Agricultural Holdings Certificate.**

(b) **"owner" means a person having a freehold interest or a leasehold interest the unexpired term of which is not less than seven years, or, in the case of development consisting of the winning and working of minerals, a person entitled to an interest in a mineral in the land (other than oil, gas, coal, gold or silver).**

Insert:

(c) **description of steps taken**

(d) **name of newspaper circulating in the area where the land is situated**

(e) **date of publication (which must be not earlier than the day 21 days before the date of the application or appeal)**

Town and Country Planning (General Development Procedure) Order 1995

CERTIFICATE UNDER ARTICLE 7

Certificate D(*a*)

I certify that:

- **I/The applicant/The appellant* cannot issue a Certificate A in respect of the accompanying application/appeal*.**

- **I/The applicant/The appellant* have/has* taken all reasonable steps open to me/him/her* to find out the names and addresses of everyone else who, on the day 21 days before the date of the application/appeal*, was the owner *(b)* of any part of the land to which the application/appeal* relates, but have/has* been unable to do so. These steps were as follows:**

  (c) ....

  ....

- **Notice of the application/appeal*, as attached to this certificate, has been published in the**

  (d) ....

  ....

  on *(e)* ....

Signed ....

†On behalf of ....

Date ....

***delete where inappropriate**

(a) **This Certificate is for use with applications and appeals for planning permission (articles 7 and 9(1) of the Order). One of Certificates, A, B, C or D (or the appropriate certificate in the case of certain minerals applications) must be completed, together with the Agricultural Holdings Certificate.**

(b) **"owner" means a person having a freehold interest or a leasehold interest the unexpired term of which is not less than seven years, or, in the case of development consisting of the winning and working of minerals, a person entitled to an interest in a mineral in the land (other than oil, gas, coal, gold or silver).**

Insert:

(c) **description of steps taken**

(d) **name of newspaper circulating in the area where the land is situated**

(e) **date of publication (which must be not earlier than the day 21 days before the date of the application or appeal)**

Town and Country Planning (General Development Procedure) Order 1995

CERTIFICATE UNDER ARTICLE 7

Agricultural Holdings Certificate

Whichever is appropriate of the following alternatives must form part of Certificates A, B, C or D. If the applicant is the sole agricultural tenant he or she must delete the first alternative and insert "not applicable" as the information required by the second alternative.

* • **None of the land to which the application/appeal* relates is, or is part of, an agricultural holding.**

or

* • **I have/The applicant has/The appellant has* given the requisite notice to every person other than my/him/her* self who, on the day 21 days before the date of the application/ appeal*, was a tenant of an agricultural holding on all or part of the land to which the application/appeal* relates, as follows:**

Tenant's name	**Address at which notice was served**	**Date on which notice was served**

Signed . . . .

†On behalf of . . . .

Date . . . .

***delete where inappropriate**

(a) **This Certificate is for use with applications and appeals for planning permission (articles 7 and 9(1) of the Order). One of Certificates A, B, C or D (or the appropriate certificate in the case of certain minerals applications) must be completed together with the Agricultural Holdings Certificate.**

Town and Country Planning (General Development Procedure) Order 1995

CERTIFICATE UNDER ARTICLE 7

(for use with applications and appeals for planning permission for development consisting of the winning and working of minerals by underground operations)

I certify that:

* • **I have/The applicant has/The appellant has* given the requisite notice to the persons specified below being persons who, on the day 21 days before the date of the accompanying application/appeal, were owners *(a)* of any part of the land to which the application/appeal* relates.**

Owner's *(a)* name	Address at which notice was served	Date on which notice was served

• **There is no person (other than me/the applicant/the appellant*) who, on the day 21 days before the date of the accompanying application/appeal*, was the owner *(a)* of any part of the land to which this application/appeal* relates, whom I/the applicant/the appellant* know/s* to be such a person and whose name and address is known to me/the applicant/the appellant* but to whom I have/the applicant/the appellant has* not given the requisite notice.**

• **I have/The applicant/The appellant has* posted the requisite notice, sited and displayed in such a way as to be easily visible and legible by members of the public, in at least one place in every parish or community within which there is situated any part of the land to which the accompanying application/appeal* relates, as listed below.**

Parish/Community	Location of notice	Date posted

• **Save as specified below* this/these* notice/s* was/were* left in position for not less than seven days in the period of 21 days immediately preceding the making of the application/appeal*.**

* • **The following notice/s* was/were*, however, left in position for less than seven days in the period of not more than 21 days immediately preceding the making of the application/appeal*.**

Parish/Community	Location of notice	Date posted

This happened because it/they* was/were* removed/obscured/defaced* before seven days had passed during the period of 21 days mentioned above. This was not my/the applicant's/the appellant's* fault or intent.

I/The applicant/The appellant* took the following steps to protect and replace the notice:

(b) ....

....

• **Notice of the application/appeal*, as attached to this certificate, has been published in the**

(c) ....

....

on *(d)* ....

Agricultural Holdings Certificate

Whichever is appropriate of the following alternatives must form part of this certificate. If the applicant is the sole agricultural tenant he or she must delete the first alternative and insert "not applicable" as the information required by the second alternative.

* • **None of the land to which the application/appeal* relates is, or is part of, an agricultural holding.**

or

* • **I have/The applicant has/The appellant has* given the requisite notice to every person other than my/him/her* self who, on the day 21 days before the date of the application/ appeal*, was a tenant of an agricultural holding on all or part of the land to which the application/appeal* relates, as follows:**

Tenant's name	**Address at which notice was served**	**Date on which notice was served**

Signed . . . .

***On behalf of** . . . .

Date . . . .

***delete where inappropriate**

(*a*) **"owner" means a person having a freehold interest or a leasehold interest the unexpired term of which is not less than seven years or a person entitled to an interest in a mineral in the land (other than oil, gas, coal, gold or silver).**

Insert:

(*b*) **description of steps taken**
(*c*) **name of newspaper circulating in the area where the land is situated**
(*d*) **date of publication (which must be not earlier than the day 21 days before the date of the application or appeal)**

SCHEDULE 3

Article 8

NOTICE OF APPLICATION FOR PLANNING PERMISSION

Town and Country Planning (General Development Procedure) Order 1995

NOTICE UNDER ARTICLE 8

(to be published in a newspaper, displayed on or near the site, or served on owners and/or occupiers of adjoining land)

Proposed development at *(a)*. . . . .

I give notice that *(b)*. . . . .

is applying to the *(c)*. . . . . Council

for planning permission to *(d)* . . . .

The proposed development does not accord with the provisions of the development plan in force in the area in which the land to which the application relates is situated*

Members of the public may inspect copies of:

- **the application**
- **the plans**
- **and other documents submitted with it**

at *(e)*. . . . . during

all reasonable hours until *(f)* . . . .

Anyone who wishes to make representations about this application should write to the Council

at *(g)* . . . .

. . . . . by *(f)*. . . . .

Signed . . . .

. . . . .
Council's authorised officer

On behalf of . . . . Council

Date . . . .

***delete where inappropriate**

Insert:

- ***(a)*** **address or location of the proposed development**
- ***(b)*** **applicant's name**
- ***(c)*** **name of Council**
- ***(d)*** **description of the proposed development**
- ***(e)*** **address at which the application may be inspected**
- ***(f)*** **date giving a period of 21 days, beginning with the date when the notice is first displayed on or near the site or served on an owner and/or occupier of adjoining land, or a period of 14 days, beginning with the date when the notice is published in a newspaper (as the case may be)**
- ***(g)*** **address of Council**

NOTICE OF APPLICATION FOR PLANNING PERMISSION

Town and Country Planning (General Development Procedure) Order 1995

NOTICE UNDER ARTICLE 8 OF APPLICATION FOR PLANNING PERMISSION ACCOMPANIED BY AN ENVIRONMENTAL STATEMENT

(to be published in a newspaper and displayed on or near the site)

Proposed development at *(a)* . . . .

I give notice that *(b)*. . . . .

is applying to the *(c)*. . . . . Council

for planning permission to *(d)* . . . .

and that the application is accompanied by an environmental statement

The proposed development does not accord with the provisions of the development plan in force in the area in which the land to which the application relates is situated*

Members of the public may inspect copies of:

- **the application**
- **the plans**
- **the environmental statement**
- **and other documents submitted with the application**

at *(e)* . . . . during

all reasonable hours until *(f)* . . . .

Members of the public may obtain copies of the environmental statement from *(g)* . . . .

. . . . .

so long as stocks last, at a charge of *(h)* . . . .

Anyone who wishes to make representations about this application should write to the Council

at *(i)* . . . .

. . . . . by *(f)*. . . . .

Signed . . . .

. . . . .

Council's authorised officer

On behalf of . . . . Council

Date . . . .

***delete where inappropriate**

Insert:

(a) **address or location of the proposed development**
(b) **applicant's name**
(c) **name of Council**
(d) **description of the proposed development**
(e) **address at which the application may be inspected**
(f) **date giving a period of 21 days, beginning with the date when the notice is first displayed on or near the site, or a period of 14 days, beginning with the date when the notice is published in a newspaper (as the case may be)**
(g) **address from where copies of the environmental statement may be obtained (whether or not the same as *(e)*)**
(h) **amount of charge, if any**
(i) **address of Council**

SCHEDULE 4

Article 24

TOWN AND COUNTRY PLANNING ACT 1990: SECTIONS 191 AND 192 (as amended by section 10 of the Planning and Compensation Act 1991)

TOWN AND COUNTRY PLANNING (GENERAL DEVELOPMENT PROCEDURE) ORDER 1995: ARTICLE 24

CERTIFICATE OF LAWFUL USE OR DEVELOPMENT

The *(a)*. . . . . Council hereby certify that on *(b)*. . . . . the use*/operations*/matter* described in the First Schedule to this in respect of the land specified in the Second Schedule to this certificate and edged*/hatched*/coloured* *(c)*. . . . . on the plan attached to this certificate, was*/were*/would have been* lawful within the meaning of section 191 of the Town and Country Planning Act 1990 (as amended), for the following reason(s):

. . . .

. . . .

. . . .

. . . .

Signed . . . . (Council's authorised officer)

On behalf of *(a)*. . . . . Council

Date . . . .

First Schedule
(d)

Second Schedule
(e)

Notes
1 This certificate is issued solely for the purpose of section 191*/192* of the Town and Country Planning Act 1990 (as amended).

2 It certifies that the use*/operations*/matter* specified in the First Schedule taking place on the land described in the Second Schedule was*/were*/would have been* lawful, on the specified date and, thus, was not*/were not*/would not have been* liable to enforcement action under section 172 of the 1990 Act on that date.

3 This certificate applies only to the extent of the use*/operations*/matter* described in the First Schedule and to the land specified in the Second Schedule and identified on the attached plan. Any use*/operations*/matter* which is*/are* materially different from that*/those* described or which relate/s* to other land may render the owner or occupier liable to enforcement action.

***4 The effect of the certificate is also qualified by the proviso in section 192(4) of the 1990 Act, as amended, which states that the lawfulness of a described use or operation is only conclusively presumed where there has been no material change, before the use is instituted or the operations begun, in any of the matters relevant to determining such lawfulness.**

***delete where inappropriate**

Insert:
- ***(a)*** **name of Council**
- ***(b)*** **date of application to the Council**
- ***(c)*** **colour used on the plan**
- ***(d)*** **full description of use, operations or other matter, if necessary, by reference to details in the application or submitted plans, including a reference to the use class, if any, specified in an order under section 55(2)(f) of the 1990 Act, within which the certificated use falls**
- ***(e)*** **address or location of the site**

SCHEDULE 5

Article 28

STATUTORY INSTRUMENTS REVOKED

1 *Title of Instrument*	2 *Reference*
The Town and Country Planning General Development Order 1988	S.I. 1988/1813
The Town and Country Planning General Development (Amendment) Order 1989	S.I. 1989/603
The Town and Country Planning General Development (Amendment) (No. 2) Order 1989	S.I. 1989/1590
The Town and Country Planning General Development (Amendment) (No. 3) Order 1991	S.I. 1991/2805
The Town and Country Planning General Development (Amendment) (No. 2) Order 1992	S.I. 1992/658
The Town and Country Planning General Development (Amendment) (No. 4) Order 1992	S.I. 1992/1493
The Town and Country Planning General Development (Amendment) (No. 5) Order 1992	S.I. 1992/1563
The Town and Country Planning General Development (Amendment) (No. 6) Order 1992	S.I. 1992/2450
The Town and Country Planning General Development (Amendment) Order 1994	S.I. 1994/678
The Town and Country Planning General Development (Amendment) (No. 2) Order 1994	S.I. 1994/2595
The Town and Country Planning General Development (Amendment) Order 1995	S.I. 1995/298

INDEX